Thank you!

Jane

THE LIBERATING PROMISE
OF PHILANTHROPY

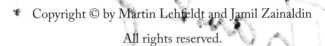

First Storyline Group edition 2019

Manufacturing: Falcon Press, Nashville

Book design: Alex Burmenko

Managing editor: Adam Volle

Library of Congress Cataloging-in-Publication Data

Names: Lehfeldt, Martin, 1940—author. | Zainaldin, Jamil, 1948—author.

Title: The liberating promise of philanthropy: stories of grant-makers in the south / by Martin Lehfeldt and Jamil Zainaldin.

Description: First Storyline Group edition. | Atlanta: The Storyline Group, 2019. | includes biographical references and index.

Identifiers: LCCN 2019914184. | ISBN 978-0-9887963-1-7 (hardcover) | ISBN 978-0-9887963-2-4 (pbk.) | 978-0-9887963-0-0 (ebook)

Subjects: LCSH: Charities—Southern States—History. 2. Nonprofit organizations—Southern States—History. 3. Humanitarianism—Southern States—History. 4. Endowments—Southern States—History.

THE LIBERATING PROMISE OF PHILANTHROPY

Stories of Grant-Makers in the South
(including a history of the Southeastern Council of Foundations)

Martin Lehfeldt & Jamil Zainaldin

The Storyline Group

Atlanta, Georgia

A Personal Dedication…

…to two remarkable spouses, Ingrid Kelly and Linda Lehfeldt, who were generous in both their editorial suggestions and their silent forbearance while this book took shape.

A Professional Dedication…

…to the Hull Fellows (board and staff of Southeastern Council of Foundations members) who were selected to prepare themselves further for the 21st century leadership responsibility to sustain and advance philanthropy in the South and elsewhere.

TABLE OF CONTENTS

Dedications   v

A Foreword by Janine Lee   viii

A Foreword by Laura McCarty   xii

Introduction   1

Chapter 1: Philanthropic Impulses And Their Obstacles   23

Chapter 2: The Widening Abyss (1830-1865)   45

Chapter 3: Reconstructing A Nation (1865–1877)   75

Chapter 4: Old Times Not Forgotten (1877–1895)   105

Chapter 5: New Order And New Philanthropy In A New Age   121

Chapter 6: The Footprint Of Government   147

Chapter 7: Julius Rosenwald   169

Chapter 8: The End Of A War And A Return To "Normalcy"   181

Chapter 9: A Personal And Regional Reclamation   203

Chapter 10: Emerging Southern Wealth And Philanthropy   219

Chapter 11: Peace, Prosperity. . . . And Change   243

Chapter 12: A New Attack On Foundations   275

Chapter 13: Grant-Makers Going On Defense   287

Chapter 14: An Organization For Southern Philanthropy   301

Chapter 15: Expansion And Maturing Of The Field   329

Chapter 16: Enhancing Diversity And Relevance   365

Afterword   375

Authors' Acknowledgments   386

Appendices   394

Index   408

The Authors   431

A Foreword by Janine Lee

For nearly a decade, I have had the honor of leading the South-eastern Council of Foundations, which represents philanthropy not only across an 11-state footprint, but also in places like the U.S. Virgin Islands and even in cities like Seattle and New York, where large, national foundations have recognized the urgency of investing in this region, its communities and its people.

SECF has come a long way since its founding 50 years ago. When we were founded in 1969, only a year had passed since Dr. Martin Luther King, Jr. was assassinated while standing on the balcony of his room at the Lorraine Motel in Memphis, Tennessee. A few years prior to that, civil rights activists attempting to cross the Edmund Pettus Bridge in Selma, Alabama, were met by police on horseback who shot them with tear gas and beat them with clubs.

The struggles of African Americans in the Southeast at that time, as well as the abject poverty faced by many rural whites in the region, would be reason enough for grant-makers to come together and discuss ways to collaborate to address these and other concerns. Yet when SECF was formed, these issues were not front of mind—the priority, instead, was tax policy. Specifically, the Tax Reform Act of 1969 which, for the first time in American history, had imposed significant regulations and requirements on private foundations—while some had sounded the alarm that federal oversight was coming, foundations were, by and large, asleep at the wheel.

Philanthropy at that time was not strongly focused on the systemic disparities that dominated so much of life in the South. Combined with a failure to self-regulate, it is little surprise that our field, back then, was seen as disconnected and unresponsive.

Much has changed since then—for the better. The South remains a region where philanthropy is strongly place-based, but while foundations may focus on one town, or a few counties, they are more willing than ever to learn from others, work in cooperation with community leaders and share what they've learned with the broader philanthropic community. Evaluation backed by research and data is considered essential. Equity is an area of growing concern and action. This evolution has resulted in philanthropic work that has improved the lives of countless people.

Yet when we look at the broader picture, some things have changed very little since 1969. We see division and turmoil, including ugly episodes of racism, every day. Economic mobility, once taken for granted, is on the decline—where you were born still largely determines your income, your education and even your lifespan. People feel that their voices are not being heard. Even the definition of truth has become a matter of partisan politics.

We all know the saying—those who forget history are condemned to repeat it. At a time when wounds of the past are being reopened, the study of history is essential. In this book, Martin Lehfeldt and Jamil Zainaldin provide a history of philanthropy in the South, one that I believe can provide some insight into lessons learned and possibilities for change as we move toward an uncertain future.

As we struggle with the issues of today, and ask ourselves about the role of philanthropy, there are larger questions that we now must face: What is philanthropy willing to fight for? What does philanthropy stand for? What happens if we choose to do nothing at this critical time in our history?

These times demand courage, leadership and collective voice. The question, for philanthropy, is whether we are willing to put our considerable resources—not just money but also our moral voice, social capital, reputation and thought leadership—to use in service of these pressing needs. We say we are dedicated to the common good, but missions and visions are only as powerful as the work that flows from them.

When David Dodson, president of the research firm MDC, talks about the state of the South, he likes to remind audiences that we should "read reality truthfully and take action responsibly." With this book, Martin and Jamil have given us their truthful reading of reality, one influenced by years of experience, research and scholarship.

Taking action responsibly, however, is up to all of us. We must look at the history of philanthropy in the South with clear eyes—the stories of success and progress, as well as the stumbles, miscalculations and failures. We must absorb that history into our hearts and minds and allow it to shape our intentions, thoughts and actions.

If we succeed in doing this, we can help ensure that the next chapter in Southern philanthropy's history, and the history of the South itself, does not repeat the errors of the past, but instead builds on the progress we have made to tell a powerful story—a story of hope, justice and love for all humankind.

Janine Lee
President & CEO
Southeastern Council of Foundations
July 2019

A Foreword by Laura McCarty

Georgia Humanities' work is sharing stories that move us and make us, as well as bringing people together in learning and conversation. As we listen to each other's stories, as well as to the ideas and cultural traditions of those who came before, we are equipped to make decisions for the future and to interact with the opportunities and challenges of life in new ways.

Philanthropy is sharing treasure, time, and talents for the purpose of serving others or "loving humankind." Like a humanities program, philanthropy involves exchange in order to benefit other people and the greater good.

This book, as well as programs that accompany it, provides an exemplary opportunity for reflecting on the people, ideas, and organizations that have been involved in philanthropy in the South throughout American history. It is appropriate that it is being published in conjunction with the 50th anniversary of the Southeastern Council of Foundations, a vibrant network that brings grant-makers together in identifying the most pressing needs of the region, in exchanging best practices, and also building a common vision for service to the people and communities of the South.

As Georgia Humanities approaches its own 50th anniversary in 2021, we are honored to help support this book. The authors are Georgia Humanities president emeritus Jamil Zainaldin and former board member Martin Lehfeldt, who have collaborated and formed partnerships between Georgia Humanities and the Southeastern Council of Foundations for nearly 25 years. These collaborations have endured, because of the deep resonances between the work of philanthropy and the public humanities.

Laura J. McCarty

Laura McCarty
President
Georgia Humanities
July 2019

THE LIBERATING PROMISE OF PHILANTHROPY

INTRODUCTION

We hold these truths to be self-evident, that all men are created equal, that they are endowed by their Creator with certain unalienable Rights, that among these are Life, Liberty and the pursuit of Happiness.—That to secure these rights, Governments are instituted among Men, deriving their just powers from the consent of the governed.

—Declaration of Independence

...to form a more perfect Union, establish Justice, insure domestic Tranquility, provide for the common defence, promote the general Welfare, and secure the Blessings of Liberty to ourselves and our Posterity...

—Preamble, U.S. Constitution

The Promise and Our Focus

At the heart of these sacred lines from our country's earliest documents, carefully crafted by our nation's Founders, is a promise of liberty and equality to their descendants. Our book seeks to describe some of the ways that Americans have tried to keep that promise—especially through the activities of foundations at work in the South.

Because "foundation" has no legal definition, both not-for-profit and for-profit organizations may claim the name—and often do. Our references and generalizations refer for the most part to grant-making foundations whose primary purpose is to disburse the return on investment of assets earmarked for charitable purposes to other not-for-profit institutions. As the spirit and philosophy of generosity and philanthropy have evolved and contributed to the formation of grant-making foundations in the United States, so too have the laws and courtroom decisions that regulate these organizations. From the early days of Elizabethan exploration and colonialism through the rise of capitalism and the supplanting of Church authority by the rule of the State, there has been a steady movement in the direction of private management of charitable resources in the United States in collaboration with the federal government.

Grant-making foundations constitute a deeply entrenched delivery system of American generosity in which compassion and capital come together for the public good. For religious or secular reasons, individuals and corporations determine to share a portion of their assets. Strongly encouraged by tax laws that permit charitable deductions and exemptions, they transfer those assets to foundations, which invest them and generate earnings that can then be disbursed to not-for-profit institutions and causes. Through the "miracle" of compound interest, it is possible for well-managed assets to increase even as the foundations give away a portion of the yield from the investment. Foundations thereby have the potential to operate in perpetuity.

Like the recipients to which they disburse funds, foundations are part of a distinctly American form of social organization that occupies an essential middle ground between citizens and their government. At their best, they help to protect the interests of people whose needs are not met by their government, even as they enhance the services that government does provide.[1] Foundations may come in for criticism from the press, the public, or the rest of the nonprofit sector, but, strictly speaking, they are accountable only to the Congress of the United States. Yet, although regulated by the government, there exists a long tradition of the two working closely together. Congress has periodically called them to account but as yet has not seen fit to abolish their right to exist. Indeed, the nation's lawmakers continue to encourage the formation and growth of foundations by providing tax benefits to their donors.

It would be naive to overlook the fact that some foundation donors have taken personal advantage of laws that permitted them to shield private assets from taxation. However, it also would be wrong to characterize the creation of all foundations as a monumental tax dodge. The overwhelming majority came into being as an expression of their donors' charitable impulses or interest in social reform, as well as a desire to give back to the communities in which they prospered financially.

Donors' interests and styles vary greatly. Dorothy Ridings, a former president of the Council on Foundations, was fond of saying, "If you've seen one foundation, you've seen one foundation." Their missions may be as broad as the betterment of life for all humankind or as focused as the protection of a single endangered species. Their donors may have biases. Doris Buffett, sister of the renowned billionaire philanthropist Warren Buffett, is reputed to have had an aversion to her foundation supporting "SOBs" (as she termed symphonies, operas, and ballets). Although their grants total only about 16% of all giving in the United States, foundations have the ability and even greater potential to be a force for positive change in the achievement of the American dream by all of our country's citizens.[2]

The South upon which we have chosen to focus is composed essentially of the states that formed the Confederacy, with the omission of Missouri and Texas and the addition of Kentucky: Alabama, Arkansas, Florida, Georgia, Kentucky, Louisiana, Mississippi, North Carolina, South Carolina, Tennessee, and Virginia. This list also constitutes the service area, since the 1970s, of the Southeastern Council of Foundations.

Context

Not all of our narrative is directly tied to the formation and performance of grant-making foundations. Like other human-shaped instruments, they draw their values and style of operation from the social structure of their surroundings. For that reason, we have tried to portray with some detail the changing civic climate (including both national and global developments) in which these foundations came into being and exercised their philanthropy.

Thus, we have taken the time and space to describe phenomena like the economic development required to generate the capital resources that became foundation assets. Other background information we have examined includes political movements, the role of taxation, wars, population change, and the nature of government—all of which figure into the establishment of America's grant-making foundations as resources for the region.

Because of the importance of context, this book is also about the way in which American attitudes about race, slavery, civil rights, and equity influenced the spirit of benevolence and the creation of foundations and, conversely, how some of those foundations attempted to change those same attitudes.

Philanthropy

Because its literal translation from Greek is "the love of humankind," *philanthropy* can be and often is the word used to describe a multiplicity of benevolent behaviors: an act of kindness to a stranger, volunteer service at a not-for-profit organization, advocacy for a humanitarian cause, a dollar placed into a Salvation Army kettle, or multimillion dollar gifts and grants to universities and hospitals. Generous benefactors may choose to concentrate their attention upon the relief of suffering, the improvement of living standards, the provision of amenities for the "good life," the promotion of social reform, or the support of civic engagement.[3]

Scholars of philanthropy increasingly use that word to describe strategic giving by foundations and corporations and thereby to set it apart from acts of often individualistic charity which may be more impulsive. In its many forms, it weaves itself through all of American life. Inspired by both religious and humanistic values and fueled by the creation of private capital, the citizens of the world's wealthiest country disburse a significant portion of their time, talent, and treasure for what they perceive to be the public good.[4] Claire Gaudiani describes the phenomenon of American philanthropy this way: "Citizen generosity has, for almost two hundred years, created a social environment where capitalism could flourish without destroying democracy."[5] We might add that it also is an environment where democracy can flourish without destroying capitalism.

As students and practitioners of philanthropy, we applaud all generosity that seeks to advance the common good, and we have witnessed countless examples of its positive impact. However, we do not believe that all giving offers equal benefit to the human condition. In support of that condition we cite Moses ben Maimonides, the great Jewish philosopher and physician of the 12th century, and his reflections on human benevolence.

Moses ben Maimonides
Wikimedia Commons

Maimonides, a Sephardic Jew who became one of the most prolific and influential Torah scholars of the Middle Ages, contended that there are gradations in the way that we express care for each other. He sought to capture them on a scale that describes eight forms of giving. Ranked lowest is a gift that is given grudgingly. As one translation puts it, the noblest (and highest ranked) of all forms of generosity occurs when one assists a poor fellow human being by providing that person with a gift, a loan, or an opportunity for a business partnership or by helping that person to find employment.[6] We would paraphrase further by stating that the greatest demonstrations of philanthropy are those that liberate fellow human beings from a state of dependency and move them toward independence and dignity, thereby helping to build an inclusive society.

Being Southern

All regions of the United States can properly lay claim to some measure of uniqueness. In the Northeast, Boston and Philadelphia may debate which is the true Cradle of Liberty, but all of the New England and Middle Atlantic states share the history and pride of being the birthplace of the Industrial Revolution and the center of stupendous corporate en-

terprise and wealth accumulation during the Gilded Age. Midwestern-
ers in turn understand their region's historic role to have been that of the
nation's breadbasket and later a central commercial and transportation
hub. The story of "the West" is transfused with the so-called frontier
spirit, and the coastal Pacific states blend a boom-town ethos with the
centuries-old influence of both Spanish and Asian culture.

Nevertheless, it is doubtful whether any section of the nation has
elevated the celebration of its peculiar "sense of place" to a higher plane
than has the South.[7] When asked to describe our region, we who claim
it as home are quick to point to a less frenzied pace of life than elsewhere
in the country. Tapping into our decidedly agrarian roots, both white
and black Southerners can with some accuracy describe their land as
a bucolic (at least in the past) setting of distinct dialects and colorful
colloquialisms expressed by tightly knit, church-going families.

Southerners proudly cite the remarkably diverse environmental
beauty of the region. Authors by birth or ancestry like Erskine Caldwell, Truman Capote, Pearl Cleage, Pat Conroy, Ralph Ellison William
Faulkner, Carson McCullers, Toni Morrison, Flannery O'Connor,
Alice Walker, and Eudora Welty anchor its rich and poignant literary
heritage and traditions. Also high on the list of defining characteristics
are the South's legendary hospitality, the importance of family, and its
unique culinary heritage. The soundtrack for this story of the South
includes folk music with European roots, but it draws even more heavily
upon the African American traditions of the blues, gospel, jazz, and
eventually rock and roll and hip-hop. Some would be quick to add the
popularity of NASCAR, the primacy of football, and a preoccupation

with politeness and gentility to the list of defining features.[8]

Southerners also are capable of defining themselves by emphasizing what they are *not*. James Sellers, a theologian writing in and about the South in the late 20th century, offered a fresh gloss on some familiar themes when he wrote that the Southerner has

> A sense of place, which may be contrasted with the Northerner's sense of time. A high valuation on the rootedness and personalness of man, which may be contrasted with the Northerner's high valuation on the equality of man. A passion for concreteness, which may be contrasted with the Northerner's thirst for universality in the abstract. A longing for stability, which may be contrasted with the Northerner's hankering for progress.[9]

Many of these features are highly marketable and have served to underscore some of what sets the South apart from the rest of the nation. More problematic for white Southerners are two painful pieces of history: 1) the region is the only one in the nation ever to be devastated by a war that it started and then lost; and 2) the Southern states more rigidly codified racial inequity for a century after it had been outlawed than any other section of the country. To attempt to tell any part of the Southern story without acknowledgment of these documented facts is to misstate our complex past. No honest accounting of the South's history from any perspective, including a look at its foundations, can skirt the crippling damage of slavery and the subsequent legal and cultural insistence upon white supremacy, both of which warped its patterns of generosity and delayed the arrival of an inclusive society for all Southerners.

One can speculate that the highlighting of the South's many cultural charms and amenities during the past century and a half constitute a defensive mechanism to avoid confronting the more shadowy portions of our past. As Robert Penn Warren opined, it was "in defeat the solid south was born—not only the witless automatism of fidelity to the Democratic Party, but the mystique of prideful 'difference,' identity, and defensiveness."[10] We will explore these themes later in our review of the "Lost Cause" movement.

The "sense of place" and the "way of life" that the South cherishes encompass an appreciation of all that is good about the region, its people, and their history. However, protecting those values also has sometimes required the conscious decision by many of the region's white citizens to set themselves apart from others in order to resist change. The South historically has represented a struggle between wanting to belong and share in the good life that all Americans hold virtually sacred and yet to cling tightly to old norms and beliefs at whatever cost. That struggle continues to roil beneath the surface of the region today. It is central to an understanding of why the formal institutions of philanthropy and civil society developed as they did.

History and Memory

Southerners often proclaim their love of history.[11] Yet, as Karl Stauber, former CEO of the Danville (VA) Regional Foundation, observed, "Philanthropy in the South largely ignores that history is part of what divides us."[12] For many Americans—perhaps even more in the South—history and memory are easily confused with each other. The killings at Emanuel AME Church in Charleston, SC in 2015 that were motivated by racism painfully re-opened a public debate about the appropriate display of Confederate flags and other memorials of the past. Then, in August, 2017, a white supremacist rally in Charlottesville that became violent further enflamed the conflict.

Todd Groce, president and CEO of the Georgia Historical Society, has reflected upon this contentious conversation and points to the words of the historian David Blight of Yale University for guidance in navigating the murky waters separating fact from memory:

> History is what trained historians do, a reasoned recon-struction of the past rooted in research. [On the other hand], memory is often treated as a sacred set of absolute meanings and stories, possessed as the heritage or iden-tity of a community. Memory is often owned, history in-terpreted. Memory is passed down through generations; history is revised. Memory often coalesces in objects, sites, and monuments; history seeks to understand contexts in all their complexity. History asserts the authority of academic training and canons of evidence; memory carries the often more immediate authority of community membership and experience.[13]

Groce then shares a story to illustrate these points:

> During the 150th anniversary of the Civil War, the Georgia

Historical Society installed two new historical markers about the March to the Sea that attempted to de-mythologize the subject. Despite decades of scholarly research demonstrating that Sherman's destruction was primarily limited to foodstuffs, livestock, factories, and railroads, the suggestion that most private homes escaped unscathed triggered an angry reaction from those raised on stories of Southern victimization. "Some of us still remember," declared one outraged older Savannahian when she read the marker text. "My grandmother told me that Sherman burned all the houses to the ground. Are you telling me she was a liar?" Obviously, this woman wasn't alive during the Civil War, but memory is not confined to eyewitnesses. It is transmitted across time.[14]

To be sure, nearly two decades into the 21st century, some of the Southern veneration of the region's collective memories is waning. After all, even though it took more than a hundred years, it is now more widely, although not universally, accepted that the Civil War was fought over the issue of slavery. We can thus acknowledge, as a matter of historic record, that on March 21, 1861, speaking extemporaneously to an overflow crowd at the Athenaeum in Savannah, Georgia, Alexander H. Stephens, vice president of the Confederate States of America, declared, "Our new government is founded upon...the great truth, that the negro is not equal to the white man; that slavery—subordination to the superior race—is his natural and normal condition."[15]

On the occasion of the removal of four Confederate monuments from places of prominence in the city of New Orleans, Mayor Mitch Landrieu delivered a powerful speech that cited the above statement by Alexander Stephens and further included these remarks:

> I want to speak about why we chose to remove these four monuments to the Lost Cause of the Confederacy, but also how and why this process can move us towards healing and understanding of each other. So, let's start with the facts.
>
> The historic record is clear, the Robert E. Lee, Jefferson Davis, and P.G.T. Beauregard statues were not erected just to honor these men, but as part of the movement which became known as The Cult of the Lost Cause. This 'cult' had one goal—through monuments and through other means—to rewrite history to hide the truth, which is that the Confederacy was on the wrong side of humanity. First erected over 166 years after the founding of our city and 19 years after the end of the Civil War, the monuments that we took down were meant to rebrand the history of our city and the ideals of a defeated Confederacy. It is self-evident that these men did not fight for the United States of America, they fought against it. They may have been warriors, but in this cause they were not patriots. These statues are not just stone and metal. They are not just innocent remembrances of a benign history. These monuments purposefully celebrate a fictional, sanitized Confederacy; ignoring the death, ignoring the enslavement, and the

terror that it actually stood for.[16]

The South's search for the true roots of the region's history has heightened its visibility and broadened the national discussion about memory and history. Other distinctions between the South and the rest of the country also are blurring. This is especially the case in the sprawling urban areas muddled by the relentless migration of Americans from other parts of the country and new waves of immigration from Latin America, Asia, Africa, the Middle East and Central Europe. By 2025 the populations of California and Texas will have increased more than any other states, but Florida, Georgia, North Carolina, and Virginia together will add some 14 million people to their rolls.[17]

And yet, the past, as Southern writer William Faulkner famously noted, "is never dead. It's not even past."[18] That cautionary note is especially instructive when one considers the people and institutions of a region like the South that selectively treasures what has been.

Southern Foundations[19]

Our initial interest in philanthropy and foundations led us to the discovery that no one seemed to have attempted to capture the history of foundation formation and activity in the southern United States. Southern foundations also have received scant attention in most of the scholarly study of national philanthropy.

Some individual foundations had chronicled their own histories. The ones we have read are interesting and even colorful but understandably not always reflective or self-critical. Organizations like the Foundation Center, the Southeastern Council of Foundations, and the Council on Foundations have periodically issued useful statistical reports about the growth and giving patterns of foundations in the region (Alabama, Arkansas, Florida, Georgia, Kentucky, Louisiana, Mississippi, North Carolina, South Carolina, Tennessee, and Virginia). Those studies, though, offer little interpretation of the factors that helped to shape them.

We anticipate that the coming years will see a new willingness by all of America's foundations to examine their past. A new generation seems ready to explore, among other factors, the relationship of their histories to the national climate of racism and segregation, the practices of which helped to generate the profits that made possible the formation of some of those foundations.

Our search for the origins of Southern foundations took us on three different trails. The first led us to the Founders of the new American Republic—some of the most influential of whom were Southerners (and future presidents). As we will describe in the first chapter of the book, they ranked liberty and a commitment to service among the highest values. As Benjamin Franklin observed, the Founders were "establishing government by human wisdom" and not leaving it to "chance, war, or conquest."[20] Their vision was the creation of a new kind of social order—an inclusive society whose hallmarks were inter-dependence and mutuality. They did not fully achieve that vision, but they laid the foundation for a distinctly American form of philanthropy.

The second path led us to the "new birth of freedom" and a new kind of nation that emerged after a Civil War—our country's second revolution. The interrupted vision returned as influential donors from the North, newly freed citizens, and others in a war-shattered South came together to forge an evolving civil society. The first revolution had been rooted in the rhetoric of liberty. This one found its soul and spirit not just in the founding principles of the Declaration of Independence but also in the further and fuller legal expression of those ideals in the 13th, 14th, and 15th amendments to the U.S. Constitution. Idealism began to be translated into pragmatic service.

Then we turned to the end of the 19th century when Southerners controlled the U.S. Congress. As we will discuss, the South also can make a case for having played a decisive role in the passage of the 16th Amendment and legislation that led to the adoption of regulations governing charitable exemptions and deductions and thereby the encouragement of philanthropy by the newly-wealthy.

Until the years just before the Great Depression, the number of indigenous Southern foundations with significant assets was small. Most notable was the Duke Endowment in North Carolina. A dozen or so community foundations (some of which did not survive) and an uncertain but small number of family foundations with narrow geographical foci rounded out the sprinkling of grant-making institutions across the Southern states.

Thus, had we titled this work "The History of Southern Foundations," the result would have been a much shorter manuscript, covering barely a century. However, we uncovered a story that cannot be told without reference to foundations that were first established in the North but chose to become active in the affairs of the South. These institutions began making their presence felt immediately after the Civil War.

Indeed, it may be said that the South functioned as a kind of field laboratory in which new and large foundations tested their concepts about how to use private resources to bring about positive change to serve the public good. If they had not appeared on the devastated Southern landscape when they did, the true return of the former Confederate states to the Union might have been delayed much longer, as also would have been the modern civil rights movement. These Northern benefactors are therefore an essential part of the Southern story.

In 1977 Charles S. Rooks, the first salaried executive director of the Southeastern Council of Foundations, undertook a study of grant-making in the region served by his organization. Drawing in part upon limited data gathered by the Foundation Center in 1974, he concluded that more than a century after the end of the Civil War, grant-makers from outside the South were responsible for fully one-third of all grants to not-for-profit Southern institutions.[21] The philanthropic balance of trade definitely favored the South, which exported relatively few grants to other parts of the country. Non-Southern foundations continue to have an influence upon the enhancement of Southern life.

Authors' Leanings

As our readers consider the cultural and political climate in which all of these philanthropic institutions came into being, we invite them to draw their own conclusions about the relationship between the past and present as well as the role of the South in the advent of a new and distinctly modern form of philanthropy—the grant-making foundation.

To be sure, many thousands of Southern foundations, like their

JAMES OGLETHORPE

He never captured great wealth; he never established a foundation. But unusual if not unique among the founders of colonial America, James Oglethorpe dreamed of a truly classless and enterprising civil society. In 1733 he brought with him to Yamacraw Bluff, in what would become the town of Savannah, the layout for a model city, the official motto of which was *Non Sibi Sed Aliss* (not for self, but for others). Undergirded by peaceful habitation with the Creek Indian tribe led by Tomochichi, this new settlement restricted the amount of land an individual could own, had a plan for the cultivation of silk, banned slavery, prohibited the consumption of rum, and welcomed most persecuted religious minorities. (Acknowledging the threatening presence of Spain in Florida, Catholicism was banned). It also prohibited the presence of lawyers.

The vision of Oglethorpe and his trustees was realized—but only for a short while. By 1751, the example of neighboring South Carolina's slavery-based rice and cotton wealth proved irresistible and Parliament (in response to a powerful faction of the Georgia colony's settlers) lifted the ban on slavery. If philanthropy at its best contributes to the building of civil society, then for a time during the 18th century this planned colony was a truly pace-setting model of philanthropic organization.

Source: Jamil Zainaldin, from a speech given at a donor event of the Community Foundation for Greater Atlanta.

The Creek Indians meet with James Oglethorpe.
Courtesy of Hargrett Rare Book and Manuscript Library / University of Georgia

counterparts throughout the U.S., continue to contribute to the general wellbeing of their fellow creatures, and for that we can all be grateful. We also would be among the first to defend the right of all foundations to support institutions and causes that they believe will enhance the lives of at least some of the earth's inhabitants and protect some portion of the planet. Nonetheless, as we have considered the century-old arc from our nation's beginning to its re-establishment in 1865, and then its continuing re-invention and evolution, we confess to having developed a special affection for those foundations whose programs and grant-making were and continue to be guided or at least strongly influenced by that early dream and latent promise of a civil society.

Closing Thoughts

In the last section of this book we offer some observations and raise some questions about the future of Southern-based and Southern-oriented philanthropy. Which distinctive features of foundation activity will remain in place in the South during the 21st century? Can Southern grant-making, itself a product of unique historical forces, play a meaningful and moderating role between a complex past and the forces of change? In short, what are the prospects for the grant-making foundations of the South?

Finally, we hope that our work will help to generate new interest by other writers and historians. The universe of Southern foundations offers rich material for anyone interested in discovering how they came into being, what they have accomplished, and what their future may hold.

Our hope for this kind of continued study stems directly from one deep regret: we were unable to tell the stories of more foundations and the individuals associated with them. To be sure, it was never our intention to compile an encyclopedia. Yet, the quantity of valuable new information we encountered was beyond the scope of a single book. We can only hope that the individuals and institutions we did not mention will recognize their spirit and style in their colleagues' examples of philanthropy that we have described.

Martin Lehfeldt and Jamil Zainaldin
Atlanta, Georgia, 2019

ENDNOTES

1   See Thomas Adam, ed., *Philanthropy, Patronage, and Civil Society: Experiences from Germany, Great Britain, and North America* (Bloomington: Indiana University Press, 2004).

2   *Giving USA*. 2018 was a record year for all forms of giving by American individuals and institutions.

3   Adam Davis and Elizabeth Lynn, eds., *The Civically Engaged Reader* (Chicago: Great Books Foundation, 2006).

4   Remarkable celebrations (and defenses) of philanthropy and its variety may be found in *The Almanac of American Philanthropy*, edited by Karl Zinsmeister and published by the Philanthropy Roundtable. It includes more than 1,300 pages of highly readable stories, articles, and charts plus a timeline of American charitable giving beginning in 1636.

5   Claire Gaudiani, *The Greater Good: How Philanthropy Drives the American Economy and Can Save Capitalism* (New York: Henry Holt and Company, 2003), 1. Gaudiani's work is an admirable overview of the many ways in which the spirit of personal generosity has expressed itself throughout American history.

6   Amy A. Kass, ed., *Doing Well, Doing Good: Readings for Thoughtful Philanthropists* (Bloomington: Indiana University Press, 2008), 95-96. Why it is important not to forget Maimonides is explained by Maxwell King, "Maimonides and Me: Lessons from Up and Down the Ladder of Giving," in *Philanthropy Magazine* (May/June 2004).

7   Although we have attempted our own gloss on a brief description of the South, we highly recommend the insightful and highly readable *Away Down South: A History of Southern Identify* by James C. Cobb (Oxford, 2003).

8   The classic study of the South's complex and at times ephemeral identity, one that is as readable today as when first published in 1960, is C. Vann Woodward, *The Burden of Southern History* (Baton Rouge, 1960). Also see further thoughts on particularity by James C. Cobb, *Away Down South: A History of Southern Identity* (Oxford, 2003), 288-339.

9   Quoted in Thomas Allen, "A Review of the South and Christian Ethics, Part 1," accessed Dec. 24, 2017 at: *http://tcallenco.blogspot.com/2015/09/a-review-of-south-and-christian-ethics_14.html*.

10   Quoted in Dewey W. Grantham, *The Life and Death of the Solid South* (Lexington: University Press of Kentucky, 1992), 1.

11   Consider some of the founding dates of the region's historical societies: Virginia (1831); Louisiana (1835); Kentucky (1836); Georgia (1839); Tennessee (1849); South Carolina (1855); Mississippi (1858).

12   Correspondence with Karl Stauber, April 4, 2018.

13   David W. Blight, *The Battlefield: Race, Memory, and the American Civil War* (Amherst & Boston: University of Massachusetts Press, 2002), 1-2.

14   W. Todd Groce, *https://saportareport.com/when-history-and-memory-collide*, retrieved December 15, 2017.

15   Henry Cleveland, *Alexander H. Stephens, in Public and Private: With Letters and Speeches, Before, During, and Since the War* (Chicago & Philadelphia: National Publishing Company, ca. 1866), 717-729. Accessed March 22, 2018 at: *http://teachingamericanhistory.org/library/document/cornerstone-speech/*.

Further evidence of the reason for secession can be found on page 18 of the *Journal* of the state convention of South Carolina held in April, 1852: "Resolved by the people of South Carolina in Convention assembled, That the frequent violations of the Constitution of the United States by the federal Government, and its encroachments upon reserved right of the sovereign States of the Union, **especially in relation to slavery,** [*boldface added for emphasis*] simply justify this State, so far as any duty or obligation to confederates in involved, in dissolving at once all political connection with her co-Stated; and that she forbears the exercise of this manifest right of self-government from considerations of expediency only."

16 *New York Times*, May 23, 2017 and retrieved March 22, 2018 at:
    https://www.nytimes.com/2017/05/23/opinion/mitch-landrieus-speech-transcript.html.

17 *https://www.census.gov/prod/2/pop/p25/p25-1131.pdf,* retrieved March 22, 2018.

18 William Faulkner, *Requiem for a Nun*, act 1, scene 3. See A. Nicholas Fargnoli, W. Michael Golay, and Robert W. Hamblin, *Critical Companion to William Faulkner* (Facts on File, Inc.: New York, 2008), 232.

19 Southern foundations historically have directed a significant portion of their giving to religious institutions and causes. The Southern philanthropic landscape also includes so-called "Christian foundations," denominational foundations, and Jewish federations (some quite large) established to support the building of churches and synagogues, the work of seminaries and colleges, and other, more narrowly focused, ecclesiastical ventures like evangelism and mission work. Many of them, like community foundations, function as vehicles for personal giving. Like many of the topics upon which we have touched, they merit a study of their own.

20 Jeffery Alan Smith, *Franklyn and Bache: Envisioning the Enlightened Republic (*New York and Oxford: Oxford University Press, 1990), 14.

21 Charles S. Rooks, *Foundation Philanthropy in the Southeast* (Atlanta, Southeastern Council of Foundations, 1977).

CHAPTER 1

Philanthropic Impulses and Their Obstacles

The Revolutionary Roots of Philanthropy

The seeds of our nation's grant-making foundations were planted by the Founders. To be sure, Thomas Jefferson, the inveterate inventor of everything from a swivel chair to a machine for making elbow macaroni, did not envision the modern foundation that we recognize today. It is further likely that Mr. Jefferson would be suspicious of today's multibillion-dollar foundations, as he was of all great wealth concentrated in the hands of a small minority. However, it also seems clear that he and Mr. Franklin and Mr. Madison and Mr. Washington and their colleagues—idealists of the highest order—had a very clear sense of the civic behavior that would be required for the establishment of the republic they had in mind as they prepared to sever their ties to England.[1]

For the Founders, classical philanthropy (the "love of humankind") both mirrored and promoted a spirit of generosity, moral correctness, and the desire to serve. This concept of public virtue—since dubbed the "republican synthesis"—stemmed from their deep study of

Bust of Cicero
Credit: José Luiz Bernardes
Ribeiro / CC BY-SA 4.0

CICERO

"With the disappearance of Latin from the schoolroom, the greatest statesman of ancient Rome, Marcus Tullius Cicero, is now a dimly remembered figure. He does not deserve this fate and it is time to restore him to his proper place in the pantheon of our common past.

One powerful motive for doing so is that, nearly two thousand years after his time, he became an unknowing architect of constitutions that still govern our lives. For the founding fathers of the United States and their political counterparts in Great Britain, the writings of Tully (as his name was Anglicized) were the foundation of their education. John Adams's first book and proudest possession was his Cicero."

Excerpt from Anthony Everitt, *Cicero: The Life and Times of Rome's Greatest Politician* (New York: Random House, 2003).

the past.[2] These intellectual politicians who comprised the Revolutionary Generation delved into classical Greek and Roman thinkers like Pericles and Cicero (whose works they read in the original languages). They consumed the writings by the civic humanists of the Renaissance. They pondered the thinking by philosophers in 17th-century England and France and during the later Enlightenment, those who celebrated the power and influence of reason to advance society.

They especially imbibed the thoughts of Scottish philosophers like Francis Hutcheson, David Hume, and Adam Smith, as well as the Englishman John Locke. It was Locke who enshrined "fellow feeling" and "empathy" as inherent human attributes that made self-government and the resulting civil society not only possible but supremely desirable. That they believed their new government to be a "gift" to posterity seems clear. Whether it could be made to work for the elevation of human community was another matter. As Benjamin Franklin emerged from the final day of the Constitutional Convention's proceedings and into the streets of his city, a lady asked him, "Well, Doctor Franklin, what have we got, a republic or monarchy?" "A republic," replied Franklin, "if you can keep it."[3]

Unlike charity (which the Founders regarded as more of a religious duty), philanthropy was a broadly inclusive state of mind and activity. It stood in opposition to aristocracy, monarchy, and ecclesiastical control and supported the formation of a republic. Philanthropy, an attitude of interdependence, held the promise of being the glue that would hold together this experiment to secure life, liberty, and the pursuit of happiness for all of the new country's citizens.

It might even be interpreted that the ultimate purpose of philanthropy for the Founders was liberation, the same goal that ignited the American Revolution. George McCully imaginatively, and even inspirationally, illustrates the harmony of philanthropy and revolution in a remarkable study that traces the word's origin to *Prometheus Bound* by Aeschylus, the ancient Greek playwright. Prometheus is the mythical Titan who created humankind from clay. His creatures initially lived in dark caves and in constant fear for their lives. When Zeus determined to destroy them, Prometheus—motivated by his *philanthropos tropos* (humanity-loving character)—gave them fire (symbolizing all the knowledge and skills that make civilization possible) and thereby the hope for a meaningful future.[4] Certainly the visionary designers of the American Republic in the 18th century were

A TRIBUTE TO PHILANTHROPY

On June 28, 1805, the Lewis and Clark expedition was surveying a portion of the Louisiana Purchase territory that is now southwestern Montana. When the party came to a confluence of three rivers that flowed into the Missouri, Captain Meriwether Lewis was moved to honor his mentor, President Thomas Jefferson, by naming one of the rivers after him. (He christened the other two after James Madison, Jefferson's Secretary of State, and Albert Gallatin, Secretary of the Treasury.) A few weeks later, they encountered other tributaries flowing into the newly named Jefferson River. Lewis designated them Wisdom and Philanthropy—which he described as two of Jefferson's "cardinal virtues." The Philanthropy River later came to be called Stinking Water, but today bears the more salubrious name of Ruby River.

Source: The story of this remarkable journey of exploration and the naming of the rivers is told in Stephen E. Ambrose, *Undaunted Courage: Meriwether Lewis, Thomas Jefferson, and the Opening of the American West* (New York: Touchstone, 1997).

onto something significant, and they knew it. George Washington wrote, "However unimportant America may be considered at present, and however Britain may affect to despise her trade, there will assuredly come a day, when this country will have some weight in the scale of Empires."[5]

A New Adam

The Founders (and some of their European contemporaries) understood themselves to constitute a "new Adam,"[6] inhabiting a new kind of Eden. Just as the biblical Adam had been unfettered by anything that may have come before him, Americans were establishing a new relationship with their environment, with their fellow human beings, with technology, and with their new form of government.

Having begun clearing the land of its native inhabitants and secured their freedom from a colonizing power, white Americans could indeed characterize what they had established as heaven on earth—surely a sign of God's endorsement and grace. In the new American republic, the biblical evocation made sense and at times seemed even to be the point of it all. As a generally God-fearing people, Americans found it easy to believe that societal progress and scientific improvements signaled a divine blessing and perhaps even destiny.

The most visible evidence of divine bounty was the building and accumulation of wealth. As early as 1816, the congressman and historian Timothy Pitkin could write (exultingly), "No nation, it is believed, has ever increased so rapidly in wealth as the United States."[7]

Slavery and Wealth

In post–Revolutionary War America, change was the watchword of the day. It was palpable in every quarter—so much so that even the rising tension over the issue of slavery was for white people at times more of a distraction than an obstacle. The nation was growing and spreading, peopled by immigrants with Scottish burrs, Old World pronunciations of the English language, French and "Dutch" (German) accents, and after 1845, Irish brogues. For all that, though, the land, still sparsely settled, continued to be home to an essentially pastoral society. The chief modes of transportation were the horse and wagon for those who could afford one or both, with carriages for the wealthy. Because water-borne vessels were the most effective way to transport bulk goods, the emerging commercial towns and handful of cities naturally bordered navigable rivers, tidal bays, harbors, and canals (the best-known being the Erie Canal in New York State).[8]

Much of the new American wealth, in the North as well as the South, was increasingly generated by slavery. A visitor traveling through the South in 1790, however, could easily have inferred that slavery was well on the road to extinction. Soil depletion and erosion from the plantation-style agriculture that grew tobacco, rice, and indigo extracted a heavy toll from the land, reducing profitability. The cost of owning slaves was becoming a financial drain; the typical Virginia planter was debt-ridden. Perhaps Thomas Jefferson's expectation was to be fulfilled: the country's embarrassing—and "peculiar"—institution would eventually exhaust itself and die away. Economic salvation came from an unlikely source. Eli Whitney, a New Englander and Phi Beta Kappa graduate of Yale University, had come south to work as a tutor for a South Carolina planter's children. When that job failed to materialize, Whitney became a guest at Mulberry Grove, a rice-producing plantation a dozen miles upriver from Savannah, Georgia, in 1793. There, he was encouraged to design a device to separate the fiber of short-staple cotton from the seed. His invention of the cotton engine (the "gin") revolution- ized the harvesting of that crop, reinvigorated the institution of slavery, and changed the course of American history.[9] In short order, large-scale cotton plantations worked by slaves using gins that were manufactured in New Haven, Connecticut, became highly profitable—at least for the 17% of the white population that owned 66% of the land.[10]

Picking cotton, Savannah, Georgia
Courtesy of the Library of Congress, LC-DIG-ppmsca-39592

The 1860 Census records 13% of all the nation's 31.443,321 million inhabitants as enslaved.[11] Leaving aside the ideology of those who would abolish it and those who defended it, slavery was a mon- ey-generator. One reliable study estimates "the value of the labor per- formed by black slaves in America between 1619 and 1865" at $71.1

trillion (compounded at 6% interest).[12] Cotton, rice, tobacco, and sugar cane were becoming elements of a national and international market system that involved massive capital investments to generate new wealth. Into the craw of this vigorous Atlantic economy were thrust not only millions of men, women and children but also untold numbers of "assorted overseers, business managers, clerks, brokers, warehousemen, factors, bankers, ginners, carpenters, blacksmiths, tenants, hoe help, sharecroppers, shippers, common farmers, and planters, to say nothing of oxen and mules and horses and machinery."[13]

Southern planters wanted even more land and pushed westward. The steamboat was the great penetrator, navigating the Mississippi River and its tributaries, connecting the Ohio, Tennessee, Missouri, Arkansas, and Red Rivers. By 1817 the portion of Upper Louisiana that would become Missouri petitioned to become a state. The debate over whether it would be a "free" or a "slave" state was soon raging. Those planters seeking more territory to grow more cotton would need more slaves. Furthermore, slave states were mindful of retaining their power in Congress. The addition of a new state to the Union also meant two more Senate seats and a proportional number of House votes. (One enslaved individual counted as three-fifths of a person for the purposes of Congressional apportionment.)

Missouri's 1820 admission into the Union as a slave state, with Maine joining as a free state (what became known as the Missouri Compromise), helped to preserve the balance of power between the two regions. It also added a substantial land mass to a Southern economy that continued to be controlled by a small percentage of the population.

(That lawmakers spoke and thought in these terms rocked the political veterans who watched from the sidelines, and for whom the debate clanged, Thomas Jefferson said, like the dreaded "fire bell in the night.")

While economic historians debate the precise place of slavery in the antebellum era's industrial revolution, all would agree that the Missouri Compromise altered the playing field—geographically and otherwise. The Southern economy soon matched the strength of the industrializing North. Indeed, within a few years, the South's cotton production became the raw fuel that sustained New England textile mills, helped in the financing of railroad and turnpike development in the Northeast and Midwest, and promoted international trade. By 1850 the region would become a critical link in America's burgeoning system of markets.

A slaveholding domain now stretched from Maryland, the District of Columbia, "old" Virginia, and the Carolinas into Georgia, the Black Belt region (so named because of the land's rich fertility) of North Florida, Alabama, and Mississippi, on to the Upper South states of Tennessee, Arkansas, and Missouri, and further into Louisiana and Texas. Of the world's global cotton supply, about 80% derived from the Southern states and accounted for 55% of the nation's exports. When adding to this picture of trade those regional specialties of tobacco, sugar, and rice, it is small wonder that at the advent of the Civil War more than half of the richest 1% of the U.S. population lived in the Southern states, while the average Northerner was one-fifth as wealthy as the average planter in a cotton-producing state.

This astounding wealth made it possible for some Americans to enjoy a most glamorous and self-indulgent lifestyle. As an example,

Southern planter and trader families in cities like Charleston, New Orleans, Richmond, Mobile, Memphis, and Savannah felt as much at home in the drawing rooms of New York and Philadelphia as in their own gracious parlors.

They spent summers in the North as part of the social set that dominated Ballston Spa, Saratoga Springs, and Newport, and traveled to England and France. The distribution of Southern slaveholding was not democratic. In the 1860 federal census, although 69.2% of white households did not own slaves, the South's per capita wealth was $3,978 compared to the North's $2,400. "With only 30% of the nation's free population, the South had 60% of the wealthiest men."[14]

Northern vacation spot (Saratoga Springs, New York) for southern planters
Larry Gottheim Collection, Prints & Photographs Division, Courtesy of the Library of Congress

As early as 1710, South Carolina had become a world apart. In this planters' paradise, landowners were the first true merchant princes who imagined themselves also to be monarchs and culture mavens. In their own way, they were. They capitalized on the European markets for rice, indigo, and cotton, grown in a coastal climate and Low Country landscape that made slavery highly profitable. By the eve of the Civil War, slaves accounted for more than 70% of South Carolina's population, and many of the nation's wealthiest citizens lived there. (When he died in 1773, Peter Manigault of Charleston was regarded as the richest man in British North America.)[15]

Organized Benevolence

We also recognize that a portion of this enormous cache of wealth did flow into the conduits of generosity as a wealthy white minority funded religious, educational, and cultural institutions for themselves, their families, and those closest to them. Among the more established cities in the region, their wealthy citizens built churches, theaters (e.g., Dock Street Theatre in Charleston), opera houses (in New Orleans), and other cultural amenities. Illustrating the magnitude of this wealth is the following partial listing of white Southern institutions of higher learning, both private and public, that its charitable owners helped to establish and support before the Civil War:

Table 1.1 Sample of White Higher Education Recipients of Southern Charity during the Antebellum Years		
1749	Washington and Lee	VA
1770	College of Charleston	SC
1772	Salem	NC
1775	Hampden-Sydney	VA
1780	Transylvania	KY
1785	University of Georgia	GA
1794	Tusculum	TN
1794	University of Tennessee	TN
1795	University of North Carolina	NC
1801	University of South Carolina	SC
1819	Centre	KY
1819	University of Virginia	VA

1825	Centenary	LA
1826	Furman	SC
1830	Randolph-Macon	VA
1830	Spring Hill	AL
1831	University of Alabama	AL
1833	Mercer	GA
1835	Oglethorpe	GA
1836	Emory	GA
1837	Davidson	NC
1848	Rhodes (started as Southwestern)	TN
1848	University of Mississippi	MS
1853	Louisiana State University	LA
1854	Wofford	SC
1855	Berea	KY
1855	Huntingdon	AL
1857	University of the South	TN

Compiled by the authors.

University of Alabama – Washington College, Rotunda and Jefferson College, ca. 1840
Courtesy of the University of Alabama Libraries Special Collections

The American sense of God-given destiny, the early organization of self-government after a successful revolution, and especially, the expanding wealth of the country inspired a growing interest in other charitably inspired reform. It in turn opened the door to another distinctly American phenomenon: stimulated by their rapid accumulation of new wealth, citizens began forming "associations." These new voluntary contrivances were really localized civic creations that busily began supplanting the historic roles of the church and state. They were the very embodiment of communal obligation dreamed of and anticipated by the Founders. As we will describe later, in both the North and South, the philanthropic impulse began to formalize; historian Lawrence J. Friedman paraphrases the oft-quoted but seldom-read Alexis de Tocqueville to explain:

> To be sure, charity still existed as a fundamental attitude and a way one person helped another with an immediate local difficulty. But the charitable impulse was being directed toward a more systematic institution-centered approach to long-term problems emerging from the new social order—organized philanthropy. Therefore, benevolence came to be equated less with the considerate feelings and charitable acts of individuals than with the actions of voluntary societies and other institutions through which citizens proceeded to shape public policy and the welfare of their more complex communities. Societies became more civil.[16]

This philanthropic impulse had deep roots that can be traced back to, among others, John Winthrop, the Puritan governor of the Massachusetts Bay Colony. In 1630 he sermonized about a "city upon a hill" that had a special pact with God to create a new, holy community in which the "care of the public" would be more important than private gain. What's more, the rich possessed a sacred duty to care for the poor.[17] Then, by 1710, Cotton Mather published *Bonifacius: Essays to Do Good*, wherein he encouraged congregants to create voluntary organizations for social reform. Mather heavily influenced Benjamin Franklin (born in 1706 in Boston), who would go on to introduce a series of institutional precursors of modern philanthropy in Philadelphia.

During the first half of the 19th century, social movements that sought the perfection of society and humankind and political and egalitarian reforms gained momentum. They included utopian experiments like the Transcendentalism-inspired Brook Farm in Massachusetts, efforts to expand the electoral franchise to the property-less in New York, improvements in child welfare in cities, and the construction of massive prison complexes everywhere (in cities and in the countryside) as the more democratic mission of rehabilitation and reform replaced punishment for sin. Especially far-reaching were the feminist sentiments that would find a voice in the 1848 Seneca Falls, New York, convention, as well as the push to establish universal compulsory education, led by Horace Mann in states like Massachusetts.

Financial charity, at least as practiced by whites on behalf of their fellow European Americans, had been ubiquitous in the South since the early days of the colonies. Thus, for example, the Reverend George Whitefield's itinerant ministry led to the creation of the Bethesda Orphan House and Academy in Savannah in 1740. (What made it unique was its use of colony-wide fund raising that broke with the tradition of localized public relief for the poor.)[18] Other charitable enterprises, especially for orphans, were also present later in the more established Eastern cities like Baltimore, Richmond, Petersburg, and Charleston.

In the South, the progress of social reform initially ran according to a somewhat slower clock than in the North. When De Tocqueville traveled through the region in 1831, he wrote of "the primeval forest... at every turn; society seems to be asleep, man to be idle...." He contrasted this picture with Northerners' "temporal prosperity," which seemed to be their "chief aim," one marked by "avidity in the pursuit of gain that resembles a species of heroism."[19] Had he been present two decades later, though, he might have experienced an altogether different world below the Mason-Dixon line. The historian of antebellum Southern charity, Timothy James Lockley, writes,

> I was able to document more than six hundred antebellum benevolent societies in the slaveholding states, which does not include hospitals or poorhouses paid for with public funds and organized locally. . . . It is evident that benevolence flourished in the antebellum South in proportions roughly similar to their presence in the North, taking into account the smaller white population in the South.[20]

Nonetheless, despite the parallel development of Southern and Northern civic and associational efforts, one area in which the South fell sharply behind was in publicly supported education. As astutely highlighted by James C. Cobb,

> Only 35 percent of the South's white children were enrolled in school in 1860 as compared to 72 percent outside the region, where the average school year was also 70 percent longer. This deficiency could be traced in part to

the simple reluctance of planters who educated their own children privately to part with tax dollars in order to school the offspring of the yeomanry. [21]

This discrepancy established a pattern whose shadows can still be detected in the support of public education throughout the region.

The Missouri Compromise certainly did much to magnify geography as another inescapable demarcation (together with slavery) of the emerging national divide. Although it had stiffened the line that separated the regions, at least for another two decades or so, only moderate differences seemed to distinguish the charitable behavior of New England, the Mid-Atlantic, and the South. In all three regions, depending on the local unit of government (city, borough, township, or county), provisions were made for the care of the "deserving" poor (orphans, the disabled, and widows) through a system of local taxation. In the South, tax-supported "relief" was overseen by county or municipal courts, vestries, and specially appointed commissions like the "wardens for the [white] poor."[22]

The Differing Roles of Women

Private benevolence in the South, like elsewhere in the country, tended to follow patterns of population density, trade, and the concentration of wealth. Many of the Southern states founded "asylums" for criminals that emphasized not punishment but reformation, and care for the insane as well as schools for the deaf and blind. Foremost among the advocates for these efforts was Dorothea Dix, the Northern reformer welcomed throughout the South (although she was among those, however, who turned a blind eye to the needs of African Americans).[23]

For a time, Southern women reformers, especially the generation that came of age between 1776 and 1820, formed part of a "Republican motherhood." They shared with their husbands, North and South, high hopes for the success of the American experiment in liberty and self-rule.[24] Other Southern women, organized in sewing circles, church groups, and benevolent societies, agitated for the education of white boys and girls: free schools for them, literacy, and the teaching of patriotic values.

In the antebellum North, especially important among the traits that women were said to uniquely possess were nurturing, caretaking, moral uplift, and emotional support—exactly those traits associated with "benevolence" (a term commonly used to distinguish a charitable purpose from a profit-oriented goal or legally mandated poor relief). Many Northern women came to recognize a connection between their role inside the family and their responsibility for societal improvement.

As has recently become more widely known, the example of New England's Peabody sisters (Elizabeth, Mary, and Sophia) and their influence upon Ralph Waldo Emerson, Nathaniel Hawthorne (whom Sophia married), and Horace Mann gives influential Northern women their due.[25] Not surprisingly, it was the young Republic's mothers who, like the Peabody sisters, became the foot soldiers of Northern reform and intellectual movements. Historians Robert A. Gross and Mark D. McGarvie describe women's expanding civic role as a new kind of power that was also fundamentally philanthropic.[26]

A classic 1970 study by Anne Firor Scott, *The Southern Lady:*

From Pedestal to Politics, since amplified by much other research, demythologized the old stereotype of the "idle, pampered Southern belle."[27] Catherine Clinton, one of the most important historians of gender roles in the South, agrees: "White women may not have been the initiators of expansion, but they were forced into full partnership in the building of the plantation South."[28] As historian of philanthropy David Hammack has observed, these partnerships included a multitude of small and large generosities—including a successful movement among "the free women of Petersburg, Virginia," to build an orphanage that would help "prevent white girls from being exploited and abused in ways that were not uncommon for African-American slave girls." [29]

Angelina Emily Grimké (1805-1879)
Courtesy of the Library of Congress,
LC-USZ61-1609

Sarah Moore Grimké (1792-1873)
Courtesy of the Library of Congress,
LC-USZ61-1608

Perhaps, then, we should not be too surprised when reminded that the modern human rights movement also traces its roots to two South Carolina women, Sarah and Angelina Grimké. During the antebellum era the sisters moved to the North and became abolitionists who also "spoke out for women's rights." [30]

It must be noted that despite these progressive examples, however, a significant difference between the North and the South is that the women of white planter families lived in an essentially patriarchal society. [31]

Torn between Two Legacies

In this chapter we have sought to acknowledge and even honor the zeal of our country's Founders to set its moorings upon the bedrock of an enlightened and mutually dependent citizenry that is free from all sorts of tyranny. Their idealism has been an inspiration to their successors and to people around the world.

However, the "new Adam," as many interpreted the United States to be, became infected by an old and powerful virus: the doctrine of white supremacy. It evolved from the worldwide and age-old practice of human slavery. Initially endorsed by organized Christianity, it attached itself to the imperial efforts of European nations to colonize the rest of the world. In the United States, even after the disavowal of slavery by many Christians and the abolition of slavery by the government, it found new expression in the conviction that white Christians had superseded Israel as God's covenant people. As we shall describe, it continued to undercut the liberating impulses of philanthropy. [32]

Chapter 1 Endnotes

1   The history of the United States (including that of its philanthropic organizations) can never escape the paradox that many who articulated the principles of liberty were themselves slaveholders. It continues as a metaphor of our nation's "original sin." See Jim Wallis, *America's Original Sin: Racism, White Privilege, and the Bridge to a New America* (Grand Rapids, MI: Brazos Press, 2016).

The Englishman Samuel Johnson, in his forty-page defense of Parliament in a 1775 pamphlet titled "Taxation No Tyranny," asked "How is it that we hear the loudest yelps from the drivers of negroes?," accessed March 22, 2018, http://www.samueljohnson.com/tnt.html.

At the U.S. Constitutional Convention twelve years later, George Mason, a Virginia delegate and slaveowner, confronted a foreboding truth: "Every master of slaves is born a petty tyrant. They bring the judgment of Heaven on a country. As nations cannot be rewarded or punished in the next world, they must be in this. By an inevitable chain of causes and effects, Providence punishes national sins by national calamities." Jonathan Elliot, ed., *Debates on the Adoption of the Federal Constitution, in the Convention Held at Philadelphia in 1787, as Reported by James Madison, a Member and deputy from Virginia* (Washington: Printed for the Editor, 1845), 458.

2   Four masterworks of the late 20th century have done more than any others to understand republicanism as a distinct Western ideology: Bernard Bailyn, *The Ideological Origins of the American Revolution* (Cambridge, MA: Harvard University Press, 1967); J. G. A. Pocock, *The Machiavellian Moment: Florentine Political Thought and the Atlantic Republican Tradition* (Princeton, NJ: Princeton University Press, 1975); Linda K. Kerber, *Women of the Republic: Intellect and Ideology in Revolutionary America* (Chapel Hill: University of North Carolina Press, 1980);and Gordon S. Wood, *The Creation of the American Republic, 1776-1787* (Chapel Hill: University of North Carolina Press, 1998).

3   Lee Ann Potter, "A Republic, If You Can Keep It," *Teaching with the Library of Congress* (blog), September 8, 2016, https://blogs.loc.gov/teachers/2016/09/a-republic-if-you-can-keep-it/.

4   George McCully, *Philanthropy Reconsidered: Private Initiatives—Public Good—Quality of Life* (Bloomington, IN: AuthorHouse, 2008). Contrast these observations with the contention of Maimonides that the highest form of charity was a gift that freed the recipient from dependency upon others.

5   Letter from Washington (sent from Mount Vernon) to Marquis de Lafayette, August 15, 1786, http://teachingamericanhistory.org/library/document/letter-to-marquis-de-lafayette-5/.

6   The homespun wit and wisdom of Benjamin Franklin, that polymath in his coonskin hat, did much to personify the new American Adam as he charmed and secured the admiration of the Parisians while courting French support of the Continental Congress. He was less successful across the English Channel, where he was known as "the chief of the rebels." Stacy Schiff, "Franklin in Paris," *The American Scholar* (Spring 2009), https://theamericanscholar.org/franklin-in-paris/#.

This Adamic theme traces its literary origin to J. Hector St. John de Crèvecoeur's *Letters from an American Farmer* (1782), widely read in Europe at the time because it addressed the matter of "what exactly an American is." His linkage of a "new man" with nature and the unspoiled New World environment emerged as a recognizable undertone in 19th- (as well as 20th-) century U.S. literary efforts that positioned "the American" in a "world without a past."

7   Timothy Pitkin, *A Statistical View of the Commerce of the United States of America* (Hartford, CT: Printed by Charles Hosman, 1816), 33.

8   Before 1820, few gravel or even dirt roads existed. The most notable building enterprise by the federal government, which had virtually no resources for this purpose, was the National (aka Cumberland) Road, built between 1822 and 1837 to connect the Potomac and Ohio Rivers. Other roads outside cities were usually produced under state charters to private developers who built "turnpikes" of stone

and soil and recovered their costs and generated profits by charging tolls. Turnpikes derived their name from the stick or pike placed across the road to halt traffic until the toll was paid.

9   While some scholars quarrel over whether Whitney actually invented the cotton engine, its effect is undeniable. Ironically, Whitney's advocacy for the use of interchangeable parts in manufacturing later contributed to the North's increased production capabilities and thereby to its victory in the Civil War.

10   Edward Pessen, "How Different from Each Other Were the Antebellum North and South?," *American Historical Review* 85, no. 5 (1980): 1119–49.

11   https://www.census.gov/history/pdf/histstats-colonial-1970.pdf.

12   Brendan Wolfe, "Slavery by the Numbers (Redux)," (blog), *Encyclopedia Virginia,* August 24, 2017, https://www.evblog.virginiahumanities.org/2017/08/slavery-by-the-numbers-redux/.

13   William W. Winn, "The View from Dowdell's Knob," in *The New Georgia Guide* (Athens: University of Georgia Press, 1996), 378. On the "new history of capitalism" in economic history, see Edward E. Baptist, *The Half Has Never Been Told: Slavery and the Making of American Capitalism* (New York: Basic Books, 2014).

14   Source: 1860 Census, "Selected Statistics on Slavery in the United States" and "The Civil War Home Page" at *civilwarcauses.org* and *civil-war.net* . This data is derived from a now-inactive census archive at the University of Virginia.

The 1619 Project" is "a major initiative of the New York Times that marks the 400th anniversary of slavery's beginning in America. Reliant on the ongoing work of historians and recent scholarship, the purpose of the series in this anniversary year is to "reframe the country's history, understanding 1619 as our true founding, and placing the consequences of slavery and the contributions of black Americans at the very center of the story we tell ourselves about who we are." An invaluable public resource, the series can be accessed at *https://www.nytimes.com/interactive/2019/08/14/magazine/1619-america-slavery.html.*

15   John Arthur Garraty and Mark Christopher Carnes, *American National Biography* (London: Oxford University Press), vol. 14, 411.

16   Lawrence J. Friedman, "Giving in America: From Charity to Philanthropy," in, *Charity, Philanthropy, and Civility in American History,* ed. Lawrence J. Friedman and Mark D. McGarvie, (Cambridge: Cambridge University Press, 2003), 29–48.

17   In yet another example of the paradoxes and ironies that weave their way through American philanthropy, the "city on the hill" reference that has become much beloved by politicians and other speechmakers overlooks that Winthrop was no great fan of dissent or democracy. His call for charity most certainly did not embrace the notion of religious freedom.

18   George Whitefield, raised in England and perhaps the most important evangelist of the 18th-century's Great Awakening, is yet another problematic figure when it comes to the issues of race and slavery. In the English colonies during the 1730s, he publicly indicted Southern slave masters for their abuse of slaves and further demonstrated a personal interest in African Americans who responded to his preaching. He believed they could become serious (and educated) Christians. However, after wealthy friends persuaded him to accept their gift of a plantation in South Carolina with a complement of slaves, he accepted without protest, convincing himself that he needed the income from the plantation to support the work of his orphanage. He did so, despite Georgia's ban on slavery, and went on to become a leading advocate for legal slavery in the state. See Thomas S. Kidd, author of *George Whitefield: America's Spiritual Founding Father* (New Haven, CT: Yale University Press, 2014).

19   Quoted in Peter Dobkin Hall, *Inventing the Nonprofit Sector and Other Essays on Philanthropy, Voluntarism, and Nonprofit Organizations* (Baltimore, MD: Johns Hopkins University Press, 1992).

20   Timothy James Lockley, *Welfare and Charity in the Antebellum South* (Gainesville: University Press of Florida, 2007), 3.

21 James C. Cobb, *Away Down South: A History of Southern Identity* (New York: Oxford University Press, 2005), 51.

22 Among the purposes of Alexis de Tocqueville's visit to America in 1831 was the study of these American *civic* "inventions." Tocqueville's perception, that a rising freedom for some parallels its decline for others in the New World (the criminal, the insane, and of course enslaved people), captures the enduring irony in the American experiment.

23 Traveling throughout the South, promoting prison reform and care for the mentally ill, Dix was critical of Northern abolitionists and outspoken in her opposition to Lincoln's emancipation plan: "I'm not a fan of his antislavery stance, but he seems like an intelligent, reasonable man." Dorothea Dix, "I Tell What I Have Seen," *The Reports of Asylum Reformer Dorothea Dix, Memorial to the Legislature of Massachusetts* (Boston: Munroe & Francis, 1843). Excerpted in Manon S. Parry, "Dorothea Dix, 1802-1887," *American Journal of Public Health,* April 2006. This "blind spot" was not atypical of New Englanders. Her contemporary Nathaniel Hawthorne was outspoken in his criticism of Lincoln, abolitionism, and the war. See Brenda Wineapple, *Hawthorne: A Life* (New York: Random House, 2004), 380. Herman Melville, while a great admirer of Lincoln, was also repulsed by the war's horror. In time, and in keeping with his family's background, he grew sympathetic with northern Democrats seeking a negotiated end to the conflict.

24 A 20th-century term coined by historian Linda Kerber to describe the 18th- and 19th-century belief that the patriots' daughters should be raised to uphold the ideals of republicanism, in order to pass on republican values to the next generation. In this way, the "Republican mother" was considered *the* custodian of civic virtue's future. Linda K. Kerber, "The Republican Mother: Women and the Enlightenment—An American Perspective," in *Toward an Intellectual History of Women: Essays* (Chapel Hill: University of North Carolina Press, 1997).

25 Megan Marshall, *The Peabody Sisters: Three Women Who Ignited American Romanticism* (New York: Houghton Mifflin Company, 2005).

26 Robert A. Gross, "Giving in America: From Charity to Philanthropy," in *Charity, Philanthropy, and Civility in American History,* ed. Lawrence J. Friedman and Mark D. McGarvie (Cambridge: Cambridge University Press, 2003), 29–48; Mark D. McGarvie, "The Dartmouth College Case and the Legal Design of Civil Society," in Friedman and McGarvie, *Charity, Philanthropy,* 91–106.

27 Quoted in Gerda Lerner, review of *The Southern Lady: From Pedestal to Politics*, by Anne Firor Scott, *Journal of American History* 58 (June 1971): 162–63.

28 Quoted in Daphne V. Wyse, "To Better Serve and Sustain the South: How Nineteenth-Century Domestic Novelists Supported Southern Patriarchy Using the 'Cult of True Womanhood' and the Written Word," *History Theses,* paper 8, State University of New York College at Buffalo—Buffalo State College, 18.

29 David Hammack, correspondence with author, March 12, 2019. . See also Suzanne Lebsock, *The Free Women of Petersburg: Status and Culture in a Southern Town, 1784–1860* (New York: W.W. Norton & Co., 1984)*,* excerpted in *Making the Nonprofit Sector in the United States: A Reader,* ed. David Hammack (Bloomington: Indiana University Press, 1998), 224–47.

30 Faye E. Dudden, "Women's Rights, Abolitionism, and Reform in Antebellum and Gilded Age America," Oxford Research Encyclopedias, April 2016, doi:10.1093/acrefore/9780199329175.013.20.

31 See Elizabeth Fox-Genovese, *Within the Plantation Household: Black and White Women of the Old South* (Chapel Hill: University of North Carolina Press, 1988) and Jane Turner Censer, *The Reconstruction of White Southern Womanhood, 1865-1895* (Baton Rouge: Louisiana State University Press, 2003).

32 Professor Elizabeth Johnson of Columbia Theological Seminary, made this suggestion in correspondence with authors; Johnson draws upon Willie James Jennings, *The Christian Imagination: Theology and the Origins of Race* (New Haven, CT: Yale University Press, 2010).

CHAPTER 2

The Widening Abyss (1830-1865)

The year 1830 marked the 41st anniversary of the young nation-state's existence. A generation of iconic leaders—Adams, Jefferson, Washington, Monroe, Hamilton, Franklin—had passed or were about to pass from the scene. The great and still unresolved questions of the Constitutional Convention (the status of slavery in the nation's expansion and the balance of power between the states and the federal government) were left to a new generation. The country was entering a period that would see social division intensify, disagreements harden into hatred, and debate escalate into violence and warfare. Because the scars of that separation still affect even our noblest behavior, it seems worthwhile to describe in some detail the forces that were at work.

Ambivalence about Slavery

As described in the previous chapter, well-meaning, God-fearing, and idealistic citizens—both Northern and Southern—sought to move their country in the direction of a new democracy and civil society that could accommodate the existence of slavery.

Some slaveowners were still looking for a way to avoid condoning the more barbarous features of human enslavement while stopping short of advocating abolition. In *The Legacy of the Civil War* (1961), Robert Penn Warren's classic reflection on that conflict's 100th anniversary, he wrote: "More than one slaveholder is on record as sympathizing with the distress of a certain Gustavus Henry, who admitted to his wife that 'I sometimes think my feelings unfit me for a slaveholder.'"[1]

Aiding the search for a resolution of the issue were some of the faculty members at Columbia Seminary, a Presbyterian institution then located in South Carolina. James Henley Thornwell (1812–62) and his colleagues tried

> to develop a theology that was guided by natural law, commonsense realism, and Protestant scholastic traditions. They were seeking a theology that avoided what they regarded as the dangerous extremes in American life—an extreme individualism and an extreme organicism. What they were advocating was a theology and philosophy of a *via media*, a middle way which would serve as both an ideological prop for slavery and a conservative utopian vision for the future of the South.[2]

Abraham Lincoln, during his first debate with Stephen Douglas in Ottawa, Illinois, on June 24, 1858, captured another side of the dilemma in what literary scholar John Burt calls Lincoln's penchant for "tragic pragmatism":

Doubtless there are individuals on both sides who would

not hold slaves under any circumstances; and others who would gladly introduce slavery anew, if it were out of existence. We know that some southern men do free their slaves, go north, and become tip-top abolitionists; while some northern ones go south and become most cruel slave-masters.[3]

Christian Instruction, Philanthropy, and Manumission

From the earliest days of their arrival in America, some slaves in the urban South had been exposed to Christianity and even become church members. Efforts to evangelize and provide Christian education to them were far less common on the rural plantations, although an unusual proponent for religious instruction was Charles C. Pinckney, a prominent planter from South Carolina. In 1829 Pinckney argued that religiously educated slaves managed by Christian overseers were the most efficient way to produce the greatest crop yield.[4]

The movement among clerics for the religious instruction of slaves, led by Charles Colcock Jones of Liberty County, Georgia, conceded them their humanity. The more radical movement of manumission (the granting of freedom to an enslaved person), foremost among Quakers, reflected a liberationist impulse in harmony with Northern millenarian reform.[5] It was perhaps the purest expression of Christian benevolence for the time.

Before 1830 the South had allowed masters to set their slaves free because this action was an inherent right of property ownership. During the Revolutionary and Constitutional periods, especially, some Southern leaders believed that manumission was consistent with the ideology of the new nation, and the number of free nonwhites in the South until the time of the Civil War seems always to have outnumbered the total of free nonwhites living in the Northern states.[6]

When the country was founded, ten of the thirteen states permitted free blacks to vote. As the Civil War neared, however, only the five New England states (not including Connecticut) continued that voting policy. Thus, with the exception of Wisconsin in 1848, all of the twenty states admitted to the Union after 1790 denied free black males the vote. Historian William D. Green describes their lives as a "paradoxical existence... they were free, yet never fully free, frozen in a state of civic ambiguity. They would be included in the census as residents but nothing more."[7] Historian Leon Litwack believes that the views of a great majority of Northerners before the Civil War can be explained as "not a departure from democratic principles, as certain foreign critics alleged, but simply the working out of natural laws, the inevitable consequence of racial inferiority of the Negro."[8]

Membership certificate of the American Colonization Society
Courtesy of the Library of Congress, Records of the American Colonization Society

The American Colonization Society

In 1816 the Society for the Colonization of Free People of Color of America came into being with the express goal of sending the approximately

200,000 free African Americans back to Africa. The new cause attracted the early support of James Monroe (president from 1817 to 1825) and other leaders like Andrew Jackson and Henry Clay. Both liberal and conservative critics (North and South) believed that the American Colonization Society, as it became known, was an urgent form of charitable work—more widely endorsed than abolitionism at the time. The Society's membership soon also included George Washington's nephew, Bushrod Washington; Robert Finley, who later would become president of the University of Georgia; and Francis Scott Key of Maryland, the author of "The Star Spangled Banner." As they looked into the future of their young republic, this hopeful amalgam of pro- and antislavery proponents all seemed to accept the proposition that blacks and whites could not forever live together and expect to prosper.[9]

By 1819 Monroe had coaxed $100,000 from the Congressional coffers to launch the first ship of returnees. Continuing efforts led to the establishment of a settlement on the coast of West Africa in 1822.[10] Christened Christopolis, it was renamed Monrovia two years later to honor President Monroe. In 1845 the Society held a convention there to draft a constitution, and in 1847 the Republic of Liberia was born and declared independence.

James Monroe, president of the United States
Courtesy of the Library of Congress,
LC-DIG-pga-03759

During the quarter-century emergence of the new country, more than 13,000 free and liberated people made the transatlantic passage with the assistance of the Society. However, the spread of a polarizing abolitionism in the North during the mid-1830s and thereafter finally led to the Society's "virtual destruction" in the South, while in the North the organization became "little more than a debating society."[11]

Fear of Rebellion

By 1830 most Southern states already had begun to limit manumission. Their primary concern was the justifiable fear that rebellious slaves—especially literate ones—were a threat to public safety. The planned Denmark Vesey uprising in Charleston in 1822, although discovered and aborted, nonetheless moved the state of South Carolina to authorize construction of the state arsenal in Charleston. Known as the "Old Citadel" because of its fortress-like construction, it was completed in 1829.

If South Carolina needed further confirmation of its precautionary instincts, it could cite Nat Turner's rebellion in 1831, an electrifying slave uprising that claimed the lives of at least fifty-five white people in southeastern Virginia. (The insurrection was the subject of *The Confessions of Nat Turner*, the 1967 Pulitzer Prize-winning novel by William Styron.)

The Citadel College, Charleston, South Carolina, 1865
Courtesy of the Library of Congress, LC-DIG-cwpb-02419

In 1842 the state legislature founded the South Carolina Military Academy, setting aside the grounds of the Old Citadel as its Charleston site. While endowing the new institution with a higher education mission (transferring the "academy" in Columbia to Charleston), the legislature also made "maintenance of public order" a co-equal responsibility of the new Citadel.

The State of Charitable Reform

The laudable American impulse to reform society had arrived at a boundary line in the South beyond which it could not cross. It was slavery. Even though fewer than one-third of all Southern households owned slaves, slavery was the defining feature (as further evidenced by the Missouri Compromise) that distinguished the South from the rest of the states.

Necessarily, the perpetuation and justification of slavery's legality inevitably took on the character of an ideology when it became articulated in law, culture, social practice, and even religion. Furthermore, it required heavy investment to suppress one-third of the region's population (about 20.5% of the upper South and 43.1% of the lower South were enslaved) and to rationalize that suppression.[12] Such expenditure of resources did not encourage the adoption of fervent, crusade-like movements to improve society and the lot of all classes of people. Completely unacceptable to most of the South, whose economy depended on enslavement, were the increasingly emphatic calls from the North for the abolition of slavery.

Religious expressions of reform also differed in the two regions after 1800. The Second Great Awakening (the first was during the colonial era) began in 1790 and gained strength through the 1850s. This Protestant movement of revivals, characterized by religious enthusiasm, called for repentance and conversions. It "burnt over" the North and gained much of its energy from the descendants of the New England Puritans and other clergy who assumed a responsibility for the reform of society and the eradication of social sin in preparation for Christ's Second Coming. Among the improvements they sought was the end of slavery.[13]

By contrast, the liberating message of evangelical Protestantism became more personal in the South—with a greater emphasis upon the salvation of the individual's soul. This slant left the public sphere of slavery in the South to fend for itself (or more accurately, to *de*fend itself). The preceding generation of Washington and Jefferson had viewed slavery as a "necessary evil," a burden and caretaking task of Christian responsibility with which slaveowners simply learned to live. Most Episcopalians, Anglicans, Methodists, and Baptists could agree on this tenet. By the 1840s, however, Southern evangelicals, according to historian Christine Leigh Heyrman, were seeking a competitive advantage when they repositioned slavery as a "divine experiment in Christian nationhood" with its own higher and glorified purpose.[14] Slavery (and its necessity) was becoming recast in positive terms and societal purpose, as a benevolent social institution.

Southern charity steadily contracted into those safer and more traditional arenas of benevolence that reinforced rather than disturbed the foundations of society. One's compassion for the white, poor, and orphans (and even occasional care for destitute blacks without homes or owners) all exemplified Christian virtues of charity without necessarily upsetting the existing order.[15]

These differing regional approaches to the care of others pointed to a widening crack that was more than cultural. An industrial, urbanizing, and democratizing North, sprouting voluntary associations, new types of philanthropy, and reform movements (some in league with government), was moving away from an agrarian and more hierarchical, communal South that saw charity in more traditional terms as one's duty to family and neighbors. It is also appropriate to note here, in the words of David Hammack, historian of philanthropy, that

> the North was far more diverse on matters of faith traditions, with some Protestant denominations almost entirely absent in the South, as well as many more Catholics and Jews, whose demands (regarding religion in public schools, the care of orphans, the authority of their hierarchy) created a different context for Protestants than existed in the South.[16]

Wealthy antebellum Southerners showed themselves most adept at living with the contradictions involved in embracing some modern cultural conventions while holding fast to a quasi-feudal concept of social hierarchy. Even as they contributed to the dynamism of the New World, they were espousing affinities for the so-called Old World values of family, honor, and chivalry. They also were capable of practicing a racially restricted benevolence.[17] The evolving civil society in the North, energized by what Alexis de Tocqueville had described as Americans' penchant for forming voluntary associations of all kinds, was taking root in an atmosphere of optimism about universal freedom's future. In the South that spirit became stifled.

Global Benevolence:
The Bequest of James Smithson

James Smithson, founder of the Smithsonian Institution
Courtesy of the Smithsonian Institution Archives

In 1829 one of the most unusual episodes in American history began to unfold against this backdrop of moral and ethical divergences along regional lines. James Smithson was a wealthy, Cambridge University-educated scientist and member of the Royal Society of London. He proclaimed himself part of a scientific movement in Europe whose members saw themselves as "citizens of the globe and pledged allegiance first of all to truth and reason. Their highest aspiration was to be a benefactor of all mankind."[18]

Smithson left his fortune, valued at more than $500,000, to his nephew. Under the terms of his will, in the event of the nephew's early demise, which in fact occurred in 1835, the estate was to revert to the United States of America, which Smithson admired because of its revolutionary commitment to liberty. The young country was to establish in the city of Washington, under the name of the Smithsonian Institution, an "establishment for the increase and diffusion of knowledge."[19]

In 1836 legislation was introduced in Congress to accept the gift. It would eventually pass both legislative houses, but not before the representative from Massachusetts (former President John Quincy Adams) and the senator from South Carolina (John C. Calhoun) wrangled over the gift's legitimacy.

They knew each other very well. Calhoun had served a term as Adams's vice president, and they had challenged each other over issues of slavery and states' rights, both of which Calhoun championed. (See also chapter 6 for their battle over federal tariffs.) On the Smithson matter, Calhoun opposed the government's acceptance of the bequest, because he believed "charity" to be purely personal and separate from government's strictly legalistic role; consequently, he contended, government lacked the authority to accept a purely private bequest. Adams held up the Smithson bequest as a model of philanthropy and its acceptance as a legitimate purpose of government in the advancement of the public good.

Interestingly, Calhoun's position on the Smithson bequest was not much different from one taken by Thomas Jefferson some years earlier. While governor of Virginia, Jefferson successfully resisted the creation of a private charitable corporation—in this case an endowment fund held by the Anglican Church. He saw it as a strategic first step in the clergy's effort to reestablish a state church.

In other respects the two differed: Jefferson, who in a traditional act of civic philanthropy bequeathed his books to the Library of Congress to replace those burned by the British in the War of 1812, and whose personal support and guidance led to the establishment of the University of Virginia in 1825, almost certainly would have applauded the English donor.

And so would have George Washington, possibly the richest American in his day. As president, in 1796 he saved Liberty Hall Academy (the institution that would become Washington & Lee University) from insolvency by an endowment gift of $20,000 in James River Canal stock in what then was the single largest gift to a private educational institution in the country. By way of explanation, Washington wrote the trustees, "To promote Literature in this rising Empire, and to encourage the Arts, have ever been amongst the warmest wishes of my heart."[20]

The Amistad Case and the "Sacred Circle"

Not long after the Smithson gift, Adams (still in the U.S. House) and Calhoun (back in the Senate) would tangle again in court. This time (1841) the dispute was one that had worked its way up to the Supreme Court. The issue was a property case that had to do with the disposition of Africans kidnapped from the British protectorate of Sierra Leone by Portuguese slave hunters and transported across the Atlantic for sale in Cuba. While being moved from one port in Cuba to another aboard the inaptly named *La Amistad* (Friendship), the captives mutinied. Their effort to sail back to Africa, however, was thwarted by the ship's Spanish navigators, who steered the vessel by night into Long Island Sound. There, they were detained by a U.S. revenue cutter and held pending

Smithsonian Institution Building (the Castle), ca. 1858
Courtesy of the Smithsonian Institution Archives

trial. The question before the court was whether the captives became free when entering U.S. territorial waters, or remained the property of their Spanish "owners."

A majority of the court's justices were slaveholding Southerners, but Adams, the ex-president, again carried the day, and the former slaves were freed and permitted to return to their homes in Sierra Leone. (The Court found that their enslavement and transport from Africa to the New World constituted a violation of international law, while their presence in the United States violated the 1807 Act Prohibiting *Importation of Slaves* [italics ours].)

The *Amistad* case was yet another headline-grabbing incident that served to intensify the conflict between North and South. Infuriated by the rising Northern clamor for slavery's abolition, Southerners went on the offensive. The region's publicists argued that their stratified, familial culture and economy, of which race was a linchpin, was more highly evolved than the North's egalitarian society. No one was more passionate in this view than John Calhoun. Two years earlier, on February 6, 1837, he had risen in the Senate to argue not that slavery was a necessary evil, as his predecessors had conceded, but rather a positive good: "Never before has the black race of Central Africa, from the dawn of history to the present day, attained a condition so civilized and so improved, not only physically, but morally and intellectually."[21]

In doing so he was anticipating the views of a rising class of Southern writers, poets, educators, and publicists after 1840, a "sacred circle" of slavery defenders that included William Gilmore Simms, Edmund Ruffin, and Nathaniel Beverley Tucker. They portrayed plantation life as an intimate community where ties of history, obligation, and mutual affection abounded.[22] As much social reformers, aware of the region's and nation's deficiencies, as they were defenders, these Southern intellectuals eschewed the North's heartless greed and exploitive "wage slavery." It was the South that took care of its own.[23]

George Fitzhugh (1806–1881), a Virginian, put a unique spin on the subject. He conceded that South and North shared a common set of values, and that it led to the exploitation of human labor—as had historically been the case for all civilizations. There seemed to be no other way in a society for wealth and industry to advance. "The central question is what form of society most effectively curbs their appetites."[24]

What set Southern owners of slaves apart was the financial responsibility they had for their labor source in a way that Northern and British capitalists did not and could not expect to assume. This led Fitzhugh to ask which system, slavery or free labor, exploited workers less. He concluded that slavery was more humane, more charitable than "wage labor," and made his case in the 1857 book, *Cannibals All! Or Slaves Without Masters.*

The Supreme Court (Again) Confronts Slavery

Perhaps the most ominous example of the South's determination to preserve the status quo in the region was the Fugitive Slave Act of 1850. Authored by Senator Henry Clay from the slave state of Kentucky and Senator Daniel Webster from the free state of Massachusetts, it was presented as a grand compromise under which California would enter the Union as a free state. Instead, the legislation appeared to many as a capitulation to Southern interests that further upset an already tenuous accommodation between pro- and antislavery states.

It is instructive to remember that the words "slave" or "slavery" appear nowhere in the 1789 U.S. Constitution. Article 4, sec. 2 mandated that

> No Person held to Service or Labour in One State, under the Laws thereof, escaping into another, shall in Consequence of any Law or Regulation therein, be discharged from such Service or Labour, but shall be delivered up on Claim of the Party to whom such Service or Labour may be due.

The Founders' use of the word "claim" identifies a legal process that makes no distinction between federal and state legal systems. And therein lay the problem. Beginning in 1830, nine Northern state legislatures had passed "personal liberty laws" that denied masters and slave catchers a legal remedy in retrieving their runaway "property." Because slave law was considered a local ordinance and because the natural state of humankind was freedom, in effect, slaves became legally (or, to be more accurate, theoretically) free when they crossed into a free state, whether as runaways or with sojourning masters.

The Congressional remedy hit upon in 1850 was the abolition of the slave trade in Washington, D.C., and the amendment of the Fugitive Slave Act. The latter imposed a radical (virtually desperate) enforcement duty upon all judicial institutions, state legislatures, and local, state, and national enforcement officials. It even extended those duties to uninvolved bystanders. Paul Finkelman writes:

> The most outrageous and unfair aspect of the law involved the testimony of the alleged fugitive. According to the law, "In no trial or hearing under this act shall the testimony of such alleged fugitive be admitted in evidence." Under this law someone could be dragged south as a slave and never be allowed to offer his or her own voice as evidence that he or she was free.[25]

Entirely upsetting the Missouri Compromise of 1820, which set slavery's northernmost boundary line at 36 degrees - 30 minutes, was the 1857 Kansas Nebraska Act. This new law repealed the Missouri

Compromise's restriction on slavery when it gave people in the new territories of Kansas and Nebraska the "popular sovereignty" option to decide the matter of slavery for themselves.

Making matters even worse for fugitives (as well as black citizens living in free states) was the U.S. Supreme Court's 1857 ruling in *Dred Scott v. Sandford.* Dashing any last hope of freedom and citizenship for African Americans, Chief Justice Roger Brook Taney's opinion ruled that no persons of African ancestry could ever become citizens of the United States because they were not part of the original founding community:

> The words "people of the United States" and "citizens" are synonymous terms, and mean the same thing. They both describe the political body who, according to our republican institutions, form the sovereignty and who hold the power and conduct the Government through their representatives. . . . The question before us is whether the class of persons described in [this legal dispute] compose a portion of this people, and are constituent members of this sovereignty? We think they are not, and that they are not included, and were not intended to be included, under the word "citizens" in the Constitution, and can therefore claim none of the rights and privileges which that instrument provides for and secures to citizens of the United States. On the contrary, they were at that time considered as a subordinate and inferior class of beings who had been subjugated by the dominant race, and, whether emanci-

pated or not, yet remained subject to their authority, and had no rights or privileges but such as those who held the power and the Government might choose to grant them.[26]

The Supreme Court's bold and clarifying line in the sand was intended to settle once and for all a tormenting dispute. Instead, it set in motion an irreversible stream of confrontational events. The search for a civil society was repeatedly being slowed by the corrosive and continually expanding domain of slavery.

And the War Came

The country prepared for the 1860 elections against a backdrop of exploding political parties and a fiery sectionalism that had erupted with armed clashes in "Bleeding Kansas" and Harper's Ferry over the issue of slavery.

Abraham Lincoln was the 1860 nominee of the new Republican Party—an 1854 yoking together of disgruntled Democrats and antislavery Whigs who opposed the Kansas-Nebraska Act. Their standard-bearer interpreted Congress's adoption of the Northwest Ordinance of 1789 that prohibited the spread of slavery to the new territories of the North as evidence that the Founders never intended it to spread beyond its Southern boundary.

The candidate for the Party of the Democracy (the "Democrats") was Stephen A. Douglas, lead author of the 1854 Kansas-Nebraska Act and the man who had defeated Lincoln two years later in the Illinois senatorial race. He was among the most influential leaders in the U.S. Congress and identified with the Democratic doctrine of "popular sovereignty" that delegated to the people of each new state the choice about adopting slavery.

The newly forming party of the Southern Democrats nominated President James Buchanan's sitting vice president, John C. Breckinridge of Tennessee, for president. Although a one-time senator from Tennessee and large slaveholder, he opposed the expansion of slavery north of the line established in the 1820 admission of Missouri. His running mate was Edward Everett of Massachusetts, a respected state and national politico, U.S. minister to England, and former president of Harvard.

The Constitutional Union Party was an appeal to conservative Whigs who opposed Jackson's Democratic Party and to Southern Democrats who opposed secession over the issue of slavery. Nominating John Bell of Tennessee for president, the party sought common ground in law and legal process: the "Constitution of the country, the Union of the states, and the Enforcement of the Laws." Bell was a planter and politician who served in the U.S. House, where he was speaker (1834–35), and in the U.S. Senate (1847–59). A slaveowner who believed the Constitution protected the institution of slavery in states where it already existed, Bell campaigned against slavery's expansion.

The spark that would set the South ablaze was Lincoln's election in November 1860, with 180 electoral votes (39.8% of the popular vote), followed by the Democrat Douglas (29.5%), Breckinridge (18.1%), and Bell (12.6%). Lincoln carried all the northern states (he did not even appear on the ballot in three Southern states), while Breckinridge won in the majority of Southern states. Douglas claimed only Missouri.

Within days of the election, South Carolina's General Assembly passed a "Resolution to Call the Election of Abraham Lincoln as U.S. President a Hostile Act and to Communicate to Other Southern States South Carolina's Desire to Secede from the Union." South Carolinian Alfred P. Aldrich of Barnwell (a prominent lawyer, legislator and judge) described what he believed to be the stakes of the presidential campaign: "It is not who shall be President, it is not which party shall rule—it is a question of political and social existence."[27]

South Carolina's decision to leave the Union became official with a declaration on December 24, 1860, which drew selectively from the 1776 Declaration of Independence in its defense. Historian Harry Jaffa writes:

> South Carolina cites, loosely, but with substantial accuracy, some of the language of the original [1776] Declaration. That Declaration does say that it is the right of the people to abolish any form of government that becomes destructive of the ends for which it was established. But South Carolina does not repeat the preceding language in the earlier document: "We hold these truths to be self-evident, that all men are created equal. . . ."[28]

He states that the omissions were for reasons that everyone at the time understood:

> In no sense could it have been said that the slaves in South Carolina were governed by powers derived from their consent. Nor could it be said that South Carolina was separating itself from the government of the Union because

that government had become destructive of the ends for which it was established. South Carolina in 1860 had an entirely different idea of what the ends of government ought to be from that of 1776 or 1787. That difference can be summed up in the difference between holding slavery to be an evil, if possibly a necessary evil, and holding it to be a positive good.[29]

On December 25, the day after South Carolina's declaration of secession, a South Carolina convention delivered an "Address to the Slaveholding States." Its description of regional differences elevated them to a grander level beyond mere politics or public opinion:

> We prefer our system of industry, by which labor and capital are identified in interest, and capital, therefore, pro-tects labor—by which our population doubles every twenty years—by which starvation is unknown, and abundance crowns the land—by which order is preserved by unpaid police, and the most fertile regions of the world, where the white man cannot labor, are brought into usefulness by the labor of the African, and the whole world is blessed by our own productions. . . .We ask you to join us, in forming a Confederacy of Slaveholding States.[30]

As Lincoln watched from the sidelines while preparing for his March 4 swearing-in, secession was moving at a frantic pace: South Carolina, Mississippi, Florida, Alabama, Georgia, and Louisiana left the Union in January. The Confederate states organized and adopted a

"Dictator" Mortar in front of Petersburg, Virginia, October, 1864
Courtesy of the Library of Congress, LC-DIG-ppmsca-12834

constitution in February, the same month that Texas joined. On April 12, six weeks after the president's inauguration, Confederate troops fired on Fort Sumter and accepted its surrender. Between April and June, Virginia, Arkansas, North Carolina, and Tennessee (the 11th state) followed. The election of 1860 was by now a distant memory. Americans were at war with each other.

It became a war that the North several times came close to losing. Only gradually did the Union forces gain the upper hand. For Union generals Ulysses Grant and William Sherman, waging war meant not only finding and destroying Lee's forces but also destroying all foodstuffs and livestock the Union's armies could not consume, and laying waste to factories, rail lines, roadways, bridges, warehouses, and public buildings (i.e., much of the South's commercial and governance infrastructure). "[W]e have devoured the land," Sherman wrote in a letter to his wife. "All the people retire before us and desolation is behind. To realize what war is, one should follow our tracks."[31]

War Time Benevolence: The U.S. Sanitary Commission

Both Northern and Southern noncombatants extended generous personal support to the war effort, but it was not a time of much structured benevolence. One notable exception was the formation in 1861 of the U.S. Sanitary Commission. Established that summer as a federal relief program supported entirely by philanthropy, the Commission raised $25 million for the personal and medical needs of the Union troops.

Dorothea Dix became its first superintendent. She followed the example of the British Sanitary Commission and Florence Nightingale in the Crimean War (1853-56), relying exclusively on a workforce of volunteer women for the care of the wounded and dying.

Civil War nurse
Courtesy of the Library of Congress,
LC-DIG-ppmsca-57149

They became aides to surgeons, dressed wounds, administered medicine, transcribed soldiers' dictated letters home, and offered cheer and comfort. Southern nurses performed similar roles for the Confederacy, organizing their own volunteer groups and establishing private hospitals in homes and public buildings.

A second structured private effort, this one operating in the South as well as the North, was the Daughters of Charity. The members of this Roman Catholic religious community from Emmitsburg, Maryland, served as nurses in both Federal and Confederate hospitals. According to scholars, as many as

> 232 nursed at one time or another in general hospitals, in field hospitals, and on hospital ships. . . . They also nursed on the battlefields at Antietam and Boonsboro, Maryland, and Vicksburg, Mississippi, and worked on hospital ships up and down the Mississippi River, the Potomac, and in the Chesapeake Bay, plus rode with the ambulance corps at Manassas, Virginia, and Harpers Ferry, West Virginia.[32]

Daily existence was harrowing for the women thus engaged on both sides. Their death rate was high. Modern nursing would not emerge as a profession until after the Civil War, but its roots are profoundly altruistic, civic, and benevolent—a magnificent demonstration of public philanthropy.[33]

By the time General Lee signed the surrender documents at Appomattox, the South was in physical, psychological, and emotional ruin.[34] In military terms alone, of the approximately 800,000 troops fielded by the Confederacy, close to 500,000 were killed, wounded, or missing. States that had become vital economic partners in the nation's expansion for the first six decades of the 19th century found themselves five years later utterly devastated by the enemy against which they had chosen to fight. One of the most telling illustrations of these desperate conditions is historian Shelby Foote's oft-repeated observation that one-fifth of the postwar budget of Mississippi was allocated to the purchase of prostheses for Confederate veterans.[35]

Unfinished Work Deferred

In Abraham Lincoln's Second Inaugural Address on March 4, 1865, he referred to "unfinished work" as he sketched the outline of a new civil society—one characterized by "malice toward none, with charity for all." He also reflected on the steps leading up to the Civil War:

Abraham Lincoln, 1864
Courtesy of the Library of Congress, LC-DIG-ppmsca-19204

On the occasion corresponding to this four years ago, all thoughts were anxiously directed to an impending civil war. All dreaded it; all sought to avert it. While the inaugural address was being delivered from this place, devoted altogether to saving the Union without war, insurgent agents were in the city seeking to destroy it without war—seeking to dissolve the Union and divide effects by negotiation.

Both parties deprecated war; but one of them would make war rather than let the nation survive, and the other would accept war rather than let it perish, *and the war came* [italics ours].[36]

Lincoln's interpretation of the Founders' vision would require a long time to be realized. On April 10, a day after Robert E. Lee's surrender, the president delivered an impromptu evening speech from a White

House porch to a milling late-night crowd. He offered his view that "intelligent" freedmen and those who had served in the Union Army deserved the right to vote alongside whites. In the audience that night was John Wilkes Booth, one of six co-conspirators who together had been planning Lincoln's kidnapping and spiriting away to Richmond before its fall eight days earlier. The full meaning of Lincoln's observation and the reality of the war's final days delivered a clear message to Booth. They meant "n----- citizenship. Now, by God, I'll put him through."[37] Four days later Booth shot Lincoln, and Vice President Andrew Johnson—a Southerner—became the nation's president. Many doubted whether the country could resume its pilgrimage toward the civil society envisioned by the Founders.

CHAPTER 2 ENDNOTES

1   Robert Penn Warren, *A Robert Penn Warren Reader* (New York: Random House, 1987), 302.

2   Erskine Clarke, *Dwelling Place: A Plantation Epic* (New Haven: Yale University Press, 2005), 273-4.

3   Quoted and discussed in John Burt, *Lincoln's Tragic Pragmatism: Lincoln, Douglas, and Moral Conflict* (Cambridge: Harvard University Press, 2013), 65.

4   Lawrence Neale Jones, *African Americans and the Christian Churches, 1619-1860* (Cleveland, OH: Pilgrim Press, 2007), 70.

5   An ironic, unintended consequence of manumission involves Johns Hopkins, whose Quaker parents freed the slaves on their tobacco planation in Anne Arundel County, Maryland, in 1795. That decision necessitated him leaving school to work on the property. He then joined his uncle's grocery business in Baltimore. After seven years, he and three brothers began their own dry goods company, selling to farmers in the Shenandoah Valley and often receiving "moonshine" as payment. They in turn sold the beverage to city folks. Hopkins invested his profits in Baltimore & Ohio Railroad stock and earned the sizeable fortune that he bequeathed to the Johns Hopkins University and the Johns Hopkins Hospital. *The Writer's Almanac,* May 19, 2016, *https://www.writersalmanac.org/index.html%3Fp=8047.html.*

    The 12th-century Jewish philosopher, Moses ben Maimonides, in his famous "Eight Levels of Giving," postulated that helping a fellow Jew move from a condition of dependence to one of independence was the greatest gift one could bestow. Surely, freeing one's slaves (and the recognition of a common humanity) qualifies for this high ranking.

6   Jenny Bourne, "Slavery in the United States," EH.Net Encyclopedia, ed. Robert Whaples, March 26, 2008, *http://eh.net/encyclopedia/slavery-in-the-united-states/.*

7   William D. Green, "Minnesota's Long Road to Black Suffrage, 1849–1868," *Minnesota History Magazine* (Summer 1998): 70, *http://collections.mnhs.org/mnhistorymagazine/articles/56/ v56i02p068-084.pdf.*

8   Leon F. Litwack, *North of Slavery: The Negro in the Free States, 1790–1860* (Chicago: University of Chicago Press, 1961), 254.

9   David S. Reynolds, *Waking Giant: America in the Age of Jackson* (New York: Harper, 2008), 26–29.

10   Preceding the Society's founding of Liberia were two earlier settlements of free Africans that grew from British anti-slavery sentiments: the Providence of Freedom (1787–89) and Freetown Colony (1792–1808) in today's Sierra Leone. Each settlement involved the British Sierra Leone Company, Granville Sharp and other English abolitionists, free Africans living in England, and American slaves freed by the British during the Revolutionary War who had been subsequently resettled in Britain's Caribbean colonies and British Canada (Nova Scotia). Freetown today is the capitol of the Republic of Sierra Leone, a British colony from 1816 until 1961. It was not until Parliament's Slavery Abolition Act of 1833 that an estimated 800,000 slaves in its Caribbean colonies and South Africa finally won their freedom (see also "Slavery Abolition Act," *Encyclopedia Britannica Online, https://www. britannica.com/topic/Slavery-Abolition-Act.*

11   Bruce Rosen, "The Formation of the American Colonization Society," *Phylon* 33, no. 2 (1972): 177.

12   Inter-university Consortium for Political and Social Research, "Historical, Demographic, Economic, and Social Data: The United States, 1790-1970" [Computer file] (Ann Arbor, MI: Inter-university Consortium for Political and Social Research, 1997).

13   J. William Harris, "The Demise of Slavery," TeacherServe, National Humanities Center, June 11, 2019 at: *https://nationalhumanitiescenter.org/tserve/freedom/1609-1865/essays/demslave.htm.*

14   Quoted in Harry S. Stout, "Religion in the Civil War: The Southern Perspective," Divining America, TeacherServe, National Humanities Center, *http://nationalhumanitiescenter.org/tserve/nineteen/*

nkeyinfo/cwsouth.htm. See also Harry S. Stout, *Upon the Altar of the Nation: A Moral History of the Civil War* (New York: Penguin, 2007) and C. C. Goen, *Broken Churches, Broken Nation: Denominational Schisms and the Coming of the American Civil War* (Macon: Mercer University Press, 1985). The story of the Bible Belt's rise in the 20th century is the subject Christine Leigh Heyrman's *Southern Cross: The Beginnings of the Bible Belt* (New York: Knopf, 1997). The journalist and satirist H. L. Mencken coined the term "Bible Belt" in 1925 while reporting on the Scopes Monkey Trial in Dayton, Tennessee.

15 The full range (and close study) of charitable activities appears in Timothy James Lockley, *Welfare and Charity in the Antebellum South* (Gainesville: University Press of Florida, 2007), 60–115.

  The urban setting of reform in the South is discussed in Barbara L. Bellows, *Benevolence among Slaveholders: Assisting the Poor in Charleston, 1670-1860* (Baton Rouge: Louisiana State University Press, 1993).

16 David Hammack, correspondence with authors, March 2, 2019.

17 According to Bertram Wyatt-Brown, the distinctive character of this system that can hold contradictions in check is honor-based. Bertram Wyatt-Brown, *Southern Honor: Ethics and Behavior in the Old South* (New York: Oxford University Press, 1982).

18 Heather Ewing, *The Lost World of James Smithson: Science, Revolution, and the Birth of the Smithsonian* (New York: Bloomsbury, 2007), quoted in *Inside Smithsonian Research,* no. 16 (Spring 2007): 15. Though Adams won, and Congress agreed to accept the gift, another decade would pass before federal representatives actually secured it (in the form of gold bullion transported by ship to the United States). That action in turn initiated a second proceeding, to secure the granting of a formal charter that would make it the nation's first scientific research foundation. Calhoun (still in the Senate) unsuccessfully challenged the effort, once again led by Adams.

19 Smithson, as it turned out, had never set foot in the United States. However, he *is* buried at the Smithsonian. He died in 1829 at the age of seventy-five and was interred in Genoa, Italy. His final resting place at the organization that bears his name is the result of a crusade in 1903 by Alexander Graham Bell to find the grave in Italy and transport Smithson's remains to the United States. That fascinating story is told by Nina Burleigh: "Digging Up James Smithson," *American Heritage* 62, no. 2 (Summer 2012), *https://www.americanheritage.com/content/digging-james-smithson.*

20 Lee Family Archives, accessed January 2, 2019, *https://leefamilyarchive.org/references/the-washington-connection.*

21 The full speech, "Slavery a Positive Good," is reproduced at Teaching American History.org: *http://teachingamericanhistory.org/library/document/slavery-a-positive-good/.*

22 Charles Dickens painted a grimly different picture of slavery in a special publication after his 1842 tour of the United States. One of its most horrific sections was the copy of newspaper advertisements describing the physical appearance of runaway slaves, with detailed accounts of the many ways in which they had been physically mutilated. ed., Charles Dickens, *American Notes for General Circulation,* ed. Patricia Ingham, revised edition (New York: Penguin Classics, 2000), 136–38.

23 Drew Gilpin Faust, *A Sacred Circle: The Dilemma of the Intellectual in the Old South, 1840–1860* (Baltimore, MD: Johns Hopkins University Press, 1977) is the classic work describing the emergence of an intellectual class in the South. Writes Faust, "their simultaneous love and hate for the South, in their need both to justify and to reform, [James Henry] Hammond, [George Frederick] Holmes, [Edmund] Ruffin, [Nathaniel Beverley] Tucker, and [William Gilmore] Simms embody not just the dilemma of the thinking Southerner, but the universal plight of the intellectual." (xii).

24 Quoted and discussed in "A Pro-Slavery Argument, 1857," America in Class, National Humanities Center, *http://americainclass.org/a-pro-slavery-argument/.*

25 Paul Finkelman, *Millard Fillmore: The 13th President, 1850–1853,* The American Presidents Series (New York: Times Books, 2011), 86–88.

26 *United States Supreme Court, The Dred Scott Decision: The Opinion of Chief Justice Taney, 1860,* Teaching American History, *https://teachingamericanhistory.org/library/document/dred-scott-v-sandford/*.

27 Harry V. Jaffa, *A New Birth of Freedom: Abraham Lincoln and the Coming of the Civil War* (Lanham, MD: Rowman & Littlefield, 2000), 231.

28 Ibid.

29 Ibid.

30 J.B.D. DeBow, *DeBow's Review*, Vol. XXX (New Orleans, LA and Charleston, S.C., 1861), 357.

31 Sherman was writing of his "March to the Sea." Quoted in James C. Cobb, "Georgia Odyssey," in *The New Georgia Guide* (Athens: University of Georgia Press, 1996), 18.

32 Barbara Mann Wall, Kathleen Rogers, and Ann Kutney-Lee, "The North vs. the South: Conditions at Civil War Hospitals," *The Southern Quarterly,* 53, nos. 3/4 (Spring/Summer 2016): 37–55, *https://muse.jhu.edu/article/630229/summary.*

33 Judith Golden, " 'For the benefit of mankind:' Nightingale's Legacy and Hours of Work in Australia, 1868-1939," in Anne Marie Rafferty, Jane Robinson, and Ruth Elkan, eds., *Nursing History and the Politics of Welfare* (Routledge: London, 1997), 184.

34 Mark E. Neely Jr., "Was the Civil War a Total War?," in *On the Road to Total War: The American Civil War and the German Wars of Unification, 1861–1871,* ed. Stig Forster and Jorg Nagler (Cambridge, Eng.: Cambridge University Press, 1997), 29–52.

35 Richard Carter, "A Visit from Historian Shelby Foote," *Humanities Magazine* 21, no. 1 (January-February 2000).

36 "Lincoln's Second Inaugural," at: *nps.gov.*

37 While many historians (including James M. McPherson) believe Booth uttered these words, Harry Jaffa also notes their original source has not been found. See Pat Young, host, "Civil War Talk" at *civilwartalk.com.*

CHAPTER 3

Reconstructing a Nation (1865–1877)

The Brewing of Philanthropic Resources

The post–Civil War South may have been in ruins, but the industrial complex that had supported the Northern military machine continued to generate products—and profits—for its leaders. Cauldrons of wealth, brimming over in amounts never before imagined, were transforming the country. From them, in remarkably short order, would be distilled the beginning assets of American philanthropy.

The estimated GDP (gross domestic product) of the United States in 1820 was $12.5 billion.[1] Before the outbreak of the Civil War, it stood at about $16 billion. By 1870 estimated U.S. GDP had expanded almost eightfold since 1820, to $98.37 billion. By far, it was the largest and fastest growth period registered by any nation or state in the known world's history.

The United States was not entirely alone in this achievement. In all of Western Europe, the other fastest-growing region of the world, the GDP from 1820 to 1879 more than doubled, from $159.8 billion to

$367.4 billion.[2] Such economic explosion on both sides of the Atlantic was "a startling departure from the norms that had prevailed for 4,000 years" and indicated "the arrival of a new mentality, one that permitted private investors to pursue profits at the expense of older values and customs."[3] It was the revolution launched by capitalism.

Over that span of time in the United States, the amount of oil refined, the production of coal and steel, the advance of electrification, and the ballooning numbers behind immigration and population, urban growth, agricultural production, travel, and commerce would all cross once-unimaginable thresholds.

Before 1867 only a handful of individuals in the United States could claim the status of a "millionaire" (a word that made its first print appearance in English in 1843).[4] The wealthiest of this embryonic cohort were bankers and shippers in the burgeoning China trade after the Revolutionary War and included John Jacob Astor of New York (1763–1848), worth $8.7 million; Stephen Girard of Philadelphia (1750–1831), $8.5 million; and the Bostonian Thomas Perkins (1754–1864).[5] Among the wealthiest in the South were planter and banker Stephen Duncan of Natchez, Mississippi (1787–1867), worth $3.5 million, and Nathaniel Heyard, a rice planter in South Carolina (1766–1851), $2 million.[6]

The known number of individuals in this millionaire class in the United States grew to more than 100 in the 1870s and to 4,047 by 1892. According to the *New York Tribune* of that year, "almost half of them were living in the New York area."[7] The idealized "new Adam" of the antebellum era was now an industrial behemoth.

Actually, the same industrial pattern of invention, planning, and management that had enabled the factories of the North to undergird victory in the Civil War was already underway before 1861. It comes as no surprise to Joyce Appleby, the historian of that era in the 19th century. "There can be no capitalism... without a culture of capitalism," she observes.[8] As only a sample of technological breakthroughs, she points to the introduction of the cotton gin in 1794 (itself a radical economic change agent), the McCormick reaper in 1831, the Colt revolver in 1836, the Morse telegraph in 1843, and the 1851 Singer sewing machine.

The Express Train, 1870
Courtesy of the Library of Congress, LC-DIG-pga-08647

Most transformative of all was the impact of the steam locomotive. In 1840 some 3,000 miles of railroad track ran through the North and South. During the Civil War that total reached 30,000 miles. Three years after Lee's surrender at Appomattox, the Transcontinental Railroad, begun with the support of Lincoln and the Congress in 1863, had connected the Atlantic and Pacific oceans.

By every measure, the U.S. economy in the North and West was exploding. One example illustrates the frenzy for wealth that swept the country. Oil had been discovered in northwestern Pennsylvania in 1859. By the end of the Civil War, Ron Chernow writes,

> Perhaps no industry so beguiled the. . .veterans with promises of overnight wealth than the oil industry. In astonishing numbers, a ragtag group of demobilized soldiers, many still in uniform and carrying knapsacks and rifles, migrated to northwest Pennsylvania. The potential money to be made was irresistible, whether in drilling or in auxiliary services; people could charge two or three times as much as they dared to ask in the city.[9]

Both driving and serving this industrial expansion was an eighty-year flood of German, British, and Irish immigrants in search of opportunity. After 1865 came other new millions that included Greeks, Poles, Italians, and Slavic language speakers fleeing wars, the European revolutions of 1848, and poverty. Migrating to American cities, they became part of that enabling industrial labor pool that worked long hours for low pay in wretched conditions. Three or more families would often occupy a single dwelling in a run-down apartment house in the poorest sections of a city.

Whether it was the expansion of opportunity, the loss of idealism, or simply old-fashioned greed that energized this massive industrial leap, the new wave of business development was further marked by a flinty opportunism and even ruthlessness, with all means justifying the profitable ends.

It was not simply increased production that generated wealth. Equal credit belongs to the managerial style (some would call it "ruthless genius") perfected by Rockefeller in oil, Andrew Carnegie in steel, J. Pierpont Morgan in banking, Russell Sage in stock speculation, and Cornelius Vanderbilt in shipping and railroads. These corporate titans created monopolistic organizations that stretched from the Atlantic to the Pacific.[10]

Certainly one condition that made it possible for ambitious entrepreneurs to flourish in an economy that hurdled state lines was a federal government with only a smattering of employees and no interstate regulatory mandate from Congress. (The later Sherman Anti-Trust Act of 1890 was aimed specifically at monopolies like Rockefeller's Standard Oil—the largest of them all—which the U.S. government, in fact, sued, but with mixed results.)

Thomas Iron Works at Hockendauqua, Pennsylvania, ca. 1857-1866
Courtesy of the Library of Congress, LC-DIG-pga-13843

Described technically, the source of these fortunes involved both the vertical and horizontal integration of their industries. More simply, critics of Standard Oil charged it with predatory pricing and conspiratorial agreements with owners of oil refineries and the railroads. Whether blatantly illegal or not, the effect was to give the company control over 90% of the nation's oil production. Rockefeller's was a competitive ingenuity that biographer Ron Chernow sees as rooted in Rockefeller's own childhood: "Since they were very poor his mother repeated maxims on frugality." One especially that she "drilled into him" was "Willful waste makes woeful want." Famously typical of the workaday economy of Standard Oil was that it *did everything from build its own oil barrels to employ scientists to figure out new uses for petroleum by-products.*[11]

In 1911 the U.S. Supreme Court ruled Standard Oil in violation of antitrust laws and ordered its dissolution. Rockefeller had long since stepped aside as president, yet he still owned one-fourth of the company's shares, which had doubled in value, making him "the richest man in the world."[12]

With near-total control of essential markets in a heavy industrial and modernizing economy, an entirely new kind of national and even international enterprise generated extraordinary wealth for owners, partners, and shareholders. These so-called robber barons (a colorful metaphor first applied in 1859 to Cornelius Vanderbilt) created what Mark Twain and Charles Dudley Warner dubbed a "Gilded Age" in their 1873 book of the same name.

In the 1880s and 1890s the wealthiest of white citizens were living lives of almost unimaginable luxury. It was a desperate and dangerous condition of inequality that steadily set the stage for almost four decades of unceasing warfare between the predominantly white labor movement and a new managerial class.

Radical Reconstruction

Against this historically unprecedented background of explosive capital formation, efforts were underway to bring the defeated South back into the Union. Before his assassination, Abraham Lincoln had favored a lenient plan for Reconstruction that Congress unsuccessfully opposed. In his second inaugural address, he extended a hand to the southland:

> With malice toward none; with charity for all; with firmness in the right, as God gives us to see the right, let us strive on to finish the work we are in; to bind up the nation's wounds; to care for him who shall have borne the battle, and for his widow, and his orphan—to do all which may achieve and cherish a just, and a lasting peace, among ourselves, and with all nations.[13]

Within a year of Andrew Johnson's ascension to the presidency, the Radical Republicans in Congress were on the warpath. They were determined to punish the Southern states for their transgressions, especially those who had led the effort to secede. Because Johnson (although a Tennessean) had been a harsh critic of Southern secession, the Radical Republicans assumed he would enact their proposed policies. To their shock, Johnson offered general amnesty to most former Confederates, vetoed proposed legislation that extended civil rights and financial support to former slaves, and rescinded an earlier order that would have returned all confiscated Southern lands to them. Johnson's actions cleared the way for many of the Southern states to enact so-called black codes, intended to restrict the activity and movement of freed slaves and to control their availability as a labor force.

However, the midterm elections of 1866 (influenced by Johnson's own political bumbling) generated Republican majorities in Congress. The Radicals overcame Johnson's veto of their civil rights legislation and seized control of Reconstruction. (Johnson's veto, although overridden, would lead to the Republicans' attempt to impeach him two years later.)

This "Radical Reconstruction" called for the freedmen to be completely integrated into the civil life of the South—now organized into five military districts. Freedmen were to live and work side-by-side with whites, governing in a new democracy mandated by the 13th Amendment (1865), which abolished slavery and involuntary servitude; the 14th Amendment (1870), which granted civil and legal rights to African Americans and former slaves (including them under the umbrella phrase "all persons born or naturalized in the United States"); and the 15th Amendment (1875), which prohibited the federal government and each state from denying a citizen the right to vote based on that citizen's "race, color, or previous condition of servitude."[14]

The Freedmen's Bureau: A Philanthropic Partnership

Leading the coalition of federal and primarily Northern private interests seeking to reinvent the South was the U.S. Bureau of Refugees, Freedmen and Abandoned Lands, soon known simply as the Freed-

Man representing the Freedman's Bureau stands between armed groups of Euro-Americans and Afro-Americans
Courtesy of the Library of Congress,
LC-USZ62-105555

Marriage of an African American soldier at Vicksburg by Chaplain Warren of the Freedmen's Bureau, 1866
Courtesy of the Library of Congress,
LC-USZ62-138383

men's Bureau. Established by Congress in 1865, two months before the end of the Civil War, it would go on to feed millions of people, build hospitals and provide medical aid, negotiate labor contracts for ex-slaves, and settle labor disputes. It also helped former slaves to legalize marriages and to locate lost relatives, and assisted black veterans. In addition, the Freedmen's Bureau attempted, with little success, to settle former slaves on Confederate lands confiscated or abandoned during the war. Intended as a temporary agency to last the duration of the war and one year afterward, the Bureau was placed under the authority of the War Department, and the majority of its original employees were Union soldiers.[15]

The Bureau was effective working closely with volunteers and other private, charitable organizations. It was instrumental in building elementary schools for African Americans, and it helped to establish institutions of higher education: Howard University (D.C.), Fisk University (Nashville, TN), Hampton Institute (Hampton, VA), and

Atlanta University (GA), the latter in partnership with the American Missionary Association.[16]

First African American senator and representatives during Reconstruction
Courtesy of the Library of Congress, LC-DIG-ppmsca-17564

This massive and new kind of undertaking was the prototype of the European Recovery Program eight decades later (popularly known as the Marshall Plan). That program waged a kind of combat that Secretary of State George C. Marshall (for whom the later plan was named) would describe in 1947 as a war "not against any country or doctrine but against hunger, poverty, desperation, and chaos."[17]

The overarching goal of the Freedmen's Bureau and its partners, according to historian Olivier Zunz, was the implementation of policies and programs that would make it possible for the South not only to rejoin the Union but also to participate in the construction of an evolving national civil society in the new United States of America.[18] For nearly a decade, this bold venture, sustained by the Lincolnian vision of a "new nation, conceived in Liberty," and financed in part by the aggregation of new industrial wealth and philanthropic will, gave some evidence of working.

Perhaps most significant, a reconstructed South was offering promise that it might indeed ameliorate some of its most glaring racial inequities. By 1870 all of the states of the former Confederacy had been readmitted to the Union. Between 1868 and 1873, seven Southern states put laws on the books that barred segregation in transportation and public facilities. Two Southern states, Louisiana and South Carolina, enacted legislation that assured integrated schools. Black elected officials sat in the region's state legislatures and occupied local political offices. In the North, the trend decidedly was in the direction of implementing Congress' 1875 Civil Rights Act, which removed barriers to discrimination in public accommodations and transportation.

George Peabody, Philanthropic Pioneer

One of the first generous spirits from the private sector to become a major partner in these Reconstruction efforts was George Peabody (1795–1869). A talented financier, Peabody began with virtually nothing and became fabulously wealthy.

Born into a poor family north of Boston (in what was then Danvers) and having little schooling, Peabody worked his way up as a dry goods importing merchant and eventually

George Peabody, 1866
©National Portrait Gallery London

relocated to Baltimore, where in 1822 he established warehouses of his own in New York City and Philadelphia. In 1837 his connections took him to London, where he worked for Maryland officials "who commissioned him to sell abroad that state's $8 million bonds to finance its Baltimore and Ohio canal and later the Baltimore and Ohio Railroad."[19] In time he expanded his efforts and his business base, operating as George Peabody & Co. He specialized "in selling U.S. state bonds to finance canals, railroads, telegraph, the Atlantic Cable...thus helping modernize and industrialize the U.S."[20] In 1854 he took in Junius Spencer Morgan (father of J. P. Morgan) to form Peabody, Morgan & Co. and retired in 1864 in the city where he made his wealth and financial fame. He remained in London until his death in 1869, after which his financial creation took on the new name of J. S. Morgan & Co., and in time, J. P. Morgan.

Years before Andrew Carnegie composed his "Gospel of Wealth," the prudent Peabody advocated that the new rich had a special responsibility to give back to society. As with Carnegie, Peabody's humble beginnings together with an open door of opportunity clearly left a mark upon him and contributed to his empathy for those in greatest need.

Peabody likely was also influenced by the writings of Charles Dickens, by the horrendous poverty he himself saw firsthand in London, and by the deep impression of William Wilberforce's abolitionism on that city. Already directly responsive to the needs of the poor in London, before the Civil War, Peabody had also considered establishing a fund to aid New York City's poor. It never materialized, but as he thought about the prospect, he wrote, "I see our country, united and prosperous, emerging from the clouds which still surround her, taking a higher rank among the nations, and becoming richer and more powerful than ever before."[21]

Peabody was the last great 19th century philanthropist born in the 18th century. As such, he was a bridge between traditional American benevolence and an emerging conviction that philanthropy, like one's business interests, could and should be purposeful as well as *strategic*. He distanced himself from forms of charity that seemed influenced by "theology" and sectarian objectives and was a great admirer of John, Abigail, and John Quincy Adams. In them he recognized a rootedness in the same non-sectarian Enlightenment tradition espoused by James Smithson, an Englishman he knew and admired.

Peabody further believed in universal education not only as a tool for self-improvement but as a pragmatic mechanism for the improvement of society. In a letter to a nephew whose education he was supporting at Yale College he wrote:

> Deprived as I was, of the opportunity of obtaining anything more than the most common education, I am well qualified to estimate its value by the disadvantages I labor under in the society which my business and situation in life frequently throws me, and willingly would I now give twenty times the expense attending a good education could I now possess it, but it is now too late for me. . . . I can only do to those who come under my care, as I could have wished circumstances had permitted others to have done by me.[22]

Given that background and those emotions, Peabody's next major philanthropic enterprise was not surprising. He was appalled by the extent of the devastation about which he had been reading and hearing, and then personally witnessed during a visit to what he described as a "stricken South." In 1867 he converted more than $2 million of his assets to create the Peabody Education Fund. Its stated purpose was to "encourage the intellectual, moral, and industrial education of the destitute children of the Southern States." He stated also that he wished to include "the entire population, without other distinction than their needs and opportunities of usefulness to them."[23]

According to Stanley Katz and Barry Karl, the Peabody Fund anticipated the legal model of corporate philanthropy that emerged in the late 19th century from the fabulous wealth of John D. Rockefeller and Andrew Carnegie. It ranks among the earliest examples of modern, structured philanthropy.[24]

One of his first steps was to appoint a board of trustees chaired by Charles Robert Winthrop, a Massachusetts attorney and former speaker of the U.S. House (and a descendant of John Winthrop, first governor of Massachusetts Bay Colony). During the next forty-seven years, 1867–1914, that board's membership would include three U.S. presidents, leading national and state jurists, members of Congress, cabinet members, ambassadors, former military leaders of the Union and the Confederacy, and financiers, thereby setting a premier (and impressively modern) standard for a rising generation of philanthropic leaders and advocates.

Winthrop, in turn, sought the advice of Barnas Sears, the president of Brown University in Rhode Island. Sears could well be the first model of the modern, philanthropic administrator. Before coming to Brown, he had been a Baptist theologian and president of Newton Theological Seminary. He also had succeeded Horace Mann, the noted reformer and educator, as secretary of the Massachusetts Board of Education. Sears urged the new fund to appoint an "executive agent" who would visit schools, consult with Southern leaders, aid deserving public schools where they existed, or establish them, and use limited Peabody funds for schools that local authorities would support and the state would perpetuate through taxes. He also recommended the awarding of scholarships for those students in state teacher education schools (called "normal schools") who would then teach for two years after graduation.

Impressed not only by the power and clarity of his vision but also by the unusually wide range of his experience and leadership, the trustees immediately urged him to become their general agent. He accepted the position and moved with his family in 1867 to Staunton, Virginia, where he would live until 1880. From this base of operations over the next thirteen years of his life, he made extensive trips throughout the South.

The broad purpose of the Fund was to support separate Southern black and white public schools, as well as some legally mandated "racially mixed" schools and teacher education institutions in twelve Southern states. By pushing against a Southern preference for private schools for the privileged, Sears may be said to have launched the drive to bring public education to the region, or what he called "free schools for the whole people."[25]

Another Peabody Fund strategy, used to increase impact, was to give preferential assistance to those schools in more populous towns or cities. Affirming his confidence that it would produce a positive outcome, Sears pointed to the region's "deep Christian commitment" which "must, in the end, adopt and carry out the same rule for both races."[26] Moreover, all grants were conditional upon a pledge by local authorities to raise taxes to maintain the schools. The Fund also instituted the novel requirement of local matching support, and retained the power to appoint a subagent to work with schools and employ discretionary power to spend Peabody funds as needed in keeping with local concerns.

The Fund published annual reports on its expenditures. It further tracked and compiled data on legislation, school attendance, age, and literacy of the school-age population (6-21), and public expenditures by each state. Grant recipients in turn provided detailed reports on how money was spent. Fund dollars usually supported teachers, scholarships for their further education, "teacher institutes" or summer training sessions, and occasional "aid" for students, equipment, and supplies. Because grants were limited to public schools, most of them had only white students, although "colored" institutions established by the states did receive support.

Each year the Fund also recorded state expenditures. In 1879, as an example, it tracked a total of $7,037,046 in state appropriations. A Peabody Education Fund disbursement for public education that same year was $74,850, about 1% of public spending.[27]

The Fund's trustees also turned their attention to the acute shortage of qualified teachers in the South. In 1875 they entered into an agreement with Tennessee's state legislature that split off the University of Nashville's teaching branches into the new State Normal School, the students of which were all white. In 1889 that institution became Peabody Normal School, a two-year education institution.

In addition to his investments in the war-torn South and his gifts in support of all grade levels of education in his home state and in the wider region of New England, this widely recognized "modern father of philanthropy" gave to libraries, the arts, museums, and a forward-looking community development initiative (the London Peabody Donation fund), still active today in the city he loved and came to call his second home.

New White Southern Universities

Vanderbilt University in 1901
Courtesy of the Library of Congress,
LC-D4-13561

Also underway in the aftermath of the war was both the creation and the rebuilding of Southern white institutions of higher education. In 1873 Bishop Holland N. McTyerie of Nashville persuaded "Commodore" Cornelius Vanderbilt (with whom he had a familial relationship) to make a personal donation of $1 million to endow a university that would soon bear the commodore's name. It is believed to be the only major charitable gift that

HONORS FOR GEORGE PEABODY

In 1869, before Robert Campbell Brinkley opened his new hotel in Memphis, he learned about George Peabody's death in England. His great respect for the philanthropist and his many benefactions to the South moved Brinkley to name the hotel in Peabody's honor—a name it continues to bear 150 years later, albeit at a different location. The British royal family wished to bury Peabody in Westminster Abbey, but his will explicitly called for him to be laid to rest in his hometown of Danvers, Massachusetts. A further honor to the great man came when the officials of his birthplace renamed the town Peabody.

Sources: "History of the Peabody Memphis," Peabody Memphis, accessed July 1, 2019, https://www. peabodymemphis.com/about-en.html; The Almanac of American Philanthropy, ed. Karl Zinsmeister

Vanderbilt made during his lifetime. His intent, he declared, was to "contribute to strengthening the ties which should exist between all sections of our common country."[28]

Later, the Vanderbilt venture led indirectly to the formation of two other universities. Southern Methodist bishop Warren Akin Candler, younger brother of Asa Candler (founder of the Coca-Cola Company), and some of his ecclesiastical colleagues on the Vanderbilt University Board of Trust lost their denominational control of the institution. (Essentially, a $1 million gift from Andrew Carnegie for Vanderbilt's medical school stipulated that the school be free of sectarian, or religious, control. The university chancellor and the Methodist Episcopal Church, South faced off in court, and a ruling from the Tennessee Supreme Court went against the Methodist bishops.) That led them to acknowledge the new Southern Methodist University in Dallas, Texas, as their western university, and to seek a location for a second school somewhere east of the Mississippi River. The Candler brothers combined their influence and financial resources to win this role for a small Georgia Methodist college—Emory. Indeed, Asa Candler pledged $1 million to help endow the new

university, and he donated land for a new campus beside the fashion-
able Druid Hills neighborhood he was developing on the eastern edge
of Atlanta.[29] (The historic grounds of antebellum Emory College are
today "Oxford College of Emory University," thirty-eight miles from
the Atlanta campus.)

During this same period, Tulane University in New Orleans also
was the beneficiary of a major grant. Josephine Louise Le Monnier
Newcomb was the daughter of a wealthy businessman in New Orleans,
who arranged for her education in Europe. After her mother died,
Newcomb returned to the United States and lived in New Orleans
with her father. She met and in 1845 married a prosperous wholesale
grocer, Warren Newcomb. He retired in 1863, and they divided their
residencies among New Orleans, Louisville (Newcomb's place of birth
and upbringing), and New York City, organizing their life around their
young daughter, Sophie, and her education.

After her husband died, the estate Newcomb inherited grew sub-
stantially in her lifetime under her own astute management. In 1886 and
in memory of her daughter, who had died of diphtheria, she endowed
the Sophie Newcomb Memorial College of the newly established Tulane
University. It was the first self-sufficient independent women's college
in the United States connected with a men's university. (Her lifetime
donations and bequest exceeded $3 million.)[30]

Education for the Freedmen

Although the Freedmen's Bureau ceased operations in 1871, many other
schools and institutions that would become centers of higher learning

Main building of Claflin University, Orangeburg, South Carolina, ca. 1899
Courtesy of the Library of Congress, LC-USZ62-107844

for African Americans came into being in the Southern states. Their founders and benefactors included African American and white individuals, the American Missionary Association, Northern white denominations, black denominations (especially the African Methodist Episcopal Church), and state legislatures. Out of necessity, many of these institutions that would become private colleges and universities began by offering elementary school curricula and vocational courses.[31] However, within a relatively short time many of the courses of study expanded to include the liberal arts. Northern Presbyterians led all others, establishing seventy-five schools in the South, twenty-five in South Carolina alone.[32] In fact, as James M. McPherson's study of 300 abolitionists and their descendants confirms, their presence and philanthropic impact in the South was multidimensional and long-term, extending to the creation of the NAACP in 1909.[33]

The historian and sociologist W. E. B. Du Bois's exhaustive study *Economic Cooperation Among Negro Americans*, published in 1907 by the press of Atlanta University (where Du Bois was also a faculty member), confirms that black generosity was the greatest of all.[34] Tuskegee Institute's *Negro Yearbook* in 1915 noted that African Americans, during the fifty years after the Civil War, contributed more than $25 million (approximately $500 million in current value) to build and sustain educa-

CHALLENGES TO BLACK EDUCATION

Not all new schools for African Americans succeeded. The difficulty in creating and especially sustaining them is well illustrated by the somewhat gnarled history of higher education relations in Nashville, Tennessee (already home to what would become Fisk University). Also in that city was the Nashville Normal and Theological Institute, which evolved from classes first taught in 1864 by the Reverend Daniel W. Phillips, of the American Baptist Home Mission Society, in his home to African American teachers and preachers with rudimentary literacy. Nashville Normal relocated to former Union Army barracks in 1865, and then to the basement of a church. Contributors included Northern and local black and white church members. In 1883 it was formally incorporated as Roger Williams University (thereby honoring the former Puritan who became the leader of the Free Baptist movement in Rhode Island). The rechristened institution hired several African American faculty members and trustees, added a master's degree program, and purchased thirty acres of land in an outlying part of the city, where Vanderbilt University was then under construction. There, the trustees erected two impressive buildings for classrooms, offices, and dormitories: Mansion House and Centennial Hall.

Roger Williams and neighboring Vanderbilt enjoyed good relations, and students and faculty visited each other's campuses. However, as Nashville's population expanded into the desirable Belmont area and encroached on the boundaries of the two schools, tensions began to build. When the trustees of Roger Williams declined to sell their property in 1901, two mysterious fires destroyed campus buildings. (That same year fire mysteriously destroyed the main College Hall on the Vanderbilt campus.)

No longer able to operate, Roger Williams University sold its property for $170,000 to all-white Peabody Normal College and relocated to a smaller lot along Nashville's Whites Creek Pike, closer to the city's African American neighborhoods. There, it was joined by American Baptist College, which added a building of its own. Unable to sustain itself financially, it finally merged with Howe Junior College in Memphis (later LeMoyne-Owen College).

The purchase of the Roger Williams campus enabled Peabody Normal College to leave its downtown campus (near a red-light district), move next to Vanderbilt University, and change its name to the George Peabody College for Teachers.

Sources: Bill Carey, "The Roger Williams Legacy," *The Tennessee Magazine*, July 2012; *https://www.tnmagazine. org/the-roger-williams-legacy/*; George Peabody College for Teachers," Lost Colleges, accessed December 18, 2017, *http://www.lostcolleges.com/george-peabody-college-for-teachers.*

tional institutions.[35] Indeed, the tradition of black community building, intramural support, education, association-building, and philanthropy, which extends as far back as the American colonial era, was a constant in the African American community, even when conditions created the severest of obstacles.[36]

Table 3.1 - Southern Historically Black Colleges and Universities
Established Between 1865 and 1876

Current Name	Current Location	Year of Founding
LeMoyne College*	Memphis, TN	1862
Virginia Union University	Richmond, VA	1864
Atlanta University**	Atlanta, GA	1865
Shaw University	Raleigh, NC	1865
Rust College	Holly Springs, MS	1866
Edward Waters College	Jacksonville, FL	1866
Fayetteville State University	Fayetteville, NC	1867
Johnson C. Smith University	Charlotte, NC	1867
Saint Augustine's University	Raleigh, NC	1867
Morehouse College	Atlanta, GA	1867
Talladega College	Talladega, AL	1867
Barber-Scotia College	Concord, NC	1867
Alabama State University	Montgomery, AL	1867
Claflin University	Orangeburg, SC	1869
Clark College	Atlanta, GA	1869
Dillard University	New Orleans, LA	1869
Tougaloo College	Tougaloo, MS	1869
Straight University***	New Orleans, LA	1869
New Orleans University	New Orleans, LA	1869
Allen University	Columbia, SC	1870
Benedict College	Columbia, SC	1870
Alcorn State University	Lorman, MS	1871
University of Arkansas at Pine Bluff	Pine Bluff, AR	1873
Bennett College	Greensboro, NC	1873
Knoxville College	Knoxville, TN	1875
Alabama A&M University	Huntsville, AL	1875
Meharry Medical College	Nashville, TN	1876
Stillman College	Tuscaloosa, AL	1876
Morris Brown College	Atlanta, GA	1881

*1968 merger of LeMoyne College (1862) and Owen Junior College (1954) to form LeMoyne-Owen College
**1988 merger of Atlanta University (1865) and Clark College (1869) to form Clark Atlanta University
***1935 merger of Straight University and New Orleans University (both 1869)

Source: Compiled by the authors.

Note: In 1862 President Lincoln signed the Morrill Act, which enabled the creation of so-called land-grant universities in every state. However, when post-Reconstruction state laws made it impossible for African American students to attend these institutions, Congress passed a second Morrill Act in 1890 that established eighteen land-grant institutions in the South for black students. Shifted to that category were Alabama A&M and Alcorn State Universities, which had been created under the first Morrill Act. See *http://www.aplu.org/library/land-grant-but-unequal-state-one-to-one-match-funding-for-1890-land-grant-universities/file.*

The almost spontaneous manner in which white and black individuals, churches, religious denominations, and other not-for-profit organizations swept into the South to establish a network of educational institutions is truly overwhelming. Unlike the work of the Freedmen's Bureau, this enterprise was never an organized campaign. Yet it is one of the most massive philanthropic efforts in the history of the United States.

A War-Weary Nation and a Radical Reversal

Despite the incursion of philanthropic capital and compassion into the South, the countervailing forces against positive change remained strong. Even those leaders of the Republican Party who yearned most deeply for a successful Reconstruction were growing weary of dealing with ungrateful and recalcitrant white Southern "partners." David Hammack, in his study of Gilded Age philanthropy, quotes a Southern Baptist leader who in effect credited the denomination with rebuilding itself from the ashes of the Civil War entirely with donations from Southerners, while proudly refusing all offers of aid from Northern Baptists.[37] To be clear, racism and racial segregation were alive and well in both the North and the South, as evidenced by segregated housing patterns and other forms of discrimination throughout the country. However, as noted in chapter 2, belief in white supremacy and African American inferiority had woven itself deeply into the doctrine and polity of much of Southern Protestantism. Despite a high level of political violence against the occupying Northern army and the frequency of attacks on blacks "daring to vote" (and the whites who aided them), the prospects for social change were actually bright. Du Bois, in his book *Black Reconstruction*, recites a catalogue of achievements in a short period of time, including the establishment of public health departments and public schools, all the more remarkable since just a decade before, literacy for the enslaved was against the law.[38] In his examination of Reconstruction's legacy, historian Eric Foner agrees:

> Although black schools and colleges remained woefully underfunded, education continued to be available to most African Americans. And the autonomous family and church, pillars of the black community emerged during Reconstruction, remained vital forces in black life, and the springboard from which future challenges to racial injustice would emerge.[39]

Ironically, given President Ulysses Grant's friendship for the freedmen, the most serious crack in the dike of the Reconstruction effort was the corruption exposed in the president's own administration (Grant became "the dupe of the Gilded Age's greediest men").[40] The unfortunate—and history-changing—side effect of the political turmoil was to push "liberal abolitionists. . .to let their pieties get the better of their priorities" when "they made common cause with the Democrats who were ending democracy in the South."[41]

A crumbling presidency was not the only problem. An economic depression in 1874 left much of the South in even greater poverty, helping the Democrats win control of the House of Representatives. Already in a weakened state and facing an ambiguous result in the election of 1876 that permitted each presidential candidate to claim victory, the Republicans made a devil's bargain. Extracting from white Southern congressmen a pledge of support for their Republican candidate, Rutherford B. Hayes, the party of Lincoln promised to end federal occupation of the South and not to seek a second term. Even "Stalwart Republicans" took a more calculating approach as national power threatened to slip away.

When the dust settled, Republican Rutherford Hayes occupied the White House (part of the agreement was that he serve only one term), and four million freedmen had essentially lost their government's protection. The Southern Democrats returned to power as their states' "Redeemers" and congressionally driven Reconstruction came to a close.[42]

Chapter 3 Endnotes

1   Gross domestic product may be defined as the total monetary value of all goods and services produced over a specific time period.

2   Angus Maddison, *Contours of the World Economy, 1-2030 AD: Essays in Macro-Economic History* (Oxford: Oxford University Press, 2007), 379, and cited in: "List of Regions by Past GDP (PPP)," Wikipedia, last modified April 10, 2019, *https://en.wikipedia.org/wiki/List_of_regions_by_past_GDP_ (PPP)#cite_note-maddison-4.*

3   Stephen Mihm, "Capitalist Chameleon," review of *The Relentless Revolution: A History of Capitalism* by Joyce Appleby, New York Times, January 22, 2010, Sunday Book Review, *https://www.nytimes. com/2010/01/24/books/review/Mihm-t.html.*

4   Not all the wealth was being created in the United States. See Eric Jay Dolin, "How the China Trade Helped Make America," *The Daily Beast*, November 4, 2012, *https://www.thedailybeast.com/how-the-china-trade-helped-make-america?ref=scroll.* See also James Bradley*, The Imperial Cruise: A Secret History of Empire and War* (New York: Little Brown & Co., 2009), 289–90, in which the author documents that some of the great fortunes of the day (Warren Delano, FDR's grandfather; the Cabots of Boston; and others) derived from opium dealing in the Far East. See also, "The Opium Kings: Opium Throughout History," *Frontline*, PBS, retrieved February 16, 2019, *https://www.pbs.org/wgbh/ pages/frontline/shows/heroin/etc/history.html.*

5   H. T. Peck, F. M. Colby, D. C. Gilman, eds., "Astor, John Jacob: An American Merchant," *New International Encyclopedia* (New York: Dodd, Mead Publishing Company, 1917); Donald Adams, *Finance and Enterprise in Early America: A Study of Stephen Girard's Bank, 1812–1831* (Philadelphia: University of Pennsylvania Press, 1978); Christopher Levenick, "Thomas Perkins," *Philanthropy Roundtable, https://www.philanthropyroundtable.org/almanac/people/hall-of-fame/ detail/thomas-perkins..* The Wikipedia entry for "Thomas Handasyd Perkins" lists "$3 million" but provides no source. The Harvard Square Library ("a digital library of Unitarian Universalist biographies, history, books, and media") describes his "fortune" as "massive" and points to his "shipping business . . . and his many investments at home: mining, quarrying, hotels, and the creator of America's first railway." Harvardsquarelibrary.org.

6   "Stephen Duncan (1787-1867): Planter and Banker," Ted Ownby and Charles Reagan Wilson, eds., *Mississippi Encyclopedia* (Oxford: University Press of Mississippi, 2017), 368-369; Robert T. Oliver, "Heyward, James and Nathaniel Heyward," *South Carolina Encyclopedia* (University of South Carolina Press, 2012) accessed at: *http://www.scencyclopedia.org/sce/entries/heyward-james-and-nathaniel-heyward/.*

7   Quoting "Q: statistics on millionaires, late 1800s" in Google Answers, *http://answers.google.com/ answers/threadview/id/280120.html.* To be sure, the South had its own millionaires (e.g., bankers, brokers, landowners) but not with the same concentration and conspicuousness.

8   Mihm, "Capitalist Chameleon."

9   Ron Chernow, *Titan: The Life of John D. Rockefeller, Sr.* (New York: Vintage, 1998), 99.

10 Arizona and New Mexico were the final territories to achieve U.S. statehood in 1912, thereby completing the "lower 48."

11 *https:/history.com/topics/early-20th-century-us/john-d-rockefeller.*

12 Daniel Yergin, *The Prize: The Epic Quest for Oil, Money, and Power* (New York: Simon and Schuster, 1991), 910. *https://history.com/topics/early-20th-century-us/john-d-rockefeller.*

13 Library of Congress, Primary Documents in American History: *https://www.loc.gov/rr/program/bib/ ourdocs/lincoln2nd.html.*

14 The classic study of Reconstruction is Eric Foner, *Reconstruction: America's Unfinished Revolution,*

1863-1877, updated ed. (New York: Harper Perennial, 2014). The author situates Reconstruction (which he dates as beginning, significantly, in 1863 with Lincoln's Emancipation Proclamation) amid the possibilities of new freedom and citizenship for the freedmen, the enlarging role of the federal government and its relations with the states, and the influence of this era (which ended in 1877) on an unfolding civil rights movement of the next century. The study moves the focus of the Reconstruction story from reaction and "redemption" in 1877 with the return of white supremacy, to the core story of freedom and government's relations with the states that extends into our own day.

See also Chris Kromm, "Fables of the Reconstruction: Why Clinton's Comments about Southern History Matter," Facing South, January 28, 2016, *https://www.facingsouth.org/2016/01/fables-of-the-reconstruction-why-clintons-comments.* Kromm, executive director of the Institute for Southern Studies notes, "[There is] a longstanding but now-discredited idea that Reconstruction—the period of political, economic and social upheaval after the Civil War from 1863 to 1877—was a mistake, a period of violent and incompetent rule forced on the South by vengeful Northerners.

"This view of Reconstruction, first made popular by scholars connected to Columbia professor William Archibald Dunning, took hold in the early 1900s and persisted as the dominant narrative through the 1960s. This view was challenged, most forcefully in 1935 in historian W. E. B. Du Bois' classic work, *Black Reconstruction,* which argued that not only was Reconstruction a critical moment of progress—for example, the multiracial governments created the South's first systems of state-funded public education—but that the period's failures were largely because Reconstruction didn't go far enough."

15 "Freedmen's Bureau," *History.com,* last modified October 3, 2018, *https://www.history.com/topics/black-history/freedmens-bureau.*

16 William Troost, "Freedmen's Bureau," EH.Net Encyclopedia, edited by Robert Whaples (June 5, 2008) at *http://eh.net/encyclopedia/the-freedmens-bureau.*

17 From Marshall's speech at the Harvard College commencement on June 5, 1947, quoted in Scott Lucas, *Freedom's War: The U.S. Crusade Against the Soviet Union.* As a young man living in Virginia and attending Virginia Military Institute at the end of the 19th century, Marshall would have learned of total war's impact on the land and its people as well.

18 For a thorough delineation of this shift, see especially Olivier Zunz, *Philanthropy in America: A History* (Princeton: Princeton University Press, 2012).

19 Quoted in Franklin Parker and Betty J. Parker, "How Research on George Peabody (1795-1869) Changed Our Lives," Franklin and Betty Parker Writings (blog), *http://bfparker.over-blog.com/article-how-research-on-george-peabody-1795-1869-changed-our-lives-by-franklin-parker-and-betty-j-park-79599036.html.* Franklin Parker, *George Peabody: A Biography* (Nashville: Vanderbilt University Press, 1995), is the standard biography.

20 Ibid.

21 Franklin Parker and Betty J. Parker, "Education Philanthropist George Peabody (1795-1869), George Peabody College for Teachers, Nashville, and the Peabody Library and Conservatory of Music, Baltimore (Brief History)," unpublished document, 1997 (ERIC), 3. Also Louis R. Harlan, *Separate and Unequal: Public School Campaigns and Racism in the Southern Seaboard States,* 1901-1915 (Chapel Hill: University of North Carolina Press, 1958).

22 Parker, *George Peabody,* 25.

23 The "stricken South" and the fund's purpose appear in the appendix to the Washington *Congressional Globe* (February 13, 1867), 122.

24 Barry D. Karl and Stanley N. Katz, "The American Private Philanthropic Foundation and the Public Sphere, 1890–1930," *Minerva* 19 (June 1981): 236–70. See also West, *History of Education Quarterly,* 3–21.

25   John Swett, *American Public Schools: History and Pedagogics* (New York: American Book Company, 1900), 95. See also James D. Anderson, *The Education of Blacks in the South, 1860–1935* (Chapel Hill: University of North Carolina Press, 1988); Eric Anderson and Alfred A. Moss Jr., *Dangerous Donations: Northern Philanthropy and Southern Black Education, 1902–1930* (Columbia: University of Missouri Press, 1999); and Harlan, *Separate and Unequal.*

26   Earle H. West, "The Peabody Education Fund and Negro Education, 1867-1880," *Higher Education Quarterly,* Vol. 6, No. 2 (Summer 1966), p. 17.

27   Proceedings of the Trustees of the Peabody Education Fund, Annual Report, 1879, vol. 2, p. 237.

28   *Vanderbilt University Quarterly*, vol. 1, no. 1 (Nashville: Vanderbilt University, 1901), 117.

29   Gary S. Hauk, *Emory as Place: Meaning in a University Landscape* (Athens: University of Georgia Press, 2019), 88.

30   *Encyclopaedia Britannica Online,* s.v. "Josephine Louise Le Monnier Newcomb," *https://www. britannica.com/biography/Josephine-Louise-Le-Monnier-Newcomb#ref669577.* The college has been shuttered since Hurricane Katrina, owing to Tulane's restructuring plan.

31   The African Methodist Episcopal (AME) Church, established by Richard Allen and others in Philadelphia in 1816, was responsible for establishing some 2,000 schools for African Americans throughout the South during the post–Civil War period.

32   See generally: Elizabeth Jacoway, *Yankee Missionaries in the South: The Penn School Experiment* (Baton Rouge: Louisiana State University Press, 1980); Jacqueline Jones, *Soldiers of Light and Love: Northern Teachers and Georgia Blacks, 1865–1873* (Chapel Hill: University of North Carolina Press, 1980); Joe M. Richardson, *Christian Reconstruction: The American Missionary Association and Southern Blacks, 1861–1890* (Athens: University of Georgia Press, 1986); and Leon F. Litwack, *Been in the Storm So Long: The Aftermath of Slavery* (New York: Vintage, 1980), 450–55.

33   James M. McPherson, *The Abolitionist Legacy: From Reconstruction to the NAACP* (Princeton: Princeton University Press, 1975).

34   W. E. B. Du Bois, *Economic Cooperation among Negro Americans* (Atlanta: Atlanta University Press, 1907), excerpted in *Making the Nonprofit Sector in the United States: A Reader,* ed. David C. Hammack (Bloomington: Indiana University Press, 1998), 264–80.

35   Adam Fairclough, *Teaching Equality: Black Schools in the Age of Jim Crow* (Athens: University of Georgia Press, 2001); Emmett D. Carson, "The Evolution of Black Philanthropy: Patterns of Giving and Voluntarism" in *Philanthropic Giving: Studies in Varieties and Goals,* ed. Richard Magat (New York: Oxford University Press, 1989), 92-102; John H. Stanfield II, "Philanthropic Regional Consciousness and Institution Building in the South, 1865-1920," in *Philanthropy in American Society,* ed. Jack Salzmann (New York: Columbia University, 1987); John H. Donohue III, James J. Heckman, and Petra E. Todd, *The Schooling of Southern Blacks: The Roles of Legal Activism and Private Philanthropy, 1910–1960* (Chicago: University of Chicago Press, 2000).

36   Wendy Gamber, "Antebellum Reform: Salvation, Social Control, and Social Transformation" in *Charity, Philanthropy, and Civility in American History,* ed. Lawrence J. Friedman and Mark D. McGarvie (Cambridge: Cambridge University Press, 2002), 148.

The New Englander William Lloyd Garrison commonly is credited as the founder of the abolitionist movement. In fact, it began in 1817 with "3,000 African Americans gathered in Philadelphia to protest colonization." During the Great Migration of the 20th century, blacks formed the NAACP, the National Urban League, the African American branches of the YMCA and YWCA, and Marcus Garvey's Universal Negro Improvement Association (UNIA). Claude A. Clegg III, "Philanthropy, the Civil Rights Movement, and the Politics of Racial Reform," in Friedman and McGarvie, *Charity, Philanthropy, and History,* 344.

W. E. B. Du Bois devoted his scholarship to documenting the initiatives and improvement efforts of blacks during Reconstruction to buttress his argument that it was racism, and not lack of ability, that made the prospects of African Americans in the South and the United States so bleak. Hammack, ed. *Making the Nonprofit Sector,* 264–80.

37   David Hammack, "Nonprofit Organizations, Philanthropy, and Civil Society," in *The Gilded Age: 1870 to 1900,* Handbook to Life in America, ed. Rodney P. Carlisle, vol. 4 (New York: Facts on File, 2009), 219.

38   Adam Gopnik, "The Takeback," *New Yorker,* April 8, 2019, 82.

39   Erik Foner, *Forever Free: The Story of Emancipation and Reconstruction* (New York: Vintage, 2005), 212.

40   Elizabeth D. Samet, "Brief History of the Image of a Hero: 1822–1885," *Harvard Magazine* (January-February 1919), 43.

41   Gopnik, "Takeback," 78.

42   Although his perspective has been contested, the historian C. Vann Woodward (like Du Bois) was able to see hope and possibility in Reconstruction. In *The Strange Career of Jim Crow* (Oxford: Oxford University Press, 1955), Woodward asserts it was the failure of a growing populist movement in the 1880s and 1890s and not the reactionary politics that brewed during Reconstruction that spoiled prospects for equality. As evidence, he points to the South's custom and tradition of race interaction— not radical separation—that historically characterized the region's history.

CHAPTER 4

Old Times Not Forgotten (1877–1895)

"Slavery by Another Name"

Many white Southerners, disheartened and even enraged by their new lot in life, now felt emboldened by the profound political upheaval taking place. Here at last was an opportunity to remove all vestiges of racial equality and to restore a climate of white supremacy.

In 1865–66, immediately after the war's end, several Southern legislatures had already begun to enact so-called black codes—essentially reincarnations of the old slave codes (without the slave-as-property provision) that had existed in both the South and the North. There followed a series of poll taxes and literacy tests (and later the "white primary") to curb black voting as well as restrictions of movement to seek employment. Especially destructive were broadly defined vagrancy laws that enabled the freedmens' arrest for minor infractions and sentencing to involuntary labor. It was the start of the notorious convict lease system—the subject of Douglas Blackmon's Pulitzer-Prize-winning study, *Slavery by Another Name*.[1]

Tennessee Coal, Iron & Railroad Co.'s furnaces, Ensley, Alabama, ca. 1906
Courtesy of the Library of Congress, LC-DIG-det-4a09958

African Americans seeking to flee these hostile conditions[2] by moving to the North encountered varied challenges. They often had to compete for jobs with immigrants, themselves desperate for work to support their families and willing to labor under brutal conditions for paltry wages. The ups and downs of the business cycles, including deep economic depressions, only worsened conditions, since it was the working men, women, and children who endured massive layoffs or hourly wage cuts during difficult times.

Economic hardship was a major impetus for flight from the South, but even more intimidating was the reign of terror against all African Americans, unchecked by any law, that revealed itself in the spread of vigilante and hate groups. The Ku Klux Klan (its formal creation in Pulaski, Tennessee is variously dated December 24, 1865 and 1866), the Knights of the White Camellia (founded in 1867 by Confederate Army Colonel Alcibiades DeBlanc in Franklin, Louisiana), and other terrorist organizations gained new strength and started to flourish. The only limited countermeasure was the military force available as a result of President Ulysses S. Grant's authorization of the Reconstruction Force Act (known as the Ku Klux Klan Act) in 1871.[3]

Ralph Ginzburg's definitive study, *100 Years of Lynchings*,[4] documents 4,075 cases of lynching of African Americans in twelve Southern states between 1877 and 1950. Unusual because it lacks any narrative, Ginsburg's exhaustive presentation relies entirely upon reprints of the thousands of news stories and press reports that comprise a "red record of racial atrocities."[5]

Racially motivated lynching was not limited to Southern states nor was every lynching a homicide. Ginzburg's book cites this press notice of April 18, 1870, from the New York *Truth Seeker*, the oldest continuously published small press in the United States:

> WEST POINT, N.Y. – James Webster Smith, the first colored cadet in this history of West Point, was recently taken from his bed, gagged, bound, and severely beaten, and then his ears were slit. He says that he cannot identify his assailants. The other cadets claim that he did it himself.[6]

Anti-black violence was not isolated, nor was it restricted to attacks on individuals. It included riots, to give only a few examples, in Wilmington, North Carolina (1898); New York City (1900); Atlanta (1906); Springfield, Illinois (1908); East St. Louis, Illinois (1917); Chicago (1919); Tulsa, Oklahoma (1921); and the rural community of Rosewood, Florida (1923).[7]

The John F. Slater Fund for the Education of Freedmen

John F. Slater (1815–1884) was undeterred by the opposition to racial equity. In 1882, no doubt influenced by the progressive writings of

John F. Slater
Rutherford Birchard Hayes, Memorial of John F. Slater, of Norwich, Connecticut, 1815-1884 (University Press: 1885)

Henry George (see chapter 5) and inspired by his own Christian beliefs and the example of George Peabody, Slater established a million-dollar fund (the equivalent of twenty-five million in 2018 dollars) bearing his name to support higher education for southern African Americans.

A native of Rhode Island whose family owned and operated textile mills in New England, Slater had made his earliest contribution to education when he endowed the Norwich Free Academy in Connecticut in 1842. He became aware that the federal census of 1880 revealed 70% of the nation's black adult population (overwhelmingly in the South) to be illiterate.[8] At the time the entire region had only thirty-nine public schools for African Americans, six of which offered college-level courses.

Slater's gift followed in Peabody's organizational footsteps. Incorporated in New York state in 1882, his fund was to be managed by a ten-person board. Its members included former U.S. president Rutherford B. Hayes, a chief justice of the United States, a prominent and wealthy abolitionist, an Episcopal bishop, a financier who also helped found the YMCA, and the presidents of Columbia and Cornell universities.

However, unlike the Peabody Education Fund, whose distributions were limited to established public institutions in the South (and thereby touched a limited number of black students), the John F. Slater Fund for the Education of Freedmen targeted both public and private colleges for African Americans from Virginia to Texas. Even after significant disbursements, the fund's assets grew to $1.5 million by 1906.[10]

As its first general agent the fund hired Atticus G. Haygood, a native of Watkinsville, Georgia, a progressive bishop of the Methodist Episcopal Church, South, and the distinguished president of Emory College. Haygood's 1881 book, *Our Brother in Black: His Freedom and His Future,* which emphasized the productive role of the newly freed people during Reconstruction, had caught the attention of the Slater Fund. His 1885 book, *The Case of the Negro,* made his and the Fund's efforts "inextricably linked. . .in behalf of Negro education, voting, and ownership of property."

New times were demanding new approaches. The Slater Fund, drawing upon the path-finding administrative experience of the Peabody Education Fund, modeled a corporate form of professional management and control that drew its inspiration from the unprecedented and transforming forces in the society at large. One of the early reports of the Slater Fund (see table 4.1) exemplifies the range of its work, the breadth of its geographic reach, and the variety of its expenditures. It maintained a strict record of accounting for all of the details associated with its grants, typically including a letter from the president of the recipient institution or the supervisor of the program involved.

Committed to racial justice, the Slater Fund was convinced of the necessity of higher education as the best route to equity for African Americans. As reported by the general agent, the Fund offered support for universities, colleges, industrial institutes (two-year training programs), normal schools (so-called because they educated high school graduates in the norms of teaching), a medical school, and theological seminaries. Occasionally it made grants for the additional education of classroom teachers, student expenses, student financial aid, supplies, equipment, and other implements.

By the standards of 1888, these were not insubstantial grants. According to the U.S. Bureau of Labor Statistics, a distribution of $45,000 was the equivalent of $1,128,602 in 2018.

Table 4.1. Report of the General Agent for Apportionments for 1887–1888

Atlanta University, Atlanta, Ga.	$1,600.00
Beaufort Normal Academy, Beaufort, S.C.	$700.00
Benedict Institute, Columbia, S.C.	$1,000.00
Biddle University, Charlotte, N.C.	$1,200.00
Brainerd Institute, Chester, S.C.	$700.00
Central Tennessee College, Nashville, Tenn.	$1,100.00
Claflin University, Orangeburg, S.C.	$1,400.00
Clark University, Atlanta, Ga.	$2,150.00
Fisk University, Nashville, Tenn.	$1,300.00
Gilbert Seminary, Baldwin, La.	$500.00
Hampton Institute, Hampton, Va.	$3,000.00
Hartshorn Memorial Institute, Richmond, Va.	$650.00
Howard University, Washington, D.C.	$600.00
Jackson College, Jackson, Miss.	$800.00
Jacksonville Graded School, Jacksonville, Fla.	$1,000.00
Kentucky Normal University, Louisville, Ky.	$700.00
Leonard Medical School, Raleigh, N.C.	$500.00
Leland University, New Orleans, La.	$1,000.00
LeMoyne Institute, Memphis, Tenn.	$1,500.00
Lewis Normal Institute, Macon, Ga.	$500.00
Livingston College, Salisbury, N.C.	$700.00
Meharry Medical College, Nashville, Tenn.	$1,000.00

Moore Street Industrial School, Richmond, Va.	$540.00
Montgomery Normal University, Montgomery, Ala.	$1,200.00
Mt. Albion State Normal School, Franklinton, N.C.	$400.00
Mt. Hermon Female Seminary, Clinton, Miss.	$1,000.00
New Orleans University, New Orleans, La.	$1,000.000
Paul Quin College, Waco, Texas	$460.00
Payne Institute, Augusta, Ga	$800.00
Philander Smith College, Little Rock, Ark	$800.00
Roger Williams University, Nashville, Tenn.	$1,300.00
Rust Nornal Institute, Huntsville, Ala.	$300.00
Rust University, Holly Springs, Miss.	$1,500.00
Schofield Normal Institute, Aiken, S.C.	$500,00
Scotia Female Seminary, Concord, N.C.	$700.00
Shaw University, Raleigh, N.C.	$1,800.00
Spelman Female Institute	$2,000.00
State Normal School, Huntsville, Ala	$700.00
State Normal School, Tuskegee, Ala	$1,000.00
Straight University, New Orle, La.	$1,000.00
Talladega College, Talladega, Ala.	$1,400.00
Tillotson Institute, Austin, Texas	$900.00
Tougaloo University, Tougaloo, Miss.	$1,500.00
Training School, Knoxville, Tenn.	$600.00
To special projects	$500.00
Total	**$45,000.00**

Source: *Proceedings of the Trustees of the John F. Slater Fund for the Education of Freedmen, 1888,* 7–10.

Jim Crow, Another New South, and the Lost Cause

Even as the Slater Fund pursued its goals, Southern states in the 1880s and 1890s continued to enact "Jim Crow" laws that steadily extended a color line of separation. In 1892 Homer A. Plessy, a black New Orleans shoemaker, legally challenged the ordinance that segregated passengers racially on streetcars in that city. The judge in that case, John Howard Ferguson, ruled that the "separate but equal" concept was constitutional, provided that the transportation facilities were of equal quality. The court cited as precedent two state Supreme Court cases, one in Massachu-

Drinking at "Colored" water cooler, 1939
Courtesy of the Library of Congress, LC-DIG-fsa-8a26761

setts and one in Pennsylvania, to the effect that to "assert separateness is not to declare inferiority."

The U.S. Supreme Court drew the final curtain on the possibility of a transformed South when it upheld the State of Louisiana's "Separate Car Act" of 1890. By affirming that the Act was not a violation of the 14th Amendment's "equal protection" clause, it swept aside the last of the constitutional barriers to an emerging white supremacy.[12]

Racial segregation quickly extended to drinking fountains, restrooms, public accommodations and services, and entrances to buildings. With that and other reversals, in the words of the biographer of W. E. B. Du Bois, "the afterglow of abolitionism and Reconstruction was to be extinguished in Washington for more than fifty years."[13]

If legally sanctioned reprisals against those who dared violate these new laws failed to encourage compliance, unpunished vigilante terrorism, as noted, continued in full force. Although racial apartheid was hardly a regional phenomenon, as evidenced by housing and other discrimination elsewhere in the country, the South's reliance on law and extralegal violence began to isolate it further from the rest of the nation's voluntary segregation practices.[14]

Henry W. Grady (1850–1889) was determined to capture a share of the burgeoning Northern wealth for his region. In bustling, business-hungry Atlanta (which became the Georgia capital in 1868), the entrepreneurial managing editor of that city's *Constitution* launched a marketing campaign. His goal was to fashion the kind of identity for Atlanta and what he promoted as the "New South" that would attract more Northern investment. Like any good salesperson, though, he recognized the need to paper over and soft-pedal the less appealing sides of Southern reality. His newspaper and other image-conscious publications like the *Memphis Daily Appeal* and *De Bow's Review* of New Orleans sought to portray the image of a region marked by robust economic resurgence, North-South financial cooperation, and interracial harmony. Helping to promote Grady's New South was the surfacing of a parallel historic invention. It was the "Lost Cause"— an affirmation of the rightness and nobility of the South's self-defense in the face of overwhelming Northern aggression.

BEREA COLLEGE

Among the institutional victims of re-segregation was Berea College in eastern Kentucky, established in 1855 on land contributed by the abolitionist and politician Cassius Marcellus Clay. Its nearly four-decade commitment to interracial education was overturned in 1904 by the state legislature's passage of the Day Law, which prohibited the education of black and white students together. When the U.S. Supreme Court upheld that new state statute, Andrew Carnegie made a $200,000 challenge grant to the trustees of Berea to assist them with funding for the continued education of African American students being forced to leave the college. (President Theodore Roosevelt was among those who wrote fund-raising letters on behalf of the campaign to match the challenge.) In 1910 the trustees established the Lincoln Institute (the only institution in the state to bear the former president's name) as a boarding school for black high school students in Shelby County. (The trustees also underwrote the tuition of all black students who transferred to other institutions.)

Graduates of Lincoln included Whitney M. Young Jr., who later became executive director of the National Urban League, and Carter G. Woodson, historian and founder of Negro History Week, which would become Black History Month.

After the Day Law was amended in 1950 to permit integration above the high school level, Berea (whose motto is the biblically inspired "God has made of one blood all peoples of the earth") was the first college in Kentucky to reopen its doors to black students.

Sources: Berea College website, https://www.berea.edu/about/; "Our History," Lincoln Foundation, http://lincolnfdn.org/about-us/our-history; "Lincoln Institute," Notable Kentucky African Americans Database, http://nkaa.uky.edu/nkaa/items/show/415.

One of its most outspoken proponents was Jubal Anderson Early, a bitter Virginian, lawyer, and former Confederate general whose troops had advanced to the suburbs of Washington, D.C., and burned Chambersburg, Pennsylvania. During the 1870s he became the first president of the Southern Historical Society. His written and oral reminiscences of the war were the basis for the establishment of, among other organizations, the Sons of Confederate Veterans in 1896.[15]

In Virginia, and eventually all of the Confederate states, Memorial or Decoration Day was promoted and celebrated "as a sign of renewal and rebirth." Each community selected an annual day (usually connected with a symbolic or particularly memorable event) that was set aside for the ceremonial decoration of the graves of war veterans.

With the spring months, for example, Caroline E. Janney recounts how

> Fredericksburg, Lynchburg, and Richmond's Oakwood association all selected May 10, the anniversary of Confederate general Thomas J. "Stonewall" Jackson's death following the Battle of Chancellorsville in 1863. The women of Hollywood agreed on May 31, the anniversary of the day Richmonders first heard the cannons of war during the Battle of Seven-Pines-Fair Oaks (1862). Winchester selected June 6, the day Confederate general Turner Ashby was killed in 1862 near Port Republic.

In addition, Ladies' Memorial Associations, "locally organized groups of southern white women... tracked down the scattered remains

Stuart Monument, Richmond, Virginia
Library of Congress, Prints & Photographs
Division, HABS VA,44-RICH,149--1

of Confederate soldiers and reinterred them in Confederate cemeteries."[16]

Gathering momentum in the 1880s, the Lost Cause movement took on the personality of a cultural religion as it "recalled" the age-old, knightly virtues of Southern honor and valor as the true and lasting legacies of the "recent unpleasantness." By 1912 Confederate memorials, often supported through private fund-raising appeals, were standing on 501 public grounds throughout the South. The Lost Cause interpretation of history, which quickly found its way into Southern school textbooks, stated clearly that Northern aggression was the cause of the war; the South's forces were overrun by superior numbers; and the period preceding the conflict had been marked by Southern racial concord and opulence. Now, according to the proponents of this interpretation of history, those prewar conditions were at last returning, resurrected by the Southern Democrats' overthrow of Radical Republicans and the "Redemption" of antebellum traditions like states' rights and local control.[17]

Seven years after the formation of the Slater Fund and a few days before his death in 1889, Henry Grady was still selling a South that simply did not exist. He proclaimed to a Boston audience,

This hour little needs the loyalty that is loyal to one section and yet holds the other in enduring suspicion and estrangement. Give us the broad and perfect loyalty that loves and trusts Georgia alike with Massachusetts that knows no South, no North, no East, no West, but endures with equal and patriotic love every foot of our soil, every state of our Union.[18]

Booker T. Washington's Compromise

Booker T. Washington was the president of Tuskegee Institute in Alabama, a model of vocational education for African Americans. Having helped white leaders to secure funding for the Cotton States and International Exposition in Henry Grady's hometown of Atlanta, Washington was asked to be an opening speaker for the September 1895 event. In what would become known as the "Atlanta Compromise," his response to the dismal state of African American economic and social conditions and nasty race relations was to encourage black Southerners to "cast down your bucket where you are... Cast it down in agriculture, mechanics, in commerce, in domestic service, and in the professions."

Having essentially endorsed black economic subordination by calling upon African Americans to "dignify and glorify common labour," he then sought to calm white fears about the foolish goal of social integration by explaining that the two races could be "as separate as the fingers, yet one as the hand in all things essential to mutual progress." He asked his white audience, in response, to trust black people and provide them with opportunities so all Southerners could advance in industry and agriculture. Future privileges for African Americans would come from "constant struggle rather than of artificial forcing."[19]

The speech received a standing ovation, and the text was tele-graphed to every major newspaper in the country. Washington almost instantly became the most influential black leader in the United States. In retrospect, it seems he had little choice but to endorse the gospel of the New South. Whether the white people who applauded his remarks realized it, Washington was describing a realistic strategy. It may have had no appeal to a black intellectual like W. E. B. Du Bois, who would go on to cofound the NAACP,[20] but Washington realized it was a dangerous time during which to ally oneself with radical social change.[21] He was seeking space and time—and funds from Northern philanthro-pists—for an emotional, educational, and spiritual recovery of a cen-turies-oppressed population. Only then, he reasoned, could his people safely challenge their oppressors.

CHAPTER 4 ENDNOTES

1   Douglas A. Blackmon, *Slavery by Another Name: The Re-Enslavement of Black Americans from the Civil War to World War II* (New York: Doubleday, 2008).

2   It was the early wave of an exodus (the so-called Great Migration) that would extend from 1916, when Europeans fighting in World War I triggered a demand for industrial laborers in the North, until 1970.

3   The Klan would be resurrected in 1915 atop Stone Mountain in Georgia and spread rapidly beyond the South.

4   Ralph Ginzburg, *100 Years of Lynchings* (Baltimore: Black Classic Press, 1962).

5   His use of this painfully descriptive phrase is a tribute to the pioneering work of Ida B. Wells and her 1895 pamphlet, "The Red Record: Tabulated Statistics and Alleged Causes of Lynching in the United States," Project Gutenberg, *https://www.gutenberg.org/files/14977/14977-h/14977-h.htm*.

6   A native of South Carolina, Smith was dismissed from the Academy one year before his graduation. He went on to a distinguished teaching career at South Carolina Agricultural and Mechanical Institute (now South Carolina State University). More than a century later, the army awarded him his second-lieutenant's bars posthumously. The unpublished full story of his lynching is told by U.S. Army captain Matthew Oliver, "Society's Sacrifice: The First Black Cadet at West Point, James Webster Smith," December 1, 1993, United States Military Academy Library, *http://digital-library.usma.edu/cdm/ref/collection/p16919coll1/id/23*.

7   See detailed listings for each city in *Encyclopedia of American Race Riots: Greenwood Milestones in African American History,* ed. Walter Rucker and James Nathaniel Upton (Westport, CT: Greenwood Press, 2006).

8   U.S. Department of Commerce, Bureau of the Census, *Historical Statistics of the United States, Colonial Times to 1970*; and U.S. Department of Commerce, Bureau of the Census, Current Population Reports, Series P-23, *Ancestry and Language in the United States: November 1979*. (This data was issued in September 1982.)

9   Leslie H. Fishel Jr., "The John F. Slater Fund," *Hayes Historical Journal* (Fall 1988): 47-51.

10 Harold W. Mann, *Atticus Greene Haygood: Methodist Bishop, Editor, and Educator* (Athens: University of Georgia Press, 1965), 182.

11 In an interesting twist of history, today the Plessy *and* Ferguson Foundation, established by descendants of both men, erects historical markers in New Orleans to celebrate singular African American achievements.

12 Jackson Lears adds this: "Equally important was the [Supreme] Court's gradual redefinition of the Fourteenth Amendment as a substantive defense of corporate property rights. The culmination of this process was the Court's decision in *Santa Clara County v. Southern Pacific Railroad* (1886), which extended the definition of the word 'persons' in the Fourteenth Amendment to include legal persons—i.e., corporations. What began as a measure to confer rights on ex-slaves became a boon for big business." Lears, *Rebirth of a Nation: The Making of Modern America, 1877–1920* (New York: Harper, 2009), 87–88.

13 David Levering Lewis, *W. E. B. Du Bois: Biography of a Race, 1868–1919* (New York: Henry Holt, 1993), 119. Preceding *Plessy* was the Supreme Court's 1883 *Civil Rights Cases* decision, which ruled that the Fourteenth Amendment did not give Congress authority to prohibit "private" (non-state) discrimination, as it attempted to do in the 1875 Civil Rights Act. See J. Morgan Kousser, *The Shaping of Southern Politics: Suffrage Restriction and the Establishment of the One Party South, 1880–1910* (New Haven, CT: Yale University Press, 1974).

14 Kevin Boyle, *Arc of Justice: A Saga of Race, Civil Rights, and Murder in the Jazz Age* (New York: Henry Holt, 2004) explores urban and rural patterns of KKK operation, membership, political participation, and violence.

15 Charles C. Osborne, *Jubal: The Life and Times of General Jubal A. Early, CSA, Defender of the Lost Cause* (Baton Rouge: Louisiana State University Press, 1994).

16 Caroline E. Janney, "Ladies' Memorial Associations," *Encyclopedia Virginia,* last modified March 8, 2012, *http://www.encyclopediavirginia.org/Ladies_Memorial_Associations.*

17 On the subject of "Southern mythology" and the denial of slavery's role in the Civil War, see Margaret MacMillan, *Dangerous Games: The Uses and Abuses of History* (New York: Modern Library, 2008), 56–58.

18 These lines are inscribed on the Atlanta statue of Grady. While in Boston to deliver the speech from which they are taken, Grady caught a cold that led to a severe case of pneumonia from which he soon died. *http://www.ocaatlanta.com/public_art/henry-w-grady/.*

19 Quoted in Jacqueline M. Moore, *Booker T. Washington, W. E. B. Du Bois, and the Struggle for Racial Uplift* (Wilmington, DE: Scholarly Resources, 2003), 128. See Derrick P. Alridge, "Atlanta Compromise Speech," *New Georgia Encyclopedia,* last modified March 1, 2019, *https://www. georgiaencyclopedia.org/articles/history-archaeology/atlanta-compromise-speech. The full text of the speech is available at www.emersonkent.com/speeches/atlanta_compromise.htm.*

20 Du Bois was a member of the faculty of Atlanta University at the time of Washington's "Atlanta Compromise" speech and initially endorsed the theme and the efforts of Washington. His subsequent experience in Atlanta, capped by the city's bloody 1906 race riot, convinced him to adopt instead an activist civil and human rights strategy combined with Pan Africanism. In 1909 he cofounded the National Association for the Advancement of Colored People (NAACP). Soon after, he accepted the position of editor of the NAACP's monthly journal, *The Crisis,* and moved to New York City, where the association established its national office.

21 Robert Penn Warren, *The Legacy of the Civil War* (New York: Random House, 1961), 11.

CHAPTER 5

New Order and New Philanthropy in a New Age

"Survival of the Fittest"

In 1859, after years of research and observation, Charles Darwin, the English naturalist and biologist, had published a book that revolutionized humankind's understanding of itself. It was called *On the Origin of Species by Means of Natural Selection, or the Preservation of Favoured Races in the Struggle for Life*. Darwin postulated that superior creatures derived from lower-order ancestors in a never-ending battle for survival. It was nature itself and its evolutionary mechanism of "natural selection" that steered the process. From his findings it was possible to infer that not all disappearance of or damage to some species was necessarily bad or lacking in purpose. Contrary to some popular understanding, Darwin's assertions were welcomed and accepted by many educated scientists and theologians alike.

Five years later, another Englishman, Herbert Spencer, a political theorist and anthropologist, was among the first individuals to apply Darwin's biological theory to human history. He asserted that the raging, post–Civil War industrial struggle and explosion of the economy transforming the United States constituted the societal equivalent of a new stage of human evolution. To explain and affirm not only its necessity but also its inevitability, Spencer employed a term: "survival of the fittest."[1]

It quickly became a mantra that many Americans supported. The de facto public policy implications of this "social Darwinism" deemphasized the role of government or other "artificial" forces that impeded or diverted society's natural evolutionary process. On the political front, Republicans generally favored only the mildest form of intrusion in economic affairs; Democrats opposed government interference in personal life and clung to a strict states-rights agenda.[2]

However, that "hands-off" interpretation did not necessarily mean that society should ignore the conditions of the disadvantaged. Some social Darwinists in both England and in the United States advocated "for the elimination of slums, the enactment of public health legislation, crusading for the elimination of child labor, championing mandatory school attendance laws, and fighting for the creation of parks and playgrounds—all this premised on the Darwinist idea that a healthy, orderly, and just society fostered the conditions for social, political, and economic progress."[3]

Nonetheless, the economic contrasts were extreme, as enormous wealth continued to gloss over a world of unregulated business, unfettered exploitation of the working class, and unchecked immigration.

One historian described the period as "surreal." Yet, although virtually unrestrained, the so-called robber barons of the time were not without spiritual or philanthropic instincts. Portions of their wealth found their way into the establishment, support, and endowment of major educational and social service institutions (often church-related) as well as cultural institutions in both the North and the South.

Clearly, though, no one seemed to be in charge of the nation's public affairs. As Henry Adams, the descendant of two presidents, would put it, the challenge was how to oversee "so complex and so concentrated a machine" as a massive, modernizing, coast-to-coast industrial nation in a democracy where most commercial law was state and local.[4] Industrialization, urbanization, immigration, corruption, and poverty all required attention. New and previously unimagined organizing principles were needed, not simply to maintain national order but also to manage the needs, opportunities, and threats to communities and society undergoing so abrupt a change. In every area of life, the elements of performance, expertise, productivity, advocacy, education, and communication were gaining new importance—nowhere more so

Mrs. William K. Vanderbilt as a "Venetian Renaissance Lady" at the Vanderbilt Ball, March 26, 1883
Courtesy of The Preservation Society of Newport County

Not all of the new wealth found its way immediately into philanthropic channels. Alva Vanderbilt, a native of Mobile, Alabama, had grown up wealthy and then married into far greater wealth. In the middle of the devastating Depression of 1882-1884, this ambitious woman decided to hurdle her way to the top rung of New York society that had been controlled by Mrs. Caroline Astor. Mrs. Vanderbilt and her husband, the grandson of "Commodore" Vanderbilt, achieved her goal by hosting a costume ball in 1883 in their extravagant new mansion on Fifth Avenue for 1,200 of the city's wealthiest citizens. The cost of the event is estimated to have been the equivalent of $6 million currently. As if the parallels with pre-Revolutionary France were not already transparent, her father-in-law was one of the guests who came attired as King Louis XVI.

By contrast, in later life, Mrs. Vanderbilt, by then re-married, devoted much of her time and money to the support of the women's suffrage movement.

than in the emerging philanthropy of the post–Civil War era that the South evoked.

The Seeds of Progressivism

In 1879 Henry George, an American political economist and journalist, published *Progress and Poverty: An Inquiry into the Cause of Industrial Depressions and of Increase of Want with Increase of Wealth: The Remedy.* In it he contended that poverty was the result of unearned wealth concentrated in the hands of a small number of the wealthy. He also argued for "solutions" like a land-based tax and the abandonment of protectionism. By 1890 only the Bible had a greater number of readers.[5]

George's ideas fell on especially receptive ears in rural America. The price of cotton during the postwar years had been falling steadily in the South. Exorbitant railroad freight rates added to the misery of farmers. Seeking relief, a rural political and social movement called the Farmers' Alliance swept across the South and Midwest, enrolling more than 100,000 members. Arguing that the American political and economic systems were tipped to serve the interests of the rich, the Alliance demanded that the government expand the money supply by printing more money and coining more silver. Such action would cause inflation (a general increase in the cost of goods and services) and drive up the prices of cotton and other farm produce.[6]

The opponents of the Alliance denounced these ideas, claiming they would encourage governmental paternalism and undermine free enterprise. When neither Democrats nor Republicans would adopt the demands, the Alliance's more reform-minded members created the

People's Party—more commonly called the Populist Party. Among its leaders was Tom Watson, an attorney and fiery orator from Georgia. Watson had been elected to the U.S. Congress in 1890 as a Southern Alliance Democrat candidate but resigned before completing his term to join the Populists and to launch the People Party's Paper.[7]

The Panic of 1893 was one of the worst depressions in American history. Railroads, banks, and businesses collapsed, and millions of people lost their jobs. The average price of cotton fell to the ruinous level of less than five cents a pound. The Democrats' failure to respond positively further seemed to offer the Populists hope for political success.

The Populists (and especially Watson), realizing the need for help to defeat the Democrats in the South, reached out to find common cause with African American voters, most of whom belonged to the Republican Party (the so-called Lincoln Republicans). However, it seems that these black Republicans rather quickly recognized that opportunism rather than idealism was the chief motivating factor for the Democrats' invitation and soon withdrew their support.

Before that happened, however, the Democrats lashed out not just against what they perceived not just as potential "rule by negroes" but also against leadership by a "lower class of whites." In his extraordinary study, "Populist Dreams and Negro Rights: East Texas as a Case Study," Lawrence C. Goodwyn offers a front-row view of a single community in which this reactionary, race-baiting form of politics led to the splintering and gradual disappearance of the Populist Party.[8]

It is a story that was repeated across the South; C. Van Woodward's classic study *Tom Watson: Agrarian Rebel*, charts a similar process in Georgia with Watson's switch from being a nationally-renown Populist who welcomed black voter support to a racially and ethnically motivated Southern Democrat who called for black disfranchisement. (He was also anti-Catholic, anti-Jewish, and anti-immigrant.)

The dashing of Southern Populism and its moderately biracial reforms helped ensure one-party rule in the South as well as the backroom dominance of moneyed interests who had the most to gain from Populism's decline. The result, in the words of C. Vann Woodward, was "mint juleps for the few and pellagra for the crew, a façade of Greek columns and a back yard full of slums."[9]

The Populists managed to sustain a measure of momentum for a few more years, but the 1896 national elections were their last hurrah. This dynamic but short-lived political party sought to maintain credibility by awkwardly joining the Democrats in nominating William Jennings Bryan for president and then naming Tom Watson as their vice presidential candidate. The Republicans, led by William McKinley, won handily.

The Emergence of Organizations

Although Progressivism failed to achieve great electoral success, its ideals continued to gain popularity. By the 1890s, both major political parties would witness the growth of "progressive" wings that sought to bring value-based organization to the American social order. In doing so, they were fashioning an appreciation of the interdependence of all human relations. Progressive leaders believed that social problems (class warfare, poverty, violence, corruption, greed, inequity) could best be addressed by the provision of good education, a safe environment, and an efficient workplace.

Against this backdrop of shifting understandings, a new set of national, not-for-profit organizations was coming into being. One such assemblage was the American Bar Association, formed in 1884, the same year that high school teachers and college professors established the American Historical Association. Skilled craftsmen created the American Federation of Labor in 1886, and during the depression of the 1890s, the business community incorporated the National Association of Manufacturers (a powerful lobbying force in Congress). Also, in 1895, professional economists organized the American Economic Association, and they were followed by medical doctors, nurses, social workers, librarians, bakers, and real estate brokers in establishing professional organizations.

These affinity groups (which would in later years become part of the so-called nonprofit sector) set standards of practice in the professions and workforces that crossed state lines. They advocated their members' interests, monitored rapidly changing developments at the state and national levels, and became a strong enough voice to attract the attention of national government.

A Flurry of Philanthropy

As the 19th century drew to an end, a relatively small group of Northern foundations found their attention being drawn to the needs of a still-devastated South. Several of them (e.g., Rockefeller, Carnegie) had an almost-religious devotion to the saving power of education. Their common analysis of the situation further suggested that the South's economic recovery would depend upon an educated population. These foundations' interests and instincts could not have found a more appropriate target. In 1890 the average public expenditure per pupil in the North equaled $20; the corresponding figure in the South was just under $2. Even more alarming was the widening spending gap between white and black children in Southern states after 1900. Focusing on one city (Birmingham, Alabama) in the throes of an industrial emergence in the late 18th century, the historian Carl V. Harris carefully documents how "economics and social class" (including race) shaped not only educational investments but also "extraction of revenue, allocation of city services, and regulatory activity."[10]

These new philanthropic activists quickly recognized that they were confronting an unprecedented crisis. Just as they had built their corporate empires through "scientific" and strategic planning, they now would need to call upon unprecedented methods to address this new challenge. Rather than simply flinging resources at the miseries of the war-torn region, they took studious note of the work by the pioneering and education-oriented Peabody and Slater funds.

Some of these new philanthropists and education reformers alike were also paying close attention to other trends in education. One promising enterprise was contemporary Germany's technical high school movement. Its emphasis was to harmonize literacy, industry, technical, and vocational training with the "rhythm and discipline of modernizing agriculture and industry."[11] Addressing the manifold demands and needs of a new industrial and commercial epoch around the world,

German tech schools challenged the skilled laborer's need of "stodgy instruction based on abstractions, rote memory, useless languages, and hoary fables."[12]

This philosophy of education focused foundation giving in America on literacy and vocational education, not only for freed slaves but also for poor whites. It therefore became a civic and economic investment, as was building libraries and schools, offering support for informal networks of mutual aid, and addressing indigenous needs for medicine and public health. The donors also hoped that the practical knowledge gained from this philanthropy would inform and stimulate new state and national public policy. The form which their corporate philanthropy took also contained "many of the features of open-endedness and trustee discretion that would later characterize modern foundations."[13]

Major Benefactors of the South

Having become the richest man in the world, John D. Rockefeller Sr. (1839–1937) retired from business and devoted much of his next four decades to philanthropy. As the "funding father" of the University of Chicago in 1891, he ranked research and education high on his list of priorities. For Rockefeller the least imaginative use of money was to give it to people outright instead of delving into the causes of human misery: "Money is a feeble offering without the study behind it which

John D. Rockefeller, Sr., 1884
Courtesy of the Rockefeller
Archive Center

will make its expenditure effective."[14]

Strongly influenced by a report from his son, John Jr., about a tour of black schools in the South the previous year, Rockefeller in 1902 funded the creation of the General Education Board (incorporated by Congress on January 1, 1903) to strengthen public education for Southern children. One of its principal mechanisms would become the provision of salary support for agents appointed by each state for white and black schools.[15]

Rockefeller also was a major benefactor of the Atlanta Baptist Female Seminary, established for African American women in 1881 in the basement of Atlanta's Friendship Baptist Church. It would be renamed Spelman College in 1884 to honor Rockefeller's wife, Laura Spelman, and her abolitionist parents.[16]

George Foster Peabody, ca. 1907
Courtesy of the Library of Congress, LC-DIG-ppmsca-17490

The Rockefellers recruited George Foster Peabody (no relation to the founder of the Peabody Fund) to serve on the General Education Board. He was a native of Columbus, Georgia, and the child of parents who in 1852 moved to the South from Connecticut. Then "the Civil War... pushed the family into poverty, and by 1866 they had relocated to Brooklyn, New York, where the fourteen-year-old Peabody took a job with a wholesale dry goods firm."[17] The talented young man rapidly moved on to build a lucrative career in railroads and banking in Pennsylvania.

In addition to his work with the General Education Board, Peabody became an important philanthropist in his own right as the benefactor of the Penn Normal Industrial and Agricultural School in South Carolina, Hampton Institute, and Tuskegee Institute. He also advocated successfully for the creation of Episcopal Church colleges for African Americans in the South. In 1923 it was he who brought the young Franklin Roosevelt to Warm Springs, Georgia, for polio therapy (see chapter 9), an act that would change the course of history.[18]

The Rockefeller family's support of education led it to become more involved in health-related endeavors. The discovery that the near-epidemic incidence of hookworm (often contracted through bare feet) was keeping significant numbers of Southern children away from school prompted the launching and funding of a massive and successful public health program to eradicate this disease.[19]

The Northern antislavery movement had some of its deepest roots among members of the Society of Friends, or Quakers, in Philadelphia. One Quaker philanthropist, Anna T. Jeanes, in 1905 created a trust, the Negro Rural School Fund, to assist schools in Southern states. Administered by the General Education Board, the fund's primary thrust was the employment of so-called Jeanes Supervisors, African American industrial supervision instructors who emphasized vocational education and school improvement.[20] By 1910 there were 129 Jeanes Supervisors working as education circuit riders in 130 counties in 13 Southern states. They were teachers, to be sure, but they also functioned as experienced, strategic dynamos who were remarkably effective at assessing, inspiring, and leveraging community resources to

Katharine Drexel
Dominican Sisters - Grand Rapids / Public
Domain

SAINT KATHARINE DREXEL

A lesser-known Philadelphia
philanthropist than Anna Jeanes
was Katharine Drexel, the daughter
of a socially prominent, wealthy,
and pious Roman Catholic family.
Born in 1858, she became a nun in
1891. Sister Katharine subsequently
received papal permission to use her
inheritance to establish the Sisters
of the Blessed Sacrament—an
order with the mission of education
for Native Americans and African
Americans. The order established
and staffed schools around the
South and Southwest and in
1915 founded Xavier University
of Louisiana, the only Catholic
institution of higher education for
African Americans in the country. At
the time of her death in 1955, more
than 500 Sisters were teaching in
63 schools around the country and
involved with more than 50 missions
for Native Americans. Katharine
Drexel in 2000 became only the
second American-born saint of the
Roman Catholic Church.

Source: *www.catholic.org-Saints & Angels*

raise education standards.

These foundations and other benevolent agencies developed a strong affinity to what came to be called the Social Gospel. This new train of thought which began to emerge toward the end of the 19th century was essentially a liberal Protestant response to the miserable working and living conditions of laborers in 19th century industrial America. It stressed the application of Jesus' teachings to public life, especially the needs of the poor and disenfranchised, with special attention to the issues of justice and equity.

Its popularity among philanthropic organizations received a valuable boost with the publication of *Christianity and the Social Crisis* by Walter Rauschenbusch in 1907. Rauschenbusch was a Baptist pastor and later professor at Rochester Theological Seminary. His book's popularity rivaled that of Henry George's *Progress and Poverty* (see above). The novels of Charles Monroe Sheldon (*In His Steps: What Would Jesus Do?*) further popularized the tenets of the Social Gospel, which rejected social Darwinism's brutish notions of competitive individualism.

Similarly, "muckraking" journalism like Lincoln Steffens's *The Shame of the Cities* (1904) cast a light on urban political corruption while other authors described the deplorable living and labor conditions that trapped working-class families in the living hell of tenement districts.

General Purpose Philanthropy

Russell Sage, born in 1816, began work as an errand boy in his brother's Troy, New York, grocery. With a natural bent for mathematics and a driving entrepreneurial spirit, he rose rapidly in that and other Hudson River trades, and soon was investing in railroads. At the age of forty-seven, he relocated his operations to New York City, the center of the nation's expanding commercial networks. He purchased a seat on the New York Stock Exchange and in time secured directorships of railroads in the Midwest. He also entered into a partnership with the infamous robber baron Jay Gould, with whom he organized the Atlanta and Pacific Telegraph Company.

After the death of his first wife, Sage married a family friend, Margaret Oliver Slocum, who worked as a schoolteacher and governess. At Sage's death in 1906, she inherited his entire $70 million estate ($1.9 billion in 2018 dollars) with no restrictions on its use. Her letter of gift one year later created the foundation bearing his name "for the improvement of living and social conditions in the United States." Then seventy-eight years old, she described her work as a philanthropist as "just beginning to live."[21]

Created the same year that Rauschenbusch's influential book was published, the Russell Sage Foundation modeled itself after the "in-

Mrs. Margaret Olivia Slocum Sage, 1910
Courtesy of the Library of Congress,
LC-DIG-ggbain-04817

formed" and effective philanthropy that Peabody, Slater, and Rockefeller envisioned but with a difference more of degree than kind. According to David Hammack and Stanton Wheeler, it was the first general purpose foundation in history to direct its support at an expansive "general wellbeing" or "the good of humankind" rather than for a more specific project or objective.[22]

The Sage Foundation's plan called for the support of surveys, studies, and the publication of social science–based monographs that could help shape policy objectives to attack the complex causes of poverty. During the first three decades of the 20th century, it sought to be a national clearinghouse for standards and social work and social welfare and established a department of surveys. Its early investigations documented slum conditions in Northern cities,[23] but the foundation would soon branch out into the South.[24]

John C. Campbell (1868–1919), a native of Indiana, studied education and theology at Williams College in Massachusetts. After graduating from that bastion of Congregationalism, he moved to the mountains of north Georgia in 1904 to become the second president of Piedmont College in Demorest.

The young college was the product of an ambitious 1897 effort, supported locally by north Georgia's Methodists, to provide collegiate opportunities for the region's mountain students. Its first two years of enrollment were strong, but the school then ran into challenges. Piedmont's isolation in the rolling foothills of the area (accessible only by roads that were "mostly crude dirt strips paved with sapling trees") and the inability to cover the institution's costs brought it to the brink of closing. It came under the wing of the New England Congregationalist Church, which invited Campbell to serve as the college's new leader.

As he traveled widely through north Georgia's communities, farmlands, and mountainous countryside, he became actively engaged in studying and improving the prospects of Southern mountain children through educational reforms. Campbell soon recognized that the educational challenges he encountered were inseparable from those of the entire Appalachian region. He approached the Russell Sage Foundation in 1908 with a proposal to support a comprehensive survey of church-based and public education in Appalachia.

Thus began a profitable partnership between the Sage Foundation and the Southern mountain region and its colleges. It led in 1913 to the opening in Asheville, North Carolina, of the Southern Highlands Division of the Russell Sage Foundation. Campbell became secretary of the regional office, from which he traveled throughout the region, collecting data and documenting his findings. That same year he helped found the Southern Mountain Workers Conference (SMWC), a network of educators and religious leaders. In 1921 the Russell Sage Foundation posthumously published Campbell's classic opus *The Southern Highlander and His Homeland* (completed by his wife, the folklorist Olive Dame Campbell, a native of Medford, Massachusetts).

Another by-product of the Russell Sage Foundation's work was the cooperative Southern Highland Handicraft Guild, spun-off in 1929 from the SMWC as a way of generating income for the region's craft workers. Through the 1930s, the Foundation saw its role, much as Campbell envisioned, as that of helping to sustain mountain culture and traditions through effective, folk-based approaches to education and regional problem solving.[25]

The Phelps Stokes Fund, created in 1911 by the will of Caroline Phelps Stokes (1854–1909), was another Northern philanthropic initiative with the aim of improving education for African Americans in the South. (Its original charter also included deliberate attention to the needs of Native Americans.) The family was not new to reform. As immigrants from England in the early 19th century, they became wealthy New York City bankers and merchants who also were active in mission and biblical tract societies as well as the American Colonization Society. Anson Greene Phelps played an important role in the American Colonization Society's 1821 creation of the state of Liberia. In 1929 the Fund was among those benefactors who established a free school for the poor in Liberia and named it after Booker T. Washington.[26]

Caroline Phelps Stokes
Educational Adaptations, Report of Ten Years' Work of the Phelps-Stokes Fund, 1910-1920

The incorporation of the fund brought focus to the family's commitment for the educational and human development of those historically underrepresented and marginalized, and in 1913 it issued an historic study that documented the racial disparities in the funding of Southern education. In 1917 the head of the Fund, Thomas Jesse Jones, published *Negro Education: A Study of the Private and Higher Schools for Colored People in the United States* as a guide to help Northern foundations find the most effective funding priorities. The Phelps Stokes Fund also promoted a number of published studies on critical social issues. It commissioned groundbreaking studies of black intellectual potential for college education at the University of Virginia and the University of Georgia, supported the historic Jeanes Teachers Program, and was a major benefactor of Berea College in Kentucky.

Like Peabody and Rockefeller, the steel magnate Andrew Carnegie (1835–1919) brought his own considerable entrepreneurial and managerial skills to the new field of scientific philanthropy. Putting into practice his "gospel of wealth" in an age of robber barons, he created endowment funds and foundations and challenged the new and fabulously rich to follow his model. Because public libraries were a rarity, the impressively literate and largely self-educated Carnegie embarked on a campaign that brought 1,689 "Carnegie libraries" (nearly 10% of them in the South) to communities in the United States. All were built between 1883 and 1917.[27]

Libraries were the very embodiment of Carnegie's own love of learning and books, and his support of them connected with his personal philosophy, one in harmony with the rising conviction that philanthropy should emphasize change-oriented giving rather than "careless" alms or charity. The Carnegie formula required that the community first demonstrate the need for a library, provide the space for

Andrew Carnegie, ca. 1913
Courtesy of the Library of
Congress, LC-USZ62-101767

a building, and make a commitment to meet the library's annual operating costs equal to 10% of the cost to build. The amount of the award (also systematized) was based on a per capita formula, or about $2 per person. No "free hand-outs for the poor," Carnegie Libraries were to be ladders for the advancement of the "sturdy" and the ambitious among the needy—exactly as books were to him as a child.[28] The libraries that Carnegie helped to establish in the South were all racially segregated, a policy that he made no effort to alter. Nonetheless, beginning in 1900 with Tuskegee Institute, he helped to fund twenty libraries on the campuses of historically African American schools, colleges, and universities. Then in 1908, he began contributing to the construction of public libraries for African Americans in Atlanta; Greensboro, North Carolina; Louisville, Kentucky; Meridian and Mound Bayou, Mississippi; and Savannah, Georgia.[29]

As one example of a racially restricted public facility, the Colored Carnegie Library of Savannah became a vital resource for the black community and played a major role in the education of individuals like James Alan McPherson, the first African American writer to win a Pulitzer Prize, for *Elbow Room* (1978), and U.S. Justice Clarence Thomas, until it closed in 1963.[30]

For whatever else it reveals about his feelings on the subject of race, Carnegie invited Robert Russa Moton (the black president of

Carnegie Library (for white patrons), Montgomery, Alabama, ca. 1906
Library of Congress, Prints & Photographs Division, Detroit Publishing Collection

Tuskegee Institute, who succeeded Booker T. Washington) to serve on the board of the Carnegie Corporation and came to the rescue of Berea College (see chapter 4) when it was re-segregated by state law.

Sometimes overlooked is the amount of cooperation and collaboration that existed among many of the foundations mentioned. Unlike most of their peers, the aims of these philanthropies were "generally secular or non-sectarian, emphasizing science and a cosmopolitan appreciation of many kinds of knowledge and the capabilities of people of all sorts."[31]

Concern from other Northerners and Southerners about the state of education in the South found expression in a series of gatherings, often held in the resort town of Capon Springs, West Virginia, toward the end of the 19th century. These Conferences on Christian Education in the South led to the formation in 1901 of the Southern Education Board, founded in Winston-Salem, North Carolina. One of its specific charges was to conduct a publicity campaign for education in the South and to serve as a clearinghouse to inform individuals and school systems interested in improving education.[32]

Reflections on Progressivism

As the 19th century drew to an end, the Progressive Era continued to bring about incremental social changes in many parts of the country. Voluntary associations and government bodies addressed critical issues of policy development and problem solving. Strategy-oriented philanthropy was establishing itself as a new kind of resource for the improvement of society. Among the objects of reform were child labor, literacy and education, working conditions and wages, the regulation of railroads and business, electoral corruption in government, and women's suffrage. In less than a half-century, great wealth and philanthropic zeal had coalesced to begin the rebuilding of a nation.

A portion of that energy, as described, spread into the South. Some of the region's own offspring and recent transplants had a hand in these efforts, serving as informal advisors and members of governing boards. Presumably not lost on any of these social entrepreneurs was the opportunity that the reclamation of the South would provide for the acquisition of raw materials, the building of transportation systems, and the opening of new consumer markets.

To be sure, ample evidence of the Civil War's debilitating impact upon the region was still everywhere to be seen, and more hard times lay ahead. Southern Progressivism did indeed have some influence on railroad regulation, education, child labor, and Prohibition (reflecting the priority of religious interests). Nonetheless, in most matters, Progressivism in the South bowed to tradition and the demands of white supremacy and male dominance.

It was extremely difficult for Northern philanthropy or government to effect major change. Jim Crow laws were state-based and shielded from federal intrusion by the ruling in the 1896 *Plessy v. Ferguson* case, so Southern governments once again became heavily invested in the maintenance of state's rights as a way to defend and manage the status quo.

Walter Hines Page of North Carolina (1855–1918), a journalist, education reformer, and ambassador to the United Kingdom under Woodrow Wilson's presidency, spoke for other progressives in the region when he bemoaned the true nature of the South's predicament: "We are all common folk who were once dominated by a little aristocracy, which, in its social and economic character, made a failure and left a stubborn crop of wrong social notions behind—especially about education."[33] Once again the South had placed itself inalterably on a long-term collision course with the federal government and, ultimately, its own people.

Historians are divided in their interpretation of Northern philanthropy in the South. James D. Anderson writes:

> Northern philanthropists were undoubtedly motivated by a mixture of sentimentalism, humanitarianism, and sociopolitical interests. . . . The philanthropists' policies and programs were designed primarily to develop an economically efficient and politically stable Southern agricultural economy by training efficient and contented black laborers while leaving the Southern racial hierarchy intact.[34]

Co-authors Eric Anderson and Alfred A. Moss Jr. recognize the obstacles in the way of reform and the compromises advocates also made, yet are reluctant to discount the impact of a philanthropic vision so dramatically different from that of the South's white majority:

> Both celebrators and critics of philanthropy have some-times treated blacks as more or less helpless victims or mostly passive objects of charity. Not only were northern donors often forced to take into account the education goals of African Americans, but black communities were also donors, contributing millions of dollars in educational self-help. . . . The whole South (including the black South) experienced striking educational progress in the early twentieth century, despite the fact that dominant whites treated black schools with highhanded inequity. . . . In spite of their compromises and ulterior motives, the foundation philanthropists had a vision of race relations (and black potential) that was significantly different from the ideas of the white majority. Unlike some of their public utterances, their private correspondence is full of comments on the narrowness and bigotry of the white South and earnest hopes for change.[35]

CHAPTER 5 ENDNOTES

1   David Weinstein, Herbert Spencer, *Stanford Encyclopedia of Philosophy* (Summer 2018 edition), ed. Edward N. Zalta, last modified January 19, 2017, *https://plato.stanford.edu/archives/sum2018/entries/spencer/.*

2   On the interplay between the Republican and Democratic parties and social Darwinism, see Mark Wahlgren Summers, *Party Games: Getting, Keeping, and Using Power in Gilded Age Politics* (Chapel Hill: University of North Carolina Press, 2004).

3   Peter Dobkin Hall, "Social Darwinism and the Poor," *Social Welfare History Project, http://socialwelfare.library.vcu.edu/issues/social-darwinism-poor/.*

4   Henry Adams is quoted in *The Education of Henry Adams: An Autobiography,* ed. Ira Nadel (Oxford: Oxford University Press, 2009), 344.

5   Edward T. O'Donnell, *Henry George and the Crisis of Inequality: Progress and Poverty in the Gilded Age* (New York: Columbia University Press, 2015), xxiii.

6   It also called for banking reform, government ownership of the railroads, and the direct election of U.S. senators (something that would not happen until 1913). Finally, the Alliance argued for the sub-treasury plan, which would make it possible for farmers at harvest time to borrow money against the value of crops stored in government warehouses while waiting for prices to improve.

7   Barton C. Shaw, "Populist Party," at *https://www.georgiaencyclopedia.org/articles/history-archaeology/thomas-e-watson-1856-1922.*

    On Watson, see Carol Pierannunzi, "Thomas E. Watson, 1856–1922," *New Georgia Encyclopedia,* last modified August 10, 2018, *https://www.georgiaencyclopedia.org/articles/history-archaeology/thomas-e-watson-1856-1922.*

8   Lawrence C. Goodwyn, "Populist Dreams and Negro Rights: East Texas as a Case Study," *American Historical Review* 76, no. 5 (December 1971): 1435–56.

9   Quoted in Steven A. Smith, *Myth, Media, and the Southern Mind* (Fayetteville: University of Arkansas Press, 1985), 66. C. Vann Woodward's classic and still relevant studies in the field of Southern history are *Tom Watson: Agrarian Rebel* (New York: Macmillan, 1938) and *Origins of the New South: 1877–1913* (Baton Rouge: Louisiana State University Press, 1951). Both editions have been reprinted several times.

10 Carl V. Harris, *Political Power in Birmingham, 1871-1921* (Knoxville: University of Tennessee Press, 1977), quoting review by Timothy Crimmins, *American Historical Review* 83, no. 5 (Dec. 1978) 911.

11 David Levering Lewis, *W. E. B. Du Bois: Biography of a Race, 1868–1919* (New York: Henry Holt, 1993), 118.

12 Ibid, 123.

13 Quoted in William Harvey Allen, *Modern Philanthropy: A Study of Efficient Appealing and Giving* (New York: Dodd, Mead, 1912), 214.

14 Raymand B. Fosdick, *The Story of the Rockefeller Foundation* (New York: Harper and Bros., 1952), 292.

15 "The immediate intention of the Board is to devote itself to the study and aiding of the educational needs of the people of our Southern states," in pamphlet entitled "General Education Board (Funded by John D. Rockefeller in 1902), Purpose and Program,*"* 49 West 49th Street, New York (no date), 2.

16 "Laura Spelman Rockefeller, 1839–1915," Rockefeller Archives Center, *http://www.rockarch.org/bio/laura.php.*

17 Sheila Devaney, "George Foster Peabody (1852–1938)," *New Georgia Encyclopedia,* last

modified August 9, 2013, *https://www.georgiaencyclopedia.org/articles/arts-culture/george-foster-peabody-1852-1938.*

18 Peabody also was one of the greatest benefactors of the University of Georgia. The Peabody Awards, one of the most prestigious in broadcasting, are named for him and are administered by the university's Grady College of Journalism and Mass Communications.

19 John Ettling, *The Germ of Laziness: Rockefeller Philanthropy and Public Health in the New South* (Cambridge: Harvard University Press, 1981); Allan Nevins, *Study in Power: John D. Rockefeller, Industrialist and Philanthropist* (New York: Charles Scribner's Sons, 1953); James D. Anderson, *The Education of Blacks in the South, 1860-1935* (Chapel Hill: University of North Carolina Press, 1988). Rockefeller's interest in public health continued. After the flood of 1927 devastated the Mississippi Delta, the Rockefeller Foundation used challenge grants to establish eighty city, county, and state health departments around the region. See John M. Barry, *Rising Tide: The Great Mississippi Flood of 1927 and How It Changed America* (New York: Simon and Schuster, 1997).

20 The Negro Rural School Fund was often referred to as the Anna T. Jeanes Fund or Foundation.

21 Quoted in Kathleen D. McCarthy, *Enterprise & Society*, Vol. 8, No. 4 (December 2007), 984. On Margaret Sage, see Ruth Crocker, *Mrs. Russell Sage: Women's Activism and Philanthropy in Gilded Age and Progressive America* (Bloomington: Indiana University Press, 2006).

22 The story and significance of the foundation is told in David C. Hammack and Stanton Wheeler, *Social Science in the Making: Essays on the Russell Sage Foundation, 1907-1972* (New York: Russell Sage Foundation, 1994). See also Peter Dobkin Hall, *Inventing the Nonprofit Sector* (Baltimore: Johns Hopkins University Press, 2001), 47; Elizabeth T. Boris and C. Eugene Steuerle, eds,, *Nonprofits and Government: Collaboration and Conflict*, 2d ed. (Washington, D.C.: Urban Institute Press, 2006), 54.

23 One of its most famous studies was the six-volume, heavily illustrated *Pittsburgh Survey*, edited by Paul U. Kellogg and released in 1914.

24 Its interests embraced the South, where it sought to engage Southerners involved with social work, with juvenile reformatories, with homes for the aged, with job training, with work safety, with consumer loans, and with pawnshops. *The Bibliography of Social Surveys* by Allen Eaton and Shelby Harrison (1930) lists studies in every Southern and border state. David Hammack, correspondence with authors, March 31, 2019.

25 See also Thomas R. Ford, *The Southern Appalachian Region: A Survey* (Lexington: University of Kentucky Press, 1962).

26 *https://lradmissions.com/booker-washington-institute-liberia/.*

27 Abigail A. Van Slyck, *Free to All: Carnegie Libraries and American Culture* (Chicago: University of Chicago Press, 1998). Durand R. Miller, *Carnegie Grants for Library Buildings, 1890–1917: A list of library buildings, public and academic, erected with funds provided by Andrew Carnegie and Carnegie Corporation of New York* (New York: Carnegie Corporation, 1943).

28 Andrew Carnegie, "The Best Fields for Philanthropy," in *North American Review* 149, no. 397 (December 1889); Michael Lorenzen, "Deconstructing the Carnegie Libraries," accessed March 1, 2016, *http://www.lib.niu.edu/1999/il990275.html*; Theodore Jones, *Carnegie Libraries Across America: A Public Legacy* (Hoboken, NJ: Preservation Press Series, 1997).

29 Michael Fultz, "Black Public Libraries in the South in the Era of De Jure Segregation," *Libraries and the Cultural Record* 41, no. 3 (Summer 2006).

See also Matthew Griffis, "The Segregated Carnegie Libraries of the South," *Aquila,* University of Southern Mississippi, *https://aquila.usm.edu/rocprofiles/.*The libraries are the Auburn Branch Library, Atlanta (1921–59), Cherry Street Library, Evansville, Indiana (1914–55), Carnegie Negro Library, Greensboro, North Carolina (1924–63), Colored Carnegie Library, Houston, Texas (1913–61),

Western Colored Branch Library, Louisville, Kentucky (1905–), Eastern Colored Branch Library, Kentucky (1914–75), 13th Street Colored Branch Library, Meridian, Mississippi (1913–74), Carnegie Library, Mound Bayou, Mississippi (1910–35), East Henry Street Carnegie Library, Savannah, Georgia (1914–present).

30 Beth Grashof, June 18, 2012, for a presentation by Arthur Clement to the National Association of Minority Architects and the Southeast Chapter of the Society of Architectural Historians.

31 David Hammack, correspondence with authors, February 25, 2019.

32 *https://finding-aids.lib.unc.edu/00680/,* Southern Education Board Records (1898-1925*), retrieved March 1, 2019; http://digital.ncdcr.gov/cdm/ref/collection/p249901coll37/id/351,* Proceedings of the Capon Springs Conference for Christian Education in the South, retrieved March 1, 2019.

33 Quoted in William Peterfield Trent, *Southern Writers: Selections in Prose and Verse* (New York: Macmillan, 1905), 470; Hugh C. Bailey, *Liberalism in the New South: Southern Social Reformers and the Progressive Movement* (Coral Gables, FL: University of Miami Press, 1969), 136.

34 "Northern Foundations and the Shaping of Southern Black Rural Education, 1902-1935," *History of Education Quarterly* 18, no. 4 (Winter 1978): 371–96. See also James D. Anderson, *The Education of Blacks in the South, 1860–1935* (Chapel Hill: University of North Carolina Press, 1988).

35 Eric Anderson and Alfred A. Moss Jr., *Dangerous Donations: Northern Philanthropy and Southern Black Education* (Columbia: University of Missouri Press, 1999), 2.

CHAPTER 6

The Footprint of Government

Emerging Order and Its Cost

From the roiling mix of economic forces, politics, philanthropic initiatives, and the formation of not-for-profit associations, a response to Henry Adams's search for order (see chapter 5) was beginning to appear. Among the features of the new "philosophy" was the recognition that cooperation among the sectors was essential. Even more important was the growing realization that the federal government would need to claim a larger role—in the reconciliation of labor-management disputes, the regulation of interstate commerce, the control of monopolistic corporate practices, the administration of immigration, the prosecution of large-scale corruption, and the oversight of organized philanthropy.

Less clear was the answer to the question of how to pay for increased federal leadership and oversight. The national government's cost of doing business had risen from $5 million in 1792 to $29 million in 1830, and then to $53 million in 1860. That total was supposed to cover the expenses of national defense, foreign relations, banking, administration of the federal courts, admission of new states to the Union, and relationships with the Indian nations—and it did. One reason for the low budget was the limited number of full-time, federal employees, a figure for which few records exist. (Employment was primarily a form of private patronage; a professionalized "civil service" did not appear in the United States until 1883). Another reason was that in this early era of the nation's history, the United States relied on the initiatives of local volunteerism, charity, and faith-based efforts as well as state-based government to perform social and public duties, such as care for the sick and needy, orphans, the elderly, post-secondary and professional education (colleges, medical education, teacher preparation), and even relations with foreign nations.

Taxation

From the earliest days of the new Republic (1789), and strongly influenced by a Revolution waged over "taxation without representation," the Founders saw the trade tariff as the least intrusive way of paying for their new government. It was reliable, cheap to administer, and generally covered up to 90% of government's costs. The tariff's leading advocate was the first Secretary of the Treasury, Alexander Hamilton, who was among the few people on either side of the Atlantic to recognize another important reason for the tariff: it served as a protective blanket shielding the young nation's "infant industry" (Hamilton's phrase) from external competition.

He and his compatriots had strong reason to worry. After all, their new country without a king was an untried experiment—as much a theory as a reality loose in a dangerous world. (England would get its revenge in the War of 1812 when it torched the White House). Moving briskly in response to this external threat, in 1790 Congress sent another bill to the president that created the Revenue Cutter Service (later the U.S. Coast Guard) to ensure the tariff's collection and enforcement.

The early tariff rates did favor the protection of "infant industries" and their workers in the Northern and Western states. That protection, though, came at the expense of some mid-Atlantic and more agrarian Southern states that had no option but to pay the higher cost for domestically manufactured consumer goods. The situation provoked regional conflict, and became even more intensely political because the setting of the tariff rate was an annual process that at times was politically fraught.

As an example, in 1828, President John Quincy Adams had signed into law a record-high tariff that favored Northern industry and threatened the cotton-dependent South, for whom low tariffs operated as an inducement for British traders in the highly competitive Atlantic economy. Senator Henry Clay of Kentucky and Vice President John Calhoun, a South Carolinian, responded in fury and labeled it the "Tariff of Abominations."[1]

By 1860 the tariff covered 95% of the cost of government. That comfortable state of affairs ended abruptly after South Carolina's military bombardment of Fort Sumter. President Lincoln signed the Revenue Act of 1861 that imposed a first-ever tax (3%) on annual income above $800 to pay the costs of the Union's mobilization and operations in wartime. When that act expired in 1865, the federal tariff resumed its former role of paying most federal government expenses.

However, these revenues were not well matched with the many-layered constitutional responsibilities that came with the war's ending, nor with the new realities of an expanding transcontinental economy.

Roots of the Modern Tax System

The chaotic state of economic and political affairs described in earlier chapters had reached the point where the federal government had no choice but to step in. In 1887, representing a big leap from the 1830s era of the Jacksonian Democrats, President Grover Cleveland, a Democrat, signed into law the act which created the Interstate Commerce Commission (ICC). Its prime purpose was to curb the unfair shipping rates that railroads were charging Southern and Western farmers. Although the ICC lacked the teeth to enforce its own sometimes vaguely worded regulations, passage of this new legislation represented a startling break from the Gilded Age's glorification of *laissez-faire* practices and signaled that the federal government was preparing to assume a more managerial function in the nation's affairs.[2]

It clearly was also time for the federal government to tackle the issue of paying for itself. The federal tariff was generating only about half of the needed revenues. With the Democratic Party in control of both the U.S. House and Senate in 1894, Congress had the opportunity to wrestle with the issue of the federal budget when it passed the Wilson-Gorman Tariff Act. (The new law carried the names of two Southern Democrats: William Wilson, the West Virginia chair of the House Ways and Means Committee, and Senator Arthur Gorman of Maryland.) The legislation actually reduced the federal tariff, long opposed by the South, but it did so by instituting the first peacetime income tax in American history. To further pay for the anticipated decline in federal receipts, the law provided for a flat 2% tax on corporate income as well as a 2% national tax on all personal income over $4,000 (representing the wealthiest 10% of all households).

Anti-Foundation Sentiment

The emerging philanthropic sector described in the previous chapter was not uniformly admired for its good works. As Barry Karl and Stanley Katz have described:

> Almost from the moment of the creation of the first foundation, there came into being a body of criticism, which has not significantly altered over the past 75 years. The criticism was, on the whole, populistic and was based on the assumption that the foundations represented the investment of ill-gotten gains in a manner which threatened to subvert the democratic process by giving philanthropists a determining role in the conduct of American public life. As one reads though the hostile literature...similar themes occur. Money which ought to be in the hands of the public is being retained by aristocrats for purposes beyond the control of democratic institutions; the academic freedom of universities is being subverted by control of academic budgets by the foundations; public policy is being determined by private groups; ... foundations are bastions of an elite of white, Anglo-Saxon, Protestant managers holding

out against the normal development of a pluralistic and ethnic society; and so on.[3]

Nevertheless, the Wilson-Gorman Act acknowledged the newly emerging ties linking national governance, the acquisition of great and unprecedented wealth, and modern philanthropic largesse. Because of that consideration and as a palliative to the Republicans, the legislation's sponsors provided for a personal deduction for charitable giving as well as a charitable exemption for "corporations, companies, or associations organized and conducted solely for charitable, religious, or educational purposes, including fraternal beneficiary associations" (included also in the Civil War income tax).[4]

The impact of the new act proved to be negligible: in the next year the Supreme Court ruled the law unconstitutional in *Pollock v. Farmers' Loan & Trust Company* (1895). That judicial decision, however, managed to set in motion a reactive national movement, which would culminate in the 1913 ratification of the 16th Amendment empowering Congress "to lay and collect taxes on incomes." In what essentially was a national referendum, Southern states (with the exception of Virginia and Florida) and their Western counterparts overwhelmingly supported the new amendment. A nation with a racially limited but emerging social conscience was sending a message to Congress and the president: national problems demanded national solutions. Newly elected President Woodrow Wilson, a Democrat and a Southerner, signed the Revenue Act of 1913. Most significant for the philanthropic sector, the new law also swept in the earlier Wilson-Gorman provisions for charitable exemptions. Not included were charitable deductions.

Even as momentum for a new national income tax was building, the enmity toward large philanthropic institutions became highly visible and focused in 1910 when John D. Rockefeller sought to obtain a congressional charter of incorporation for his foundation. It was fairly common during that period for congressmen to provide such charters for nationwide, not-for-profit organizations with broad public and educational missions, such as the American Historical Association. Indeed, Rockefeller's own General Education Board had received a charter in 1902.

In 1910, however, the richest man in the world (and one of the most despised, especially for the ruthless treatment of his workers) was greeted by a firestorm of protest. Rockefeller, the founder of the Standard Oil Company, which controlled 90% of the country's oil production and which the federal government had tried, unsuccessfully, to shut down by using the Sherman Anti-Trust Act of 1890, was not going to get all that he wanted. (The breakup of Standard Oil was mitigated for Rockefeller by his family's ownership of shares in successor firms, while Pennsylvanians, who thought they and their state should derive more benefit from the exploitation of oil, did benefit from a reduction in the cost of fuel and lighting.) Since he could have received a charter from the New York legislature, and subsequently did exactly that, it is assumed that Rockefeller wanted national recognition and admiration for the great good he had done with his philanthropy—and that too was true. However, the strength of the federal government was beginning to become a match for what had been the absolute power of the newly and extraordinarily wealthy.

Walsh Commission

During the final months of his administration (1909–13), President William Howard Taft took aim at the unabated challenge of labor violence throughout American manufacturing by appointing the Commission on Industrial Relations to investigate its causes. The work of the Commission did not take place in a vacuum. In 1910 the bombing of the *Los Angeles Times* Building by staunch unionists had ignited a fire that killed twenty-one of the newspaper's employees. (The bombers, members of the Association of Bridge and Structural Iron Workers, were retaliating against the strong anti-union campaign that had been led by Harrison Gray Otis, the publisher of the newspaper.)

The nine-person commission of labor and business leaders bore the name of its chairperson, Frank P. Walsh, a Kansas City, Missouri, labor lawyer and activist (who once told a friend, "I hate like hell to be respectable"). President Taft appointed four of the commissioners in 1913, his last year in office. Taft's successor, Woodrow Wilson, appointed the other five. They included Walsh (who had enthusiastically supported Wilson in his election bid). Walsh was one of three so-called neutrals—neither pro-labor nor pro-business.

The importance of the Commission's work (and further rationale for its creation) was dramatized in 1914 by an event known as the Ludlow Massacre: members of the Colorado National Guard and privately employed guards from the Colorado Fuel and Iron Company (primarily owned by John D. Rockefeller) used machine guns to fire into a tent colony of 1,200, striking coal miners and their families, killing about two dozen people and triggering retaliations and further deaths.

Reflecting on the crisis and the Commission's work over the next year (1915–16), labor historian David Montgomery concluded:

> The commission's members were intellectually unprepared for what they encountered. Their common faith that the interests of America's various social classes were basically harmonious was jolted by their discovery of unmistakable class conflict on a nationwide scale and involving native [sic] Americans as fully as it did recent immigrants.[5]

This "revelation" perhaps explains what can only be described as a symbol of the entire nation's political dysfunction.

After 154 days of hearings, in 1916 the commissioners presented not one but three contesting final reports. One was signed by five commissioners, making it the "majority report," and written by the highly regarded commission member John R. Commons, faculty member of the University of Wisconsin. A single commissioner signed a second report, which was never published.

Signed by commission chair Walsh and two others, a third, "minority report" proved "much more provocative and accusatory in its tone and conclusions. Its centerpiece was a call for industrial democracy."[6] Walsh lambasted state and local tax exemptions for private foundations, writing,

> The funds of these foundations are exempt from taxation, yet during the lives of their funders are subject to their direction for any purpose other than commercial profit. . . .
> As regards the "foundations" created for unlimited general

RETURN OF THE KLAN

Even as classism became more evident, racism continued to flourish. Progressives on the subjects of race and inclusion were deeply disheartened by the 1915 release of *The Birth of a Nation*, D. W. Griffith's nationally impactful film about the Civil War and Reconstruction. This controversial epic drama may have been the most cinematically advanced of its time; however, it glorified the Ku Klux Klan as a valiant savior of Southern dignity, womanhood, and respectability in a postwar South ravaged by Northern carpetbaggers and immoral, sexually inflamed African American men. Based on *The Clansman*, a novel by the Reverend Thomas Dixon Jr., a Johns Hopkins classmate and friend of Woodrow Wilson, the movie was the first American feature film to be screened in the Wilson White House.

Although attacked for its racial bigotry by a minority of Americans, *The Birth of a Nation* became a wildly popular attraction during a period marked by powerful anti-immigration feelings as well. With a story line widely accepted as fact, it is credited with reviving the Klan in 1915 atop Stone Mountain near Atlanta. The Klan used the film as a recruitment tool, and made that hate group a national force. By 1924, its peak year, the Klan in Detroit, Michigan, is reported to have had 35,000 members; Chicago reputedly had 50,000 on the rolls.

Source: Melvyn Stokes, *D. W. Griffith's* The Birth of a Nation: *A History of "The Most Controversial Motion Picture of All Time"* (New York: Oxford University Press, 2007).

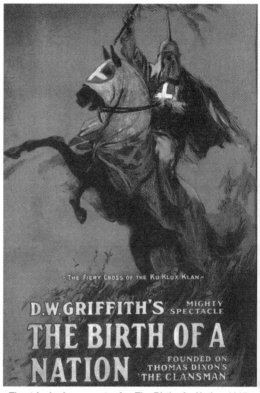

Theatrical release poster for *The Birth of a Nation*, 1915.
Wikimedia Commons

purposes and endowed with enormous resources, their ultimate possibilities are so grave a menace, not only as regards
their activities and influence but also the benumbing effect
which they have on private citizens and public bodies that
if they could be clearly differentiated...from other forms of
voluntary altruistic effort it would be desirable to recommend their abolition.[7]

As it turns out, what began as an intensified critique of philanthropic foundations during the Progressive Era, and could have grown
stronger, became sidelined by a major historic development of no less
portent for the future of foundations: the onset of World War I.

Preparations for War...
and the New Future for Philanthropy

War had been raging in Europe since 1914. The general mood of the
country initially had favored non-intervention. However, the likeli-
hood—if not the inevitability—of Americans joining the conflict grew
steadily stronger, and preparations for war intensified. Germany's determination to continue U-boat attacks on neutral ships brought the
situation to a head. Heightening public outrage was news that the
inflammatory German "Zimmerman Telegram" offering U.S. territory
to Mexico in return for its support of Germany had been intercepted.
With its declaration on April 2, 1917, the United States officially entered
the war.

In this climate, the generalized hostility against foundations by
the Democrats' labor wing and other opponents receded for the time.

Issues like the government's need for additional revenue and the necessity of national unity loomed ever larger. These conditions were helping President Woodrow Wilson to organize a new political consensus around the viability, if not the absolute necessity, of a more ambitious income tax. He and many others believed that the charitable sector could be an indispensable helpmeet in that effort.

Doughboys at Cochem, Germany, ca. 1919
Courtesy of the Library of Congress,
LC-DIG-ggbain-28510

Two particular philanthropic efforts that were dominating the news played into the president's hand. The first was the massive fund-raising campaign of the Commission for Relief in Belgium. It was the inspiration of Herbert Hoover, an Iowa-born mining engineer and humanitarian. He had been in China during the 1909 Boxer Rebellion, during which he organized relief efforts for stranded foreigners. He then went on to perform similar services to Americans trapped in Europe at the outset of World War I.

The Commission's private relief efforts on behalf of Belgium are credited with having fed and even saved from starvation some 9 million people after the invasion of that country by the German army at the start of World War I. Driven entirely by philanthropic initiative and enlisting the cooperation of governments (even the occupying Germans), Hoover brilliantly orchestrated the raising of $5 billion in private contributions and donated services. His effectiveness prompted President Wilson to appoint Hoover head of the U.S. Food Administration, which diverted American agricultural products to the overseas American troops, and subsequently to the American Relief Administration, which extended the Belgian campaign via the European Relief Council (1919–22) to all of postwar Europe. Recipients of support included the people of Albania, Austria, Turkey, Italy, Czechoslovakia, Finland, Greece, and others (including Germany, France, and England). Until the Great Depression, the world regarded Hoover as the Great Humanitarian.[8]

Equally visible in the United States and Europe were the services of the privately funded American National Red Cross (federally chartered in 1900 and partially under federal control), which named President Wilson as its first honorary president in 1913.[9] Started by Clara Barton in 1881, it had been active in the Spanish-American War and provided privately supported medical aid for both French and English civilians and armed forces long before U.S. entry into World War I. Then, its services expanded, supported by a massive volunteer effort through the Red Cross Production Corps.

Wilson called on the American public to support its charities in wartime. Besides helping to fulfill revenue expectations (income-tax dollars paid only an estimated 65% of the country's wartime expenditures), charities and local philanthropic activity helped maintain morale. In addition, women were volunteering in great numbers in the Young Men's and Women's Christian Associations, the Salvation Army, 4H, and the Girl Scouts.

In other local charities, too, they

performed their volunteer duties in communal spaces owned by the leaders of the municipal chapters of these organizations. Women met at designated times to roll bandages, prepare and serve meals and snacks, package and ship supplies, and organize community fund-raisers. The variety of volunteer opportunities gave women the ability to appear in public spaces and promote charitable activities for the war effort. Female volunteers encouraged entire communities, including children, to get involved in war work. While most of these efforts focused on support for the home front, a small percentage of female volunteers served with the American Expeditionary Force in France.[10]

By the time an armistice was declared, almost one-third of the American population claimed membership in the Red Cross (20 million adults and 11 million youth) or served as volunteers (8 million adults). The war had mobilized civilian efforts as never before.

The entire federal government's wartime budget for 1917 ($30 billion) was more than 30 times larger than the 1913 budget of $970 million. The issue of Liberty Bonds in 1917 and 1918 (redeemable in fifteen years) was another

The Doughboys Make Good, 1918.
Courtesy of the Library of Congress,
LC-USZC4-3048

public/private vehicle for raising money and support for the war effort. These bonds allowed individuals, nonprofit institutions, municipalities, and companies to invest in the war effort and to display "honor flags" for meeting or exceeding their quotas.

Charity, Government, and the Nonprofit Sector Come of Age

Perhaps the most important piece of legislation during that period was the progressive new income tax law: the War Revenue Act of 1917. Given the highly publicized position of the not-for-profit sector and the great range of ways by which citizens contributed to the war effort, it comes as little surprise that the new nationwide law included a provision for the charitable deduction. Like the progressive income tax and the charitable exemption, the charitable deduction became the newest partner in what some called "cooperative democracy's" 20th-century system of taxation.

It also spawned a proliferation of charitable and philanthropic activity in support of the war effort and the global alleviation of hardships in war areas. Of great significance—and with extraordinary long-term impact—was the informal (but also highly organized) network of faith-based, nonprofit associations and their relief efforts: the Young Men's Christian Association (founded in London, 1844), the Young Women's Christian Association (London, 1855), the Knights of Columbus (Connecticut, 1882), the Federal Council of Churches (Philadelphia, 1908), the Near East Foundation (New York, 1915, founded as the American Committee for Armenian and Syrian Relief), the American Friends

Service Committee (Philadelphia, 1917, founded by the Religious Society of Friends, or Quakers), the American Jewish Joint Distribution Committee (New York, 1917), and the National Catholic War Council (Washington, DC, 2017). Protestant missionary organizations, some active since the 18th century, also played a role on the world stage that now was in harness with national government in a global war. By 1919 the collective reach and impact of such popular public-private efforts galvanized nationwide public support not only for a permanent national system of taxation but for the charitable deduction that was now recognized as an inseparable part of it.

A partial description of what sorts of contributions were eligible for charitable deduction in the 1917 law (which has changed very little during the past century) reads in part:

> Contributions or gifts actually made within the year to corporations or associations organized and operated exclusively for religious, charitable, scientific, or educational purposes, or to societies for the prevention of cruelty to children or animals, no part of the net income of which inures to the benefit of any private stockholder or individual, to an amount not in excess of fifteen percentum (15%) of the taxpayer's taxable net income as computed without the benefit of the deduction of such contributions.

The 1917 law was neither a political phantasm nor a maneuver to soak the rich, but rather a sophisticated product of like-minded Progressive Era intellectuals and political theorists such as Edwin R.A. Seligman, a professor of political economy at Columbia University.

Seligman was a co-founder of the American Economic Association, which attracted professionally trained academics who generally opposed the nonscientific notions of *laissez-faire*. These new academic thinkers together shared a belief that the old "benefit theory" of taxation was obsolete. Extending back to Elizabethan times, it rested on a conception of government whose primary responsibility was the protection of property.

What was needed in a new age, they asserted, was a new vision—one guided by an updated and "more equitable principle of taxation based on one's . . . ability to pay." This new perception of taxation, according to legal and intellectual historian Ajay Mehrotra, regarded national government as playing an "active role in the distribution of fiscal burdens" and obligations. It was an affirmative step in the historic shift of governing responsibility from state and local levels to the sphere of the "nation state" and in harmony with principles of self-government and national democracy.[11]

War's Other Legacies

World War I was a horrendous chapter in world history. Of the 4.7 million Americans who served, casualties totaled 320,518, with 116,516 deaths and approximately 320,000 sick and wounded. These figures do not include the unknown number of those who suffered from "shell shock," the name coined during World War I for the psychological and emotional trauma soldiers suffered in addition to their physical wounds (in the Civil War such trauma was called a "heart wound"). The total number of all civilian and military killed and wounded worldwide in that war is estimated at 40 million (the equivalent of about 40% of the 1918 U.S. population).[12]

Even so, in retrospect, it clearly accelerated an appreciation of women's rights and the passage of the 19th Amendment two years later. Furthermore, one of the great by-products of the 1919 Paris Peace Conference was the founding of the League of Nations. Republican Senator Henry Cabot Lodge of Massachusetts led a successful campaign to keep the United States from membership in the League, holding it up as an intrusion on American autonomy. Nonetheless, by raising the consciousness of human rights globally during the modern era of rapidly expanding technology, it set in motion a world peace movement that would culminate in the formation of the United Nations in a later (and nuclear) age, in 1945. Finally, whatever its destructive consequences, the conflict brought together Northern and Southern citizens of the United States around a common cause.

The war also inaugurated a distinctly American brand of philanthropy twined with government, described by economist Charles Clotfelter as "American exceptionalism's social contract" for the advancement of the public good. The resulting delicate balance between federal regulation and voluntary philanthropy, as he goes on to explain, carries with it an implied warning about "tinkering" with the mechanism:

> U.S. tax policy favors charitable giving and nonprofit organizations. Not only are nonprofit organizations generally exempted from income and property taxes, but most contributions to them from living donors, corporations, and

estates are also tax deductible. This favorable tax treatment is one important component of a more general American approach to the provision of public goods. The nation's tax policy toward charitable giving has had three broad effects. First, this tax policy allows many citizens to gain a sense of participation that they might not otherwise have, by choosing the causes and organizations that will receive their donations. Institutionally, this sense of participation is reflected and enhanced by a very prominent nonprofit sector. Second, this policy has the effect of handing over to wealthy individuals an extraordinary amount of influence over the allocation of public funds. As a result of these two effects, American tax policy contains an inherent tension between participatory citizenship and elitism. Third, because it operates through a tax deduction, tax policy toward charitable giving is vulnerable to inadvertent modification simply as a result of otherwise unrelated tinkering with the income tax.[13]

With an inconclusive outcome, World War I rearranged but failed to dispel European colonialism, and it set the stage for another world war within a scant two decades. Between those two conflicts, the United States would continue to search for a way through its own social and economic dilemmas.

A major obstacle to progress was the prejudice of its own president. W. E. B. Du Bois (1868–1963) is credited with the aphorism, "As the South goes, so goes the nation." That prophetic utterance came to life negatively with Woodrow Wilson's election. Born and raised in the South, whatever his positive attributes, Wilson was a racist.

Supporting modern-day protests at Princeton (the university Wilson once lead), the New York Times critiqued his domestic performance as President:

> He inherited a federal government that had been shaped during the late 19th and early 20th centuries, when thousands of African-American men and woman passed Civil Service examinations or received political appointments that landed them in well-paying, middle-class government jobs in which they sometimes supervised white workers. This was anathema to Wilson, who believed that black Americans were unworthy of full citizenship and admired the Ku Klux Klan for the role it had in terrorizing African-Americans to restrict their political power. . . . Wilson stocked his administration with segregationists who shared his point of view. The man he chose for the postal department, which had the most black employees nationally, had campaigned on the promise that the Democratic Party could be counted on to keep black people out of its own ranks and out of the government affairs of the Southern states. In this way, his administration set about segregating the work force, driving out highly placed black employees, and shunting the rest into lower paying jobs. . . . In a few years, the Wilson administration had established federal discrimination as a national norm.[14]

CHAPTER 6 ENDNOTES

1　Calhoun went so far as to resign the vice presidency and successfully run for a Senate seat from South Carolina to fight the new law and nullify its legality. What became known as the "nullification crisis" continued in 1832 (see chapter 2) when he and his state similarly fought a revised version of the bill, signed this time by President Andrew Jackson. The crisis eventually passed, but it contributed to a deepening of regional enmity. (Andrew Jackson later said the two mistakes of his life were not shooting Henry Clay and not hanging John Calhoun.)

2　The later Republican administration of Theodore Roosevelt would go on to declare war on big trusts; his successor, William Howard Taft, signed legislation for greater regulation of interstate commerce and railroads; and Woodrow Wilson in 1913 signed the Federal Reserve Act that established a decentralized central bank for the nation. That same year he signed into law a new national income tax, only the second since the Civil War.

3　Barry D. Karl and Stanley N. Katz, "The American Private Philanthropic Foundation and the Public Sphere, 1890–1930," *Minerva* 19, no. 2 (June 1981): 236–37.

4　Sheldon D. Pollack, "The Origins of the Modern Income Tax, 1894–1913," *The Tax Lawyer* 66, no. 2 (2013): 295–330; Bernard Grossfeld and James D. Bryce, " A Brief Comparative History of the Origins of the Income Tax in Great Britain, Germany and the United States," *American Journal of Tax Policy* Volume 2, Spring, 1983, 211.

5　David Montgomery, review of *Age of Industrial Violence, 1910–15: The Activities and Findings of the United States Commission on Industrial Relations,* by Graham Adams Jr., *Technology and Culture* 8, no. 2 (April 1967): 234–37.

6　Quoted in Wikipedia, s.v., "Commission on Industrial Relations," last modified March 17, 2019, *https://en.wikipedia.org/wiki/Commission_on_Industrial_Relations#cite_note-Labor13-17.*

7　Quoted in Angela M. Eikenberry, *Giving Circles: Philanthropy, Voluntary Association, and Democracy* (Bloomington: Indiana University Press, 2009), 25.

8　In his book about Herbert Hoover, Bill Bryson is generous in his acknowledgment of Hoover's achievements, but offers a more measured tribute: "Two things accounted for Hoover's glorious reputation: he executed his duties with tireless efficiency and dispatch, and he made sure that no one anywhere was ever unaware of his accomplishments. . . . [He] was meticulous in ensuring that every positive act associated with him was inflated to maximum importance and covered with a press release." *One Summer: America, 1927* (New York: Doubleday, 2013), 55–56.

9　"Our Federal Charter," American Red Cross, *https://www.redcross.org/content/dam/redcross/National/history-federal-charter.pdf.*

10　Quoted in "World War I and Its Aftermath: America Enters the War," in *The American Yawp: A Massively Collaborative Open U.S. History Textbook* (Stanford: Stanford University Press, 2018–19), *http://www.americanyawp.com/index.html.*

11　Ajay K. Mehrotra, *Making the Modern American Fiscal State: Law, Politics, and the Rise of Progressive Taxation, 1877–1929* (Cambridge: Cambridge University Press, 2013), 86–87.

12　Ute Daniel, Peter Gatrell, Oliver Janz, Heather Jones, Jennifer D. Keene, Alan Kramer and Bill Nasson, *International Encyclopedia of the First World War: 1914–1918 https://encyclopedia.1914-1918-online.net/article/war_losses_usa.*

13　Quoted in Gabrielle Fact and Camille Landais, eds., "American Exceptionalism, the Social Contract, and Charitable Giving," in *Conference Volume: CEPR Conference,* Paris School of Economics (May 2012): 35.

14　Editorial, *New York Times*, "The Case Against Woodrow Wilson at Princeton," November 24, 2015.

CHAPTER 7

Julius Rosenwald

At this stage of our narrative, we pause to focus upon one individual whose single-minded philanthropy and disregard for the prevailing order quite possibly did more to bring positive change to the entire South than any other individual benefactor. It would take several more decades for the results to become apparent, but the transformative civil rights movement of the 1950s and 1960s and subsequent gains can, we believe, be traced directly back to the vision and determination of Julius Rosenwald (1862–1932) and his remarkable partner, Booker T. Washington (c. 1856–1915).[1]

The son of German immigrants, Rosenwald was born in Springfield, Illinois, in a house just steps from what had been the home of Abraham Lincoln. After a modestly successful early career as a clothing manufacturer, he had the opportunity to purchase 25% of the burgeoning Sears, Roebuck Company. The business had been founded in 1887 as a watch and jewelry catalog and mail-order business under the tutelage of an ingenious salesman, Richard Sears. Rosenwald bought out Roebuck's interest and took over the company's management. He began diversifying its merchandise while controlling costs to make its commodities appealing to farms and villages that lacked access to retail stores.

In 1909 Rosenwald succeeded Sears as president of the company. The U.S. Postal Service had initiated rural free delivery in 1896. The introduction of parcel post shipping in 1913, combined with the virtually universal access to customers that railroads provided, revolutionized the Sears distribution system. Its catalog became synonymous with the mail-order business, serving millions of customers and employing thousands of workers.

Historic preservationist Jeanne Cyriaque reminds us that Rosenwald's new approach to sales, whether or not originally intended, was a special boon to black people in the South. Rather than suffering the Jim Crow indignities associated with local retail shopping in white-owned stores, African Americans could simply make their choices from the mail-order catalog.

As the firm's CEO, Rosenwald was soon a man of great wealth. His interest shifted to philanthropy, an activity that was strongly grounded by his religious training. His rabbi, Emil Hirsch, reinforced the message that "property entails duties." Hirsch introduced Rosenwald to influential reformers like Jane Addams, the pioneering settlement house social worker and activist in Chicago, who inspired the Sears executive to support their work. Rosenwald's philanthropy also contributed to the building of the University of Chicago, and with Marshall Field, he helped to underwrite the construction of Chicago's Museum of Science and Industry.

In 1910 Rosenwald was deeply impressed by his reading of Booker

T. Washington's autobiography, *Up from Slavery*, first published in 1901. He was not ignorant about the South and its many difficulties. His daughter and son-in-law were progressive leaders and philanthropists in New Orleans, and the rising Sears empire in tidal-wave fashion was pushing into every corner of the predominantly rural Southern states. (The region's majority population did not shift from rural to urban until the national census of 1960.)[2]

Rosenwald chose Washington to be a mentor as he pondered what he could do to bring about meaningful change. The two met a year later. As Stephanie Deutsch describes it:

[It was over lunch] on a sweltering day in May 1911 at Chicago's elegant, new, lakefront hotel, the Blackstone. They had been anxious to meet each other. Washington regularly cultivated wealthy people who might donate money to Tuskegee Institute, the training school for black teachers he had founded thirty years earlier in rural Alabama. Rosenwald was such a man, extraordinarily rich and interested in using his money to promote the well-being of African Americans, though aware that he himself knew little about how best to do so. Each man knew the other might be of use to him. Each man was disciplined and determined, used to getting what he needed. We do not have a frank record from either one of his initial impressions of the other. We do know, though, that the results of the meeting between them would be extraordinary.[3]

Then, in 1912, Rosenwald decided to celebrate his fiftieth birthday by contributing nearly $700,000 for charitable purposes (about $16 million in 2018 dollars). Among the recipients of this generosity was Tuskegee Institute.

It was an era when most black schools in the South operated in deplorably shabby one-room buildings or church structures. Washington utilized a small portion of the $25,000 donation from Rosenwald to support an experimental "off-campus" initiative that he had launched: the construction of new school buildings for black students in rural areas of Alabama.

Julius Rosenwald and Booker T. Washington at the Tuskegee Institute in Alabama, 1915.
Special Collections Research Center, University of Chicago Library

Furthermore, the college president had documented the progress on these schools with photos and careful accounting. He included descriptions of the community enthusiasm that the erection of the new schools created among the local population—sometimes even including white citizens. Pride in the fresh facilities often stimulated the appearance of newly painted houses, improved roads, and expanded cooperation among residents that made a new school house "a focal point of community identity and aspiration."[4]

Rosenwald shared Washington's deep belief in hard work and self-reliance. He was intrigued by what the black educator had accomplished and immediately saw the potential for what else might be done. Washington died soon thereafter (in 1915), apparently of malignant hypertension. However, during the next two decades—a period when the virulence of Jim Crow ruled most of the South—his colleague's death did not deter Rosenwald and his newly formed

Sketch of Three-Teacher Community School, 1924.
Courtesy of HistorySouth.org

foundation from ramping up their school-building program throughout the South. Added to that work were correlated efforts to train teachers for the new schools and funds to provide libraries and workshops for students.

By the time of Rosenwald's death in 1932, an astonishing 4,977 Rosenwald schools and 380 complementary buildings (including 217 homes for teachers) had been erected in every Southern locale with a significant black population. That year they enrolled 663,615 students in 15 states. Fully 35% of all black children in the South (and 27% of all black children in America) were educated that year in Rosenwald schools.

It was in these schools that many of both the leaders and the foot soldiers of the civil rights movement received their educational grounding—not just readin', writin', and 'rithmetic, but also the principles of government, history, human rights, and even foreign languages. (French was very popular and likely reflected the presence in their home communities of World War I black army veterans returning home with a rudimentary knowledge of the language.) This broad foundation helped to prepare students for higher education, typically at the kinds of historically black colleges that Rosenwald and his philanthropic colleagues helped to co-found and support (e.g., Fisk University, Meharry Medical College, and Tennessee Agricultural and Industrial State College, all in Nashville), sometimes graduate school, and then social and political action.[5] Because the Rosenwald schools often were located on land shared with a community's church, on Sundays they became meeting spaces and lending libraries for the community's adult population. The Rosenwald Fund also linked forces with the Jeanes Fund and the General Education Board (see chapter 5).

The man's generosity was seemingly ubiquitous. Later in the foundation's history, it used its grants to leverage public support for so-called Country Training Schools. Allegedly established to provide "vocational training," they offered high school curricula that evolved into state-supported HBCUs, like Fort Valley College in Georgia.[6]

However, the philanthropy story goes far beyond the single-handed generosity of one white benefactor. Rosenwald did not believe in handouts. He insisted that local residents match all of his donations—and they did, despite the fact that most of them were poor

Elkton Rosenwald School (Three-Teacher) under construction, Tennessee, 1929.
Courtesy of Tennessee State Library and Archives. Image has been altered from the original.

African Americans. It is now calculated that black families contributed slightly more than 16% of the total costs of these schools with the Rosenwald Fund giving 15%. Much of the rest of the support came from funds cannily leveraged by Rosenwald from state and county education authorities.

During the course of their short but close relationship that included visits to each other's homes,[7] Rosenwald gave a speech to introduce Washington to a group of Chicago business leaders. He described the educator as someone "who was helping his own race to attain the high art of self-help and self-dependence" while simultaneously "helping the white race to learn that opportunity and obligation go hand in hand, and that there is no enduring superiority save that which comes as the result of serving."[8]

Because Rosenwald's investments were in people, it comes as no surprise that he made grants to writers and artists like Ralph Ellison, Langston Hughes, and W. E. B. Du Bois, while supporting also the research of Dr. Kenneth Clark, the psychologist, and the doctoral studies of his wife, Mamie Phipps Clark, that focused on the self-perception of black children. The Fund was phased out in 1948 (sixteen years after his death), because Rosenwald believed that foundations should not exist in perpetuity. However, the research of the Clarks that showed how black children internalized the negative racial perceptions of the dominant culture was decisive in the U.S. Supreme Court's decision to overrule *Plessy* in the 1954 *Brown v. Board of Education* decision.

Rosenwald also donated to national Jewish causes, although he opposed Zionism, and offered challenge grants for the construction of black YMCA facilities in both Southern states and black communities of the North. Even as he contributed to institutions that operated within the strictures of racial segregation, he also was generous to organizations like the Commission on Interracial Cooperation and the later Southern Regional Council that worked to eliminate racial barriers.

After the passing of a century, it is perhaps inevitable that further scrutiny of the remarkable Rosenwald-funded school program should yield hind-sighted criticism.[9] It is a fact that the schools he funded were segregated and that the curriculum nominally stressed vocational training. However, they were established during a period when everything in the region was sharply divided along racial lines, and "Negro education," as Washington's well-known Atlanta speech (see chapter 4) made clear, had to depend for survival upon accommodation to the prevailing order. Also, soon after Washington's death, the program's administration was indeed transferred to the newly created and white-staffed Rosenwald Fund, but it is possible that mismanagement crept in after the Tuskegee president's demise.

Overlooked (and certainly not emphasized publicly at the peak of the program's success) was its role in stealthily undermining white supremacy in a variety of ways. As already described, teachers taught more than the stated vocational curriculum. The imaginative design of the new buildings was often an architectural rebuff to conventional style. Even more important, because the black community had to raise matching funds, African Americans gained a strong sense of ownership in this communal project. A Rosenwald School was a recognizable space of pride and achievement.[10]

John H. Stanfield II, a scholarly critic of Northern philanthropy, delivers this observation: "During the pre-Civil Rights era, all but one of the few foundations that officially reported an interest in race relations areas [the Julius Rosenwald Fund] respected racial caste traditions in the South and North."[11] Perhaps the last word should go to another leader, W. E. B. Du Bois, who, on hearing of Rosenwald's death, declared him "a subtle stinging critic of our racial democracy."[12]

CHAPTER 7 ENDNOTES

1   Peter M. Ascoli, *Julius Rosenwald: The Man Who Built Sears, Roebuck and Advanced the Cause of Black Education in the American South* (Bloomington: Indiana University Press, 2006).

2   John F. McDonald, "Urban Areas in the Transformation of the South: A Review of Modern History," *Urban Studies Research* (2013), *http://dx.doi.org/10.1155/2013/376529.* For an in-depth study of the region's transformation in the second half of the 20th century and the forces driving urban and suburbanization, see Bruce J. Schulman, *From Cotton Belt to Sunbelt: Federal Policy, Economic Development, and the Transformation of the South, 1938–1980* (New York: Oxford University Press, 1991).

3   Stephanie Deutsch, *You Need a Schoolhouse: Booker T. Washington, Julius Rosenwald, and the Building of Schools for the Segregated South* (Evanston, IL: Northwestern University Press, 2011), "Prologue, 1911."

4   "National Treasures: Rosenwald Schools," National Trust for Historic Preservation, *https://savingplaces.org/places/rosenwald-schools#.XHgco9F7nBI.*

5   Mary S. Hoffschwelle, "Julius Rosenwald Fund," *Tennessee Encyclopedia*, last modified March 1, 2018, *https://tennesseeencyclopedia.net/entries/julius-rosenwald-fund/.*

6   See *https://georgiashpo.org/sites/default/files/hpd/pdf/AfricanAmericanHistoricPlaces/March%20 2009.pdf about a county training school.* For Fort Valley University, see: *https://georgiashpo.org/ sites/default/files/hpd/pdf/AfricanAmericanHistoricPlaces/December%202010.pdf.*

7   His daughter, Edith Stern, recalled spending the night in a Tuskegee Institute dormitory when the family accompanied Rosenwald to a board meeting on the campus. Philip M. Stern, *The Stern Fund* (New York: Institute for Media Analysis, 1992).

8   Hoffschwelle, "Julius Rosenwald Fund."

9   Discussed in Marian Wright Edelman, "Rosenwald Schools: Reclaiming a Legacy," *Child Watch*, February 19, 2010, *https://www.childrensdefense.org/child-watch-columns/health/2010/rosenwald-schools-reclaiming-a-legacy/.*

10 Mary S. Hoffschwelle, *The Rosenwald Schools of the American South* (Gainesville: University Press of Florida, 2006).

11 John H. Stanfield II, "Private Foundations and Black Education and Intellectual Talent Development," in *Philanthropic Giving: Studies in Varieties and Goals,* ed. Richard Magat (New York: Oxford University Press, 1989), 336.

   Not all historians agree with this perspective. Perhaps the staunchest modern critic of philanthropists working in the South in the post–Civil War era is Donald Spivey, who believes that "industrial education was a major force in the subjugation of black labor in the New South." This was also a view of W. E. B. Du Bois, who argued for a stronger emphasis on education for liberation rather than rural farm work that he believed instead served dominant industrial and commercial business interests. Donald Spivey, *Schooling for the New Slavery: Black Industrial Education, 1868–1915* (Westport, CT: Greenwood Press, 1978), ix.

   A more recent study by Hasia R. Diner, *Julius Rosenwald: Repairing the World* (New Haven, CT: Yale University Press, 2017), contains these prefatory remarks: "I am completing this book at a trying moment in the history of the United States, a moment which gives me pause and allows me to rethink the meaning of Julius Rosenwald. He made many millions through business but never saw money as an end in itself, as a way to augment his own political power or that of his class of the wealthy and well-connected. Money, he believed, brought responsibility to those who had it, and that responsibility meant seriously thinking about how to make the world a better place. He had no interest in slapping his name on buildings, no desire to see it boldly projected on public spaces. His money let him expand opportunities for others, to foster the welfare of those whom prejudice had ground down. Not a meaningless antidote to the present moment" (xi).

12 Stuart Rockoff, "Review Essay: Measuring Julius Rosenwald's Legacy," *Journal of the Southern Jewish Historical Society* 10 (2007): 235–38.

CHAPTER 8

The End of a War and a Return to "Normalcy"

An Awakening and Reuniting Country

On June 3, 1914—intentionally selected because it was the anniversary of Jefferson Davis's birth—President Woodrow Wilson presided over the reburial of Confederate war dead in the national cemetery at Arlington and the installation of a new Confederate memorial. Three

years later, for a second time since the Spanish-American War of 1898, great numbers of Southerners proudly and enthusiastically responded to Congress's declaration of war and joined ranks in battle with their Northern brethren against a common enemy.

Black Americans also saw the opportunity to demonstrate their patriotism. Georgia-born Eugene Bullard served as the world's first black fighter pilot in the French Air Force (and earned the prestigious Legion

Eugene Bullard, posthumously promoted to first lieutenant in the U.S. Air Force.
US Air Force/US Army Air Corps

of Honor award from the French government) while the "Harlem Hell-fighters," the 369th Infantry Regiment, spent more time in combat than any other infantry unit in the U.S. Army. Two of its members were the first Americans to receive the coveted French Croix de Guerre. Though the survivors could return home with a sense of great pride, these African Americans quickly discovered that their military service conferred no guarantee of equality in citizenship. The postwar period was marked by unabated white mob violence and lynchings.

As disastrous as the First World War was for Europe, the peace that America's late entry ensured brought a new sense of America's global importance and dynamism—not to mention a dependence upon her seemingly bottomless resources. (France and Great Britain were still paying off their WWI debts when they entered the 21st century.)

The Spanish Flu and Other Tumult

Even as Americans gathered to parade and cheer the war's end in 1918, moving silently through those crowds and indeed throughout the world was the misnamed "Spanish" influenza pandemic.[1] An estimated 675,000 Americans died of influenza, 10 times as many as in the war. Half of the American soldiers who died in Europe were felled by the disease. One-fifth of the world's population (28% of all Americans) were infected.[2]

The period between the two World Wars was one of the most tumultuous and consequential eras in the young nation's history. For the United States the 'Twenties opened new horizons for commerce, industry, trade and world leadership. U.S. GDP doubled in that decade. Government was experiencing a return to "normalcy." The U.S. Congress decidedly disapproved of joining the League of Nations. Instead it considered the appointment of Herbert Hoover as secretary of commerce a more useful melding of the American model of philanthropic purpose, the nonprofit sector, government, and business interests. President Harding appointed Andrew Mellon, one of the richest men in the U.S. (and a future philanthropist), as Secretary of the Treasury, a position he held from 1921 to 1932.

The sale of more than 100 million phonograph records in a single year (1927) together with the reign of cultural icons as varied as "the Babe" (George Herman Ruth Jr.), F. Scott Fitzgerald, Amelia Earhart, "Jelly Roll" Morton, Al Capone, and Mary Pickford signaled the birth of a new "mass culture" of interest and entertainment. By 1930, two out of three Americans attended a movie theater at least once a week.

The advent of advertising signaled the presence of a new consumer society and high on that list of desirable commodities was the automobile. Radio, newspapers, advertising, cinema, and tabloids connected people in new ways and even shaped a common public consciousness. Women now had the vote, while prohibition (1920-1933) testified to a persistent and crusade-like reformist impulse deep within at least part of the American spirit.

Exodus from the South

As the war came to an end and Americans ventured into the 20th century, most of those who were living in the North, Midwest, and West could look to the future with some optimism. In the South, though, the barriers to dignity, opportunity, and progress for most black and many white citizens seemed almost insurmountable.

Earlier chapters described the African American emigration from the South immediately after the Civil War and thereafter. The exodus continued steadily until what has come to be called the "Great Migration"—when the expanding demands of war-time factory production (even before U.S. entry into World War I) drew an estimated 700,000 black Southerners to employment in Northern cities. This trend continued through succeeding decades, eventually reaching an estimated total of 6,000,000 emigrants. The number of African Americans in the South as a percentage of the national black population was 89% in 1910, dropped to 85% in 1920, 79% in 1930, 77% in 1940, 68% in 1950, and continued its downward plummet through 1969. In 2000, for the first time in more than a century, it rose, to 55%.[3]

Drawing upon U.S. Census decennial records, historian James N. Gregory, in his study *America's Great Migrations*, documents that "white migration grew especially heavy in the two decades after the Civil War, with many leaving for farming opportunities and others heading for the North's big cities—New York, Philadelphia, Boston, and Chicago."[4] Resettlement brought many challenges, and not the least was the absence of a welcoming committee. Migrating Southerners were called "Okies" in the West, "hillbillies" in the East.

Gregory characterizes this long-term demographic upheaval as a "Southern Diaspora"—the beginning of a national epoch filled with history-changing repercussions.[5] The cultural achievements of black and white Southerners who flooded into other American cities, he notes, left a lasting impact upon the nation's music, literature, and community life. Racism and even inter-racial violence did not disappear among those who left the South, but Staci Glover describes both the white and black emigrants as "intuitive people capable of adjusting to their surroundings and using the infrastructure of those environs to spread southern culture and create new lives for their families."[6]

"Southern out-migration" may have been a constant since 1865, but Gregory sees a shifting variety of "pulls" that made it transformational

> right from the start of the new century, with flows accelerating in the second decade thanks to the job opportunities of World War I. By 1920 southerners living outside their home region numbered more than 2.7 million, in 1930 more than 4 million. Another, even larger surge during World War II raised that total to 7.4 million in 1950, 9.9 million in 1960, 10.8 million in 1970 [and] 12 million in 1980. That was the peak. As the Sunbelt basked and northern cities rusted, the population of southern expatriation began to decline, dropping to 11.7 million in 1990 and 10.2 million in 2000.

> The number of migrants was much larger than these census counts which do not account for return migration and mortality.... More than 7 million black southerners, nearly 20 million white southerners and more than one million Southern-born Latinos participated in the diaspora, some leaving the South permanently, others temporarily.[7]

As for life in the South, nobody rushed in to fill the labor void. The immigration waves of the 1880s, again in the 1920s (despite efforts to curb it), and after WWII that swept into the U.S. skirted the South. In any event, Southerners did not put out a welcome mat for potential newcomers. Flannery O'Connor's 1952 short story ("The Immigrant") speaks with a "revelatory honesty" about the entire region's lack of allure to outside investors.[8]

Commission on Interracial Cooperation (CIC)

Southern white liberal opposition to lynching, mob violence, peonage, and other racial abuse found a voice in the creation of the Commission on Interracial Cooperation (CIC) in Atlanta in 1918. Its first executive director was Will W. Alexander, a local white Methodist pastor, who had been active in the Atlanta Christian Council and the YMCA War Work Council. The first board chair was John J. Eagan, an Atlanta-based in-

dustrialist who had become a deeply engaged disciple of the social gospel movement.

Eagan, owner of the American Cast Iron Pipe Company in Birmingham, Alabama, was a member of Atlanta's Central Presbyterian Church and superintendent of the denomination's largest Sunday school. At the turn of the century, Josiah Strong, one of the most renowned leaders of the Social Gospel movement, came to Atlanta and stayed in Eagan's home. The experience

John J. Eagan
Courtesy of the Atlanta
History Center

transformed Eagan, who radically changed his business management practices and adopted other Progressive social positions. Before his death, he acquired all the stock of his company and gave the shares to the employees.[9]

Other CIC leaders were Tuskegee Institute president Robert R. Moton, New York investment banker George Foster Peabody, Virginia governor Harry F. Byrd, Wake Forest College president William Louis Poteat, and John Hope, the president of Morehouse College.

The CIC remained based in Atlanta but eventually had state-level committees throughout the region and some 800 local chapters. With most of its funding coming from northern philanthropies (Rockefeller Foundation, Rosenwald Fund, and Carnegie Foundation), CIC leaders were able to adopt cautiously liberal goals (e.g., opposition to lynching, mob violence, and peonage, and promotion of the economic development of the region). However, they did not attack racial segregation, believing that their most effective strategy was to bring together the "best people" of both races to discuss racial problems.[10]

Considered a progressive move at the time, this response must have seemed woefully pallid to African Americans, whose daily existence was threatened by the oppression of Jim Crow and the potential for violence against them. Northern philanthropy supported efforts to enact federal anti-lynching legislation in the 1920s and 1930s. As historian and political scientist Ira Katznelson documents in *Fear Itself: The New Deal and the Origins of Our Time*, none of those attempts was a match for the Southern Democrats' stranglehold on Congress.[11]

Warren G. Harding, not always highly regarded by historians,

Warren G. Harding addresses a crowd in Birmingham, Alabama on race relations, October 26, 1921.
The Literary Digest, November 19, 1921.

WARREN G. HARDING: A VOICE IN THE WILDERNESS

On October 26, 1921, President Warren G. Harding (whose parents had been abolitionists) spoke to a segregated crowd of 20,000 whites and 10,000 African Americans in Birmingham, Alabama. Acknowledging that racial differences could not be bridged, he nonetheless urged equal political rights for black Americans and supported literacy tests only if they applied to everyone.

"'Whether you like it or not,' he told his audience, 'unless our democracy is a lie, you must stand for that equality.' The white section of the audience listened in silence, while the black section cheered."

Source: "Warren G. Harding," Wikipedia. Last modified June 25, 2019

was perhaps the most racially progressive U.S. president since Ulysses S. Grant. In Harding's April 1921 address to Congress, he called on both bodies "to wipe the stain of barbaric lynching from the banners of a free and orderly representative democracy."[12] His proposal of an anti-lynching law made little headway, however, against legislative intransigence. One version passed the House but never made it through the Senate. Harding also was unsuccessful in reversing the segregation of the federal government departments that had been imposed by Woodrow Wilson (see chapter 6).

Early Southern Foundations

For all of the misery affecting the South, beginning before and continuing after World War I, a small measure of financial health was returning to the region—stimulated in part by the wartime economy. As evidence, a few philanthropic foundations began to take root.

The first grant-making foundation to be established in the South by Southerners (other institution-specific, operating foundations came earlier) may have been the Feild Co-Operative Association. Actually started in Tennessee, it was

organized on November 12, 1919, by the sons of
the late Dr. and Mrs. Montfort Jones of Kosciusko,
Mississippi, to honor their mother, Sallie Thomas
Feild. Its primary interest was in education with a
focus on individual scholarships. In 1925 the foundation's directors established a self-perpetuating,
revolving educational loan fund. (With current
assets of approximately $21 million, it continues
to provide low-interest, supplemental support to
post-secondary students.)[13]

Relocated to Mississippi, Feild Co-Operative was to be that state's primary claim to philanthropic fame for a long time. In 1890 the state
legislature had banned married people from leaving
more than one-third of their estates to charity. The
move was a heavy-handed reaction to a spate of
spurious deathbed "conversions" by which some
unscrupulous clergymen had robbed presumed
heirs of anticipated homes and land.[14] Mississippi,
like other Southern states, had a long and strong
history of individual charitable giving. However,
this law stunted the establishment and growth of
private foundations as well as university endowments for nearly a century, since it was not repealed
until the 1987–88 legislative session.

Elsewhere, a democratization of foun-

**Emblem of the Feild
Co-Operative Association**,
based in Mississippi and
possibly the first organized
grant-making foundation
created by Southerners in
the South.

dation-based philanthropy was underway with the formation of the first community foundation in Cleveland, Ohio, in 1914.[15] The new concept of pooling and investing endowed charitable funds for the broad benefit of a community was the brainchild of Frederick H. Goff, an attorney, banker, and business colleague of John D. Rockefeller. Goff's thinking about philanthropy had been strongly instructed by Rockfeller's formation of the General Education Board.[16] The Cleveland model was copied rather quickly in other industrialized Northern cities, but the movement made only scant headway in the South.[17]

The South's first community foundation was launched in Winston-Salem, North Carolina, in 1919 by a $1,000 endowment gift from "Colonel" Francis Fries, banker and railroader, much of whose wealth derived from the textile mill that he built on the banks of the New River in Grayson County, Virginia, in 1903.[18] Hard times capped by the Great Depression years delayed the formation of the next sustainable community foundation until 1943, when Walter Scott Montgomery's leadership and initial gift of $10,000 created the Spartanburg (SC) County Foundation.[19]

The Duke Endowment

During this era, the first—and only—major foundation (as measured by assets) in the South was created by James Buchanan ("Buck") Duke, who signed the Indenture of Trust creating The Duke Endowment with $40 million in December 1924.[20]

He had been only two years old when his mother died and seven

Portrait of James B. Duke, circa 1924
Courtesy of James Buchanan Duke Papers, David M. Rubenstein Rare Book & Manuscript Library, Duke University

years old when his father, Washington Duke, was drafted to serve in the army of the Confederacy. After the Civil War, the father and his two sons, Buck and Benjamin, and their sister, Mary Duke Lyon, slowly built a family tobacco business in Durham, North Carolina, selling pouches of the product from the back of a wagon. Their decision in 1884 to begin the mechanized mass production of cigarettes proved to be highly successful and led to the acquisition of other companies that evolved into the American Tobacco Company. The federal government's successful antitrust prosecution against this enormous and complex corporation did not dissipate the family fortune, for the Dukes had also invested in both the textile industry and hydroelectric power, forming the Duke Power Company in 1925.

Even as they prospered, the Dukes demonstrated an instinct for generosity through their support of Trinity College, affiliated with the Methodist Church, as well as hospitals and orphanages. However, after the death of their father and sister, the two brothers steadily systematized their giving in North Carolina and South Carolina. The 1924 Indenture of Trust is a uniquely detailed document that not only sets forth the causes and institutions eligible for support from it but also cites the reasons for their eligibility and mandates many of the administrative procedures.

It specifically names Duke University (the former Trinity College in Durham, North Carolina), Davidson College (a Presbyterian institution outside of Charlotte, North Carolina), and Furman University (a Baptist school in Greenville, South Carolina) as perpetual beneficiaries but also includes Johnson C. Smith University (an historically African American institution founded in Charlotte as the Freedmen's Institute of North Carolina in 1867). It further prescribes support for not-for-profit hospitals and children's homes in the Carolinas, rural Methodist churches in North Carolina, retired pastors, and their surviving families.[21] The document even delineates the compensation of the endowment's trustees as a fixed percentage of the assets. Although generally regarded as a Southerner, Duke spent most of his adult life at homes in New York City and New Jersey, in which state the Indenture of Trust was drawn up and signed. Duke died in 1925, less than a year after the foundation's formation, and his will left it an additional $67 million to bolster the initial gift of $40 million.[22]

The Great Depression

Neither the Duke millions nor other philanthropic assets in the South could stave off the devastation of the Great Depression. It is doubtful that any region of the country was harder hit. Then again, the lives of many Southerners were already miserable. In a sense, the Great Depression for the South did not begin in 1929; rather, it started for them in 1865 and just continued to worsen. The region, after all, was still crippled by limited public health, poor working conditions, the absence of electricity and of widespread education, rural isolation, joblessness, the oppressions of Jim Crow and racial violence for one-third of the population, and a political heritage that kept all but local government almost invisible.

The Desperation of Southern Farming

It is difficult to overstate the unfortunate lot of Southern farm families—69% of the South's population in 1930. (The distribution of farm families as a percentage of the nation's population was 21%.) By the time the Great Depression hit, much of Southern agriculture was taking place on the relics of bygone, slave-owning plantations of overworked land. Since the late 19th century, the typical family-owned farm leased out "shares" of the property to as many as ten landless and usually desperate families in need of work.

After the harvest, the owner divvied out to each tenant family its share of the cash proceeds (hence "sharecropper"), after subtracting the advance of loans for the use of a mule and equipment, seeds, clothing, minimal medical attention, and the rent of "sufficient quarters." Nobody could get ahead financially. Tenants were forever in debt to the landowners, and the owners themselves often were mired in bank loans. One bad year in cotton prices could wipe out years of hard work. Yearly gross income in 1929 was $186 for the typical Southern farm family, compared with $528 for American farmers outside the South.[23]

The killing blow to agriculture in the region was the arrival of the boll weevil, a beetle that devoured the buds and flowers of cotton plants. Hordes of these insects entered the United States from Mexico in 1892 and had reached southeastern Alabama in 1909. By the mid-

1920s the plague had infested all cotton-growing regions of the country, traveling 40 to 160 miles per year. Naturally, it seriously disrupted or even destroyed local communities and significantly reduced the value of land—then still the most important economic asset of the American South. Small wonder that this Southern version of farming, the bleakest and most hopeless of agrarian enterprises, drove people into the cities and to other employment.

Glimpses of Positive Change

As already noted, it was, admittedly, possible during this harsh period to catch occasional glimpses of positive change. Important writers of the period were coming into their own as part of a "Southern Renaissance," and included William Faulkner, Ellen Glasgow, Will Percy, Lillian Smith, Allen Tate, Eudora Welty, Thomas Wolfe, Richard Wright, and Frank Yerby. Visionaries like Frank Porter Graham, president of the University of North Carolina, and sociologist Howard W. Odum promoted a social science of reform. Emissaries of a "New Southern Liberalism" included political scientist V. O. Key (Johns Hopkins and Harvard), acclaimed poet and writer Robert Penn Warren (a native of Kentucky), and historian C. Vann Woodward (an Arkansas native and educator at Johns Hopkins and Yale).[24] So far behind was the region, though, that popular journalists and commentators regularly continued to describe this part of the country as a social hellhole, an educational disaster, and a cultural wasteland.

Still seared into popular consciousness was the coverage of the 1925 Scopes "Monkey Trial" in Tennessee by the columnist and essayist H. L. Mencken. His steady flow of columns created in the national imagination a hellish and indelible image of the region. In his oft-re-printed "The Sahara of the Bozart" he described the business boosters of the New South as "the most noisy and vapid chamber of commerce," and went on to proclaim that the entire South, "for all the progress it babbles of," as being "almost as sterile, artistically, intellectually, cultur-ally, as the Sahara Desert."[25]

Wilbur J. Cash's paradigmatic "Mind of the South" essay, a tour de force published in the October 1929 issue of the *American Mercury*, was a frontal assault on the mythology of the Old South and its cavalier legend. For Cash, the South's traditions of violence and racism consti-tuted a form of social pathology. Twelve years later, his published book of the same name became an instant classic, influencing a rising genera-tion of Southern intellectuals, writers, and historians.[26]

Two widely read novels of the time offered up their own "radical contrast to the traditionally genteel and romantic views of the region, that would be popularized most notably by Margaret Mitchell."[27] They were Georgia native Erskine Caldwell's *Tobacco Road* in 1932 and *God's Little Acre* in 1933, the latter named one of the Modern Library's hundred best novels of the 20th century. In *God's Little Acre* the author dissected the effects, the cruelties, and the constricted worldviews that were born of poverty, racism, lack of education, and lives bound to the soil and the mill. Reflecting on his work years later, Caldwell wrote:

> I could not become accustomed to the sight of children's
> stomachs bloated from hunger and seeing the ill and the
> aged too weak to walk to the fields to search for some-

thing to eat. In the evenings I wrote about what I had seen during the day, but nothing I put down on paper succeeded in conveying the full meaning of poverty and hopelessness and degradation as I had observed it.[28]

Years later, Harry Crews, the Southern author of dark fiction, recalled of his childhood that one did not have to be poor to feel the precariousness of daily living. The margin for "error" or "bad luck" was so thin "that when something went wrong, it almost always brought something else down with it. It was a world in which survival depended on raw courage, a courage born out of desperation and sustained by a lack of alternatives."[29] The South was still primarily agricultural, but an inferior system of roads made it almost impossible to move the yield of the land to markets where it could be sold. The system of white supremacy further poisoned everything it touched, and the absence of air conditioning kept the pace of life moving at a crawl.

Against this distressing portrayal, a group of twelve Southern writers known as "the Agrarians," whose unofficial leader was John Crowe Ransom, launched a counterattack.[30] Major contributors to the revival of Southern literature and connected with Vanderbilt University in Nashville, the Agrarians took strong exception to the prevailing negative depictions of Southern life. In 1930 they delivered a manifesto, *I'll Take My Stand: The South and the Agrarian Tradition*.[31] This collection of essays, whose title was taken from the chorus of "Dixie," celebrated the nobility of the ideal "yeomen" who tilled the soil—a figure that had been highly extolled by Thomas Jefferson 150 years earlier. By contrast, it characterized the advent of Northern-style industrialization and urbanization into the South as a descent into a paved, soilless, and soul-less hell. The introduction set the tone:

> All the articles. . .tend to support a Southern way of life against what may be called the American or prevailing way. . . . An agrarian society is hardly one that has no use at all for industries, for professional vocations, for scholars and artists, and for the life of cities. Technically, perhaps, an agrarian society is one in which agriculture is the leading vocation, whether for wealth, for pleasure, or for pres-tige—a form of labor that is pursued with intelligence and leisure, and that becomes the model to which the other forms approach as well as they may. The theory of agrar-ianism is that the culture of the soil is the best and most sensitive of vocations, and that therefore it should have the economic preference and enlist the maximum number of workers.[32]

The earlier "Lost Cause" revisionists who had once described the pre-1861 region as populated solely by an aristocracy of honorable plan-tation owners and nearly four million happy black slaves clearly ignored the facts. Just as clearly, not every non-black individual in the postwar period was "poor white trash." However, the Agrarians also erred in their reactionary and romanticized defense of an antebellum South that ignored the darker sides of the region's history. Ransom himself later denounced the work as a fantasy.[33] Nonetheless, its major themes continued to surface in sermons, political speeches, and other nostalgic memorials to the past.

The world war to end all wars had come to an end, and, to be sure, there were positive signs in the South that kinder and gentler times might lie ahead. Nonetheless, the battle to establish justice, insure domestic tranquility, promote the general welfare, and secure the blessings of liberty in the South continued to flounder.

CHAPTER 8 ENDNOTES

1   The disease did not originate in Spain, but was first detected and publicized there, after allegedly killing millions of citizens.

2   *https://virus.stanford.edu/uda/.*

3   U.S. Census Bureau, Historical Census Statistics on Population Totals by Race, 1790–1990 (Washington, D.C., 2002). In 2017, an estimated 15% of the U.S. population was African American. Of the nation's ten largest cities with the highest black population, six of the ten are outside the states of the old Confederacy.

4   Isabel Wilkerson's prize-winning *The Warmth of Other Suns: The Epic Story of America's Great Migration* (New York: Random House, 2010) tells the story of three successive generations of African Americans, from 1917 to 1970, who ventured to cities in the North and West seeking a better life.

5   James N. Gregory, "The Southern Diaspora (Black, White, and Latino)," America's Great Migrations, *http://depts.washington.edu/moving1/diaspora.shtml.*

6   James N. Gregory, *The Southern Diaspora: How the Great Migrations of Black and White Southerners Transformed America* (Chapel Hill: University of North Carolina Press, 2005), 12. See also the interactive map of the Northern migratory destinations for each U.S. Census year since 1900: James N. Gregory, "The Southern Diaspora (Black, White, and Latino)," America's Great Migrations, *http://depts.washington.edu/moving1/diaspora.shtml.*

7   Staci Glover, "The Southern Diaspora: How the Great Migrations of Black and White Southerners Transformed America," *https://networks.h-net.org/node/512/reviews/818/glover-gregory-southern-diaspora-how-great-migrations-black-and-white.*

8   Gregory, "The Southern Diaspora…": *http://depts.washington.edu/moving1/diaspora.shtml.*

9   Hilton Als, "This Lonesome Place," *The New Yorker* (Jan. 21, 2001), *https://www.newyorker.com/magazine/2001/10/29/this-lonesome-place.*

10   Robert E. Speer, *John J. Eagan: A Memoir of an Adventurer for the Kingdom of God on Earth* (Privately Printed, Anerucan Cast Iron Pipe Company, Birmingham, Alabama 1939). Lois Trigg Chaplin, John J. Eagan: *The Golden Rule for Life and Business*, 2003, American Cast Iron Pipe Company. The company continues to be owned and operated by its employees.

11   Nancy MacLean, *Behind the Mask of Chivalry: The Making of the Second Ku Klux Klan* (Oxford: Oxford University Press, 1994), 30. As MacLean notes, and according to internal documents, the CIC believed that World War I had "changed the whole status of race relationships" and that African Americans had grown resolved to obtain "things hitherto not hoped for." The group's leaders identified three types of Southern African American leaders—those "openly rebellious, defiant and contemptuous. . .thoughtful educated Negro leaders. . .and the great mass of uneducated Negroes." The CIC sought to increase the popularity of those who advocated patience.

By 1930 financial difficulties occasioned by the Great Depression led the CIC to forsake its expensive fieldwork and to focus primarily upon research and educational activities like the promotion of race relations courses in Southern high schools and colleges. Ann Ellis Pullen, "Commission on Interracial Cooperation," *New Georgia Encyclopedia*, last modified August 5, 2013, *https://www.georgiaencyclopedia.org/articles/history-archaeology/commission-interracial-cooperation.*

12   Democrats controlled one or both Houses of Congress from 1911 to 1921, and at least one branch of Congress from 1931 through 1997 (except for two two-year periods). In 1931 Southerners occupied leadership positions on twenty-nine of forty-seven congressional committees, including the most powerful of all: Ways and Means, Rules, Rivers and Harbors, Naval Affairs, Military Affairs,

Judiciary, Interstate and Foreign Commerce, Banking and Currency, Appropriations, and Agriculture. Southerners also held two of the top three positions in House leadership. Katznelson describes the South's Congressional power during the New Deal as a "Southern cage" that restrained FDR's actions on civil rights in exchange for the region's critical support of his programs and national defense initiatives. The Democratic Party's nearly unbroken control of the House from 1933 to 1997 was an element in the region's transformation from an agricultural to a commercial, industrial, and Cold War national defense economy. See *Fear Itself: The New Deal and the Origins of Our Time* (New York: W. W. Norton, 2013), 156–224.

13 Quoted in Maxwell Bloomfield, *Peaceful Revolution: Constitutional Change and American Culture from Progressivism to the New Deal* (Cambridge: Harvard University Press, 2000), 92.

14 Archives of the Feild Co-Operative Association, Jackson, Mississippi.

15 Correspondence from David Hammack notes that the 19th-century practice of favoring family heirs over charities was not unique to the South. In New York it enabled a distant relative to thwart a major bequest to Cornell University and made possible the defeat of the founding bequest from Samuel J. Tilden to the New York Public Library. See Stanley N. Katz, Barry Sullivan, and C. Paul Beach, "Legal Change and Legal Autonomy: Charitable Trusts in New York, 1777–1893," *Law and History Review* 3 (Spring 1985): 51–89. Also see Kristine S. Knaplund, "Charity for the 'Death Tax': The Impact of Legislation on Charitable Bequests," *Gonzaga Law Review* 45 (2009/2010): 236.

16 One comprehensive definition of a community foundation, found at *COF_Community%20 Foundation%20Definition_3-8-08.pdf,* states: A community foundation is a tax-exempt, nonprofit, autonomous, publicly supported, nonsectarian philanthropic institution with a long term goal of building permanent, named component funds established by many separate donors to carry out their charitable interests and for the broad-based charitable interest of and for the benefit of residents of a defined geographic area, typically no larger than a state.

17 For a carefully researched exploration of the relationship between the two men, see Eleanor W. Sacks, "Frederick Harris Goff, Rockefeller Philanthropy and the Early History of U.S. Community Foundations," Rockefeller Archive Center Research Reports Online, accessed December 28, 2017, *http://rockarch.org/publications/resrep/sacks.pdf.* On the Cleveland Foundation and its founding, see Diana Tittle, *Rebuilding Cleveland: The Cleveland Foundation and Its Evolving Urban Strategy* (Columbus: Ohio State University Press, 1992).

18 David Hammack, "Community Foundations: The Delicate Question of Purpose," in *An Agile Servant: Community Leadership by Community Foundations,* ed. Richard Magat (Ithaca, NY: Cornell University Press, 1989), 23–50.

19 *https://www.wsfoundation.org/our-story. A* small number of other Southern community foundations formed during this period but failed to survive the Great Depression.

20 *https://spcf.org/about/.*

21 Robert F. Durbin, *The Dukes of Durham, 1865–1929* (Durham, NC: Duke University Press, 1975).

22 See *https://dukeendowment.org/video-history-franklin* for a reflection about the legacy of Mr. Duke by Dr. John Hope Franklin, the renowned African-American historian who served on the Endowment board from 1993 to 2004.

Today, with assets of approximately $3.3 billion, it is the largest charitable foundation in the region. In recent years the endowment also has found imaginative ways to loosen some of the dictates of the original Indenture of Trust to broaden its scope of giving. In recent years, under the leadership of Gene Cochrane, President from 2005 to 2016, his senior staff and the board, the Endowment also has found imaginative ways to loosen some of the dictates of the original Indenture of Trust to broaden its scope of giving. Other details about the Endowment and its personnel provided in correspondence with Charity Perkins and Kimberly Webb, Duke Endowment staff, May 29, 2019.

23 Jeff Wallenfeldt, editor, *A New World Power: America from 1920 to 1945,* Documenting America: The Primary Source Documents of a Nation (New York: Rosen Publishing, 2013), 87.

24 Richard H. King, *A Southern Renaissance: The Cultural Awakening of the American South, 1930–1955* (New York: Oxford University Press, 1980).

25 Quoted in James C. Cobb, *Away Down South: A History of Southern Identity* (New York: Oxford University Press, 2005), 109. See Fred C. Hobson Jr., *Serpent in Eden: H. L. Mencken and the South* (Chapel Hill: University of North Carolina Press, 1974).

26 W. J. Cash, *The Mind of the South* (New York: Knopf, 1941).

27 Edwin T. Arnold, *"Tobacco Road" and "God's Little Acre," New Georgia Encyclopedia,* last modified May 16, 2016, *http://www.georgiaencyclopedia.org/articles/arts-culture/tobacco-road-and-gods-little-acre.*

28 Erskine Caldwell, *Call It Experience: The Years of Learning how to Write (*Athens: University of Georgia Press, 1996), 102.

29 Harry Crews, *A Childhood: The Biography of a Place* (Athens: University of Georgia Press), 44.

30 The group also included Donald Davidson, John Gould Fletcher, Henry Blue Kline, Lyle H. Lanier, Andrew Nelson Lytle, Herman Clarence Nixon, Frank Lawrence Owsley, Allen Tate, John Donald Wade, Robert Penn Warren and Stark Young.

31 *I'll Take My Stand: The South and the Agrarian Tradition* (New York: Harper and Brothers, 1930).

32 Quoted in Robert Jackson, *Seeking the Region in American Literature and Culture: Modernity, Dissidence, Innovation* (Baton Rouge: Louisiana State University Press, 2005), 77.

33 John Crowe Ransom, "Art and the Human Economy," *Kenyon Review* 7 (Autumn 1945): 686.

CHAPTER 9

A Personal and Regional Reclamation

FDR and the South

In many ways, the modern economic salvation of the South begins with the story of a man—himself a damaged creature—who had to reclaim himself before he could extend relief and restoration to others. The story's beginning predates the arrival of the Great Depression.

Franklin Delano Roosevelt was a vigorous man, born to wealth and privilege. In 1920 he had been a candidate for the vice presidency of the United States. A year later, at the age of thirty-nine, he came down with the effects of infantile paralysis while at his summer retreat on Campobello Island off the coast of Maine (in Canada's Bay of Fundy). William Leuchtenburg records the moment:

> After a swim in the cold waters and a two-mile hike home,
> he went to bed very tired. The next morning he was fever-
> ish and his left leg felt numb. By the following day he was
> partly paralyzed from the abdomen down. He had polio-
> myelitis—a viral inflammation of the spinal column.[1]

One possible source of the virus was a canteen of unsanitary water from which he drank just days earlier while attending a Boy Scout Jamboree in the mountains of New York.[2]

Contracting polio at his age was unusual, but the presence of the disease, uncommon before 1900, had become a national scourge. That year the borough of Brooklyn, New York, registered America's first polio epidemic, with 27,000 reported cases and 2,000 fatalities. For the next thirty-eight years, dreaded polio epidemics appeared annually throughout the United States, ritually spreading panic during the summer months, when the risks of contagion and infection were highest. The disease's incidence was directly related to urbanization and unsanitary drinking water; although some physicians recognized a connection between polio, viral infection, and water, the nature of the disease remained baffling.[3]

After the first few years of living with the incurable disease that crippled him from the waist down, Roosevelt plunged into the depths of a grave personal crisis. He descended into a state of depression and incipient alcoholism. Withdrawing from politics, he purchased a houseboat that one friend called a "floating dump," and spent the next several winters in the Florida Keys, indulging in a self-prescribed treatment of basking in warm sun, swimming in warm sea water, drinking martinis, fishing, partying, and keeping a written log.[4]

That regimen did nothing to improve his health. Then, encouraged by George Foster Peabody (no relation to the George Peabody described in chapter 3), he paid a visit in October 1924 to Peabody's Warm Springs resort in Georgia.[5] Untold generations of native inhabitants since the archaic and woodlands periods—and in the 18th century, the Muscogee Creek Indians—had partaken of the "healing waters" (88°F) of Warm Springs, the product of an ancient meteorite fracture in the earth's crust.[6] After his first visit, Roosevelt became convinced that the waters were offsetting polio's damage to his body. He also was inspired by the courage of other patients recuperating at the resort, especially young children stricken with paralysis. He sold the houseboat and started the routine of regular visits and extended stays at Warm Springs that would continue until his death there.

By 1926 Roosevelt had invested two-thirds of his inheritance in property at Warm Springs and incorporated the Georgia Warm Springs Foundation. The institution added an enclosed pool, funded by Edsel Ford, son of automotive pioneer Henry Ford, and other improvements followed. Over the years physicians and physiotherapists worked with Roosevelt to develop muscle exercises. The "spirit of Warm Springs" and its treatment facility (cultivating more a family than a hospital atmosphere) became firmly entrenched as patients relearned how to function in society and to live with greater enjoyment.[7]

Franklin Delano Roosevelt, Warm Springs, Georgia, sometime between 1927 and 1935
Selections from the Records of the Georgia Warm Springs Foundation, 1924-1974. Courtesy of the Roosevelt Warm Springs Vocational Rehabilitation Campus

A rejuvenated Roosevelt returned to politics. As New York's

governor Al Smith prepared to campaign against Herbert Hoover for the U.S. presidency, the state's Democratic leaders prevailed heavily and successfully upon Roosevelt to make a run to succeed Smith. Smith lost to Hoover, but Roosevelt became the governor of New York. While still governor, he built the home he intended to occupy when visiting Warm Springs. It became known as "The Little White House" because of its modesty and exterior color.[8]

Depression Days

Elected in 1932 as the Democratic Party's candidate for president in an electoral landslide against Herbert Hoover, FDR arrived at the real White House as the nation's deepening slide into the Great Depression grew grimmer by the day. He did not need his inspirationally progressive wife, Eleanor, to tell him about rural poverty, poor public health,

destructive agricultural practices, and economic distress. He had already seen those conditions with his own eyes. While in Georgia, he had spent portions of his days taking afternoon jaunts through the countryside in his specially equipped car, mingling freely and chatting with mostly white farmers, merchants, and other folk. For him, the rural poor had faces and names.[9]

Depression-era bread line in 1932.
Courtesy of Franklin D. Roosevelt Presidential Library & Museum

Not all of his new friendships were with the poor. Roosevelt also visited regularly with the wealthy textile magnate Cason Callaway and his family at their estate, a short drive from Warm Springs. They occupied opposite poles of the political sphere, but they had a lot in common. Callaway had served in the U.S. Navy, and Roosevelt had been assistant secretary of that department. They both were good salesmen. They also shared a strong interest in the people of the area as well as farming and agricultural experimentation and reform.[10]

The New Deal Underway

Under President Roosevelt's direction, federal funds began pouring into the South to support a seemingly endless array of new, often highly experimental programs with an alphabet-soup mix of acronymic and initialized titles. Nowhere was their impact felt more dramatically than the rural areas of the region. As an example, the Tennessee

THE CARMAKER AND THE CHEMIST

At least one Southern community survived the Great Depression quite well.

Ways Station was a whistle-stop hamlet some twenty miles south of Savannah that Henry Ford had spotted while on a train trip to Florida. He purchased the property that had been the site of an antebellum plantation house overlooking the Ogeechee River and constructed a winter home that he christened Richmond Hill. Eventually, he acquired some 85,000 acres of farm and timber land on which he constructed an experimental agricultural station. From 1929 through World War II, Ford made sure the residents of the community were well paid and cared for.

Another remarkable part of the story is that a periodic visitor to the Ford property was George Washington Carver, the renowned African American chemist from Tuskegee Institute whom Ford had visited and with whom he had corresponded. (Carver also traveled to Dearborn, Michigan, for visits and consultations with Ford.) They shared an interest in converting agricultural products to industrial purposes and later would even fashion an automobile body from soybeans.

The "rest of the story" is that Tuskegee Institute received generous support from Ford and from the Ford Foundation for many years thereafter. In 1981 Benjamin F. Payton, a Ford Foundation program officer, became the president of Tuskegee and held that position until 2010.

Sources: *http://www.edisonfordwinterestates.org*; *http://www.fordplantation.com*.

THE VIRGINIA PLAN

The difficulties of the Great Depression distracted many Americans from thinking about international affairs. Yet, during the years leading up to World War II, many American Jews engaged in efforts to rescue European Jews from persecution in Nazi Germany and other countries and to slip past the many stiff immigration barriers established by the U.S. Department of State.

On a trip to Germany with his family in the 1930s to visit relatives and business contacts, William B. Thalhimer Sr., founder of Thalhimers department store in Richmond, Virginia, was deeply disturbed by the anti-Semitism he witnessed and became determined to take some action. After meeting a representative of Gross Breesen, a Jewish agricultural training institute in Germany, Thalhimer launched a plan to furnish its students with visas as trained farmers and to relocate them safely to the United States. In 1938 he purchased a 1,500-acre farm in rural Burkeville, Virginia (Hyde Farmlands), where they could safely settle and work.

Thalhimer and other family members would later establish foundations in Richmond through which they and their descendants could disburse their philanthropy.

Source: Robert H. Gillette, *The Virginia Plan: William B. Thalhimer and a Rescue from Nazi Germany* (Charleston, SC: History Press, 2011).

Valley Authority, which still has high visibility today, not only provided electrification to farms and remote communities but also offered jobs, educational instruction, and of course, hope to a desperate population inhabiting some of the most removed and isolated regions of seven Southern states. Other programs targeted agricultural improvements (including the eradication of the boll weevil), and supports for farmers and their families.[11]

Many Southerners also benefitted from national programs like improved hours and wages for textile workers, the removal of children from the workplace, a national minimum wage (twenty-five cents per hour), and the promise of social insurance for retirees. The 1938 Fair Labor Standards Act "disproportionately affected low paid southern workers, and brought southern wages within the reach of northern wages" for the first time.[12]

The Civilian Conservation Corps (CCC) and the Works Progress Administration (WPA) put people to work with a paycheck while building and improving roads and bridges, constructing or rehabilitating thousands of public buildings like city halls, courthouses, schools, libraries, hospitals, and post offices and undertaking an extraordinary collection of public works projects, including public murals. At the same time, a continued rise to powerful leadership positions in Congress by Southern Democrats—their social views notwithstanding—was giving new political leverage to the region and a corresponding rise in national stature.

Despite the desperately needed focus upon the South by the federal government and by some foundations, the South remained in deep trouble. In 1938 a special commission appointed by President Roosevelt issued its *Report to the President on the Economic Conditions in the South*. The document did not single out the poverty-ridden counties in the low country of South Carolina, the slums of Atlanta and Richmond and Memphis, or the Delta portion of Mississippi, which had not yet recovered from the catastrophic flood of 1927. It labeled the entire region as "the Nation's No. 1 economic problem."[13]

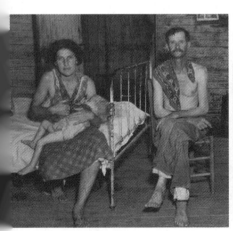

Fields family, Hale County, Alabama, 1936
Courtesy of the Library of Congress,
LC-USZC4-4832

Vicksburg, Mississippi, March 1936
Courtesy of the Library of Congress,
LC-DIG-fsa-8c52213

CHET ATKINS

"I didn't have any idea
we were poor. Back then,
nobody had any money.
We were so poor, and
everybody around us was
so poor, that it was the '40s
before any of us knew there
had been a Depression."
Chester Burton "Chet" Atkins
(1924-2001), legendary,
Tennessee-born guitarist.

"The Writer's Almanac with Garrison
Keillor," June 20, 2019

As the haunting photography of Walker Evans and the prose of James Agee in *Let Us Now Praise Famous Men* would later (1941) make abundantly clear, the financial collapse of the South crossed the color line; both poor whites and poor blacks who had been unable to escape the region suffered. This classic documentation of the period recorded not only the extent but also the nature of poverty. Much more than economic, it was also physical, psychological, and spiritual.[14]

And yet the mythology of agrarian values and states' rights endured in the region, presumably distancing the New South's brand of progress from Yankee materialism. Its magnetic appeal to a watching and reading nation was still evident in 1939 when the opening lines in the film version of *Gone With the Wind*, one of Hollywood's more notable distortions of history, described the Old South as a place of "cavaliers and cotton fields" where gallantry "took its last bow."

Appalachia

Further emblematic of the already-described distress of the South was Appalachia, a region within a region that possessed a proud lineage and mountain culture as old as the nation itself. However, when timber cutting and later coal-mining began their decline in the 1920s, the region's only real alternatives to subsistence farming began to disappear. As described in Harry Caudill's classic *Night Comes to the Cumberlands*, Appalachia's people fell into a state of extreme poverty that was both exacerbated and also well hidden from the rest of the South and the nation by the geographic isolation created by its mountains and "hollers."[15]

A modest but noteworthy effort to respond to this need occurred in 1930 when the New York State Legislature granted a charter to the Algernon Sydney Sullivan Foundation, whose initial philanthropic focus was upon the educational needs of Appalachia. The person whose name it bears was an Indiana native and New York attorney who founded Sullivan & Cromwell, still one of the nation's most prestigious law firms. His wife, Mary Mildred Sullivan (1836–1933), and he were both opposed to slavery. They also shared Irish familial roots in Virginia (Sullivan's grandfather immigrated there from Ireland) and they honored the South without apology. During the Civil War, Sullivan (1826–87) opposed warfare as a means of preserving the Union (a "Peace Democrat"), and the couple did what it could to provide legal aid to Southerners and promote more humane treatment of Confederate prisoners of war in the North.

Among his actions to promote greater interregional harmony was becoming the first president of the New York Southern Society, whose membership included President Grover Cleveland. In his inaugural remarks, Sullivan proposed some aspirational goals for that association. One was "to care for and uphold those of our fellow citizens, without distinction of race, whose lot is affected by any burdens of the past."[16] He also sponsored the first African-American member of the New York State Bar Association. Interestingly, the first Algernon Sydney Sullivan Medallion from the Memorial Association of the same name was presented in 1925 to the George Peabody College for Teachers in Nashville. (See chapter 3).

Going to War

Millions of dollars in funds from the programs of the New Deal had fallen upon the cash-parched South like a rainy night in Georgia. Those expenditures, though, were but a drizzle when compared with the deluge of additional billions of federal dollars that arrived to support the buildup for a global war. Between 1938 and 1945, according to economic historian Taylor Jaworski, more than $20 billion flowed into and through the South.[17] Southern historian James Cobb estimates that the region absorbed $11.5 billion more in federal expenditures than it paid in taxes.[18]

The region's thousands of square miles of vacant and untilled acreage that were not too distant from population centers paired with a warm climate made the South a near-ideal location for military encampments, aviation and infantry training grounds, and bombing ranges. Railroads linked almost all significant municipalities, and coastal port cities with easy access to the Atlantic Ocean and Gulf of Mexico were ideally suited for shipyards and the deployment of personnel and materiel. Aircraft plants, steel and textile mills, synthetic rubber factories, tin smelting operations, and pulpwood processors working around the clock

Preparations for World War II, Fort Story, Virginia, 1940.
National Archives and Records Administration

further broadened the picture of a country going to war.

That all of this activity was taking place in the South was no accident of climate or available land. As noted above, powerful Southern legislators like Richard Russell and Carl Vinson of Georgia, who chaired the armed services committees in, respectively, the U.S. Senate and House, made sure their region was not forgotten in this time of national preparation.

Many of the barriers that had separated North from South became far more porous after the United States became fully engaged in international hostilities. New business relationships flourished, Northern corporations opened Southern sales offices, long-interrupted conversations between individuals and organizations resumed, and romantic liaisons ripened. Many a young Yankee draftee showed up for basic training at a Southern base, met a local belle, and figuratively speaking, never returned home.

All sorts of other demographic shifts were underway. Those young Southern men, white and black, who were not drafted, ventured northward and westward—in search of employment and other opportunities. Jewish refugees from Nazi persecutions (their passage often underwritten by Jewish family foundations) came to Southern cities, and a significant number of the academics among them found positions on the faculties of historically black colleges in the South. Perhaps the most dramatic change in daily life occurred as America's women found themselves in demand by both the military and the world of private business.

Clearly, the U.S. South was no longer the nation's "number-one economic problem." Historian Christopher Tassava notes "the war's global scale severely damaged every major economy in the world except for the United States, which thus enjoyed unprecedented economic and political power after 1945."[19] The U.S. Gross Domestic Product's (GDP) annual rate of change was -8.5% in 1930 (one year after the beginning of the Great Depression), 8.9% in 1935 (the advent of Social Security), 8.8% in 1940 (national defense spending), and 8.0% in 1944 (more increases in defense spending).[20]

Southern Regional Council

As described by Randall L. Patton and Ann Ellis Pullen, during the latter years of the Great Depression, Jessie Ames, longtime head of women's work for the Commission on Interracial Cooperation (CIC) (see previous chapter), assumed leadership of that organization's day-to-day operations. She began to revive the interracial committees around the region that had been disbanded for financial reasons and started publishing a monthly newsletter, *The Southern Frontier.*[21]

CIC's executive Will Alexander and its president Howard W. Odum (a Georgia native, University of North Carolina professor, and widely regarded sociologist and writer) advocated for another strategy. They believed CIC's early focus on speaking out against mob violence, lynching, and peonage should shift to seeking economic and educational improvements for all Southerners. Virginia Union University sociologist Gordon Hancock took a strong exception to that position. He spoke for many African American intellectuals when he called for the dismantling of "legally enforced segregation" as the highest priority.[22]

The CIC and those seeking a new direction fused in 1944 as the Southern Regional Council (SRC) with headquarters in Atlanta. From the beginning, though, this next-generation organization remained divided between the regionalists who preferred to focus on broad structural reforms (racial problems, they argued, could best be remedied through improving economic conditions for all Southerners) and those who advocated a principled stand against segregation.

The author Lillian Smith is best known for her novel *Strange Fruit* and her nonfiction treatise *Killers of the Dream.* Courtesy of Hargrett Rare Book and Manuscript Library / University of Georgia

The influential Lillian Smith was among those who argued strongly that the SRC had to take the latter position. The debate continued until 1949, when the position Smith supported prevailed, and the SRC declared officially that segregation "in and of itself constitutes discrimination and inequality of treatment." That declaration cost the organization in the short term, as many white members left—they were not yet ready to abandon the "separate but equal" doctrine.

After the 1954 *Brown v. Board of Education* decision, "SRC sponsored the formation of state Councils on Human Relations, committees of concerned citizens who worked to encourage and ease the process of desegregation." With the help of Northern foundations (see chapter 13), the organization survived and ultimately remained an influential force in the South's postwar transformation.[23]

Philanthropy Expanding

With new windows open to the rest of the world, some Southerners, especially those with military contracts, began to create capital of their own and subsequently converted portions of this wealth into philanthropic assets. Only some thirty-plus foundations were active in the South in the 1930s; however, during the next two decades, more than two hundred new private foundations rooted themselves on the Southern scene. Among the most significant were those tightly bound to the fortunes of the relatively small number of families who learned how to make money in the distinctively Southern occupations of textiles, tobacco, timber, and of course, carbonated beverages.

CHAPTER 9 ENDNOTES

1   William E. Leuchtenburg, "Franklin D. Roosevelt: Life Before the Presidency," Miller Center, University of Virginia, *https://millercenter.org/president/fdroosevelt/life-before-the-presidency.*

2   Amy Berish, "FDR and Polio," Franklin D. Roosevelt Presidential Library and Museum, *https://fdrlibrary.org.*

3   David M. Oshinsky, *Polio: The American Story* (New York: Oxford University Press, 2005), charts the first epidemics in the United States and dates their earliest appearance in Vermont in 1894. He writes: "No disease drew as much attention, or struck the same terror, as polio. And for good reason. Polio hit without warning. There was no way of telling who would get it and who would be spared. It killed some of its victims and marked others for life, leaving behind vivid reminders for all to see: wheelchairs, crutches, leg braces, breathing devices, deformed limbs." 5.

4   Karen Chase, ed., *FDR on His Houseboat: The Larooco Log, 1924–1926* (Albany: State University Press of New York, 2016).

5   George Foster Peabody was a progressive philanthropist, banker, and wealthy investor who "left his mark on society through his philanthropic work." The two men had first met earlier that year at the Democratic Party's state convention at which FDR had been urged to put Al Smith's name into nomination as the Democratic Party's candidate for governor. See Sheila Devaney, "George Foster Peabody (1852–1938)," *New Georgia Encyclopedia,* last modified August 9, 2013, www.georgiaencyclopedia.org/articles/arts-culture/george-foster-peabody–1852–1938.

6   Evan Miller, "Franklin D. Roosevelt's Healing Waters," *Guideposts*, June 21, 2018, *https://www.guideposts.org/inspiration/miracles/gods-grace/franklin-d-roosevelts-healing-waters.*

7   In 1938, years after election to the White House, Roosevelt founded the wholly private National Foundation for Infantile Paralysis and promoted its financial support through the annual March of Dimes campaign timed to coincide with his birthday (January 30), and so named at the suggestion of entertainer Eddie Cantor. Grants from these funds would later help to support Dr. Jonas Salk's successful search for a vaccine that would virtually eradicate polio from the United States and the world.

8   Filmmaker Ken Burns offers his own theory of Roosevelt's emotional and psychological "recovery." Comparing Theodore Roosevelt with FDR, his fifth cousin, Burns notes: "Both men were unstable and always had to be in motion. It fell to FDR, who could not move, to figure out a way to outrun his demons." Quoted in Jeffrey Kluger, "FDR's Polio: The Steel in His Soul," *Time Magazine,* September 12, 2014, *http://time.com/3340831/polio-fdr-roosevelt-burns/.*

9   Kaye Lanning Minchew documents FDR's travels in Georgia, as well as his speeches, photographs, public appearances, and local news coverage in *A President in Our Midst: Franklin Delano Roosevelt in Georgia* (Athens: University of Georgia Press, 2017). As federal relief came to the South, the operator of the Warm Springs Hotel wrote that a "poor dirt farmer" from Gadsden, Alabama, "walked a hundred miles barefoot to make a gift of a country ham to FDR."

10   The friendship of Cason Callaway and FDR along with their mutual interest in agricultural improvement in the U.S. South is documented in William W. Winn, "The View from Dowdell's Knob," *The New Georgia Guide* (Athens: University of Georgia Press, 1996), 384.

11   James C. Cobb and Michael V. Namorato, eds., *The New Deal and the South* (Jackson: University Press of Mississippi, 1984) looks at the "turning points" in the region that were products of New Deal policy. A story needing wider circulation is the often ignored "red-lining" that prevented many African Americans from taking advantage of the benefits offered through the New Deal and the legislative compromises involving the denial of civil rights and limited access to New Deal benefits by African Americans. Roosevelt accepted these limits as a negotiating reality with Southern congressional leadership. In his second term, as he gained support outside the South, he took a more critical stance toward Southern opposition to civil rights.

12 "The New Deal in the South," *The American Yawp: A Massively Collaborative Open U.S. History Textbook* (Stanford: Stanford University Press, 2018–19), *http://www.americanyawp.com*. See also Gavin Wright, "The New Deal and the Modernization of the South," Stanford Institute for Economic Policy Research, *https://siepr.stanford.edu/research/publications/new-deal-and-modernization-south*. Wright emphasizes the conditionality of progress and views the New Deal era as "a turning point in regional economic development, a watershed if not an instantaneous revolution."

13 The full text of the report *Economic Conditions of the South* appears at *http://www.archive.org/stream/ reportoneconomic00nati/reportoneconomic00nati_djvu.txt*.

14 James Agee and Walker Evans, *Let Us Now Praise Famous Men* (New York: Houghton Mifflin, 1941). Danny Heitman notes that the photographic portrayal, of "Depression-era Alabama sharecroppers, was a commercial flop when it was released in 1941" but "now stands as a landmark piece of social documentary." "Let Us Now Praise James Agee," *Humanities Magazine* 33, no. 4 (July/August 2012).

15 Harry M. Caudill, *Night Comes to the Cumberlands: A Biography of a Depressed Area* (Boston: Little Brown and Co., 1962) aroused the U.S. Congress to authorize the creation and funding and funding of the Appalachian Regional Commission. Like much of the South, Appalachia too has been the subject of stereotyping and caricature that does not add to our understanding of the region. See John C. Inscoe, "The Discovery of Appalachia: Regional Revisionism as Scholarly Renaissance," in *A Companion to the American South,* ed. John B. Boles (Oxford, UK: Blackwell, 2002), 369–86.

16 "Southern Society of New York, III," *Magazine of Western History*, vol. 16 (1892), 215. The Society established the Sullivan Award, which honors him by providing service-based scholarships that continue to this day. The initial emphasis upon Appalachia by his widow and son, George Hammond Sullivan, has since broadened to support scholarships and grants to institutions elsewhere in the South, with a special interest in the promotion of social entrepreneurship. Based for many years in New York City, the foundation now has its office in Oxford, Mississippi. Also see Gray Williams Jr., *The Sullivan Heritage* (Oxford, MS: Triton Press, 2014).

17 Taylor Jaworsky, "World War II and the Industrialization of the American South," in *Journal of Economic History* 77, no. 4 (June 2017): 1048–82, *http://www.nber.org/papers/w23477*.

18 James C. Cobb, *The Selling of the South: The Southern Crusade for Industrial Development, 1936–1990* (Baton Rouge: Louisiana State University Press, 1982), 196.

19 Christopher J. Tassava, "The American Economy during World War II," EH.Net Encyclopedia, ed. Robert Whaples, February 10, 2018, *http://eh.net/encyclopedia/the-american-economy-during-world-war-ii/*.

20 Kimberly Amadeo, "U.S. GDP by Year Compared to Recessions and Events," *The Balance*, June 25, 2019, *http:// https://www.thebalance.com/us-gdp-by-year-3305543*.

21 Randall L. Patton, "Southern Regional Council," *New Georgia Encyclopedia*, last modified February 20, 2013, *https://www.georgiaencyclopedia.org/articles/government-politics/southern-regional-council*. Ann Ellis Pullen, "Commission on Interracial Cooperation," New Georgia Encyclopedia, last modified August 5, 2013.

22 Raymond Gavins, "Gordon Blaine Hancock (1884-1970)," *Encyclopedia Virginia*, *https://www.EncyclopediaVirginia.org/Hancock_Gordon_Blaine_1884-1970*.

23 Pullen, "Commission on Interracial Cooperation," New Georgia Encyclopedia, last modified August 5, 2013.

CHAPTER 10

Emerging Southern Wealth and Philanthropy

The Real Thing

It was not widely recognized at the time, but a corporate evolution of the early 20th century set in motion the building of a financial fortune that would have a major impact upon Southern philanthropy until the present time. It is the tale of a commercial success story built on a beverage that came to acquire perhaps the most widely recognized trademark in the world—Coca-Cola.[1]

In 1886 Atlanta pharmacist John Pemberton had invented a syrup that when mixed with carbonated water became a popular soda fountain beverage. Two years later he sold the formula to Asa Candler of Atlanta. By 1892 the newly formed Coca-Cola Company was flourishing, and plants were manufacturing the syrup in Atlanta and elsewhere throughout the United States.

The product's distribution and popularity expanded exponentially when Benjamin F. Thomas and Joseph B. Whitehead of Chattanooga (later joined by John T. Lupton) convinced Candler to grant them the exclusive license to bottle the beverage almost everywhere in the United States. The three pioneers divided the country into territories and sold bottling rights to local entrepreneurs. By 1909 nearly four hundred Coca-Cola bottling plants, most of them family-owned businesses, were in operation.

The firm's early rise hit a roadblock during World War I. When the U.S. government imposed strict rationing on sugar, the company soon faced total collapse. However, in 1919 a syndicate that included W. C. Bradley of Columbus, Georgia, and Ernest Woodruff of Atlanta (and a Columbus native) purchased the company and set about salvaging and rebuilding the enterprise.

In 1923 their most far-reaching decision was to hire Robert W. Woodruff, then only thirty-three years old, to run the corporation. Woodruff was a marketing genius. Even though more than a thousand Coca-Cola bottlers were operating in the United States, he began a major push to establish bottling operations outside the country. Plants were opened in France, Belgium, Italy, Spain, Guatemala, Honduras, Mexico, Peru, Australia, and South Africa. By the time World War II began, Coca-Cola was being bottled in forty-four countries and was transforming the world's drinking habits.

For our purposes, though, what set Woodruff apart was not his business acumen, the way he restored the company's strength, or the enormous personal wealth he accumulated, but rather his philanthropic instincts—coupled with a remarkable insistence upon the anonymity of his giving, as shown in two examples.

The first story concerns Woodruff and his Ichauway Plantation, a hunting preserve and working farm comprising thousands of acres of land about 200 miles south of Atlanta, in Baker County, Georgia. During a 1929 visit there, he was sitting on the front porch of House No. 1 when an elderly black tenant farmer approached to pay his respects to the "new boss." After shaking Woodruff's hand, however, he suffered a violent seizure and passed out. Like many of his fellow tenant farmers and 40% of the county's residents, he suffered from malaria.

Woodruff bought a barrel of quinine to distribute not just to Ichauway residents but to every resident in Baker County. Then, for the next few years, Woodruff quietly continued to purchase and give away the anti-malarial drug to anyone in the area who would agree to follow doctor's orders for its use. Eventually, he decided to fund the poverty-stricken county's first public health department in the town of Newton. The benefactor was listed simply as a "friend of the community."[2]

A visiting nurse makes a call on a family near Ichauway Plantation
Credit Line: Melvin H. Goodwin Papers, TN 72383, Stuart A. Rose Manuscript, Archives, and Rare Book Library, Emory University

By the late 1930s, Woodruff had created the Woodruff Malaria Fund at Emory University and asked the university's department of pathology and the U.S. Public Health Service to study the disease's foothold in an effort to eradicate malaria in Baker County. Conducted from a base next to the Ichauway General Store, the research was the first truly comprehensive field study of the disease.

LETTIE PATE WHITEHEAD EVANS

A large but very low-profile foundation in the South, despite being active in much of the region, is the Lettie Pate Whitehead Foundation. It provides scholarship assistance to deserving women at more than two hundred colleges and funds senior-care facilities for elderly women. Letitia ("Lettie") Pate, born into a prominent western Virginia family, married Joseph B. Whitehead, an attorney from Oxford, Mississippi. They settled in Chattanooga, Tennessee, where they had two sons. Whitehead and his colleague, Benjamin Thomas, secured the exclusive bottling rights for Coca-Cola, and in 1900, the Whiteheads relocated to Atlanta, where he opened a second bottling plant. His entrepreneurial and highly successful efforts to establish other bottlers around the South and the West was interrupted by his death six years later.

At the age of thirty-four, left with young children, Lettie Pate Whitehead, who had an acute business sense, took over the management of her late husband's massive bottling and real estate holdings. Seven years later, she married Col. Arthur Kelly Evans, a retired Canadian Army officer. During their thirty-five-year union, they kept a home in Atlanta but also established a large estate, Malvern Hill, in Hot Springs, Virginia. Mentored by Robert W. Woodruff, whose family had acquired the Coca-Cola Company from the Asa Candler family, Lettie Pate Whitehead Evans prospered. Woodruff appointed her to the company's board of directors—a position she held for almost twenty years—making her one of the first women in America to serve on the board of a major corporation.

During her lifetime she and her sons gave away millions of dollars. She died in 1935, having outlived both her husbands and her sons. Her legacy includes three foundations, all managed by the Robert W. Woodruff Foundation: the already-noted Lettie Pate Whitehead Foundation, the Lettie Pate Evans Foundation, and the Joseph B. Whitehead Foundation

Source: *lpwhitehead.org*; authors' correspondence with P. Russell Hardin

That venture would lead to the formation in downtown Atlanta of the Malaria Control in War Areas program by the Public Health Service in 1942. It in turn would become the Communicable Disease Center in 1946, and then Woodruff's anonymous purchase of 15 acres from Emory University made possible the relocation of the CDC (now the Centers for Disease Control and Prevention) to the edge of the city.[3]

A second example of Woodruff's philanthropic style is less far-reaching but equally telling. He was no social activist nor did he openly challenge the racist structures or beliefs common among Baker County's white residents. However, behind the scenes, he was deeply loyal to the black farmers and employees who made Ichauway work, although his style was distinctly paternalistic by today's standards. When a black church just beyond the borders of the property burned to the ground and its members had no funds to rebuild, Woodruff acted through an outside agent to pay for the construction of a new church. The church members quickly guessed that Ichauway's owner was responsible for their good fortune, and wanted to thank him. Respecting his insistence on privacy, the congregation ingeniously wrote a thank-you letter to God, and sent a carbon copy to Robert Woodruff.[4]

Woodruff established his own grant-making institution, the Trebor ("Robert" spelled backward to secure anonymity) Foundation in 1937.[5] The next year another family foundation bearing his parents' name (the Ernest and Emily Woodruff Fund) came into being. Clearly, new tax law played a role in these decisions: the Revenue Act of 1935 imposed taxes of 70 percent on estates of more than $50 million.

A Culture of Philanthropy

This form of philanthropy seems to have worked its way into the psyche of the Coca-Cola bottlers' network. Also in 1937, the Joseph B. Whitehead Foundation was formed in Atlanta, and the next year both the Memorial Welfare Foundation of Chattanooga (the first private foundation in Tennessee; later renamed the Lyndhurst Foundation) and the RosaMary Foundation of New Orleans (see chapter 11 sidebar) were established by bottlers in those cities. Yet another Coca-Cola fortune in Chattanooga—created by Benjamin Thomas of the Coca-Cola Bottling Company—led to the establishment of the Benwood Foundation (1944). It sometimes seemed as if every Coca-Cola bottling franchise in

ANOTHER "FIZZY" PHILANTHROPY FUND

In 1905 Claud Hatcher, a pharmacist in Columbus, Georgia, introduced a new syrup, Royal Crown Ginger Ale. For a variety of reasons, what became Royal Crown Cola and is still bottled and sold, never achieved the national or international popularity of that other carbonated beverage from Georgia. The company, which for a period operated under the name Chero-Cola and then Nehi, managed to survive the Great Depression. Legend has it that DeWitt Clinton Pickett, a business associate, played a major role in saving the company from ruin.

When Hatcher died in 1933, he left a significant portion of his estate to establish a philanthropic endowment. Also according to legend, he honored Clinton by naming it the Pickett & Hatcher Educational Fund. Since then, this remarkable, revolving loan fund has awarded more than $100 million to college students nationally, but primarily from the Southeast.

Source: Alan Rothschild, "100 Years of Philanthropy in Columbus," *Columbus and the Valley* (June 2016), 15-22.

the South brought with it a virtual license to print money, and many of those bottlers established foundations and found other ways to serve their communities.

Bradley-Turner Foundation

Another Coca-Cola story tied to philanthropy merits mention. W. C. Bradley's name is virtually synonymous with Columbus, Georgia, and closely linked with both Coca-Cola and the textiles industry. A long-time chair of the Coca-Cola Company board, Bradley prospered with Woodruff's success. Bradley and his Columbus business partner, D. A. Turner, combined their capital to build a west Georgia manufacturing empire. The W. C. Bradley Company also owned the textile mills lining the banks of the Chattahoochee River that separated Columbus and Phenix City, Alabama. Four years before Bradley's death in 1947, the two of them created the W. C. and Sarah H. Bradley Foundation (today known as the Bradley-Turner Foundation).[6] Under the later leadership of D. A. Turner's grandson, William B. (Bill) Turner[7], who also served on the Coca-Cola Company board during one of the most profitable periods in its history, the family's generosity transformed the city through its several foundations. It is questionable whether any family foundation operations, with the exception of the Woodruff-related philanthropies in Atlanta, have had as dramatic an impact upon a single municipality as the Bradley-Turner interests have had upon Columbus.

During World War II, at General Dwight Eisenhower's request, the government established sixty-four Coca-Cola bottling plants around the world to ensure that anyone serving in the armed forces could have access to a bottle of Coke for a nickel. Many of these wartime plants were later converted to civilian use, permanently enlarging the bottling system and accelerating the growth of the company's worldwide business.

The multiplier effect of this product is almost incalculable; early investments in Coca-Cola by individuals in Georgia and elsewhere created personal fortunes that in turn led to the creation of other foundations.

For the People of North Carolina

Another citadel of new philanthropy was emerging in North Carolina. There, in addition to the Duke Endowment, the Reynolds family, like Duke, built its early wealth from the growing, packaging, and marketing of tobacco products and made Winston-Salem its home. The wealth of the Reynolds family would establish four foundations that have had major statewide, regional, and even national impact.

ROBERTO GOIZUETA

Keeping alive the relationship of Coca-Cola–related wealth to philanthropy during the past quarter-century has been the Goizueta Foundation, one of Georgia's largest and lowest-profile philanthropic institutions. Its name honors Roberto Goizueta (1931–1997).

A native of Cuba and a graduate of Yale University, Goizueta began his relationship with Coca-Cola as a chemical engineer in his country and soon became chief engineer for the company's five bottling plants. After Fidel Castro seized power in Cuba, Goizueta and his family left the country with little more than $200 and 100 shares of Coca-Cola stock. They settled in Miami, where Goizueta worked for Coke's Latin American division for a few years before relocating to Coke's Atlanta headquarters. His rise up the corporate ladder was swift, and by 1980 he was named president and then board chairman. Under his lengthy stewardship, which continued until his death, the price of the company stock increased 3,500%, and the company tripled in size.

Goizueta established the foundation that bears his name in 1992. From the beginning, its primary focus has been on strategic ventures in early childhood, elementary, and high school education as well as other programs and institutions to strengthen the Atlanta metro area.

Sources: Chris Starrs, "Roberto Goizueta (1931–1997)," *New Georgia Encyclopedia*, last modified February 19, 2017, https://www.georgiaencyclopedia.org/articles/business-economy/roberto-goizueta-1931-1997; Maria Saporta, "Roberto Goizueta's Legacy Lives on in Atlanta," *Atlanta Business Chronicle*, July 4-10, 2014; www.goizuetafoundation.org.

In 1936, a year before the establishment of the Trebor Foundation in Georgia, Dick, Mary, and Nancy Reynolds, children of Reynolds Tobacco Company founder R. J. Reynolds, created the Z. Smith Reynolds Foundation to honor their brother. (In an unsolved mystery, Zachary Smith Reynolds, not yet twenty-one years old, had been found dead of a gunshot wound in the family home.)

From the start, that foundation established a tradition of imaginative and progressive generosity. Its first philanthropic act was the disbursement of its entire grant-making corpus for several years to institutional and programmatic partners for the eradication of venereal disease throughout the state. The funding of that enterprise continued for a decade. It was followed by the provision of major support for what became the Z. Smith Reynolds Airport, serving their home city of Winston-Salem and Forsyth County.

The medical school of Wake Forest University, named for the town in which it was situated, had already moved to Winston-Salem, a relocation underwritten by a 1935 bequest from Bowman Gray, president and chairman of the tobacco company. "Z. Smith" then supported the transfer of the rest of the institution to a new campus on the family's estate, Reynolds Village, and the construction of several facilities. (See additional information about Reynolds philanthropy in later chapters.)

In 1946, before her death, Katherine Bidding Reynolds, the wife of "Will" Reynolds, chairman of the R. J. Reynolds Company, and the sister-in-law of R. J. Reynolds, the corporation's founder, established the Kate B. Reynolds Charitable Trust to continue the work that she had championed during her lifetime. Its "poor and needy" division was to use its resources to improve the welfare of the people of Winston-Salem and Forsyth County, while the larger health care division was intended to serve the health and medical needs of charity patients elsewhere in North Carolina.

In 1934, soon after a visit to Sapelo Island, the fourth-largest of Georgia's barrier islands and home to perhaps the most pristine salt marsh in the world, Dick Reynolds purchased virtually all of the island from a financially strapped Howard Coffin, an industrial executive from Detroit. Fourteen years later, a chance meeting on the island between Reynolds and zoologist

Sapelo Island Lighthouse on the southern tip of Sapelo Island, Georgia, 2017.
Courtesy of the Library of Congress, LC-DIG-highsm- 43471

Wait Chapel at Wake Forest University, 2006.
Courtesy of Wikimedia Commons.

Eugene Odum from the University of Georgia (often called the "father of modern ecology") and subsequent negotiations led to the transfer of part of the island to the university's research facilities and the formation of the Sapelo Foundation.[8] Under three generations of family leadership, the foundation's mission has evolved. As it states, the foundation "promotes progressive social change affecting, in particular, vulnerable populations, rural communities, and the natural environment in the state of Georgia."

Mary Reynolds Babcock inherited $30 million from her father in 1936, making her one of the world's richest women. During her lifetime she became the principal benefactor of Wake Forest University, and in 1953, after her death, her estate made possible the creation of a fourth family-related philanthropy, the Mary Reynolds Babcock Foundation (see Afterword for further information about the foundation's unique mission).

Mary Reynolds Babcock, ca. 1928
Courtesy of the Reynolds House
Museum of American Art Archives

Taxation and Foundation Formation

According to some economists and economic historians, it was not just the war effort or innate generosity that pushed the South into this promising new philanthropic era. Sometimes overlooked is the role that federal taxation played.

The first "modern" U.S. income tax had taken effect in 1913. Its top marginal tax rate was 7% (and the new law granted an exemption to low-income earners, who comprised about 70% of the working population). To pay the expenses incurred after the U.S. entry into World War I in 1918, the highest marginal rate escalated to 77% with the same exemption in place. After the war, the top marginal tax rate ebbed and flowed from a high of 46% in 1924 (the year in which the Duke Endowment was created) to a low of 24% in 1929.

In 1933, with the country in the depths of its worst financial crisis in history, and to underwrite its national recovery efforts, Franklin D. Roosevelt and Congress raised the top marginal tax rate to 63%—and then to 79% in 1936, and 94% (its highest level yet) during the last two years of World War II.[9]

As in the World War I era, the 1930s and 1940s witnessed a combination of patriotic zeal and progressive tax policies, which stimulated a rivulet (if not yet a flood) of new foundations in the South. It seems quite clear that many of the new foundations that came into being during the New Deal and World War II period were motivated by charitable impulse but also took advantage of deductions and exemptions to avoid the high taxes being levied by the federal government.[10]

They continued to pop up across the South. Among those small

230 THE LIBERATING PROMISE OF PHILANTHROPY

foundations that remain in existence are the Charles B. Keesee Educational Fund in Martinsville, Virginia (1941); the Chapin Foundation in Myrtle Beach, South Carolina (1943); the Dickson Foundation in Charlotte, North Carolina (1944); and the Inman-Riverdale Foundation in Inman, South Carolina (1947).

J. Bulow Campbell

Many of these new foundations had relatively modest endowments. A notable exception occurred in 1940, when J. Bulow Campbell of Atlanta bequeathed approximately $7 million from his estate to establish a private foundation that now bears his name. The owner of the Campbell Coal Company, Campbell also served on the boards of the Coca-Cola Company and the Trust Company of Georgia. He was a devout Presbyterian who was deeply influenced by his fellow parishioner John J. Eagan (see chapter 9). During Campbell's lifetime he had already demonstrated great generosity not only to his church, Central Presbyterian of Atlanta, but also to Columbia Theological Seminary (whose relocation from South Carolina to Decatur, Georgia, he underwrote); Berry College (founded by his sister-in-law, Martha Berry); Agnes Scott College; and Rabun Gap–Nacoochee School, for which he served as founding chairman. Today, the Campbell Foundation continues to follow his example of giving anonymously and requesting that grant recipients not publicize the source of their support. Thus, despite being one of Georgia's largest foundations, with assets of well in excess of half a billion dollars, and despite having been a significant donor to many not-for-profit institutions in Atlanta and elsewhere in Georgia, the

Campbell Foundation and the name of its founder remain deliberately and successfully obscured.

Textile Foundations

Any reference to the creation of organized philanthropy in the South during the 1940s and 1950s demands special mention of the wealth accumulated from war-related textile manufacturing and the powerful impact it had upon many sections of the region. The first such textile-based foundation seems to have been the Gregg-Graniteville Foun-

Graniteville Mill, Graniteville, South Carolina
Library of Congress, Prints & Photographs Division, HAER SC,2-GRANV,1--3.

dation, established in South Carolina in 1941.[11] Its roots stretch back to 1845 when William Gregg, a Virginia native sometimes referred to as the father of Southern cotton manufacturing, received a charter for the Graniteville Company. A visionary who carefully studied the industry in

England and New England to seek new efficiencies, he relied on local people to build the mill as well as to operate it, and offered wages that were on the same level as those paid to Northern mill workers.

Somewhat of a utopian for his day, and certainly a practitioner of an enlightened brand of paternalism, Gregg also provided quality housing for his workers, as well as a church and a small library. Employees received medical care for a small fee and had access to gardens and woods from which to harvest timber. Gregg also created what was perhaps the first compulsory education system in the United States. He built a school for children six to twelve years old, furnished teachers and books, and fined parent workers five cents a day, withheld from their wages, for every day their children were absent from classes.[12]

A year after the formation of the Gregg-Graniteville Foundation, James C. Self, founder of what would become Greenwood Mills in the South Carolina town of the same name, incorporated the Self Foundation with the primary purpose of building a hospital for the people of the county. When the hospital opened in 1951, Self described it as a "debt of gratitude to the community that has been so good to me." The mission of the foundation (now called the Self Family Foundation) continued for many years to be "helping people help themselves." Today's version affirms that the foundation "encourages self-sufficiency in people and the communities in which they live."[13]

In 1942 a colorful World War I flying ace and textile tycoon, Elliott Springs, created the Springs Foundation in Fort Mill, South Carolina. A year later, Charles A. Cannon, the head of

Cannon Mills for fifty years, established the Cannon Foundation in Concord, North Carolina, to serve the communities in which the company had manufacturing operations.

Most of the mill owners recognized that it was in their own self-interest to extend their employees a variety of benefits, e.g., housing (the Greenwood Mills worker homes were constructed of brick), churches, elementary schools, health clinics, garden plots, and recreational facilities. Col. Elliott Springs and his family were especially solicitous. They provided their employees and their communities with swimming pools, bowling alleys, parks, tennis courts, and ballfields. Additionally, they purchased a large tract of land on the coast of South Carolina and constructed affordable, beachfront rental units for vacationing employees (Springmaid Beach) and then later a forest retreat (Springmaid Mountain) near the Blue Ridge Parkway in western North Carolina. Operations were paid from income and an annual subsidy from the family foundation.

Callaway Philanthropy

Fuller E. Callaway of LaGrange, Georgia, built a textile-centered business empire and became one of

THE COLONEL

Colonel Elliott Springs, the World War I flying ace and later aerial barnstormer, rarely did anything in a small way and usually seemed to have fun doing it. After settling down to manage the textile company he inherited from his father, Springs still found time to compose risqué copy to advertise the Springmaid bedsheets his mills produced, write fiction, and enjoy partying with celebrity friends in New York and elsewhere.

One of the family's holdings was the Lancaster and Chester Railroad, a twenty-nine-mile spur between those two South Carolina communities. In the 1930s the colonel got the idea to appoint twenty-nine vice presidents to the railway, one for each mile of track. They included playwright Charles MacArthur, golfer Bobby Jones, radio newscaster Lowell Thomas, and other friends. What garnered the most attention was his designation of Gypsy Rose Lee, the country's best-known striptease artist, as vice president in charge of unveiling.

Source: Burke Davis, *War Bird: The Life and Times of Elliott White Springs* (Chapel Hill: University of North Carolina Press, 1987).

CREATION OF FORD FOUNDATION

In 1936 Edsel Ford, president of the Ford Motor Company and the only son of Henry Ford, formed the Ford Foundation with a donation of $25,000—in part to avoid the extremely high inheritance taxes being imposed on large estates during the Great Depression. With a broadly conceived mission ("the advancement of human welfare"), and based in New York City, the Ford Foundation became a multibillion dollar global institution, and for a time was the largest foundation in the world. When Edsel Ford died in 1943 at the age of thirty-nine, he was succeeded as president of both the company and the foundation by his oldest son, Henry Ford II. The foundation soon became, and remains, an important benefactor to Southern institutions and programs.

https://www.fordfoundation.org/about/about-ford/our-origins/

the region's most-admired industrialists. Tapped by Presidents Woodrow Wilson and Warren Harding to serve on a variety of commissions, he also was profiled glowingly in a 1921 article by Ida Tarbell, the famous investigative journalist. Callaway's business acumen included a concern for employee benefits, and the title of Tarbell's profile drew upon his famous saying, that he built American citizens and ran cotton mills to pay for the expense of that enterprise.

His son, Fuller E. Callaway Jr., extended the family's long-standing support of LaGrange and the surrounding area by forming what became the Callaway Foundation (originally called the Callaway Community Foundation) in 1943.[14] (Note: despite the name, it was not a community foundation.)

During this period, further evidence of a linkage between textile manufacturing and philanthropy emerged with the formation of other foundations. They included the Dover Foundation in Shelby, North Carolina (1944); the Joanna Foundation in Sullivan Island, South Carolina (1945); the Inman-Riverdale Foundation in Inman, South Carolina (1946); the Hamrick Mills Foundation in Gaffney, South Carolina (1953); and the Abney

Foundation in Anderson, South Carolina (1957).

Although many of these textile-related foundations have been generous in support of institutions and causes elsewhere in their states, they have for the most part been primarily "place-based," focusing the bulk of their philanthropy upon the improvement of their local communities' health, education, and general welfare.[15]

A Postwar Philanthropic Spirit

Northern philanthropy had never really left the South, despite the fact that its work usually required compromise with the existing, restricted social order. Now, though, some foundations, building upon earlier strategic approaches, elected not simply to alleviate the effects of racial discrimination but instead to support studies that documented its crippling impact.

A key example came from the Carnegie Corporation, which supported the 1944 publication of Gunnar Myrdal's *An American Dilemma: The Negro Problem and American Democracy*; Myrdal's work would be cited in the Supreme Court's *Brown v. Board of Education* decision a decade later. Within a week of the Carnegie publication's issue, the Ford Foundation-funded book, *The Negro and the Schools* by Harry Ashmore, provided a comprehensive study of racial inequity among public schools in the South.

The slowly growing number of not-for-profit organizations in the South could now look to increased support from the growing number of indigenous private foundations. Churches, the primary recipients of foundation generosity in the region, were establishing social-service programs and agencies for some of the South's neediest citizens. As in the North, the South's white, middle-class women organized volunteer clubs that advocated for the improvement of schools and city beautification. A burgeoning African American middle class financially supported its HBCUs, college fraternities and sororities (many of which dated back to the 1930s and focused on the professional advancement of their members), and other such organizations as Jack and Jill of America.[16] Corporate and individual generosity contributed to the formation and sustenance of symphony orchestras, opera companies, and museums.

United Negro College Fund

Private African American colleges and universities established in the post–Civil War years (see chapter 3) had since their founding collec-

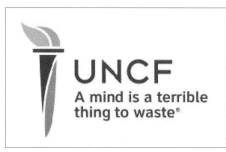

United Negro College Fund, Inc. logo
Courtesy of the United Negro College Fund, Inc.

tively functioned as one of the most significant resources to the black population of the South— laying the groundwork (against all sorts of financial odds in a Jim Crow climate) for assembling a strong black middle and professional class. Almost invisible to white eyes, the private ones especially (ineligible for the "separate but equal" support from state governments) had struggled each year to keep their doors open.

Now, though, veteran fund raisers could sense a shift of philanthropic currents; more people and businesses were garnering more disposable income and profits. In 1944 Frederick Patterson, president of the Tuskegee Institute in Alabama, and Mary McLeod Bethune, former president of what became Bethune-Cookman College in Daytona Beach, Florida, formed the United Negro College Fund. Its principal goal was to attract a stream of annual funding to twenty-seven of these institutions. This "appeal to the national conscience" attracted the early support of Franklin D. and Eleanor Roosevelt and John D. Rockefeller Jr., as well as other Northern foundations and corporations. As it tapped into post–World War II wealth, it generated significant support for this federated fund-raising program.[18]

In the South, generally speaking, most of the newly formed foundations were doing what many of their counterparts elsewhere in the country were doing—building and strengthening the educational, religious, cultural, health-nurturing, and recreational institutions and programs for white citizens that enhanced the quality of their lives and made their communities more inviting to newcomers. Those grant-makers that quietly directed a portion of their support to historically black private institutions and segregated public institutions and agencies considered this strategy of support to be fair.

The Shadow Side Resurfaces

The South clearly was in a restorative mode, but there continued to be stark reminders that the road to recovery was still far from that destination. In 1945, even as the surviving troops returned home from World War II, the Carnegie Corporation issued *The American Soldier* by Samuel Stouffer. Commissioned by the War Department and utilizing the then-novel method of opinion polling, it uncovered a deep chasm between the nation's democratic ideals and the U.S. military's practices. The War Department's response to the exposé that racism against African Americans had been rampant even as the interracial armed forces pursued victory was tempered. It did not propose desegregation of America's military, but it did recommend a "more efficient use" of personnel.

A harsh postscript to the report surfaced in February 1946. Isaac Woodward, an African American discharged from the army at Camp Gordon in Augusta, was travelling home to North Carolina in uniform on a Greyhound bus. Near Aiken, South Carolina, police detained and savagely beat him, blinding him in both eyes. President Harry Truman, upon learning of this lynching, ordered the federal prosecution of police chief Linwood Shull and his deputies. An all-white jury subsequently acquitted them. Later that same year, at Moore's Ford in Walton County, Georgia, two African American veterans and their wives (George and Mae Murray Dorsey, and Roger and Dorothy Malcom) were lynched, their bodies riddled by more than sixty bullets. No one was prosecuted for the crime.

Shocked by these news reports, as was much of the rest of the nation, Truman quickly moved forward on a plan to desegregate the armed forces via executive order rather than using the more circuitous and uncertain legislative process. Issuing the order in 1948, he declared as national policy "equality of treatment and opportunity for all persons in the armed services without regard to race, color, religion, or national origin." It would take five years to implement the order fully. By the mid-to-late 1940s, then, portions of yet another "new" South still looked very old and sadly familiar. If real change were to occur, it would depend upon a seismic shift at the core of society.

CHAPTER 10 ENDNOTES

1   Sources for information about The Coca-Cola Company and the foundations generated by its success include Constance L. Hays, *The Real Thing: Truth and Power at the Coca-Cola Company* (New York: Random House, 2004); Mark Pendergrast, *For God, Country, and Coca-Cola: The Definitive History of the Great American Soft Drink and the Company That Makes It,* 2nd ed. (New York: Basic, 2000); Mike Cheatham, *"Your Friendly Neighbor": The Story of Georgia's Coca-Cola Bottling Families* (Macon, Ga.: Mercer University Press, 1999); Frederick Allen, *Secret Formula: How Brilliant Marketing and Relentless Salesmanship Made Coca-Cola the Best-Known Product in the World* (New York: HarperCollins, 1994).

2   Andrew Land, "The Social and Civic Impacts of Robert Winship Woodruff in the City of Atlanta During the 1960s" (master's thesis, Clemson University, 2007). *https://tigerprints.clemson.edu/all_theses/103.*

3   It was the beginning of a pattern that continues today. The Woodruff-related philanthropies have over the years played a quiet but significant role in encouraging the relocation to Atlanta of the headquarters for the American Cancer Society, the Arthritis Foundation, the Boys and Girls Clubs of America, CARE, and the Taskforce for Global Health, as well as the regional office of the Foundation Center.

4   Land, "Social and Civic Impacts of Robert Winship Woodruff."

5   In 1985, after his death, the name was changed to the Robert W. Woodruff Foundation. With assets exceeding $3 billion, it is the largest private foundation in Georgia and the second-largest in the South.

6   Laura McCarty, "W. C. Bradley," *New Georgia Encyclopedia,* last modified July 10, 2018, *https://www.georgiaencyclopedia.org/articles/business-economy/w-c-bradley-1863-1947*; and Laura McCarty, "Bradley-Turner Foundation," *New Georgia Encyclopedia,* last modified July 23, 2018, *https://www.georgiaencyclopedia.org/articles/business-economy/bradley-turner-foundation.*

7   Bill Turner was deeply influenced by the concept of servant leadership, an idea first introduced by Robert K. Greenleaf, a former AT&T executive, in 1970, and became a tireless advocate of its importance. He also authored a memoir, *The Learning of Love: A Journey toward Servant Leadership* (Macon, Ga.: Smith & Helwys, 2000).

8   Thomas Brendler, *A Part of This Earth: The Story of the Sapelo Foundation,* the Sapelo Foundation, 2015.

9   A complete table of the historical highest marginal income tax rates from 1913 to 2018 can be found at the Tax Policy Center's website: *https://www.taxpolicycenter.org/statistics/historical-highest-marginal-income-tax-rates.*

10 *https://bradfordtaxinstitute.com/Free_Resources/Federal-Income-Tax-Rates.aspx; https://www.cch.com/wbot2013/029IncomeTaxRates.asp.*

Ordinary citizens also were beginning to feel the "tax bite." Four million Americans paid federal taxes in 1939, but 43 million were doing so by 1945. As Christopher Tassava describes the change: "Over the same period, federal tax revenue grew from about 8 percent of GDP to more than 20 percent. Americans who earned as little as $500 per year paid income tax at a 23 per cent rate, whole those who earned more than $1 million per year paid a 94 percent rate." "World War II Economy" in EH. Net *Encyclopedia of Economic and Business History,* RobertWhaples, ed. (2005).

11 *Southeastern Council of Foundations Membership Directory* (10th edition), 2005, 88.

12 *https://www.encyclopedia.com/people/social-sciences-and-law/business-leaders/william-gregg.*

13 Correspondence with Frank J. Wideman, III, June 24, 2019.

14 Authors' note: It is interesting that, until recently, few actual community foundations were established in mill towns—so complete was the public care-taking provided by the mill owners and their private foundations. One of the exceptions is the Greenwood County (SC) Community Foundation.

15 In 1919, years before the surge in the growth of textile-related foundations, Fuller E. Callaway established the Textile Association Foundation to support the health, educational, religious, recreational, and other needs of the community. Its assets were transferred to the Callaway Community Foundation in 1944. Buckner F. Melton, Jr. and Carol Willcox Melton, *Fuller E. Callaway: Portrait of New South Citizen* (Winston-Salem: Looking Glass Books, Inc., 2015).

16 *https://jackandjillinc.org/about-us/*. Jack and Jill of America was established in Philadelphia in 1938 after Marion Stubbs Thomas brought together 20 African American mothers to discuss creating an organization to provide social, cultural and educational opportunities for youth between the ages of 2 and 19.

17 As late as 1970, Atlanta, one of the South's largest cities, had a population of 496,000, comparable to that of Buffalo, New York, with 462,768. However, Atlanta's city expenditures were 33% less and its indebtedness 25% higher. Buffalo's per capita expenditure for public education was $309.41, compared with Atlanta's per capita expenditure of $9.60. U.S. Census Bureau, Population Reports (Characteristics of Cities of 50,000 or More), 1975.

18 See Marybeth Gasman, *Envisioning Black Colleges: A History of the United Negro College Fund* (Baltimore: Johns Hopkins University Press, 2007).

In more recent years UNCF, which includes thirty-seven institutions, added to its mission the distribution of individual scholarships (for attendance at any college) to minority students, including African Americans, Native Americans, Hispanic Americans, and Asian Americans. It also administers the Gates Millennium Scholars program, funded with $1.6 billion from the Bill and Melinda Gates Foundation. Other major supporters have included Walter Annenberg ($50 million) and Koch Industries and the Charles Koch Foundation ($25 million).

CHAPTER 11

Peace, Prosperity. . . . and Change

Further Economic Strength

The seismic shift that would eventually transform the region was still a distant rumble. In the meantime, economic growth continued. Despite the double whammy of a Great Depression and wartime restrictions, the once-hardscrabble South seemed at last to have hit pay dirt, as previously discussed: Coca-Cola was on an apparently unstoppable growth curve; modernized textile manufacturing flourished throughout the Piedmont; the tobacco industry in Virginia and the Carolinas was immensely profitable; and the Black Belt diversified from a one-crop cotton economy to raising cattle, broilers, peanuts, and eventually soybeans as well.

Behind this transformation were not only the New Deal's rural initiatives but also the demands (and scientific advances) of a wartime and postwar economy. As an example, better technology led to more efficient and affordable tractors as well as improved mechanical cotton pickers (supplemented by herbicides and pesticides). On the way out was the icon of the mule, the "foundation and symbol" of a recent past

Catalogue cover for a prominent house plan company, helping to meet the demand for homes after World War II.
National Plan Service, Inc.

that "patiently bore his lot in Southern life for more than a century."[1] In Alabama alone, where 5,000 tractors had been operating in 1930, there were 46,000 by 1950. Growing efficiency in farm output also meant fewer farm laborers. (Only 2% of the U.S. population is today engaged in agricultural work.)

The petrochemical industries in Louisiana, as in Texas, continued to accelerate, accounting for more than half of the nation's oil production by 1955, and Florida's vacation industry (and its population) boomed. Peace (for a time) and relative prosperity reigned for many Americans—no more dramatically than in yet another "new" South. The region abounded in glitz, paved highways, and suburbs.

As described by James C. Cobb in *The Selling of the South*, in comparison with the North, southern states could also offer a predominantly non-unionized workforce and a history of comparatively lower wages, a more salubrious climate, cheap cost of land, lower-cost housing, and in general, a more modest cost of living.[2] Bundled with tax exemptions and other offers from municipalities, counties, and state governments, the South presented a package that was difficult for a Northern business to resist. Not incidental to the mix was the evolving technology of air-conditioning (one million AC units were sold in 1953) that found its way into homes, offices, restaurants, schools, hotels, motels, airports, and automobiles.

The TV series *The Adventures of Ozzie and Harriet* became synonymous with 1950s ideal American values and family life.
American Broadcasting Company and Stage Five Productions

Simultaneously, and for more than a decade after the war, the Serviceman's Readjustment Act of 1944 (known as the "GI Bill") opened more Southern colleges to more students, who upon graduation were positioned to populate new business enterprises with both basic and advanced skills. Indeed, it was the GI Bill, in the opinion of historian Doris Kearns Goodwin, that became the stimulus for "remarkable postwar expansion that followed across the country" and made the United States a "more middle-class society than we have been before."[3]

An interstate-highway around Charlotte, North Carolina
Courtesy of the Library of Congress, LC-DIG-highsm-43344

By the late 1950s, television was helping to create a new national culture that began to blur regional distinctions. In 1957, 60.9 million homes (76% of all dwellings nationwide) owned at least one TV set.

American automobile production set new records every year, so it was no surprise when President Dwight Eisenhower's 1956 proposal for construction of an interstate highway system received near-unanimous endorsement from the Congress. Just as electric trollies in the 1880s had launched the construction of nearby suburbs to which employees could commute from central workplaces, now automobiles and highways fueled the "escape" from the cities.

Philanthropy Expanding

As wealth grew, new foundation formation continued around the region. Among those individuals whose sense of noblesse oblige or charitable obligation led them to establish charitable endowments was James Graham Brown of Louisville, Kentucky, a lumberman, horseman, and entrepreneur. He formally incorporated his eponymous foundation in 1954 and left the bulk of his estate to serve the citizens of his city and state when he died in 1969. Other new philanthropies were the Courts Foundation (1950), created by an Atlanta investment banking and real estate investment firm partner; the Robins Foundation of Richmond, Virginia (1957), established with assets from the A. H. Robins pharmaceutical company; and the William G. Selby and Marie Selby Foundation of Sarasota, Florida (1955), funded by a family oil-drilling company that had merged with Texaco.

The Southern Education Foundation—formed in 1937 by the consolidation of the pioneering Peabody, Slater, Jeanes, and Randolph funds—had been based in Washington, D.C., where four U.S. presidents served on its board.[4] In 1950 it relocated to Atlanta. There, under the leadership of J. Curtis Dixon, the Foundation built its own facility in order to be able to conduct its biracial board meetings (a unique practice during Jim Crow). The Southern Education Foundation's move signaled a renewed commitment to meeting head-on some of the region's fundamental inequities in education—though again there were practical limits to what it could do and the mechanisms through which it could operate.

Tzedakah

The Hebrew word *tzedakah* can be literally translated as "justice" or "righteousness." For the faithful Jew, it is a religious obligation to do what is just and right. Penelope McPhee, president of The Arthur M. Blank Family Foundation, offered these observations as part of her remarks at the opening of an art exhibit entitled "Tzedakah—The Art of Giving" at the Breman Jewish Heritage Museum in Atlanta on August 31, 2006:

> In the Jewish tradition, all people are obligated to give to their fullest capacity. . . . It's not simply a matter of generosity, kindness or goodness; it's a matter of simple justice. . . . Those who *have* are required to help those who do not. . . . And like so many other aspects of Jewish faith and culture, it's not negotiable!

In a previous chapter we held up Julius Rosenwald as a unique standard-setter, and elsewhere in this book we also reference other Jewish philanthropists. All are part of an often unpublicized yet highly significant pattern of generosity by Jewish merchants and other business-people in the South—especially after 1945.[5] Once the frequent target of discrimination, social ostracism, and even violence against themselves and their institutions, Jewish philanthropies have been key players in the building of such major civic institutions as hospitals, libraries, museums, and parks in virtually every metropolitan area of the region.[6]

Space does not permit the listing of all their names, but in Birmingham, Memphis, New Orleans, Richmond, Charlotte, Atlanta, and many other cities and towns, department stores and other commercial establishments that bore the names of their Jewish owners appeared frequently on the major donor lists of citywide fund-raising campaigns. Not to be overlooked in this pattern of giving are rabbis, regularly exhorting their synagogue members not just to be generous but also to remember the religious obligation to pursue justice.

Those Jews of a compassionate and social justice bent found it difficult—even dangerous—to advocate against intolerance and bigotry when it surfaced in the communities where they did business. Yet, they and their spiritual leaders were among the minority who remained active and whose family foundations supported a variety of initiatives to pursue the rights of African Americans and other marginalized groups (discussed later in this chapter).[7]

Assets vs. Attitudes

Economic improvement came steadily. Given the distance it had to travel, it moved at a measured pace. However, impeding progress were not the understandable limits of newly formed, indigenous public and private capital. As big a factor was the determination of many white citizens to retain a stratified society, one that turned on race, social class, hierarchy and paternalism. Thus, both organized white Southern philanthropy and the grant-making of Northern foundations during the post–

World War II years benignly helped to perpetuate the legalized racial segregation that dominated the region's life by funding separate black hospitals, educational institutions, and other helping agencies. Clearly, the social dynamics of the South would have to change radically before many more of its people (more than one-third of whom continued to live in poverty) could share in the growing prosperity being enjoyed by much of the rest of the nation. Whatever one's thoughts about racial segregation or other forms of white, male supremacy, one fact was clear: discrimination and inequity remained as distinct barriers to economic success. Until that pattern changed, any differences between the Old South and the post–World War II region would have to be measured in degree rather than kind. From that perspective, the region still looked sadly familiar: a racially divided land to which not even the personal and family generosity of some concerned white Southerners and limited Northern philanthropy seemed able to bring lasting change.

Shifts of the Wind

Yet, changes were in the air—coming from sometimes new and sometimes unexpected directions. Decades after the formation of the Negro Rural School Fund in 1905, Jeanes Supervisors (now paid by their states) and other teachers, working in Rosenwald and other segregated schools, were still going about their business. Officially tasked with the vocational education of young African Americans, they were accomplishing much more. Many of those who belonged to the National Association for the Advancement of Colored People (NAACP) or all-black state teachers organizations kept their young charges informed about the continuing work to achieve equal education and voting rights, even as they prepared them not just for the trades and home-making but also for attending the historically black colleges and universities around the region.

Brown v. Board of Education

On May 17, 1954, the Supreme Court ruling in *Brown v. Board of Education* ended the officially imposed racial segregation of public education by overruling the "separate but equal" 1896 Supreme Court decision in *Plessy v. Ferguson*.[8] The *Brown* decision, written by Chief Justice Earl Warren and supported unanimously by the other justices, generated defiant political rhetoric from white politicians, and even a campaign of "massive resistance" that triggered the ubiquitous sprouting of "IMPEACH EARL WARREN" signs in Southern fields. Truth be told, though, the ruling barely rippled the surface of everyday Southern life.

Until the *Brown* decision, it presumably had remained possible for white people of good will to favor or at least accept the concept of an educated yet still segregated African American population. As we have described, from the time of the first philanthropic forays of Northern-based foundations into the South on behalf of African American education, most of that well-intentioned work had included cautious strategies to avoid triggering explosions in the racism-charged atmosphere. The historic 1954 Supreme Court ruling blew a hole through the "separate but equal" concept, and gave philanthropy a vital resource with which to justify challenges to the status quo.

Emboldened Philanthropy

One of the first foundations to respond to this radical ruling was the idealistically named New World Foundation, established that same year, in New York. Its founder was Anita McCormick Blaine, daughter and an heiress of Virginia-born industrialist Cyrus Hall McCormick, contributing inventor of the McCormick Reaper. Blaine had supported the 1948 presidential campaign of Henry Wallace and

Martin Luther King Jr., Pete Seeger, Rosa Parks and Ralph Abernathy at Highlander Folk School in 1957.
Highlander Research and Education Center

was deeply involved in the promotion of progressive education, ethics, peace, and public health. She died before the new foundation with $7 million in assets made a single grant, but her granddaughter, Anne Blaine Harrison, steered the New World Foundation in the direction of supporting the battle for civil rights. Harrison, who herself had been an organizer for the Textile Workers of America, was drawn to the unique work of an institution that began as the Highlander Folk School.

Highlander: No Ordinary School

Established in 1932 on two hundred acres near Monteagle, Tennessee, by Myles Horton and Donald West, the Highlander Folk School offered residential adult workshops, initially with mill, timber, and unemployed

COURAGEOUS PHILANTHROPY IN NEW ORLEANS

It took many black and white heroes (named and unnamed) in New Orleans and elsewhere to bring about significant social change in the Crescent City. The names of Stern, Freeman, and Wisdom merit special mention, however. These socially prominent and courageous families and their foundations played critical roles in promoting justice and equity, especially in the struggle for racial integration of the public schools.

The oldest foundation was the Edgar B. Stern Family Fund (later renamed the Stern Family Fund), established in 1936 by Edgar Stern Sr. and his wife, Edith, the daughter of Julius Rosenwald (see chapter 7), with gifts of their own cash as well as Lehman Corporation and Sears, Roebuck stock. During the Stern Fund's early years, according to one of the founders' descendants, "it made mainly mainstream grants to mainstream groups—grants that did not seek, as in later years, to get at root causes and bring about social change."

Stern, a Jewish cotton broker and highly influential leader, despite functioning in a rampantly anti-Semitic city, was nonetheless a "traditional" Southerner when it came to racial issues. He may have been sufficiently liberal to support the concept of economic advancement and education for African Americans (he served on the board of the historically black Dillard University), but he could not bring himself to accept the idea of social integration. His wife, however, had inherited her father's deep commitment to repairing the faults of the world. After her husband's death, the foundation became increasingly supportive of key organizations in the civil rights movement.

Alfred Bird ("A. B.") Freeman, an entrepreneurial salesman with limited formal education, who described himself as "a nobody from nowhere," moved with his wife, Ella, from Georgia to New Orleans in 1906 and acquired the license for the Louisiana Coca-Cola Bottling Company. He prospered and in 1937 established the RosaMary Foundation, named after his two daughters— Rosa (the younger) and Mary. In 1941 he created the Ella West Freeman Foundation to honor his wife, although she died a few years later. Some funds from her estate were added to the RosaMary Foundation corpus.

After making her social debut in 1932, Rosa Freeman met and married Charles Keller Jr., a Detroit native and graduate of West Point and M.I.T. Following Keller's military service in World War II, during which he earned a Bronze Star, the couple settled in New Orleans. Keller became a successful businessman and eventually a dedicated historic preservationist. In 1949, using ten shares of Coca-Cola Company stock as an initial gift, Charles and Rosa founded the Keller Family Foundation, originally formed as the Lincoln Foundation (to honor the 16th U.S. president).

In 1947 New Orleans was facing a critical postwar housing shortage. The Kellers, over dinner with friends and fellow philanthropists Edgar and Edith Stern, began a discussion that led to the couples financing the construction of Pontchartrain Park, one of the first middle-class black communities in the country.

Mary Elizabeth (Betty) Wisdom, the niece of Rosa Freeman, did not establish a foundation, but she used her income as a so-called Coca-Cola heiress to support the New Orleans school system when it was threatened with closure. A fierce, independent advocate for school desegregation, Wisdom, like her aunt, received regular death threats for her highly visible support of racial integration.

1   Quotation from Philip Stern, found in The Stern Fund: The History of a Progressive Family Foundation (Institute for Media Analysis, 1992), vii.

2   See Shannon Frystak, "Rosa Keller," Encyclopedia of Louisiana, last modified January 31, 2011; Mike Scott, " A Silver Spoon, an Iron Will, and a Spine of Steel," Times-Picayune, April 13, 2018, *https://www.nola.com/300/2018/04/rosa_keller_new_orleans_300_fo.html*; "Keller, Charles Jr. (1909–1996)," New Orleans Preservation Timeline Project, Tulane School of Architecture, accessed June 28, 2019, *http://architecture.tulane.edu/preservation-project/entity/432*; "The New Orleans Heiress Who Became a Civil Rights Champion," Times-Picayune, July 27, 2018, *https://www.nola.com/300/2018/07/betty_wisdom_new_orleans_300_f.html*.

workers from the surrounding area. John Glen, author of *Highlander: No Ordinary School*, describes the importance of this remarkable institution:

> By the late 1930s, the school's reputation grew and faculty members became directly involved in the Southern organizing drives mounted by the Congress of Industrial Organizations (CIO). For most of the next decade, they helped unionize textile workers in Tennessee and the Carolinas, directed large-scale labor education programs in eleven Southern states, and developed a residential program that promoted a broad-based, racially integrated, and politically active labor movement.

> Frustrated by the continued reluctance of existing organizations to overcome racial barriers to change, Highlander's teachers began holding workshops on public school desegregation in 1953, nearly a year before the U.S. Supreme Court's momentous decision in *Brown v. Board of Education* and the subsequent emergence of the civil rights movement in the South. Residential workshops gradually encompassed the challenges of community-wide integration. The sessions attracted hundreds of black and white activists including, shortly before the Montgomery bus boycott, Rosa Parks and Martin Luther King Jr.

> Highlander-sponsored Citizenship Schools, first held in 1957 on the South Carolina Sea Islands, taught thousands

of blacks in Tennessee, Georgia, and Alabama the literacy skills they needed to secure the right to vote. In the early 1960s, as sit-in protests erupted in Nashville and across the South, college students gathered at the folk school to explore the possible directions and goals for a new era of black protest; they also learned "freedom songs" adapted by Highlander musicians, including "We Shall Overcome." Through these programs Highlander became the educational center of the early civil rights movement.[10]

As Highlander became more prominent in the struggle for racial justice, already outraged Southern white segregationists launched a sustained assault against what they described as a "Communist training school." By 1962 the state authorities had revoked Highlander's charter and confiscated its property. Undeterred, the school's leaders secured a charter for a new institution called the Highlander Research and Education Center, based first in Knoxville and later near New Market. Other progressive Northern foundations began joining New World in its support of civil rights action and advocacy.

The famous December 1, 1955, arrest of Rosa Parks on a city bus triggered the formation of the Montgomery (Alabama) Improvement Association and a one-year bus boycott that ended successfully when the Supreme Court ruled that the city's seating ordinance violated the 14th Amendment. It was an outcome that also catapulted the movement's twenty-six-year-old leader, Martin Luther King Jr., to international fame.

The Movement

Brown v. Board of Education, the successful Montgomery bus boycott, and President Eisenhower's reluctant decision to use troops in the 1957 desegregation of Central High School in Little Rock, Arkansas, were victories, but they still stood as isolated incidents that only slightly scratched the veneer of Southern society.[11]

Then, on February 1, 1960, four students from A&T University of North Carolina sat themselves at a racially segregated Woolworth's lunch counter in Greensboro, North Carolina, and asked unsuccessfully to be served. The so-called sit-in movement was underway. College students in Nashville, Atlanta, and other Southern cities soon followed suit. The South, indeed the nation, would never again be the same.

Discussing the civil rights movement today, we tend to refer to that period in the early 1960s when bands of African American and sympathetic white students, courageous attorneys, charismatic black preachers, and others determined that they were "sick and tired of being sick and tired."[12] With remarkable boldness, they declared their opposition to state-sanctioned racial segregation in the South through a wide-ranging series of protests. The movement gained further moral depth by its Gandhi-inspired commitment to nonviolence by most of those who participated. Steadily increasing televised news coverage of its battlefields galvanized national energies behind the struggle for equality and justice and eventually would serve to catalyze the university students' free speech movement and a host of battles for the rights of women, gays, and other marginalized groups.

Of course, the genesis of the movement that crested in the 1960s originated long before then. It began the first time an enslaved African American resisted the domination of a "master" or a Quaker family freed the people it "owned." It was kept alive by the rebellion on the slave ship *Amistad*, by the revolt of Nat Turner and the plans of Denmark Vesey, by the establishment of schools for African Americans, and by many decades of struggle in the courts. In a sense, it continues today. Through the years it has received varying degrees of philanthropic support.

Among the first foundations to join the New World Foundation (see above) in responding to the "movement" activities were the Taconic Foundation, the Field Foundation, and the Stern Fund.[13] All were relatively small. All were based in offices on the Upper East Side of New York City. The assets for three of them derived from Northern corporate wealth. The Stern Fund (see sidebar in this chapter) had already been established a quarter-century earlier in New Orleans by the daughter and son-in-law of Julius Rosenwald. In 1963 it shifted its offices to New York City, where David Hunter, a social worker and former Ford Foundation program officer, assumed its directorship.

The four foundations became heavily involved in funding the Voter Education Project, a program of the Southern Regional Council in Atlanta. They did so with the strong encouragement of U.S. attorney general Robert F. Kennedy, who is credited with having conceived of the program in 1961. During this Cold War period, when many African nations were declaring their independence from colonial rule, the United States was competing with the Soviet Union for the favor of these newly independent countries. Robert Kennedy and his brother, John F. Kennedy, the recently elected president of the United States,

African American lawyer Vernon E. Jordan, Jr working on a voter education project at the Southern Regional Council, Atlanta, Georgia
Library of Congress, Prints & Photographs Division, U.S. News & World Report Magazine Collection, LC-DIG-ds-05214.

were deeply concerned by the poor international image of the United States that the protests portrayed.

The Field Foundation of New York was a spin-off from the Field Foundation in Chicago, created in 1940 by Marshall Field III, the grandson of the man who founded Marshall Field's department store in that city. From its start, the original foundation was a progressive philanthropy that was supportive of President Franklin Roosevelt's New Deal. After Field's death, the foundation split into the Field Foundation of Illinois and the Field Foundation of New York. The latter, under the leadership of Field's widow, Ruth Field, became a more nationally oriented organization with an interest in social change. It was already supporting racial integration efforts in the South during the 1950s. In 1967, under Leslie Dunbar, former director of the Southern Regional Council and a native West Virginian, the foundation also began its examination of the state of poor Southern communities that led to the expansion of federal support for food-stamp and school lunch programs. It also was among the first foundations to push for the recognition and treatment of black lung disease.[14]

Stephen and Audrey Bruce Currier established the Taconic

Foundation in 1958. She was the daughter of David Bruce, the only person ever to serve as U.S. ambassador to France, the Federal Republic of Germany, and the Court of St. James. Her grandfather was the financier and philanthropist Andrew W. Mellon. Stephen Currier was a descendent of the printmaker Nathaniel Currier, of Currier & Ives. His stepfather was Edward M. M. Warburg, another noted philanthropist in New York. In addition to civil rights, their interests included housing, employment, and anti-poverty programs.

Stephen Currier played a key role in the formation of the Council for United Civil Rights Leadership (CUCRL), to which the Taconic Foundation gave an initial $1.5 million. The council was composed of leaders from a wide-ranging group of civil rights organizations (e.g., the NAACP and the Student Nonviolent Coordinating Committee) and supportive white donors. Taconic support played a key role in the organization of the 1963 March on Washington. Currier was its co-chair.[15]

Signs carried during the March on Washington, August 28, 1963
Courtesy of the Library of Congress, LC-DIG-ppmsca-37245

That enormous, peaceful demonstration in the nation's capital catapulted the civil rights movement to the forefront of national and international news. Continued and intensified media coverage of the church bombing in Birmingham that killed four little black girls just two weeks after the March on Washington; of police dogs and fire-hoses being turned on demonstrators in the same city; of the violence of "Freedom Summer" in Mississippi and the 1965 "Bloody Sunday" in Selma, Alabama, galvanized national attention and new support for the cause of voting and civil rights.

The Ford Foundation steadily increased its support of civil rights work during the 1960s, including grants to the Voter Education Project. Ford also supported the Southern Education Reporting Service, which provided coverage about the battle over segregated schools that many politically conservative Southern newspapers would not print.

During the same period Ford partnered with the Cummins Engine Foundation of Columbus, Indiana, to make early investments in the Delta Corporation, a new private enterprise mechanism for addressing poverty in the Mississippi Delta. Drawing upon the services of loaned Cummins executives, the new not-for-profit effort created the Fine Vines blue jeans company and Mid-South Stamping, which for a time were among the region's largest black-owned companies. These same foundations also launched a new industry by funding the nation's first catfish farms in Mississippi to provide jobs for low-income, rural African Americans.

In 1967 Ford officially announced its broad support of disadvantaged minorities, and by 1970 that support constituted 40 percent of its annual giving. Perhaps its greatest impact derived from its generous support of the NAACP Legal Defense and Educational Fund and other civil rights litigators for equal opportunity.[16]

Progressive Southern Leadership

John Griffin's speech that broadly critiqued Southern philanthropy for failing to support civil rights activities during the 1950s and 1960s (see chapter 14) was essentially on target. There were notable examples, however, ranging from small family foundations (e.g., the Norman Foundation, a Northern philanthropy with Southern trustees) to well-established grant-makers with a strong tradition of progressive giving and advocacy, who sought to bring about positive change in race relations.

No other Southern state was quite so fortunate as North Carolina, blessed by the presence of the Reynolds foundations (see also chapter 10). They gave evidence of a new kind of Southern philanthropy, seeking to be transformative rather than simply ameliorative. The Z. Smith Reynolds (ZSR) Foundation, which was restricted to working within its own state, collaborated with the Ford Foundation and its "cousin," the Mary Reynolds Babcock Foundation, to establish the North Carolina Fund in 1963.

Conceived by Governor Terry Sanford, the North Carolina Fund was a not-for-profit corporation that consisted of experimental projects in education, health, job training, housing, and community development. Directed by George Esser, it intentionally operated for only five years.[17] Its primary goals were to reduce minority poverty across the state and to further the cause of civil rights. During the summers of 1964 and 1965, teams of African American and white college students worked together to demonstrate how communities could be strengthened if its citizens worked across lines of race and class to solve problems of poverty. The Fund served as a model and motivator for such national programs as

A LOT OF DOUGH FOR PHILANTHROPY

Utilizing imaginative marketing techniques, including the sponsorship of a popular television show, Phillip B. Hardin (1891–1972) amassed his wealth by converting a bankrupt Meridian bakery into a state-wide operation with four production centers that also was known as a generous corporate citizen. During the 1970s, the Hardin Bakeries Corporation consolidated its operations into a single production and distribution center and became the principal supplier of hamburger buns to McDonald's restaurants throughout the mid-South.

Hardin became convinced that Mississippi needed better education programs to produce more skilled workers. That conviction, further enforced by reading an article in the *Wall Street Journal* about the Lyndon B. Johnson Foundation, led him to create the foundation that bore his name. Founded in 1964—a year of great racial turmoil in Mississippi—the foundation began its grant-making throughout a state plagued by widespread poverty and one of the worst public school systems in the country. When he died with no wife or children, the bulk of his estate went to the foundation.

Over half a century, the foundation quietly but firmly used its resources to transform education through the university levels and helped to make public education a leader in the quest for racial integration. Among the roles it played to reshape Mississippi's white and historically black public universities have been as an assistant to the governor to select board appointees and as the organizer of a board training program to promote greater collaboration. Its further efforts to raise admission standards in turn encouraged more strenuous high school curricula, especially in the math and sciences. Today the foundation focuses on encouraging a collaborative system of cradle to college support in its home town of Meridian and on improving K-12 student outcomes statewide, with an emphasis on at-risk interventions.

Much of the foundation's positive impact is attributable to C. Thompson (Tom) Wacaster. A fifth-generation Mississippian and a product of public schools in Mississippi and Georgia, Wacaster earned degrees from Yale University, the University of Virginia, and the University of Oregon, where he was a research assistant at the Center for Educational Policy and Management.

During the 30 years (1976-2007) he managed the affairs of the Hardin Foundation, Wacaster came to know seemingly every educational institution and its leaders, as well as politicians, businesspeople, writers and artists, and just plain folks. He knew the location of hundreds of historical sites and the back roads by which to reach them. He had and still has a wry sense of humor, a nuanced appreciation for Mississippi's many gothic qualities, and a "million" stories about its people.

Sources: *www.philhardin.org/the foundation.cfm*; Thomas John Carey, "The Phil Hardin Foundation," Mississippi Encyclopedia, *http://mississippiencyclopedia.org/entries/phil-harden-foundation/*; correspondence with C. Thompson Wacaster, June 23, 2019; correspondence with Lloyd Gray, July, 2019."

Head Start, VISTA, and other initiatives of President Lyndon B. Johnson's "War on Poverty."

ZSR, working with the Kate B. Reynolds Charitable Trust, also established the Area Health Education Centers, which placed doctors in rural areas around the state (funding for which was later assumed by state government). During the early 1960s ZSR also funded the first pilot kindergarten program in the state and (again with Ford) helped to introduce the minority credit union movement to North Carolina. Undergirding its work and influence during the latter part of the 20th century was its ability to forge remarkable alliances among philanthropy, state government, and public higher education to effect positive change throughout North Carolina.[18]

In 1970 ZSR, whose trustees had all been family members, elected Joseph G. Gordon, an African American physician from Winston-Salem, to the board—one of the first black trustees of a historically white Southern foundation.[19] In 1986 the foundation honored Gordon's long-standing service by establishing a $250,000 Joseph G. Gordon Fund at Wake Forest University that is used to provide scholarships annually to as many as five students "who show exceptional promise and achievement and who are members of constituencies traditionally underrepresented at Wake Forest."[20]

A Critical Not-for-Profit Sector

Without the availability of wealth, there can be no philanthropic endowments. However, without a web of not-for-profit organizations (those offspring of the American instinct for "voluntary association" that so

NORTH CAROLINA CENTER FOR NONPROFITS: EFFECTIVE PARTNERS FOR PHILANTHROPY

If philanthropy is to be effective, the not-for-profit sector is an essential partner. Yet during the second half of the 20th century, foundation growth was outstripping the spread of effective nonprofits. Exacerbating the problem was the challenge to survive being faced by many well-intended but often poorly managed and inadequately funded organizations. Things began to change when Jane Kendall, a nonprofit executive, secured a Kellogg Foundation National Leadership Fellowship to conduct an exploration of what might be done to improve the situation. In 1990 Kendall's three-year period of careful research resulted in the formation of the North Carolina Center for Nonprofits (NCCNP), based in Raleigh.

During the next twenty-five years she served as NCCNP's chief executive. The organization became a state-wide voice of the sector, advocating for laws that would enhance nonprofits. NCCNP promoted effectiveness, training staff and board members to be stronger administrators and fundraisers, and championed ethical behavior and legally sound practices. It grew to include more than 1,500 members, who provided one-third of the annual operating support through dues and fees, while the balance came from the generous support of the foundation and corporate sectors.

Equally significant, Kendall and her staff became models and mentors for other nonprofit associations throughout the region. Today, every Southern state has a similar organization dedicated to the promotion and protection of a strong not-for-profit sector.

Source: https://www.ncnonprofits.org

struck de Tocqueville), philanthropy might be the sound of one hand clapping. That sector is an essential partner of grant-making foundations as they translate the charitable impulse into societal action.

In addition to catalyzing many other changes in Southern life, the movement for racial equality inspired or strengthened alternative civic associations in the region. They included not only SNCC, the SCLC, the regional coordinating committees of the National Urban League and the Congress of Racial Equality (CORE), but also the dozens of local chapters of the NAACP, black professional organizations, and (everywhere) local churches and their spin-off volunteer groups. These grass-roots activist associations signaled not only the first stages of true democratization in the South but also the formation of a biracial, progressive civic spirit and political will that harkened back to the agrarian

Populism of the early 1890s.

The intersection of the civil rights struggle with other national developments added to the forward thrust and momentum for Southern civil society. Certainly, President Johnson's Great Society program did much to modernize state and local government, as dozens of new federal programs in environment, education, and social justice prepared the ground for nonprofit organizational growth. Indeed, President Kennedy's inaugural call to "ask not what your country can do for you—ask what you can do for your country" was nothing less than a national mandate for civic action in *every* state. As part of a new private-public, federal-state partnership fueled by federal financial outlays, private associations (formal and informal) came into existence to combat hunger and poverty, promote civil rights, care for the aged and the disabled, preserve public lands and recreational areas, seed community action organizations, plan programming for public television, attack pollution of the air and waterways, improve child nutrition, empower a "teacher corps" to work in central-city areas, and beautify the nation's cities and countryside. Though some of the Great Society programs were short-lived, others were reaffirmed and even expanded upon by the Nixon Administration in the 1970s. Not of lesser importance was the anti–Vietnam War movement that fed from and contributed to other forms of social activism and justice among young people.

The White Rediscovery of Black Colleges

It seems to be the fate of the historically black colleges and universities (HBCUs) to be rediscovered every few decades by the rest of the country. In 1965, more than a half-century after Northern philanthropists and some white Southern liberals had concerned themselves about these institutions and their futures, an attention-grabbing book by Earl J. McGrath, former U.S. commissioner of education and executive officer, Institute of Higher Education, at Teachers College of Columbia University, began making the rounds in academic circles. *The Predominantly Negro Colleges and Universities in Transition* drew back a veil that had obscured most of them from widespread white awareness for many years.[21] Knowledgeable observers knew a bit about Howard University in Washington, D.C., Hampton Institute on the eastern coast of Virginia, and Tuskegee Institute in Alabama, which had been modeled after Hampton. Others may have been aware of Fisk University in Nashville through the renowned fund-raising concerts of its student choir around the United States and Europe. But most Northern and Southern whites did not have a clue about the 123 African American junior and senior colleges as well as a few graduate and professional schools that McGrath identified (almost all of them in the South). Indeed, many white residents would have been hard pressed to offer directions to the campuses of historically black colleges in their own communities.

The revelation of their existence set in motion some interesting dynamics. First, many of the HBCUs had faculty members who had earned their doctorates at some of the country's most prestigious public and private universities elsewhere in the country after being denied admission to postgraduate institutions in the South. Seeking to integrate their faculties, those white institutions of higher learning now sought to recruit these scholars, generally by dangling much more attractive compensation packages before them than their current employers could offer.

Major corporations also were on the prowl for educated African American, entry-level men and women. Within a very short time, a large cadre of white recruiters was making the rounds of the HBCUs, entertaining students and their guidance counselors and blandishing generous employment offers. The more astute of these headhunters deduced that they might improve their access to the best candidates with corporate and corporate foundation grants to the institutions. White Southern foundations also began steadily increasing the support of HCBUs in their local communities and states.

Another result of the HBCUs' new visibility was the arrival on their campuses of young, mostly white scholars, usually at the master's degree level in their graduate studies, who offered themselves as junior, relatively inexpensive faculty members. A few of them were veterans of earlier civil rights activities like the 1964 Freedom Summer, but most simply wanted to make the best contribution they could offer while gaining important teaching experience. Usually supported at least in part by white grant-making foundations, the members of this academic wing of the movement were intelligent, occasionally naive, and often impatient and quick to challenge their colleges' more conservative administrations. For some, it was a positive, life-changing experience. One of the largest programs was underwritten by the Rockefeller Foundation, administered by the Woodrow Wilson National Fellowship Foundation, and advised by J. Curtis Dixon, the recently retired executive director of the Southern Education Foundation. Between 1963 and

A PERSUASIVE PHILANTHROPIST

In late 1964, Dr. Martin Luther King Jr. had just received the Nobel Peace Prize, and some of his city's religious and civic leaders wanted to honor him at a banquet. However, it soon became clear, and was even reported in the national press, that most of Atlanta's white corporate leaders were going to decline their invitations and boycott the event. Atlanta mayor Ivan Allen was deeply concerned. He and Paul Austin, chairman and CEO of the Coca-Cola Company, conferred with "The Boss" (Robert W. Woodruff) at his plantation in south Georgia.

Upon their return, Austin convened the business leadership of the city. He pointedly made clear his expectation that his colleagues would be present when Dr. King was honored. In almost so many words, he observed that Coca-Cola had no intention of being associated with a city that would not honor a native son who was a Nobel laureate. Atlanta needed Coca-Cola but the company did not need Atlanta to succeed.

The words came from Austin, but no one had any doubt about the source of the message. The banquet was quickly sold out, biracial relations continued to grow stronger, and new business, including a growing list of Fortune 500 corporate headquarters, began arriving in the metro area. So did an increased pool of philanthropic assets.

Source: Sheffield Hale, "An Award for All Mankind, a Dinner for One," Georgia Humanities, accessed June 15, 2019, *https://www.georgiahumanities.org/2016/11/02/an-award-for-all-mankind-a-dinner-for-one-the-atlanta-nobel-prize-party-for-mlk-given-by-the-citys-image-conscious-white-leadership/*.

1970 it placed 303 former Wilson and Danforth Foundation fellows on sixty-two campuses. A spin-off program, the Administrative Internships (added in 1967) recruited young leaders and scholars, primarily from graduate business schools, with skills in development and financial management to help HBCUs meet demands for well-trained administrators. Funded initially by the Esso Education Fund and the Jesse Smith Noyes Foundation, the Administrative Internships would continue until 1990.[22]

McGrath's research happily coincided with the unlocking of the first significant access to federal dollars by the HBCUs for nearly a century. The route to this funding was through "The Strengthening Developing Institutions Program under title III of the Higher Education Act of 1965"—a veritable cornucopia of millions of dollars in fiscal support for categories that included instruction, equipment capital improvement, library acquisitions, tutoring and counseling, faculty development, establishment of development offices, teacher education, community outreach, and even endowment.

A True New South

Opposition to black voter registration seemed even more vicious and violent than had been the reaction to other forms of protest. Yet, after a string of federal appellate court decisions, President Lyndon Johnson secured sufficient Congressional votes to pass the Civil Rights Act of 1964 (which officially ended segregation in public places and banned employment discrimination on the basis of race, color, religion, sex, or national origin), the Voting Rights Act of 1965 (to ensure state-level enforcement of the 14th and 15th Amendments to the U.S. Constitution), and the Fair Housing Act of 1968. Those Southerners with the will now also had legal means and support to do the right thing.

They also had access to financial resources. The economic transformation that followed the legal eradication of segregation was dramatic. Investors who had long been hesitant to enter a region characterized by poor race relations now began to feel more comfortable about coming South. Informed by studies like those of Dr. V. W. Henderson, a labor economist on the faculty of Fisk University, both large and small white-owned businesses discovered what for many of them had been the invisible purchasing power of African Americans.[23] Rising employment opportunities for all citizens led to greater investment in higher education that provided the training for a new work force. The ripples were and continue to be profound.

TWO INSTITUTIONS BORN OF TRAGEDY

In the aftermath of the Memphis sanitation workers strike that led to the assassination of Martin Luther King, Jr., two important community institutions came into being. The first was the Metropolitan Interfaith Association (MIFA) built on the foundation of bonds among diverse clergy and lay people who supported the sanitation workers. Originally created to find a solution for poverty and racial division in Memphis, MIFA grew to offer, among other services, the city's Meals on Wheels program, the Mid-South Food Bank, and an important provider of emergency shelter.

At the same time, a group of civic and business leaders met to consider how best to repair the scars of the sanitation strike. After meeting with leaders from other cities and further research and discussion, they determined that encouraging and driving charitable investment in Memphis was the best way to secure the future of the city. In September, 1969, they chartered what is now the Community Foundation of Greater Memphis.

Both institutions were led by the late Gid Smith (1941-2017), a visionary former Methodist minister. He was co-executive director of MIFA from the early 1970's until 1989, when he accepted the presidency of the community foundation. At the time of his retirement in 2006, his leadership had driven the value of its assets from $20 million to $280 million.

Source: Robert M. Fockler, President, Community Foundation of Greater Memphis

Another telling affirmation about reformation in the South was the beginning of a large migration into the region by African Americans. Many of them were the children, grandchildren, and great-grandchildren of men and women who had steadily fled the South from 1865 until 1969 (see chapter 8). By 2010, 55% of the nation's African-American population could claim the South as home.

A powerful chapter in a great drama—perhaps the greatest drama—in American history with its roots in the 18th century culminated with the passage of the Civil Rights and Voting Rights Acts of the 1960s. How long it would take for the final chapter to be written remained a mystery. An almost immediate setback was the assassination of Dr. Martin Luther King, Jr. Yet it could be said that Americans had productively wrestled with the kinds of questions that the Founders themselves had raised. How does one balance individual rights with public responsibilities? Public good and private interest? What is government's role, and is humankind truly capable of a just self-government? What does one person owe to another? The long journey to find answers to these questions—a journey in which some key foundations had played and would continue to play an important role—gave signs that the nation was perhaps moving in the direction of finding its long-imagined true self.

CHAPTER 11 Endnotes

1   George B. Ellenberg, *Mule South to Tractor South: Mules, Machines, and the Transformation of the Cotton South* (Tuscaloosa: University of Alabama Press, 2007), 8.

2   James C. Cobb, *The Selling of the South: The Southern Crusade for Industrial Development, 1936-1980* (Baton Rouge: Louisiana State University Press, 1982).

3   Doris Goodwin, "The Way We Won: America's Economic Breakthrough During World War II," *American Prospect* (Fall 1992), *http://prospect.org/article/way-we-won-americas-economic-breakthrough-during-world-war-ii.*

4   The website of the Southern Education Foundation is an excellent source of scholarly and documentary material on the development of education in the South, especially for African Americans. The formation of the SEF is chronicled at *http://southerneducation.org/1932.asp#passages.*

5   See Edward S. Shapiro, *A Time for Healing: American Jewry Since World War II* (Baltimore, Md.: Johns Hopkins University Press, 1992).

6   Highly notable exemplars of this tradition in recent times are Arthur Blank and Bernie Marcus, co-founders of The Home Depot (1978), each of whom has established a major foundation.

7   See Milton Goldin, *Why They Give: American Jews and Their Philanthropies* (New York: Macmillan, 1976). The civic dimension is explored in Jonathan S. Woocher, *Sacred Survival: The Civil Religion of American Jews* (Bloomington: Indiana University Press, 1986).

8   In 1953 SEF became the home for a team of researchers sponsored by the Ford Foundation to compile a definitive study of the conditions of black education in the South in anticipation of the U.S. Supreme Court's decision in *Brown v. Board of Education.* No Southern state university would accept the research project.

9   Henry Wallace was a Progressive Party candidate, and the former Secretary of Agriculture and Vice President (1941-45) of Franklin D. Roosevelt.

10 Quoted in John M. Glen, "Highlander Folk School," *Tennessee Encyclopedia*, last modified March 1, 2018, *http://tennesseeencyclopedia.net/entries/highlander-folk-school*, retrieved March 15, 2019. See also John M. Glen, *Highlander: No Ordinary School, 1932–1962* (Lexington: University Press of Kentucky, 1988). On the influence of the Highlander Folk School's training outside of Tennessee, see e.g., Stephen Schneider, "The Sea Island Citizenship Schools: Literacy, Community Organization, and the Civil Rights Movement," *College English* 70, no. 2 (Nov. 2007): 144–67.

Congressman John Lewis recounts the Highlander Folk School's nonviolent training for the Nashville college students (later SNCC) who peacefully desegregated that city's lunch counters in 1961. Lewis, *March: Book One* (Marietta, Ga.: Top Shelf Productions, 2013), 103–21.

11 Within a week of that decision, the Ford Foundation–funded book, *The Negro and the Schools*, provided a comprehensive study of racial inequity among public schools in the South.

12 The words are those of Fannie Lou Hamer (December 20, 1954), the civil rights leader from Mississippi who cofounded the Freedom Democratic Party. See Maegan Parker Brooks and Davis W. Houck, eds., *The Speeches of Fannie Lou Hamer: To Tell It Like It Is* (Jackson: University Press of Mississippi, 2011), 57.

13 For a recap of the work of these foundations, see Sean Dobson's article for the National Committee for Responsive Philanthropy, *https://bjn9t2lhlni2dhd5hvym7llj-wpengine.netdna-ssl.com/wp-content/uploads/2016/11/Freedom_Funders_and_the_Civil_Rights_Movement-FINAL.pdf.*

14 The Field Foundation liquidated its assets in 1989.

15 In 1967 the Curriers disappeared when their plane vanished over the Caribbean Sea after departing from San Juan, Puerto Rico. Neither the plane's wreckage nor the bodies of the Curriers or the pilot were ever recovered. A year later, Jane Lee Eddy, who had been an assistant to the Curriers, became the foundation's executive director. The Taconic Foundation remained in existence until intentionally spending itself out of business in 2013. Among its many achievements was pioneering the concept of "program-related investments."

16 See Steven Schindler, "Social Movements and Civil Rights Litigation: Ford Foundation, 1967," Center for Strategic Philanthropy and Civil Society at Duke University (2007), *https://cspcs.sanford. duke.edu/learning-resources/case-study-database/social-movements-and-civil-rights-litigation-ford-foundation.*

17 George Esser (1921–2006) later was a program adviser for the Ford Foundation, executive director of the Southern Regional Council, and executive director of the National Academy of Public Administration in Washington, D.C. He received the North Carolina Philanthropy Award in 1995.

18 One embodiment of this collaborative style was Thomas Lambeth, former executive director and now director emeritus of the Z. Smith Reynolds Foundation. Before coming to the foundation in 1978, he had been on the campaign staff of gubernatorial candidate Terry Sanford, served as assistant to the chair of the North Carolina Democratic Party, and was administrative assistant to Governor Sanford. From 1965 to 1969 he was an administrator at the Smith Richardson Foundation in Greensboro, and from 1969 to 1978 he worked as administrative assistant to U.S. Representative Richardson Preyer.

19 Thomas Lambeth, correspondence with authors, May 2, 2019. Also see "ZSR Timeline (1936–Present)," Z. Smith Reynolds Foundation, *https://www.zsr.org/content/zsr-timeline-1936-present.*

20 See "Joseph G. Gordon Scholarships," Wake Forest University, *https://financialaid.wfu.edu/merit/ joseph-g-gordon-scholarships/.*

21 Earl J. McGrath, *The Predominantly Negro Colleges and Universities in Transition* (New York: Teachers College, Columbia University, 1965).

22 *https://woodrow.org/about/past-programs/#AF.*

23 Henderson became president of Clark College (now Clark Atlanta University) in 1965 and subsequently also served as a board member of the Ford Foundation.

CHAPTER 12

A New Attack on Foundations

Getting Organized

Not-for-profit organizations with similar missions and foci (like the American Hospital Association and the Association of American Colleges and Universities) had been voluntarily forming themselves into membership clusters since the last half of the 19th century. Not so the grant-making foundations. Until well into the 20th century, many of them operated in silo-like isolation from each other.[1] Obviously, these grant-makers were aware of one another's existence, and certainly there were informal conversations and consultations among them. Nonetheless, the notion that they might constitute a "field" was still a distant concept.

In 1949, however, the leaders of several Texas foundations discovered that each had awarded a grant to the same program at the University of Texas. It occurred to them that they and their peers might benefit from sharing other information. Robert Sutherland, director of the Hogg Foundation, volunteered to host a meeting in Austin that was attended by the donors and trustees of ten grant-makers. The program consisted of presentations by representatives from the Carnegie Corporation, the Rockefeller Foundation, the General Education Board, and the Southern Education Foundation, who also facilitated discussions.

This initial meeting was sufficiently successful that several Houston-based foundations voted to host another gathering the next year. For eight years the pattern continued, with the Hogg Foundation assuming primary responsibility for conference planning, staffing, and operation of what was called the Conference of Texas Foundations and Trust Funds. Attendance, by invitation only, was limited to grant-makers.[2]

As in other, "younger" parts of the country, the leaders of most Texas foundations constituted a first generation of grant-makers. Many of their donors were still living and often involved in the daily operation of their foundations with the help of business or personal office staffs. They avoided publicity, lest they be swamped with requests for funds far beyond their ability to respond. For a time, because it was the only gathering of its kind in the country, the Texas convening regularly attracted foundation representatives from outside the region.[3]

During the same year that this small group of Texas grant-makers began to compare notes, the National Committee on Foundations and Trusts for Community Welfare organized itself and began operations in space provided by the Chicago Community Trust. By 1957 the organization was incorporated in New York as the National Council on Community Foundations. A year later it expanded its membership criteria to permit the inclusion of private and company foundations, and by 1964, family and corporate foundations were welcomed as full, voting members. The membership by the end of 1965 embraced 88 community, 30 corporate, and 126 private family foundations. The foundation universe was growing and steadily becoming more self-conscious about its roles and responsibilities.

Congress on the Warpath

The field's new visibility also was gaining more attention from the press, the public and—most threatening—the Congress charged with regulating it. During the early Cold War of the late 1940s and early 1950s, the anti-Communist movement led by Wisconsin senator Joseph McCarthy was highlighted by his reckless charges of subversion in government and in the nation's universities.

Legislators from the South, like Representative Eugene "Goober" Cox of Camilla, Georgia, who served in Congress as chair of the House Select Committee to Investigate Tax-Exempt Foundations and Comparable Organizations, held hearings on "subversive" philanthropy.

A long-time defender of racial segregation and an enemy of Franklin D. Roosevelt's New Deal, Cox targeted foundations like Ford and Carnegie, and universities like Columbia and Harvard, which benefitted from their tax-exempt status. He accused them of discrediting the United States, pointing to European economist and Nobel Laureate Gunnar Myrdal's *An American Dilemma* (a 1944 study of race relations concluding that Americans had a moral imperative to end legal segregation—see Chapter 10), produced with financial underwriting from Carnegie, and the Ford Foundation's area studies program as examples of un-American ideas.[4]

Following Representative Cox's untimely death, Tennessee representative B. Carroll Reece continued committee hearings in 1953. In a floor statement, Reece declared, "Some of these institutions support efforts to overthrow our government and to undermine our American way of life.... Here lies the story of how communism and socialism are financed in the United States, where they get their money. It is the story of who pays the bill."[5]

Foundation Directory

Joseph McCarthy died in 1957, and the witch-hunting he initiated receded for a few years, damaged in part by its own reckless and extreme attacks on organizations within the Christian social gospel movement and the American Historical Association. However, the national foundation community—though not critically scathed—recognized the potential severity of the threat to its existence. It took the precautionary

U.S. Capitol, Washington D.C.
Library of Congress, Prints & Photographs Division, photograph by Carol M. Highsmith, LC-DIG-highsm-12649

step in November 1956 of promoting greater transparency within its ranks by creating the Foundation Library Center (today's Foundation Center) as a repository of data about the field. Four years later, in 1960, the Center would publish the first edition of the *Foundation Directory*. It was to become the statistical bible of the field[6] and continues as the premier resource of information about foundation grant-making throughout the world.[7]

This first catalog, which acknowledged the existence of approximately 12,000 foundations in the United States, included listings for 5,202 of the largest foundations.[8] In its introduction, the editors pointedly called attention to those foundations "that refused information, or did not reply," and expressed the hope "for more cooperation in the future."[9]

Only 490 foundations from the eleven Southern states were listed. Of the 129 foundations with assets of $10 million or more, eight of them (four each from Georgia and North Carolina) were from the South. The Duke Endowment was the only Southern foundation at the time with assets of more than $100 million.[10]

The *Foundation Directory* was an important step in the direction of greater transparency of the field. Congress was not through with these foundations, however. The 1965 Treasury report on private foundations set the stage for further reforms. A 2017 analysis by philanthropic Studies Archivist Angela White and the Lilly Family School of Philanthropy explains:

> Although the Treasury Department believed "that the preponderant number of private foundations perform their functions without tax abuse," their investigation revealed many of the problems that TRA69 [Tax Reform Act of 1969] sought to address, including self-dealing, failure to use accumulated funds for charitable purposes, unrelated business income, and use of foundations to control corporate and personal property.[11]

John D. Rockefeller III was the manager for all family undertakings of social relevance. He had started the Rockefeller Brothers Fund and had chaired The Rockefeller Foundation. His concern about Congressional and public criticism of foundations next led in 1968-69 to the formation of the Commission on Foundations and Private Philanthropy (the so-called Peterson Commission, chaired by Peter G. Peterson, Chairman and CEO of Bell & Howell). Its members quickly discovered, though, that finding solid information to support their research of negative claims against foundations was extremely difficult. The Commission did not complete its work before the passage of the Tax Reform Act of 1969.[12]

Tax Reform Act of 1969

That legislative chapter only very narrowly averted the removal of the grant-making sector from the IRS tax code. A handful of populist-minded and sometimes politically motivated members of Congress once again sought to force foundations out of existence or, at the very least, to eliminate their prerogative to exist in perpetuity. Part of the impetus for the new series of attacks during the 1960s was the support that foundations (mostly Northern but also some from the South) had provided to advocate for the civil rights movement. Their opponents were highly influential and included Representatives Wright Patman of Texas (whose objection to all foundations extended back to the New Deal) and Tom Steed of Oklahoma, as well as powerful Senators Russell Long of Louisiana, J. W. Fulbright of Arkansas, and Herman Talmadge of Georgia. In the Senate debate

Senator Talmadge reminded his colleagues that

> a foundation is the only thing in the world that is perma-
> nent in scope. Individuals die, corporation charters expire
> and must be renewed, all life on earth and vegetation die.
> Has the Treasury given any thought to the fact that some-
> time the life of the foundation ought to expire?[13]

The position of Representative Patman, who earlier had proposed a "death sentence" bill that would have limited the lifespan of founda-tions to twenty-five years, was modified only slightly by a provision from Senator Albert Gore Sr. of Tennessee. Although a moderate on racial matters who had refused to sign Senator Strom Thurmond's anti-in-tegration Southern Manifesto, Senator Gore proposed that the Senate Finance Committee's tax legislation restrict the life of foundations to forty years.

For all of the charges leveled against foundations, clearly their most "offensive" fault had been the support of voter registration efforts in the South as well as the North. Furthermore, the Ford Foundation work in Cleveland, Ohio, as an example, had clearly played a role in the election of Carl Stokes as the city's first black mayor. "Are the giant foundations," Patman asked, "on the road to becoming political machines?"[14] It didn't help this particular giant foundation's position that, after Senator Robert F. Kennedy's assassination in 1968, it had awarded just over $131,000 in "travel grants" to several of his staffers, which one critic decried as "severance pay for benignly regarded political functionaries."[15] Some observers also felt that the perceived arrogance

REGIONAL ASSOCIATIONS OF GRANTMAKERS

The Southeastern Council of Foundations played an active role in the continued evolution of the regional movement. The coming together of foundations to defend themselves led to further organization as additional regional associations came into being, and all of them joined forces to strengthen themselves and become more useful to their members.

This activity inevitably led to competition with the Council on Foundations (COF). During the late 1970s, COF appointed an informal committee composed of the executives of the more-established groups to provide liaison between the regionals and the COF. A subsequent Special Committee of all regional association executives grew to twenty-four members during the 1980s, and COF expanded its services to them and their members.

The complexity of those needs led the W. K. Kellogg Foundation to underwrite a planning grant to stimulate a four-year, staffed collaboration between the COF and regional associations that consisted of five national working groups. The grant culminated in 1995 with the formation of the Forum of Regional Association of Grantmakers as a three-year test. The member organizations defined themselves as serving metropolitan, state, or multistate areas. Then, in 1997, a national funder collaborative invited the Forum to lead a new initiative to promote philanthropy throughout the country. Among the disbursements made by New Ventures in Philanthropy was a $200,000 grant to the Southeastern Council of Foundations to support its work to increase foundation assets and organization in the South.

By 1998 the Forum had twenty-nine members, representing more than four thousand grant-makers in forty-one of the fifty states. At the end of that year, it was separately incorporated as a supporting organization of COF, with its own board, president, staff, budget, audit, and policies and with continued responsibility for the administration of New Ventures in Philanthropy. Martin Lehfeldt was elected to the board in 1999 and served until 2005, the last three years as chair and representative to the board of COF.

The wealth of information and learning opportunities generated by New Ventures led the Forum to begin a knowledge management initiative, designed to capture, organize, and make available electronic resources generated by members and other stakeholders. Yet another ground-breaking initiative came with the development of consistent guiding principles for all foundations to strengthen accountability and transparency.

The timing of this venture could not have been better. After a three-decade absence from the battlefield, Congress was again declaring war on organized philanthropy (see chapter 15).

The Forum continued to evolve. Today, under the leadership of David Biemesderfer, it is called the United Philanthropy Forum, a membership organization of more than seventy-five philanthropy-serving organizations (including SECF), representing seven thousand foundations and other funders, who work to make philanthropy better. United Philanthropy Forum describes its vision this way: "We envision a courageous philanthropic sector that catalyzes a just and equitable society where all can participate and prosper."

Source: Courtney Moore and David Biemesderfer of the United Philanthropy Forum, correspondence with authors, 2019.

of the Ford Foundation's president, McGeorge Bundy, during his testimony and after arriving in a large limousine with an entourage, further offended the committee members.[16]

By the time the dust settled, supportive members of the Senate together with foundation leaders had managed to thwart the "death sentence" provision. Central to their defense was an emphasis upon the creative and evolutionary role that foundations and their trustees normally played in meeting changing societal needs.

Still, although the opposing Southerners failed in their overarching and decidedly draconian objective, they did succeed in other ways. Because of the Tax Reform Act of 1969, foundations soon found themselves much more highly regulated and accountable as well as de-politicized. The legislators usefully and productively added to foundations' public accountability and overcame one of the greatest criticisms of organized philanthropy by requiring annual charitable disbursements.[17]

If the hearings had touched upon the line between foundations and overt politics, it was also obvious that those lines only continued to blur with the Great Society's comingling of public and private resources in pursuit of common goals.

When all was said and done, the final version of the bill, broadly speaking, was moderate. Still, its bewildering complexity led Senator Russell Long of Louisiana to label it as the "Attorneys' and Accountants' Relief Act of 1969."[18]

Key Elements of the New Legislation

At the risk of oversimplification, the new law divided the not-for-profit sector into public charities (which receive broad-based public support) and private foundations (grant-making institutions supported by the contributions of individuals or small groups of people). Grant-makers now had to comply with these strictures:[19]

- A 4% tax on investment income (later reduced to 2%; see chapter 15)

- A 5% minimum distribution of income

- Limit of 20% ownership of the stock holdings of a business

- Prohibition against attempts to influence legislation or elections

- Taxation on unrelated business income

- Prohibition against self-dealing (officers and directors could not benefit financially from transactions with their foundation)

- Enhanced reporting requirements, including grants awarded; guaranteed public access to all information.

CHAPTER 12 Endnotes

1   A notable exception, dating back to the last decade of the 19th century, was the communication and collaboration among the major foundations based primarily in New York (e.g., the Rockefeller Foundations, the two leading Carnegie funds, the Russell Sage Foundation, the Commonwealth Fund, some of the Guggenheim funds, and the Rosenwald Fund). See Chapter 6 above. Unlike many other foundations, the aims of these philanthropies were "generally secular or non-sectarian, emphasizing science and a cosmopolitan appreciation of many kinds of knowledge and the capabilities of people of all sorts...." —from correspondence with David Hammack, February 25, 2019.

2   Mary L. Kelley, *The Foundations of Texas Philanthropy* (College Station: Texas A&M University Press, 2004). This well-researched volume is a model for other state histories of philanthropy.

3   At its eighth annual conference in Corpus Christi, the organization changed its name to the Conference of Southwest Foundations in order to extend membership to grant-makers in neighboring states. Today, it is called Philanthropy Southwest. See Maud W. Keeling, "Conference of Southwest Foundations," *Handbook of Texas Online*, June 12, 2010, *https://tshaonline.org/handbook/online/articles/vrc03.*

4   Olivier Zunz, *Philanthropy in America: A History* (Princeton, NJ: Princeton University Press, 2012), 194.

5   Ibid.

6   *Foundation Directory*, edition 1, 1960, x. In prior years, such foundation statistics as existed were gathered by the Russell Sage Foundation (which shared data about twenty-seven foundations in 1915), *American Foundations and Their Fields* (initiated by the Twentieth Century Fund), Raymond Rich Associates, and American Foundations Information Service.

7   As this manuscript is being completed, the Foundation Center and GuideStar (another repository of information about the entire not-for-profit sector) have announced their intention to merge and to form a new organization called Candid.

8   The average asset size of the rest was below $10,000.

9   *Foundation Directory.*

10 The financial data of foundations was not audited until the regulations of the Tax Reform Act of 1969 went into effect. Before that, foundations could make their own determination about the figures they chose to share.

11 Angela White, "Tax Reform Act of 1969," Learning to Give, *https://www.learningtogive.org//resources/tax-reform-act-1969.*

12 Ibid.

13 Zunz, *Philanthropy*, 226.

14 Neil Maghami, "Tax Reform 1969: Ford vs. Patman," Capital Research Center, August 9, 2018, *https://capitalresearch.org/article/tax-reform-1969-part-2/.*

15 Ibid.

16 Correspondence with Robert Hull (President, Southeastern Council of Foundations, 1978-1987, see Chapters 13-14).

17 Not, however, for "donor-advised funds" managed by community foundations.

18 Zunz, *Philanthropy*, 228.

19 Angela White, "Tax Reform Act of 1969."

CHAPTER 13

Grant-Makers Going on Defense

The Southeastern Council of Foundations

Much of the increased philanthropic impact upon the Southeast for the next three decades was linked to the building of relationships among its grant-makers—and nowhere more strongly than the members of the newly formed Southeastern Council of Foundations (SECF). They were primarily place-based and not especially prone to collaboration, but they began to recognize themselves as a field whose constituents had much to share with each other. For that reason we have chosen to portray further foundation growth and expansion of the field in the region against the backdrop of SECF history.

By way of background, SECF is the geographically largest regional association of grant-makers in the country, holding together a patchwork quilt of members from eleven states. Its membership, which enfolds an ever-expanding variety of organizations and individuals, includes some but not all of the South's largest foundations and some very small ones. Although most of the states in which SECF is active have their own grant-making associations, SECF offers the preeminent regional voice for the promotion and protection of philanthropy.

Now fifty years old, SECF has approximately 350 members. They constitute only about 2% of the region's 16,600 foundations, but collectively that very small number of grant-makers has responsibility for the oversight of more than $50 billion—almost half of all the philanthropic assets in the region. Since its founding, SECF has been the region's premier convener of institutions to encourage wise and imaginative grant-making, legal compliance, public accountability, exemplary governance and management, and sound financial investment practices. In recent years it has focused a great deal of energy upon the promotion of greater diversity and inclusiveness throughout the field.

Mobilization

SECF came into being as a primarily defensive reaction to government opposition. As described in the previous chapter, a cadre of U.S. legislators (many from the South), and not for the first time in history, had been harboring growing suspicions about the activities of grant-making foundations. They were determined to pass the necessary legislation to force these institutions out of existence or at least to curtail the lifespans of their influence.

Robert H. Hull, who would later become president of SECF, describes the turmoil generated by the expansion of Congressional scrutiny and oversight. When the Tax Reform Act of 1969 became law, Hull recalls:

These new regulations sent shock waves through the

foundation world, especially among those smaller foundations without professional staff to manage the compliance factors. (The Southeastern region probably had more of this type of foundation than other regions of the country.) There were rumors that some of them planned to liquidate their assets and go out of business. Even those continuing to operate doubted that they could correctly comply with the new rules.[1]

He goes on to observe that one reason the foundations were caught off guard by the new legislation was their assumption that the national Council on Foundations (COF) would have mustered sufficient testimony to defeat the measures it contained. At the very least, foundations assumed that the COF would have been ready to assist the field as it sought to comply with the new rules of conduct, a somewhat hypocritical position on the part of those who did not belong to the organization nor pay its dues.

The COF actually did its best to help with compliance. As an example, the educational materials it prepared for its members were helpful, but many foundations, as noted, were not members. The regional associations disseminated some of the COF material to their constituencies, and the Council sent speakers to the regional meetings, but overall the effort was insufficient. It also was hampered by the fact that it took years for the Internal Revenue Service to put in place the regulations that supported the legal changes. Further undercutting its defense, the COF still had not cultivated the kind of strong relationships with other national nonprofit organizations that might have served as character witnesses.

Southern foundations were among those grant-makers that felt isolated and abandoned. As they fretted, William C. Archie, executive director of the Mary Reynolds Babcock Foundation in Winston-Salem, North Carolina, took it upon himself to determine a course of action. Dr. Archie, a former professor of romance languages who had been dean of the College of Arts and Sciences at both Wake Forest University and then Emory University, was a bluff and forceful leader. (Some colleagues described him affectionately as a bull that carried his own china shop with him.) Soon after the Tax Reform Act went into effect in the spring of 1970, he quickly reached out to other foundation leaders in the region and invited them to a meeting in Atlanta. After what was later described to Hull as a weekend of "discussion and mutual anxiety," the twenty-four in attendance decided to convene a multi-state gathering of foundation representatives that fall in Atlanta to propose the establishment of a regional association.[2]

Archie drafted William L. Bondurant, his executive associate at the Babcock Foundation, to assemble an invitation list and make arrangements for the inaugural meeting of what would become the Southeastern Council of Foundations. Approximately seventy-five philanthropists and "philanthropoids"[3] assembled at the American Hotel in Atlanta in November 1970. To assist them, they recruited the services of Randolph Thrower, who had just completed a stint (1969) as commissioner of the Internal Revenue Service under President Nixon and had returned to the law firm of Sutherland, Asbill & Brennan in Atlanta.

A Regional Organization Takes Form

Before they concluded their meeting, and under Thrower's guidance, the congregants had composed a charter, completed the authorization for incorporation,[4] elected Archie to be the founding board chair, and recruited the first members,[5] each of which paid annual dues of $75.[6] For the next twenty months or so, Bondurant served the new organization as its unpaid executive director, while continuing his work at the Babcock Foundation.[7]

By the end of 1970, almost two dozen foundations constituted the new SECF. Most of them were rather large for the time, although the list also included some small family foundations. They were based in seven of the nine states that had been determined to be SECF's initial footprint[8] and included:

William C. Archie
Special Collections & Archives / Wake Forest University / Winston-Salem, North Carolina

WILLIAM C. ARCHIE

William C. "Bill" Archie, executive director of the Mary Reynolds Babcock Foundation, was the colorful sparkplug who ignited the organization of the Southeastern Council of Foundations in 1970 and served as its first board chair. He merits being called the "father of the SECF."

Mary Reynolds Babcock Foundation... Winston-Salem, NC

J. Bulow Campbell Foundation ....Atlanta, GA

Arthur Vining Davis Foundations .... Fort Lauderdale, FL
(later relocated to Jacksonville, FL)

The Duke Endowment ....Charlotte, NC

Lettie Pate Evans Foundation ....Atlanta, GA

Feild Co-Operative Association ....Jackson, MS

Foundation for the Carolinas..Charlotte, NC

James G. K. McClure Education and Development Fund..................... Asheville, NC
(later became a fund of Community Foundation
of Western North Carolina)

Memorial Welfare Foundation ....Chattanooga, TN
(became Lyndhurst Foundation)

Metropolitan Atlanta Community Foundation ....Atlanta, GA
(now Community Foundation for Greater Atlanta)

James Starr Moore Memorial Foundation .... Atlanta, GA

The Morgan Foundation .... Laurel Hill, NC

Z. Smith Reynolds Foundation .... Winston-Salem, NC

Smith Richardson Foundation .... Greensboro, NC
(later relocated to Connecticut)

Florence Rogers Charitable Trust .... Fayetteville, NC

The Self Foundation .... Greenwood, SC
(now Self Family Foundation)

Southern Education Foundation .... Atlanta, GA

Elliott White Springs Foundation .... Fort Mill, SC
(now Springs Close Foundation)

Trebor Foundation .... Atlanta, GA
(now Robert W. Woodruff Foundation)

Joseph B. Whitehead Foundation .... Atlanta, GA

Lettie Pate Whitehead Foundation .... Atlanta, GA

Emily and Ernest Woodruff Foundation .... Atlanta, GA

Although managed in the same office, the Lettie Pate Evans, Trebor, Joseph B. Whitehead, Lettie Pate Whitehead, and Emily and Ernest Woodruff Foundations all generously paid individual dues.

Arthur Vining Davis
Courtesy of the
Arthur Vining Davis
Foundations

ARTHUR VINING DAVIS FOUNDATIONS

The majority of SECF's early members, described elsewhere in the book, had been in operation for two-to-four decades, but among the newer philanthropic enterprises were the Arthur Vining Davis Foundations, established in 1965. They were created by Arthur Vining Davis, a Congregational minister's son from Massachusetts and an 1888 Amherst College graduate, who went on to make a fortune as the de facto CEO and chairman, for nineteen years, of what became the Aluminum Company of America (Alcoa).

After retiring to Florida at the age of eighty-two, he made a second fortune in real estate—including the development of Ponte Vedra. The family foundations are known primarily for their grant-making throughout the United States, especially to private institutions of higher education and graduate theological education. There is nothing stereotypically Southern about the foundations beyond their office location in Florida, but they have been highly valued supporters of the SECF since the beginning of the organization, reflecting additional credit upon the region's philanthropy.

The members of the first SECF board of trustees were drawn primarily from the planning group that Archie had assembled after passage of the Tax Reform Act. Its members were:

William C. Archie (Chair)	Mary Reynolds Babcock Foundation	Winston-Salem, NC
Boisfeuillet Jones	Emily and Ernest Woodruff Foundation	Atlanta, GA
Joel Richardson Jr.	Memorial Welfare Foundation	Chattanooga, TN
Carolyn Bufkind	Feild Co-Operative Association	Jackson, MS
James M. Clarke	McClure Education and Development Fund	Asheville, NC
John Eck	The Self Foundation	Greenwood, SC
John A. Griffin	Southern Education Foundation	Atlanta, GA
R. Carl Hubbard	Elliott White Springs Foundation	Fort Mill, SC
Franklyn A. Johnson	Arthur Vining Davis Foundations	Ft. Lauderdale, FL
John W. Red Jr.	Smith Richardson Foundation	Greensboro, NC
Robert J. Sailstad	The Duke Endowment	Charlotte, NC

Employment of an Executive

In the summer of 1972, the board's search for a full-time executive director serendipitously led them to Charles S. Rooks. Rooks was a North Carolina native who had graduated from Wake Forest University and earned master's and doctorate degrees from Duke University. He had been a member of the political science faculty at Lake Forest College in Illinois before returning to the South to work for the Voter Education Project in Atlanta.

WHAT'S A NAME?

George McLean was an imaginative, politically progressive, theologically trained, sometimes belligerent, and impatient newspaper publisher in Tupelo, Mississippi. Raised a Presbyterian, as a college student he was strongly influenced by the Social Gospel movement. McLean went on to play a major role in the economic development of northeastern Mississippi and that area's relatively peaceful transition through the days of school integration and civil rights activity during the 1960s and 1970s.

In 1972 he and his wife, Anna Keirsey, endowed the CREATE* Foundation, the state's first community foundation. Upon their deaths, that foundation became the sole stockholder of the *Northeast Mississippi Daily Journal*. The foundation now serves seventeen counties and manages more than $100 million in assets, including the $50 million Toyota Wellspring Fund, created by the automobile manufacturer when it built a plant outside Tupelo in 2007.

The eulogist at McLean's funeral in 1983 speculated that the deceased might have delivered the following remarks to the assembled congregation: "If what I have tried to say and do here for almost fifty years has meant anything to you, then you SHOW IT! By going out and DOING SOMETHING yourselves for other people, for your community, your state, and your world."

*Originally an acronym for "Christian, Research, Education, Action, Technical, Enterprise." Most people who knew McLean believe he used those components to justify the formation of the name.

Compiled with the assistance of an unpublished document by Mike Clayborne, president of the CREATE Foundation, for a forthcoming book on the life of McLean.

After a few years, Rooks's decision to look for other employment had brought him to the office of John Griffin, the executive director of the Southern Education Foundation in midtown Atlanta. Griffin kept him waiting while completing a long-distance telephone call with William Archie to discuss the employment of a full-time SECF director. When Rooks entered the room and explained his interest, Griffin encouraged him to apply for the SECF position.

As Rooks recalls, given his recent background in political activism, he was not completely comfortable with the idea of leaving the civil rights milieu of voter registration and "dealing with bankers, lawyers, and others of a more privileged class."[9] Nonetheless, he applied and warily accepted the subsequent offer. The organization set him up in a small, two-room office with a secretary in the historic, downtown Rhodes-Haverty Building.[10]

Charles S. Rooks, 2008
Courtesy of Charles Rooks

One of Rooks's primary assignments after coming to SECF was to hit the road to recruit new members throughout the Southeast. That task was not without its difficulties, as simply locating foundations could be a problem. *The Foundation Directory* was not comprehensive, and Rooks learned about some prospective members only through word of mouth. Many of the foundations had no offices, let alone employees. Once he found the persons responsible for the foundation's affairs, he then had to introduce them to the newly constituted intricacies of regulation and compliance and to explain why SECF membership could be essential to their survival. In the process, and despite his earlier misgivings about these new colleagues, he discovered that he liked most of the people he met.

The organization began to meet annually in November, shifting the location from state to state within the region. The complicated new tax legislation was sufficiently intricate to challenge the

Table 13.1 - SECF Annual Meetings		
1972	Biltmore Hotel	Atlanta, GA
1973	Callaway Gardens	Pine Mountain, GA
1974	Governor's Inn	Research Triangle Park, NC
1975	Bay Hill Lodge	Orlando, FL
1976	Williamsburg Lodge	Williamsburg, VA
1977	DeSoto Hilton Hotel	Savannah, GA

intelligence of lawyers; lay-people found it almost impossible to unravel. As a result, those early meetings were primarily training sessions in compliance. Speakers tended to be either attorneys or staff members from the U.S. House Ways and Means Committee or the Senate Finance Committee.[11]

The SECF Family

From the start, in its unique Southern way, SECF tended to operate more like a family than a professional organization. One of the early board members of the Southeastern Council was James ("Jamie") M. Clarke of Fairview, North Carolina, a farmer whose career included service as a Democratic member of the North Carolina House of Representatives and Senate, and subsequently several terms in the U.S. House of Representatives. Born in Manchester, Vermont, Clarke grew up in Asheville, North Carolina. He graduated from Princeton University in 1939 and served as a lieutenant in the U.S. Navy in the Pacific during World War II. After his military duty, he married Elspeth McClure, a cousin and the daughter of the legendary Reverend James G. K. McClure, who came south and revolutionized farming practices in Buncombe County and elsewhere in North Carolina.[12]

It became the custom during Rooks's years as executive for the SECF governing board to meet very informally in mid-summer at the Clarke fishing lodge on the Tuckasegee River. Other memorable board meetings during those early years of the Council, as Rooks remembers, "took place at Trustee Frank Wideman, Jr.'s rustic cabin on the Pee Dee River in South Carolina (at which the menu included white bread sandwiche, Vidalia onions and thick bacon); in the Florida Everglades near Frank Johnson's home ('stone crabs as the featured meal'); and Arnold Palmer's golf club in Orlando, where 'The King,' (another Wake Forest alum) came by to chat with us for a while." Rooks adds, "These kinds of experiences cemented together the SECF leadership in ways that were most helpful to a newly formed association looking for mission and method."[13]

Data collection and management for the foundation field was still in its infancy during this period. The paucity of information and Rooks's own curiosity led him in 1977 to write *Foundation Philanthropy in the Southeast*, a study of grant-making trends between regions. Drawing upon what information he could derive from the Foundation Center Library and other sources, he documented that the South's not-for-profit world was heavily dependent upon Northern philanthropy. As Rook explains:

> In six of the eleven southeastern states, …more funds were received from foundations outside the region than from foundations in their state or elsewhere in the Southeast. The most dramatic example of this was Mississippi, where 85 percent of all the foundation grants received in that state came from outside the region. The proportion of foundation funds supplied by non-southeastern foundations was 64 percent in Virginia, 60 percent in Arkansas, 57 percent in Alabama, 55 percent in Kentucky, and 52.5 percent in Louisiana.[14]

In 1978 Rooks left SECF. After a brief employment detour through Oregon for both him and his wife, Judy, they found their way to Washington, D.C. She took a position in the office of the U.S. Surgeon General, and he accepted the offer to be director of member services at the Council on Foundations, which was preparing to move from New York City to the nation's capital.[15]

Table 13.2 - SECF Board Chairs			
1970-1973	William C. Archie	Mary Reynolds Babcock Foundation	Winston-Salem, NC
1973-1975	Boisfeuillet Jones	Woodruff-related foundations	Atlanta, GA
1975-1977	Franklyn A. Johnson	Arthur Vining Davis Foundations	Miami, FL

CHAPTER 13 ENDNOTES

1   Robert Hall correspondence with Martin Lehfeldt (October 2015).

2   As described in the previous chapter, the Conference of Southwest Foundations was already established, but other regional associations of grant-makers also began organizing prior to 1970. They included, in 1965, North California Grantmakers and in 1969, Associated Grantmakers (of Massachusetts and New Hampshire), Connecticut Council for Philanthropy, and the Minnesota Council on Foundations.

3   A term sometimes humorously applied to staff people of grant-making foundations who are not related by blood to the endowments'donors (i.e. someone who gives away someone else's money).

4   The official incorporation took place on April 7, 1972.

5   It is significant to note that in order to assemble a critical mass of members, the new SECF had to draw upon a nine-state pool of foundations. Eligible members came from Alabama, Florida, Georgia, Louisiana, Mississippi, North Carolina, South Carolina, Tennessee, and Virginia.

6   Additional contributions from some of the larger early members helped to keep the dues at a modest level during the beginning years of the association.

7   Bondurant would go on to a distinguished career in philanthropy, government service, and not-for-profit board service. After graduation from Davidson College (A.B., Economics) and Duke University School of Law, and service in the U.S. Army, he was director of alumni activities and administrative assistant to the president at Davidson before being hired by Archie. After a tour of duty as secretary of administration for the state of North Carolina, he succeeded Archie as executive director of the Babcock Foundation. While there he served on the SECF board and as its chairman, and later on the board of the Park Foundation.

8   See note 5 above. The first Virginia foundation to become a member was the Charles B. Keesee Educational Fund in 1973. SECF then expanded its territory to include Kentucky and Arkansas. The first members from those states were the Steele-Reese Foundation from Lexington, Kentucky (1975) and the Ross Foundation from Arkadelphia, Arkansas (1977). Soon after their admission, their first representatives were elected to the SECF board: W.R. Broaddus Jr. from Virginia, William Buice from Kentucky, and Ross Whipple from Arkansas.

9   Rooks correspondence with Martin Lehfeldt (October, 2015).

10   The Lehfeldt Company took over the SECF space during the period when Lehfeldt directed the Community Foundation Initiative (see Chapter 14). Today those two rooms are presumed to have become part of a guest bedroom after the Rhodes-Haverty Building was converted to a boutique hotel that stands beside the building in which the SECF now has its suite of offices.

11   As Randolph Thrower moved into semi-retirement, James Hasson, a member of the same law firm of Sutherland, Asbill and Brennan, became of counsel to the organization. Hasson and Thrower were especially helpful in recruiting the Congressional committee staff members as speakers.

12   John Curtis Ager, *We Plow God's Fields: The Life of James G. K. McClure* (Boone, N.C.; Appalachian Consortium Press, 1991). McClure, the son of a Presbyterian minister and himself a clergyman, discovered the mountainous area of western North Carolina while on his honeymoon and moved there from Illinois. He and his wife, Elizabeth, were especially charmed by the old Sherrill's Inn beside an important road across the Blue Ridge, and its surrounding farm, which they subsequently acquired, restored, and maintained as Hickory Nut Gap Inn. The inn's office boasted a guest registry that included the name of Democratic president James Buchanan.

13   Rooks correspondence.

14   Charles S. Rooks, *Foundation Philanthropy in the Southeast* (Southeastern Council of Foundations, 1977), 7.

15 Rooks would later become vice president and then acting president of the Council during a period of executive transition. Now retired, he continued his distinguished career as CEO of the then-new Fred Meyer Charitable Trust in Portland, Oregon.

CHAPTER 14

An Organization for Southern Philanthropy

Robert Hull's Leadership

Succeeding Charles Rooks as executive director in 1978 was Robert H. Hull. A native Floridian, Hull was the great-grandson of one of the pioneers who established Orlando. He earned degrees from the University of Florida, Columbia Theological Seminary, and Vanderbilt University and later was employed by Emory University's Center for Research in Social Change while pursuing a graduate degree at the Institute of Liberal Arts. As a former Presbyterian minister, he served as a university pastor while at Vanderbilt and later spent nine years associated with a private city-planning firm in Atlanta.

Since the passage of the Tax Reform Act of 1969, much of SECF's concern had remained focused upon keeping its members fully observant of their legal responsibilities.

Robert Hull
Courtesy of Robert Hull

Nonetheless, there were signs that grant-makers could also concern themselves with philanthropic values and priorities. Soon after Hull's arrival he recognized this shift of emphasis when John Griffin,[1] the veteran foundation executive, shared his intention to rock the boat—at least gently—in an upcoming speech. Hull encouraged him to speak his mind.

A Cautionary Keynote Address

Griffin, the soft-spoken head of the Southern Education Foundation, was nearing retirement. He was also chairman of the SECF board that year, a fitting honor for someone who had been present at the creation of the organization. The planning committee for the annual meeting, scheduled for the next October at the Royal Orleans Hotel in New Orleans, had asked Dr. Griffin to deliver the keynote address. A thoroughly progressive Southerner of long standing, Griffin had always been a conciliatory figure, but it soon became clear that he had some critical thoughts he wanted to express to his colleagues before departing the scene.

The title of Griffin's speech telegraphed his thesis: "Charity versus Justice."[2] In his characteristically non-confrontational way, he summarized some statistics about the giving patterns of Southern foundations, noting that "it is easier to give to the safe, historically sound recipients." He further noted that he did not wish "to discount the importance of philanthropic grants for the purpose of conserving worthy institutions." However, he made clear his belief that most Southern philanthropy had erred on the side of caution:

As an example of our conservative approach to philanthropy, I point out the fact that the social revolution which
has taken place in the South since 1954 has gone forward
with little support and encouragement from the southern
foundation community, certainly little direct support.

After a brief summary of the civil rights movement and its cat-
alytic impact upon the struggle for the rights of many other minority
populations, he continued:

As this profoundly important struggle went on in the
South, we did a little—but not much. Not to chide ourselves do I speak of this. But I do believe that we might
well remind ourselves of these opportunities lost as we
think of our responsibilities in relation to the vast changes
taking place in our region and in the world beyond. Surely
it would be a tragic mistake to miss the boat again.[3]

From its beginnings, the SECF felt the keen need to promote the
establishment of more institutional philanthropy for the region. One of
the first projects launched on Hull's watch as executive director and later
as president was the 1980 publication of the booklet *Why Establish a
Private Foundation?* It was written with assistance from Jim Hasson (see
previous chapter) and the subsidy of a small grant from the Lyndhurst
Foundation that enabled the hiring of an editor and graphic designer.[4]
Recognizing that educating those who gave professional advice to generous people of wealth might be the most effective way to reach potential donors, Hull distributed the publication to as many estate attorneys

as possible. Several regional associations of grant-makers also used the booklet, and still others published their own versions.

Table 14.1 SECF Board Chairs			
1977-78	John A. Griffin	Southern Education Foundation	Atlanta, GA
1978-80	Robert J. Sailstad	The Duke Endowment	Charlotte, NC
1980-82	William L. Bondurant	Mary Reynolds Babcock Foundation	Winston-Salem, NC
1982-83	Charles A. Bundy	Springs Foundation	Lancaster, SC
1983-84	William T. Buice, III	Steele-Reese Foundation	Lexington, KY
1984-85	Deaderick C. Montague	Lyndhurst Foundation	Chattanooga, TN
1985-87	Thomas W. Lambeth	Z. Smith Reynolds Foundation	Winston-Salem, NC
1987-88	C. Thompson Wacaster	Phil Hardin Foundation	Meridian, MS
1988-89	Henry M. Carter, Jr.	The Winston-Salem Foundation,	Winston-Salem NC
1989-90	Charles H. (Pete) McTier	Robert W. Woodruff Foundation	Atlanta, GA
1990-92	Martha G. Peck	Burroughs-Wellcome Fund	Research Triangle, NC
1992-93	Jack Murrah	Lyndhurst Foundation	Chattanooga, TN
1993-95	John W. Stephenson	J. Bulow Campbell Foundation	Atlanta, GA
1995-97	Katharine Pearson	East Tennessee Foundation	Knoxville, TN

Membership Criteria

By 1981 the new SECF was seemingly settled enough to begin feeling a bit exclusive. A debate arose that year about whether corporate giving programs of companies that had no separate endowed foundations should be welcomed to membership in the association.[5] The topic was raised by Carroll Thrift, a representative of the Levi Strauss Company based in San Francisco. The company, well known for its philanthropy had several plants around the region, and Thrift had sought to attend SECF conferences.

During that year's annual meeting at Atlanta's Hyatt Regency

Hotel, Hull proposed that they be admitted as full members. The board decided to throw open the debate to the entire membership during the business meeting portion of the conference. Most of the "old-timers" favored exclusion of the corporate grant-makers, feeling that their presence would change what they considered to be the essential, regulations-driven format of the association's meetings.

The younger foundation leaders sensed that the future of SECF would need to be less about rules and more about the art of grant-making. Hull remembers that the discussion was tense but not especially heated. When one of the younger members expressed impatience with the more conservative position, Rick Montague of the Lyndhurst Foundation in Chattanooga encouraged patience. The issue, he noted, was likely be resolved by some "inevitable funerals." The SECF board resolved the matter by approving inclusion of corporate grant-making programs.[6] Not surprisingly, since its stock then constituted most of the assets of the so-called Woodruff-source funds, the Coca-Cola Company was among the first corporate grant-makers to join the SECF.[7] The Levi Strauss Company would later submit its application for membership.

Competition in the Field

The steady emergence and growth of the regional associations (or RAGs, as they came to be called) deeply concerned the national Council on Foundations (COF). Most basically, the existence of both levels of infrastructure constituted competition for dues. Among the complaints of the regional associations was their disappointment with what they perceived to be the COF's weak advocacy of their members' interests in Congress and the predominant role of large Northeastern foundations (especially those from New York City) in the leadership of the Council.[8]

Some of those larger COF members were still dissatisfied with the way in which David Freeman, the president, had dealt with Congress during the Tax Reform Act negotiations.[9] They engineered a coup of sorts that placed Robert Goheen, the former president of Princeton University, in the newly created, full-time position as chairman of the COF. Goheen's duties included building better public relations for foundations by educating and cultivating support from legislators, news media, and other opinion makers.

COF continued to be interested in bringing the members of SECF and other regional associations back into the fold. Goheen was tapped to lead the COF's delegation for a meeting between representatives from both organizations to discuss the possibility. A former classics scholar, he was a gracious Ivy Leaguer, who perhaps somewhat naively believed that the SECF would immediately recognize the reasonableness of placing itself under the wing of the national council. In advance of the gathering, Rooks did his best to discourage this expectation. However, as perhaps could have been predicted, the Southern foundations rejected the COF's advances, as did the other regional associations.[10]

The conflict actually involved a more substantive issue than regional pride. SECF (and other regional associations) placed a high priority on revising the payout requirement for foundations (which included both disbursements for charitable purposes and reasonable administrative expenses). The original and very convoluted legislation had called for an annual 6.5% payout for each foundation, based on its previous year's assets. As Rooks recalls, some foundations doubted that their investment earnings could keep pace with the required spending level. The resulting shrinkage of assets would eventually (perhaps within about a decade) put them out of business—an outcome that some members of Congress still considered to be highly desirable. A further problem was that foundations would not know the extent of their charitable obligations until they were well into the year when those payments needed to be made—a major barrier to long-term planning.

COF recognized the importance of a required payout and certainly didn't want lawmakers and regulators to think that foundations were resisting that concept. Its top priority as it continued to challenge the 1969 legislation, however, was to lower the proposed excise tax of 4% on investment income. Ostensibly intended to cover IRS expenses for the audits of private foundations and public charities, the tax generated far more income than needed for this oversight; the foundations were anxious to recover the "surplus" and use it for grant-making instead.

Lobbying Congress

Hull remembers a lot of "fussin' and feudin'" about priorities when they all might have been better served by presenting a unified front. Nonetheless, a flurry of commuting to and from the District of Columbia ensued as the philanthropic sector sought to convince the members and committees of the Congress about the merit of the foundations' positions. Charles Rooks, SECF's former executive, contributed to the strategizing.

To the elation of the foundation world, a bill to reduce the excise tax on investments was introduced, and Congressman Charles Rangel of New York scheduled hearings for the Sub-Committee on Oversight of the U.S. House Committee on Ways and Means. Hull was chairing the regional associations group (later to be named the Forum) that year and was asked by the Council on Foundations to testify on its behalf. He was joined by the presidents of the Council of Michigan Foundations (Dorothy Johnson), the Donors Forum of Chicago (Eleanor Petersen), and Associated Grantmakers (Janet Taylor), which served Massachusetts and the surrounding areas. The value of their testimony, as the COF reasoned, was that they represented a vital link between the nation's small, unstaffed foundations and Congress. The heart of their presentation included the strong avowal that the regional associations were performing valuable service by keeping these small foundations in compliance with federal law.

Hull's partial account of the experience follows:

> When we first arrived for the hearings [on June 28, 1983], the four of us met for lunch at the office of the Michigan Republican Party, next door to Capitol Hill. You could tell we were nervous; we didn't eat much. Our appearance was first on the agenda after lunch, and none of us had ever done this kind of thing before. . . . We walked into the largest hearing room and found it filled with foundation folk. . . . our table was placed in front of the rows of chairs with Members of Congress nameplates on them. The Members sat high above us, looking down on our lowly

position. Intimidated? You bet! I was to start our testimony and I hoped my voice didn't fail me. Finally, Congressman Rangel's gavel struck the table and we were on.... [Despite the absence of several Sub-Committee members, to be expected since we were not famous philanthropoids], we were duly sworn to tell the truth and we did.... I think it went well.... After we were dismissed, we took our seats in the audience and looked at each other with relief on our faces. We had made it through the ordeal without embarrassing ourselves or our purpose for being there.

After the dust settled, the foundations had secured a reduction of the excise tax on investment earnings, from 4% to 2%. The other subsequent victory was the reduction of the payout percentage to 5% of an asset figure to be determined by a twelve-month average of a foundation's endowment/non-charitable assets.

Financial Maturity

In 1984, now nearly fifteen years old, SECF was still operating on a financial shoestring—often relying upon quiet subsidies from individual foundations to balance the books. It had, to be sure, gained additional members, but their dues were not enough to cover an expanded program. Not without a great deal of nervousness, the trustees reached the decision to increase the dues. They introduced a new fee schedule and then held their breath. To their relief, the center held and the SECF constituency suffered no significant losses.

The organization had indeed expanded its work. Nowhere was

that increase more evident than in the structure and content of its annual meetings. As the worries about compliance failures and resulting penalties began to recede, the representatives of SECF foundations began to shift their attention to discussions about what constituted good grant-making. The meeting agendas included space for the sharing of management efficiencies and investment options and presentations from experts in education, health care, community development, children and

	Table 14.2-SECF Annual Meetings	
1978	Royal Orleans Hotel	New Orleans, LA
1979	Hyatt House Hotel	Winston-Salem, NC
1980	Kiawah Island Inn	Kiawah Island, SC
1981	Hyatt Regency Hotel	Atlanta, GA
1982	Grand Hotel	Point Clear, AL
1983	Peabody Hotel	Memphis, TN
1984	Hyatt Hotel	Sarasota, FL
1985	Hyatt Regency Hotel	Greenville, SC
1986	The Homestead	Hot Springs, VA
1987	Hyatt Regency Hotel	Lexington, KY
1988	Omni Hotel	Charleston, SC
1989	The Cloister	Sea Island, GA
1990	Vanderbilt Plaza Hotel	Nashville, TN
1991	The Breakers	Palm Beach, FL
1992	Jefferson Hotel	Richmond, VA
1993	Hotel Intercontinental	New Orleans, LA
1994	Omni Hotel	Charlotte, NC
1995	Marriott Sawgrass	Ponte Vedra Beach, FL
1996	The Greenbrier	White Sulphur Springs, WV
1997	Peabody Hotel	Memphis, TN

youth issues, elder care concerns, and other community-oriented topics. SECF was, to be sure, still a trade association, but it was now marked by an increased emphasis upon the building of a professional ethos.

Even without the funds to pay significant honoraria, the Southeastern Council was able to attract both "headline" speakers (Terry Sanford, McGeorge Bundy, William Simon, Landrum Bolling, Robert Coles, James Laney) as well as rising stars (Jimmy Carter, Hillary Clinton). Especially popular were Southern authors and other artists like Josephine Humphreys and William Ferris.

As the organization grew, and despite the increase in the depth and intensity of the programs, these annual gatherings retained their "family" ambience, perhaps because the number of foundation trustees (and their spouses) in attendance still outnumbered staff members. "Spouse tours" were regular features of the program, as was the Chairman's Dinner on the traditional, opening Wednesday evening. The rest of the conference called for casual garb, but the guests dressed up for this dinner and the dancing that followed. One of the traditions that continued for many years occurred when

SOUTHERN BY ADOPTION

The Knight Foundation became a "naturalized" Southern citizen when it relocated from Akron, Ohio, to Miami, Florida in 1990. Three years later it changed its name to the John S. and James L. Knight Foundation to honor the two brothers who built the highly successful newspaper chain that bore their last name.

Although a major national grant-maker with heavy emphasis upon journalism, it acquired and maintains an authentic Southern accent: two of its regional offices are in the South (Charlotte, North Carolina, and Macon, Georgia), and it also works through local community foundations to support programs in Bradenton, Palm Beach County, and Tallahassee, Florida; Columbus and Milledgeville, Georgia; Lexington, Kentucky, Biloxi, Mississippi; and Columbia and Myrtle Beach, South Carolina—all of which once had Knight or Knight-Ridder newspapers.

Source: *www.knightfoundation.org*

Henry Carter, president of the Winston-Salem Foundation, and his wife, Rhea, would lead the way onto the floor and dazzle their colleagues with elegant foxtrots and waltzes, exotic rhumba and mambos, and energetic jitterbugging.

Facility and Staff Expansion

In Atlanta during the early 1990s several of the metropolitan area's major foundations, led by the Woodruff-related philanthropies,[11] were moving into the historic Hurt Building, a former Federal Reserve Bank and later Southern Bell facility, in downtown Atlanta. With the benefit of an expanded dues base and several small grants, Hull, his assistant director, Dixie Purvis, and secretary, Becky Weaver, joined the migration.

During the next several years, the Hurt Building became "Philanthropy Central." Other foundations that took up residence included the Atlanta Women's Foundation, the CDC Foundation, the Community Foundation for Greater Atlanta, the R. Howard Dobbs Foundation, the Georgia Baptist Healthcare Ministry Foundation, the Henry W. Grady

The Hurt Building, Atlanta, Georgia
Courtesy of Beth Grashof

Foundation, the Healthcare Georgia Foundation, the Katherine John Murphy Foundation, the Tull Charitable Foundation, the Jesse Parker Williams Foundation, and a wide range of foundations and trusts managed by SunTrust Bank. They would be joined in 2002 by the J. Bulow Campbell Foundation, the Courts Foundation, the Fraser-Parker Foundation, and the Georgia Health Foundation, all administered by a single staff. The proximity of these charitable organizations and the opportunity for informal encounters in the elevators, lobbies, and the building's restaurant did much to strengthen ties among them and the Southeastern Council.

SECF began to develop an interest in recruiting more corporate members and consequently hired Danah Craft in 1994 to succeed Purvis as assistant director. As her responsibilities expanded, she subsequently became assistant director of member services and government affairs. Craft left SECF in 1997 to join the Sun Trust Endowment and Foundations group (two stories higher in the same building) and was succeeded by Jane Hardesty, who had just completed a year-long internship at the Robert W. Woodruff Foundation.

Eldridge McMillan
CAU Photograph Collection, Atlanta University Center, Robert W. Woodruff Library

ELRIDGE W. MCMILLAN

In 1990 Elridge W. McMillan became the first African American trustee of the Southeastern Council of Foundations. He also was the first African American president of the Southern Education Foundation and the first African American chair of the Board of Regents of the University System of Georgia, on which governing body he served for more than thirty-four years. As a former trustee of Clark College (his alma mater), he co-chaired the Trustee Committee that was responsible for the consolidation of Clark and Atlanta University (1987–89). McMillan was also appointed to the Center for Civil and Human Rights Global Advisory Board and is a past member of the University System of Georgia Foundation Board.

Source: SECF Archives; "Georgia's Regent Emeritus to Be Honored by Atlanta Metropolitan State College," Metro Atlanta CEO, September 25, 2018, *http://metroatlantaceo.com/ news/2018/09/georgias-regent-emeritus-be-honored-atlanta-metropolitan-state-college/*.

Donors' Discovery of Community Foundations

One of the by-products of the Tax Reform Act of 1969 was a significant surge in the number of new community foundations created. In the South, as throughout the country, charitably inclined individuals with discretionary assets were discovering that these foundations provided a remarkably flexible philanthropic alternative to conventional private foundations. Especially welcome was the relief from the onerous task of subjecting themselves to the federal government's newly mandated reporting requirements. For these new philanthropists, community foundations were increasingly becoming the vehicles for their generosity.

Keenly aware of this trend, in 1986 the Council on Foundations launched the National Agenda for Community Foundations—a $2.2 million, three-year initiative underwritten by six large private foundations, 125 community foundations, and the Council itself.[12] It was composed of five projects: On-Site Consulting, National Presence, Data Gathering, National Training, and Community Leadership. Among its accomplishments, the National Agenda promoted an assertive approach to fund raising among living donors, the development of greater staff professionalism, and community building.[13]

Until then, most of the South's older community foundations (of which there were relatively few) had built their assets in the same way their Northern counterparts had done it—by waiting for civic-minded citizens to die and leave a portion of their estates to them for unrestricted purposes. Thus, Jack Shakeley, then the CEO of the California Community Foundation in Los Angeles, was fond of describing these institutions as "United Ways for the Dead."

Shakeley was one of the "on-site consultants" from the National Agenda who helped to stimulate new thinking and otherwise "shake up things" at the community foundations they visited. Darcy Oman, CEO of the Community Foundation Serving Richmond and Central Virginia, still remembers Californian Shakeley's arrival for a meeting with her conservatively attired board wearing his powder-blue leisure suit. Another consultant, Eugene C. ("Struck") Struckhoff, raised some Richmond eyebrows when he ordered wine with lunch.[14]

"Struck" was the Johnny Appleseed of the movement. According to his estimate, he could claim responsibility for having launched 140 community foundations in the United States. He had a dogmatic set of recommendations about how best to create or strengthen a foundation, and it was for him an article of faith that no citizen should have the temerity to die without leaving behind a bequest to the local community foundation. (See below for further information about the formation of Southern community foundations.)

Donor-Advised Funds

Perhaps the most dramatic change in the field entailed the new attention being paid to the establishment of donor-advised funds at the community foundations.[15] The New York Community Trust had established the first such fund in 1931, but the use of this charitable giving instrument had not received much notice since that time. Indeed, some of the older community foundations frowned upon the notion that living donors might wish to express opinions about how their contributions would be disbursed. As an example, in those days the executive of one Mid-

Martha Peck, MD
Courtesy of Martha Peck

MARTHA G. PECK, M.D.

Dr. Martha G. Peck, the first female board chair of SECF, is a North Carolina native who earned her B.S. and M.S. degrees in pharmacy from the University of North Carolina at Chapel Hill. After employment as a clinical pharmacist, she joined the neurology division of the former Burroughs Wellcome pharmaceutical company as a clinical research scientist. In 1981 she became executive director (and later vice president) of the Burroughs Wellcome Fund. During her twenty-plus years with the fund, its endowment grew to over $500 million, and it gained national recognition for investments in medical research and science education. In 2000 Peck returned to UNC for her medical degree and residency in family medicine. She was a partner in Daniels and Peck Family Medicine until her retirement but still works part-time with UNC Physicians Network. She has been married for forty-one years to Ray F. Peck, vice president, Raymond James Investment Services; they have two grown sons and two grandchildren.

Source: Martha Peck, correspondence with Martin Lehfeldt, June 21, 2019.

western foundation proudly and pointedly described his institution's refusal to accept any restricted donations.[16]

In 1977, however, the IRS issued a new set of regulations about donor-advised funds as described in the Tax Reform Act of 1969. These clarifications essentially opened the hunting season for the more entrepreneurial foundation executives. CEOs like Darcy Oman in Richmond and Dennis Riggs in Louisville who had come to the field from careers in fund raising adapted to this new style of resource building with ease. Rather than studying obituary columns to learn from whose estates they might anticipate bequests, they could instead begin stalking live game.[17] Many of them received important support from the Charles Stewart Mott Foundation of Flint, Michigan (see below).

Change on the Way

A major break with SECF tradition occurred when Martha Peck, executive of the Burroughs Wellcome Fund in North Carolina, was elected in 1990 to be the first female chair of SECF. Under Peck's energetic leadership,

Hull and the board set in motion the first strategic planning exercise in the organization's history. They engaged the Lehfeldt Company, a local consulting firm that was well acquainted with the foundation field, to facilitate the process. The results were presented to the annual conference attendees at The Breakers in Palm Beach, Florida, in 1991.

SECF's Own Community Foundation Initiative

One of the new strategic plan's five major goals was a commitment to promote the growth of private philanthropic resources in and for the region. The wealth of the South was increasing steadily, but its charitable capital was not keeping pace. Certainly no one was amassing the kind of fortunes associated with James B. Duke and Robert W. Woodruff. The infamous "intergenerational transfer of wealth" phenomenon that would later be identified and labeled by Paul Schervish and John Havens at Boston College (see next chapter) was still undiscovered, and many of the new foundations being formed in the South tended to be relatively small family foundations with assets of fewer than $10 million. Only a few of the larger ones had paid staff, and their giving was intensely localized. If structured philanthropy was going to have a significant impact upon the South, it would require a different kind of strategy.

The board consequently determined that the needed expansion of charitable capital would be tied to the growth in the number and assets of community foundations. SECF launched the Community Foundation Development Project in March 1993. The project retained Bill Somerville, CEO of the Peninsula Community Foundation in California, to present three grant-making workshops in Florida, Georgia, and North

WEST VIRGINIA AND SECF

The Greater Kanawha Valley Community Foundation was established in Charleston, West Virginia, in 1962. In 1993 Betsy von Blond, its CEO, sought membership for her organization in the Southeastern Council of Foundations. SECF changed its by-laws to make West Virginia foundations eligible for membership, and redrew its map and logo to reflect a twelve-state service area. Two other West Virginia community foundations followed the lead of Greater Kanawha. The addition of the new territory enabled SECF to schedule annual meetings at the Greenbrier, the historic resort in White Sulfur Springs. The West Virginians retained their membership until they joined their own newly formed statewide association of grant-makers (now called Philanthropy West Virginia).

Source: SECF Archives.

Carolina and to conduct follow-up, on-site consulting to individual community foundations.[18]

Subsequent additional grants (primarily from the Robert W. Woodruff Foundation) made it possible for SECF to retain Martin Lehfeldt for three years as a part-time director of what became the Community Foundation Initiative. Beginning in July 1994, he was charged with the responsibility of helping to identify strategies that might promote extended coverage of the region by existing and new community foundations, to respond to ad hoc requests for technical assistance, and to help with the search for additional funding of the venture.

Lehfeldt functioned as a virtual staff person. Although he continued to work with a few other clients, much of his time was spent on the road for SECF, convening statewide gatherings of community foundation representatives, leading planning retreats for their boards, and meeting with local leaders who wished to explore the creation of community foundations. However, the overall goal of the initiative was not necessarily to increase the number of community foundations. Rather, as Hull often described it, SECF's vision was one of every prospective donor and grant-seeker in the

South having easy access to the benefits of a community foundation's services.

Nonetheless, in a report to the SECF board in November 1996, Lehfeldt was able to identify ninety-two community foundations (many of them newly formed) in the region—a figure that would continue to increase steadily during subsequent years. Part of that expansion was, to be sure, due to the special attention being given to these new and growing organizations. Other important contributing factors included a booming economy, business migration into the South, and a series of challenge grants from Northern funders—especially the Charles Stewart Mott Foundation, which awarded SECF a grant of $200,000 for community foundation development work.

Over a period of approximately ten years (1984–94), the Mott Foundation also awarded

MANY WAYS TO START A COMMUNITY FOUNDATION

There did not seem to be a standard way by which community foundations came into existence. The Southwest Florida Estate Planning Council established the Community Foundation of Sarasota County in 1979. The Foothills Community Foundation in South Carolina (serving Anderson, Oconee, and Pickens County) got its start with a $1 million challenge bequest from William Law Watkins, a local attorney, and began operations in 2001. Elsewhere, banks transferred small foundations and trusts they had been managing into community foundation portfolios.

The launching gift for the foundation in Columbus, Georgia came from the not-for-profit Chattahoochee Valley Fair. Construction of a softball field for the 1996 Olympics was going to force the relocation of the fair from its traditional site, and that disruption triggered the realization by the leaders that the fair "business" was increasingly being run by for-profit corporations. They decided to dissolve their organization and transfer the bulk of their assets—some $600,000—to the newly formed community foundation. They attached no strings to the use of these funds; their only provision was that the new philanthropy be called the Community Foundation of the Chattahoochee Valley rather than the Community Foundation of Columbus. Today the Chattahoochee Valley Fair Fund endowment is valued at approximately $900,000, and its yield is used to make discretionary grants across a 13-county wide service area. The entire assets of the Community Foundation of the Chattahoochee Valley now total $130 million.

Source: Communication with Betsy Covington, President, Community Foundation of the Chattahoochee Valley; *https:// foothillscommunityfoundation.org/about-us/*; *https://www. cfsarasota.org/About/About-CFSC-Community-Knowledge-Lasting-Impact.*

challenge grants to help build administrative assets and endowments, underwrite neighborhood small grants programs, and support marketing efforts by community foundations in Florida, Georgia, Louisiana, North Carolina, South Carolina, Tennessee, and Virginia. Total grants totaled $2,459,800, which in turn generated $4,441,671 in matching funds. Southeastern foundations that took advantage of this opportunity included:

Florida
Community Foundation of Broward
Dade Community Foundation
Community Foundation for Palm Beach and Martin Counties
Community Foundation of Sarasota County
Community Foundation of Tampa Bay

Georgia
Community Foundation for Greater Atlanta

Louisiana
Greater New Orleans Foundation

North Carolina
Foundation for the Carolinas
Cumberland Community Foundation

South Carolina
Central Carolina Community Foundation
Community Foundation Serving Coastal South Carolina

Tennessee
East Tennessee Foundation
Community Foundation of Greater Memphis

Virginia
Foundation for Roanoke Valley
Community Foundation Serving Richmond and Central Virginia
Virginia Beach Foundation (since merged with Norfolk Foundation)

New community foundations soon realized they could speed their growth in assets and extend their service by reaching out to adjoining counties and helping them to establish their own named affiliate funds. Thus Robert Hull's vision of every Southern donor and nonprofit having easy access to a community foundation steadily accelerated into greater focus. The Foundation for the Carolinas (FFTC) was among the first, if not the first, to adopt this strategy. As its name suggests, it had a sense of geographical destiny from the start. Established in Charlotte in 1958 with a $3,000 grant from United Way, it soon was reaching out to neighboring counties in South Carolina as well as its own state.

In similar fashion, the Metropolitan Atlanta Community Foundation, founded in 1951, followed the city's pattern of population sprawl across the Georgia landscape. Indeed, it was the Atlanta foundation that served as a kind of flagship of the movement in the region into the 21st century. Created by the city's four largest banks, it initially had appointed trustees who managed the funds and a distribution committee that determined the grants to be awarded. A decade later it created the Metropolitan Foundation of Atlanta, Inc., a corporation that could hold title to real property for local nonprofit organizations. Major contributors to capital projects could thus be assured that even if the organization whose facility they helped to build were to go out of business, the property would remain in the public trust and available for use by another agency.

During its early decades, the foundation sup-

ARKANSAS COMMUNITY FOUNDATION

The Arkansas Community Foundation is the only statewide community foundation in the South. Established in 1976, primarily by a lead grant of $258,000 from the Winthrop Rockefeller Foundation, the services of its central office staff of fifteen in Little Rock are supplemented by twenty-eight staffed affiliate offices whose coverage extends to all seventy-five counties in the state. The foundation now manages some $335 million in assets.

Source: *arcf.org*; correspondence from Heather Larkin and Pat Lile, current and former presidents of the foundation.

plemented the influence of its still somewhat limited assets (only $7 million in 1977) by drawing upon its leadership clout and convening ability to provide support for the city's major planning ventures. A focus upon soliciting donor-advised funds (see above) led to a soaring of asset totals to $280 million and a subsequent overhaul of governance, management, and investment system and strategies.

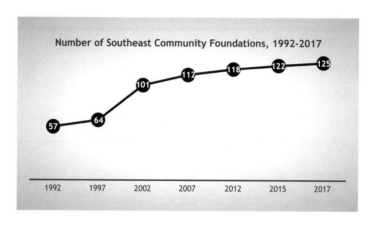

Number of Southeast Community Foundations, 1992-2017

Growth of Community Foundations in the Southeast, 1992-2017

	1992	1997	2002	2007	2012	2015	2017
AL	3	3	9	10	9	9	9
AR	1	1	3	3	3	3	3
FL	11	12	23	26	26	28	27
GA	3	5	10	12	14	14	14
KY	3	3	5	5	6	6	6
LA	3	3	3	4	5	5	5
MS	2	5	5	6	8	8	8
NC	16	13	18	19	17	19	20
SC	4	4	6	7	9	9	9
TN	4	4	5	5	4	4	4
VA	7	11	14	15	17	17	20
TOTAL	57	64	101	112	118	122	125

Source for 1992 data: Southeastern Foundations: A Profile of the Region's Grantmaking Community. New York: Foundation Center, 1994.
Source for 1997 data: Southeastern Foundations II: A Profile of the Region's Grantmaking Community. New York: Foundation Center, 1999.
Source for 2002-2015 data: Foundation Center (http://data.foundationcenter.org), ca. 2018.
Source for 2017 data: Foundation Directory Online, ca. 2018.

One of its most significant actions was to create the Atlanta AIDS Partnership Fund at a time when many foundations were fearful of having anything to do with combating this dread disease. It similarly established the reputation of providing a "Seal of Approval" to new and emerging nonprofit organizations; even a modest grant of $5,000 from the community foundation often signaled to the rest of the foundations that the nonprofit was worthy of additional support. During these years, the foundation also was the incubator of the Atlanta Woman's Fund and the Nonprofit Resource Center (now the Georgia Center for Nonprofits)—both of which became independent organizations, as well as the Metropolitan Atlanta Arts Fund.

Today, operating as The Community Foundation for Greater Atlanta, with a self-perpetuating board of regional business and community leaders, this remarkable philanthropy manages more than $1 billion in assets. A highly professional cadre of specialists focuses its asset-building activities upon the cultivation and education of professional advisors (e.g., attorneys, accountants, estate planners) who advise clients of wealth.

State	Number	Assets	Grants
AL	22	$14,577,000	$1,011,000
AR	17	$2,876,000	$508,000
FL	48	$12,015,000	$1,363,000
GA	107	$124,589,000	$4,917,000
KY	29	$15,528,000	$875,000
LA	40	$16,044,000	$1,813,000
MS	8	$651,000	$103,000
NC	84	$130,750,000	$5,898,000
SC	40	$22,916,000	$1,450,000
TN	47	$29,004,000	$2,463,000
VA	55	$20,610,000	$2,311,000
TOTALS	497	$389,560,000	$22,712,000

Source: The Foundation Directory. New York, NY: Russell Sage Foundation, 1960. Transcribed from chart on page xiv.

Alicia Philipp, president and CEO for the past forty-two years, has been a generous mentor and guide to her colleagues. The story just

Peyton Anderson, owner and publisher of the Macon Telegraph and News from 1951 to 1969, in the Macon Telegraph pressroom.
Courtesy of the Peyton Anderson Foundation

PEYTON ANDERSON FOUNDATION
"The money I have is not mine."

The Peyton Anderson Foundation in Macon, Georgia, was formed to distribute funds from the estate of Peyton T. Anderson Jr., based on his desire to improve and impact the communities of his hometown region. When Anderson died on April 24, 1988, he directed in his will that approximately $35 million of his state be used to establish the foundation.

"The money I have is not mine. It's not mine because this money was made in the community, and it was made because the community flourished," he said. "Therefore, I was able to flourish and this money rightfully should go back into the well-being of the community."

He instructed the trustees to give to "good-doers" instead of "do-gooders." The Peyton Anderson wgood will lives on long after him.

Under the inaugural leadership of Juanita Jordan, a former SECF board member, the foundation played a key role in the establishment of the Community Foundation of Central Georgia, which now serves twenty-one counties and provides administrative support to the Barnesville-Lamar Community Foundation and the Community Foundation of Coffee County. She also led the effort to establish the Peyton Anderson Community Services Building for the benefit of local nonprofit organizations, and to establish NewTown Macon, the city's leading economic development advocate.

Sources: Jaclyn Weldon White, Bestest: The Life of Peyton Tooke Anderson, Jr. (Macon, Ga.: Mercer University Press, 2005); Linda S. Morris, "Jordan Retiring from Peyton Anderson Foundation," Macon Telegraph, November 16, 2011, *https://www.macon.com/news/article28626085.html.*

shared, with its own local variations, has become a kind of template for successful community foundation development throughout the region. Today these flexible institutions of philanthropy and their affiliate funds—from the Communities of Coastal Georgia Foundation on St. Simons Island in southeastern Georgia to the Carroll County Community Foundation in northwestern Arkansas (an affiliate of the Arkansas Community Foundation)—convene, collaborate, incubate, commission studies and reports, and promote the creation of new philanthropic assets.

One of the most dramatic changes in the field has occurred with the Foundation for the Carolinas (see above), whose imaginative and innovative asset-building technique have brought its portfolio total to nearly $2 billion.

Ready for Further Growth

The Southeastern Council was now nearly thirty years old. By this time it was clear that the SECF had proven its value to a growing number of both established and new foundations in what had become (at least for a short time) a twelve-state region. It no longer needed to focus upon congressionally regulated rectitude or the recruitment of sufficient members to sustain its activities. The organization was ready to broaden and deepen its services to an increasingly varied cadre of grant-makers with specialized needs.

CHAPTER 14 endnotes

1   John A. Griffin, who died in 1997, was a native of Monroe, Georgia. He received his undergraduate and master's degrees from Emory University and his doctorate in sociology and agricultural economics from the University of Wisconsin. His career included service on the faculty and administration of Emory and the U.S. Community Relations Service, working to resolve volatile racial crises in places like Selma, Alabama; McComb, Mississippi; and Houma, Louisiana. He was one of the founders of the Southern Regional Council, and organized much of the research on the South's racially segregated schools that is credited with having influenced the U.S. Supreme Court's 1954 decision in *Brown v. Board of Education.* Peter Applebome, "John Griffin, 84, Who Helped Bridge the Gulf Between the Races," *New York Times,* January 28, 1997.

2   A written version of the speech was printed in January 1979 by the Southern Education Foundation.

3   The authors speculate that it was an oversight by Dr. Griffin to omit a reference to the Stern Fund during his New Orleans speech. This foundation (see chapter 11), established in 1936 by Edgar and Edith Stern, a prominent New Orleans family, and later headquartered in New York City, became one of the most notable supporters of civil rights activities in the South. Mrs. Stern was the daughter of Julius Rosenwald (see chapter 8). Similarly, the speech neglected references to the progressive grant-making of the Reynolds foundations in North Carolina.

4   The designer wanted to incorporate some of the details from U.S. printed currency for marginal decorations and chapter divisions, only to discover that it would require the permission of the U.S. Secret Service to reproduce the many detailed images like leaves and curlicues. The brochure's illustrations were changed.

5   Robert Hull, correspondence and interviews with Martin Lehfeldt, January 12, 2016.

6   The board instructed Hull to determine a fair dues structure to accommodate these new members. He settled upon using charitable funds disbursements as the only criterion that would work for all members, and that system became the protocol for several years.

   Hull and others also remember that year's annual meeting as the one at which Boisfeuillet Jones and Charles H. ("Pete") McTier of the Emily and Ernest Woodruff Foundation, a major supporter of the city's premier arts center, arranged for a cocktail reception there, after which the Atlanta Symphony Orchestra presented a short program for the guests, who also were invited to a private stroll through the High Museum of Art.

7   The Coca-Cola Company Foundation was established in 1984.

8   Robert Hull and Charles Rooks, correspondence and interviews with Martin Lehfeldt during January 2016. Most of the RAG executives, whatever their gripes and their desire for independence, maintained a cordial relationship with the Council leadership. Rooks remembers the especially challenging tension, however, between the Council and Joseph G. Dempsey, the founder of what eventually would become the Southern California Association of Philanthropy. Dempsey, a petroleum engineer from Tulsa, was brash and outspoken, and alarmed the Council by his proclivity for arranging unilateral meetings with legislators on Capitol Hill. The colorful Dempsey was a World War II veteran who had been wounded during the invasion of Iwo Jima and later joined the Vietnam War protests. He was an active Presbyterian layman who also was involved in interdenominational circles, and a civic volunteer. Robert Hull remembers Dempsey as a "delightful, aggressive guy." Engaged in a discussion during which he wanted to preempt other opinions, he would begin his argument by stating, "Clearly, the only way to view this issue. . . ." Hull recalls. "The rest of us called him 'Clearly'—and he loved it."

9   Rooks correspondence. As Rooks recalls, and as noted in the previous chapter, although much of the criticism was deserved, there was also an element of hypocrisy present in these complaints, since some of them came from foundations that had not joined or otherwise supported the work of the Council.

10 Ibid.

11 As reported by Russ Hardin, the foundations' president, after twenty years at 230 Peachtree Street (to which they had moved from the Whitehead Realty Building across the street to make room for the further development of John Portman's Peachtree Center), the Woodruff-related foundations relocated to the Hurt Building in 1991. They remained there for another twenty years.

12 Leadership of this imaginative program came from James Joseph, COF president; Steven Minter, chair of the National Agenda and president of the Cleveland Foundation; and Barbara Bode, the initial staff director, who was soon succeeded by Dr. Joanne Scanlan. Scanlan wrote the original proposal for the program and would go on to serve as a senior staff officer at the COF for more than twenty-two years. Lehfeldt and Associates, an Atlanta-based consulting firm, was selected to conduct the formative evaluation of this ambitious venture.

13 A significant product of the National Agenda was the publication of *An Agile Servant: Community Leadership by Community Foundations* (New York: Foundation Center, 1989), edited by Richard Magat. Published on the 75th anniversary of the founding of the first community foundation (Cleveland), it opened with a lead essay by David Hammack, "Community Foundations: The Delicate Question of Purpose," and included other essays and case studies by a variety of community and private foundation leaders and others from the not-for-profit sector.

14 Struckhoff was a graduate of Colby College and Harvard Law School. After practicing law privately for a brief period, he entered the field of philanthropy by helping to form the New Hampshire Charitable Foundation. He later was president of the Council on Foundations, executive director of the Baltimore Community Foundation, and in retirement, executive director of the York County (Maryland) Community Foundation.

15 A donor-advised fund is a contribution given to and managed by a public charity. The donors surrender ownership of their gifts, but they retain advisory privileges over how their account is invested and how its principal and/or investment returns are distributed to charities. They also receive the maximum tax deduction available while avoiding excise taxes and other restrictions imposed upon private foundations. The public charity that manages a donor-advised fund usually performs due diligence services to assure that grant recipients are eligible to receive the funds that the donors recommend be given to them and charges modest fees for these services and for investment management.

16 Informal conversation between Martin Lehfeldt and community foundation CEO in 1986. David Hammack reports that the Cleveland Foundation and similar Midwestern philanthropies emphasized general purpose gifts; Cleveland at the time also specified that the funds it managed could not support charities affiliated with religious institutions. The community foundations of New York and Philadelphia, Hammack further points out, were much more hospitable to donor preferences. Hammack, "Community Foundations: The Delicate Question of Purpose."

17 Today, donor-advised funds are the fastest growing charitable giving vehicle in the United States—more than 463,622 donor-advised accounts hold over $110.01 billion in assets, according to "Donor-Advised Fund Report," National Philanthropic Trust, 2017—more than triple the corresponding figures in 2015. The courting of living donors steadily evolved into the strategic education of the legal, estate, and financial advisors to these potential supporters, and it would not be long before commercial financial institutions (e.g., Fidelity) also began offering their clients the option of establishing donor-advised funds.

18 After directing the Peninsula Community Foundation for seventeen years, Somerville founded the Philanthropic Ventures Foundation. He has consulted with over 400 community foundations about creative grant-making and foundation operations and is the author of *Grassroots Philanthropy: Field Notes of a Maverick Grantmaker.*

CHAPTER 15

Expansion and Maturing of the Field[1]

Intergenerational Transfer of Wealth

On October 19, 1999, John J Havens and Paul G. Schervish, colleagues at the Social Welfare Research Institute of Boston College published "Millionaires and the Millennium: New Estimates of the Forthcoming Wealth Transfer and the Prospects for a Golden Age of Philanthropy."[2] In the introduction of their paper, they asserted:

> On the basis of a recently developed Wealth Transfer Microsimulation Model (WTMM), we estimate that the forthcoming transfer of wealth will be many times higher than the almost universally cited 55-year figure of $10 trillion. Our low-range best estimate is that over the 55-year period from 1998 to 2052 the wealth transfer will be $41 trillion, and may well reach double or triple that amount. Depending upon the assumptions we introduce into the model (for instance, in regard to the current level of wealth, real growth in wealth, and savings rates) we estimate

the wealth transfer will range from a lower level figure of $41 trillion to an upper level figure of $136 trillion. These estimates are not back-of-the-envelope projections. They emerge from what to our knowledge is a first-of-its-kind microsimulation model of wealth accumulation and transfer.

As noted, the most conservative of their figures more than quadrupled the estimates from a 1990 study by Cornell University professors Robert Avery and Michael Rendall who had calculated the wealth transfer between 1990 and 2040 to be about $10 trillion.

Other scholars might dispute the Boston College figures and the methodology for determining them, but evidence abounded that philanthropic coffers were expanding. For almost the next decade and until the coming of the Great Recession, foundation growth would steadily accelerate, nowhere more so than in the South.

New Leadership for SECF

After Robert Hull announced his retirement plans, SECF's subsequent search for a successor led to the hiring of Martin C. Lehfeldt in January, 1998. Lehfeldt was no stranger to SECF, to foundations, or to the South,[3] having migrated to Atlanta from Princeton, New Jersey, in 1969.

He was a graduate of Haverford College and Union Theological Seminary in New York. His *curriculum vita* included a four-year stint at the Woodrow Wilson National Fellowship Foundation, directing a program for historically black colleges throughout the South. He had then spent 10 years as a development vice president for Clark College

Martin Lehfeldt
Courtesy of Mikki Harris

and the Atlanta University Center. During the next 18 years he was president of his own consulting firm that provided fund raising, planning, and organizational development assistance to local, regional and national not-for-profit institutions and community foundations around the country.

From 1986 until 1989, he and a colleague, Dan Joslyn, had conducted a multi-year, formative evaluation of the National Agenda for Community Foundations (see Chapter 14). He also had facilitated the crafting of SECF's first strategic plan in 1990 and then directed the Community Foundation Initiative for three years (see Chapter 14).

SECF Staff Growth and Administrative Change

Anticipating the expansion of programming, Lehfeldt secured approval for the employment of additional personnel. He further decided that it was time to diversify the top-level staff and identified Imani Burnett, an African American nonprofit program director associated with the California Community Foundation. The fact that her daughter was already a student at Spelman College in Atlanta helped to encourage Burnett's relocation from Los Angeles.[4]

Some wise planning before Hull stepped down had led to the acquisition of larger SECF office space. At the beginning of January, 1998,

A SENSE OF PLACE

Southerners are notoriously proud of and defensive about the places they call home. One morning soon after the beginning of the 21st century, the president of the Southeastern Council of Foundations received a telephone call from a gentleman in a small Alabama municipality. The caller wanted to learn what would be needed to organize a new community foundation. However, before listening for the answer, he first felt the need to make sure the SECF official appreciated the importance of his community. After delivering a monologue worthy of a Chamber of Commerce membership chair, he concluded, "And I'll have you know that we're the third largest city south of Montgomery!"

Source: As told by Martin Lehfeldt

Lehfeldt, Burnett, Hardesty, and Michael Morgan, a part-time administrative assistant who had been on Lehfeldt's staff, moved into the expanded quarters on the third floor of The Hurt Building. The new space also included two other offices for possible later expansion and a work room. A grant from Pat Willis, an SECF board member and CEO of the BellSouth Foundation, made possible the installation of a telephone and computer system in the new office suite.

Robert Hull had handled all of the routine financial record-keeping and check-writing himself, and the small staff had managed logistics for the annual meetings. Several months of keeping track of payroll and other routines and the experience of dealing with insufficient member lodging at his first annual meeting in Williamsburg, Virginia, convinced Lehfeldt that his time could more profitably be devoted to other duties. After experimenting with part-time assistance, he employed Francis Holley as a bookkeeper.

Three years later, after having utilized outside assistance with annual meeting planning, Lehfeldt hired Marianne Gordon as full-time director for all SECF public functions. Her organizational skills attention to detail, cost-consciousness, and unfailing courtesy soon made it clear to everyone that her appointment may have been the president's wisest decision during his 11-year tenure.[5]

Several other management changes followed in fairly rapid order, and Lehfeldt embarked on a listening tour to present a new strategic plan to members. Thereafter came the securing of health benefits for all employees; D & O liability insurance coverage for board members; and the creation of an employee manual and written-expense accounting and financial-management procedures. The board also adopted a revised set of by-laws developed by Lawrence I'Anson, board chair.

Despite the success of staff and board fund raising efforts, it was evident to all that "SECF members themselves would have to shoulder a bigger portion of the association's expenses."[6] The board approved a dues increase.

Hull Fellows Program[7]

One of the most important programs in SECF's history got its start when John Stephenson and Katharine Pearson, former board chairs of the organization, invited Lehfeldt to lunch soon after his arrival.[8] They wanted to discuss how SECF might

---

SECF'S NATIONAL MEMBERS

In the early 2000s, SECF already had a few private foundation members based elsewhere in the country that made grants to Southern not-for-profit institutions. Martin Lehfeldt, hoping to increase this pool, reached out to Barry Gaberman, senior vice president of the Ford Foundation, and invited that gigantic institution, long an active grant-maker in the South, to join SECF. Gaberman replied that Ford had years ago attempted to become a member, but "you wouldn't let us in because we didn't have an office in your region." Lehfeldt swiftly had the bylaws changed to eliminate that restriction and sent Ford's president, Susan Berresford, a welcome letter, expressing his delight that Ford now qualified to belong. The upward bump on the income side of the ledger from Ford dues was deeply appreciated by all at SECF, as were the subsequent membership dues from other national foundations.

Source: As told by Martin Lehfeldt

Table 15.1.SECF Board Chairs			
1997–99	Lawrence W. I'Anson Jr.	Beazley Foundation	Portsmouth, VA
1999–2001	P. Russell Hardin	Robert W. Woodruff Foundation	Atlanta, GA
2001–3	Frank J. Wideman III	Self Family Foundation	Greenwood, SC
2003–5	John J. Graham	Baptist Community Ministries	New Orleans, LA
2005–7	W. E. "Chip" Gaylor	Patricia J. Buster Foundation	Venice, FL
2007–9	Peter F. Bird	The Frist Foundation	Nashville, TN

honor Robert Hull for his eighteen years of service. That conversation, further shaped by the input of Vice Chair Betsy Locke, then President of The Duke Endowment, and others, considered possibilities like an endowed annual lectureship. With further discussion, however, what emerged as the favored priority was a leadership program that would strengthen individuals in the field as well as the field itself.

Bobbi Cleveland, executive director of the Tull Charitable Foundation, led the design of what came to be called the Hull Fellows Program. Jane Hardesty, who later became executive director of the Harland Charitable Foundation, assisted her. They assembled a committee whose members were requested *not* to set up a standard leadership development curriculum. Rather, their charge was to create an experience that would "explore the history, philosophy, challenges and opportunities of philanthropy specifically in the context of the South."[9] The result was a unique, year-long, educational experience that featured reading, research, work projects, discussion, retreats, and webinars for both young trustees and staff from a variety of foundations encompassing broad diversity. So strong was the membership's affection for Hull and interest in the vision for the new program that Lehfeldt had little difficulty in raising an initial endowment of nearly $200,000 from a simple letter solicitation even before the program was fully designed or announced.

The first Hull Fellows retreat took place in 2000 at the Aqueduct Conference Center near Durham, North Carolina. Leaders included Pat Turner, an expert facilitator; George Penick, then president of the Foundation for the Mid South; and Jamil Zainaldin, president of the Georgia Humanities Council.[10] Jack Murrah, president of the Lyndhurst Foundation, joined the facilitation team the next year. As the program continued to evolve, other leaders from the foundation field and the not-for-profit sector were called upon for presentations and discussion leadership at retreats and for webinars.

Participants in that first class forged deep bonds that later influenced their careers in philanthropy—an outcome that has remained constant throughout the program's history. Several of them also went on to serve as facilitators of later classes. Hull "alumni" were soon serving on the SECF board and committees and rising to executive positions in the field. The program also strengthened the professionalism of the field, encouraging geographical mobility. During an interview by Betsey Russell for an article on the 15th anniversary of the program, Lehfeldt remembered:

> Strategically, the Hull Fellows program was the most deliberate effort SECF had ever made to promote a high level of diversity, encompassing race, ethnicity, gender, and foundation type and size. That was important because back then philanthropy was very much a white-male-dominated field. The Hull Program really gave others a chance to shine,

show their talents, and gain greater visibility. It brought people together who normally didn't have that opportunity and provided occasions for discussions about tough issues that didn't occur elsewhere. Everything took place within a safe cocoon of confidentiality that encouraged honesty.

The Hull Fellows program brought new energy to organized philanthropy in the South. It has strengthened the professionalism of both governance and management and has been an agency of positive change for the field and for the region.

Interviewed for the same article, Hull observed that the Fellows were becoming the lifeblood of SECF and the field in the South. He added this recollection:

> It was the wrap-up of the year, and as I was addressing the graduates, I told them, "Sometime in the future, maybe twenty years or more from now, some university professor or reporter or book editor will say, 'Something happened to Southern foundations about the turn of the century. It's hard to put a finger on it, but it was almost like a movement started. Corners were turned, things were discussed that had been kept in little closets here and there.' Those people in the future might never know what the motivating factor was, but you will know that a great part of what they are talking about is you."

As reported by Stephen Sherman, SECF's research and data manager, 33 of the 300+ Hull Fellows alumni are chief executives of SECF member foundations, including the presidents of The Duke Endowment and American Humane. About one-third of the alumni serve in senior leadership positions with their current organizations.[11] (See Appendix E for complete list of Hull Fellows.)

Communications

Lehfeldt as a young man had been a reporter for the Youngstown (OH) *Vindicator*. Some of those writing and editing instincts seem to have returned, as he, Imani Burnett, Betsey Russell, and later-hires Renee Vary (communications director) and Helen Ishii (membership and marketing director) went into a production mode. During the next several years, the SECF team developed a revised version of *Interchange*, the monthly newsletter to which Lehfeldt contributed a popular and sometimes controversial column.[12] The committed staff also created revised editions of *Starting a Private Foundation*, the *Foundation Desk Reference*, the *SECF Membership Directory*, *Southeastern Foundations* (with the Foundation Center), a new informational brochure, and *Southern Philanthropy Overview*. A colorful Annual Report became a regular feature, and new technology made further possible the development of a website and an e-cast. Another important communication tool became the one-page "SECF Board Briefing" with which the president kept the trustees abreast of the organization's activities during the periods between board meetings.

Table 15.2. SECF Annual Meetings		
1998	Williamsburg Lodge	Williamsburg, VA
1999	Grove Park Inn	Asheville, NC
2000	Hyatt Regency Grand Cypress	Orlando, FL
2001	Beau Rivage	Biloxi, MS
2002	The Greenbrier	White Sulphur Springs, WV
2003	Fairmont Hotel	New Orleans, LA
2004	Charleston Place	Charleston, SC
2005	Marco Island Marriott	Marco Island, FL
2006	Westin Savannah Harbor	Savannah, GA
2007	The Homestead	Hot Springs, VA
2008	Grove Park Inn	Asheville, NC

Taking a Gamble

The board was not unanimous in its support for Lehfeldt's proposal that the 2001 annual meeting be quartered at the Beau Rivage Hotel in Biloxi, Mississippi. The heavily advertised resort was the largest and most elegant gambling casino on that state's Gulf Coast. Several of the members complained, after the event began to be publicized, about meeting in a "gaming center." Helping to swing the argument in favor of a conference in Biloxi was the fact that the SECF had never convened in Mississippi and that the Beau Rivage was the only facility large enough to accommodate the 500+ expected attendees.

Lehfeldt had a far different concern—the sensitivity of some SECF members to Mississippi's recent public referendum that had approved a state flag which incorporated the design of the Confederate battle banner. He remembers arriving at the hotel well before the conference's scheduled beginning. While the staff was unpacking pro grams and other meeting materials in the main ballroom, he noticed the Mississippi and U.S. flags prominently displayed on one side of the stage. No one was paying any attention to him, so he quietly lifted the staff bearing the "stars and bars" and slipped it into a corner behind the curtain. "It never reappeared during the course of the conference," Lehfeldt recalls, "nor was its absence noted."

Meeting attendance that year suffered only slightly because of the location, said Lehfeldt, who also recollects that "a number of the guests seemed to enjoy striding (or surreptitiously slipping) into the casino portion of the facility to try their luck." As one female confided to Linda Lehfeldt, "What's all the fuss about? We've had slot machines in our country club for years."

That Family Feeling

As SECF's programs expanded and the paid staff grew, Lehfeldt sought ways to maintain the family-like ethos that had long been a hallmark of the organization. He had already started with the board: "Most out-of-town trustees had become accustomed to flying into Atlanta early on the morning of a meeting and then taking a flight home at the end of the day's work," he said. In his first year, he changed that pattern by inviting all trustees and staff to dinner at his home the evenings before the Atlanta meetings. Pre-prandial beverages and candle-lit dining in the backyard with meals usually cooked by Linda Lehfeldt became a popular custom for the next decade.[13] Periodically, other board members like Russ Hardin and Bobbi Cleveland also opened their Atlanta homes for these trustee receptions.

"CHAIRMAN'S LETTER," 2000 SECF ANNUAL REPORT

Years ago, I had the privilege of beginning my career at the Woodruff and Whitehead Foundations when Boisfeuillet Jones still served as their President. I still remember his stories about the initial meetings of the small band of philanthropic merry men—usually hosted by Jamie Clark at his cabin in the North Carolina mountains—that led to the establishment of the Southeastern Council of Foundations.

Those founders of the Southeastern Council were admirable individuals—leaders with a sense of responsibility to their field, their communities and their region. They also were just nice folks who built lifelong friendships upon the professional camaraderie they enjoyed. . . .

There's no question that the specific impetus for the formation of the Southeastern Council was the 1969 Tax Reform Act. However, from the beginning the SECF organizers also saw its potential for being more than an instrument of defense and self-preservation. They realized that it also furnished a valuable network for foundation trustees and staff to trade notes on their local experiences as well as an important professional association to promote the highest standards throughout Southern philanthropy.

Much has changed during the past 30 years, but then again, much has not. To be sure, attendance at the annual meetings has mushroomed to the level that the question now is not whether enough people will show up, but whether we can accommodate everyone who does. . .

At the same time, the Southeastern Council is playing the larger role envisioned by our founders 30 years ago. It provides a useful network for grant-makers to learn from one another; sponsors educational programs; and publishes tools that promote the highest standards in philanthropy. It also is strongly articulating the importance of organized philanthropy and actively encouraging its growth within our region. For all of our growth in recent years, I am perhaps happiest about the fact that a leading characteristic of our association—30 years after those initial cabin-in-the-woods meetings—continues to be the way in which we begin by gathering as professionals and then enjoy each other's company so much that we build personal friendships which enrich all of our lives.

P. Russell Hardin
Vice President, Robert W. Woodruff Foundation

As membership grew and the field's interests became more diversified, SECF realized that the annual meetings simply could not provide all of the specialized information-sharing and discussion that its members wanted or needed. Accordingly, board committee chairs and staff began scheduling special gatherings for family foundations and community foundations and, in time, the growing number of health legacy foundations. In 2005 SECF leadership convened the first family foundation retreat in Point Clear, Alabama.

Nor did SECF forget its historic commitment to encourage new philanthropy. Imani Burnett and Guy Lescault, director of the ABA Business Law Section Pro Bono Committee, organized a series of Continuing Legal Education courses on philanthropy, beginning in Georgia and then extending to nine of the Southern states.

Burnett and Lehfeldt also sought to continue the practice, established during Hull's tenure, of promoting state-wide associations of community foundations. Although the experiment lasted only two years, they even secured an experimental grant from the Kellogg Foundation to staff an office in Florida to coordinate work in that state.

Foundations on the Hill

Foundations on the Hill (FOH) had for several years been a co-sponsored program of the Forum of Regional Associations and the Council on Foundations. Each regional association, usually in March, would send representatives from its own staff as well as board and staff from its member foundations on a pilgrimage to Washington to educate their elected lawmakers about the value of organized philanthropy and to argue against any pending legislation that seemed to threaten foundations.

Because SECF served 11 states, Lehfeldt was embarrassed to discover on his first FOH visit that he, two other staff members, and a single foundation representative (his board chairman) were the only Southerners to make an appearance while state organizations like Michigan and Minnesota sent large delegations. During the remainder of his tenure he pushed steadily to expand and organize participation, enhancing it by the addition of a sponsored dinner and a prominent Washington figure as a speaker the night before the prearranged visits to U.S. representatives and senators.[14]

The Return of Scrutiny

Leaving aside the president's competitive spirit, it was becoming an important time for Southern foundations and their colleagues to present themselves in the most favorable possible light—a challenge they shared with their peers throughout the country.

Dorothy S. Ridings, president and publisher of the Bradenton (FL) *Herald*, was elected to succeed James Joseph as President and CEO of the Council in March, 1996. A West Virginian by birth, she was a longtime newspaper person, but her experience also included direct exposure to the world of philanthropy. She had served on the board of the Ford Foundation, been a director of the Benton Foundation, and had orchestrated the creation of the Manatee (FL) Community Foundation as a supporting organization of the Community Foundation of Sarasota County. A graduate of Northwestern University's Medill School of Journalism with a master's degree from the University of North Carolina, she had taught journalism at the universities of Louisville and North Carolina, served as a Knight-Ridder general executive while based in Charlotte, N.C., and held editorial and reporting positions at the *Kentucky Business Ledger*, *The Washington Post* and the *Charlotte Observer*. Her career further included a two-year stint as president of the League of Women Voters in the United States, speaking tours for the U.S. Department of State, fact-finding delegations for NATO, and chairing the boards of the Louisville Presbyterian Theological Seminary and the National Civic League.

By the time of her arrival in Washington, the Council had more than 2,000 members that collectively were disbursing some $18 billion in grants annually. Many of them were modestly reticent to publicize their good works. Despite the advent of an information age in which very little could be kept private, others still believed that keeping a low profile would shield them from the advances of grant seekers. Still others, somewhat more arrogantly, saw no reason to share information about their operations beyond filing tax returns.

Ridings immediately recognized the potential for trouble. The combined assets of the Council's members may have been just a pittance when compared to federal budgets, but multi-million dollar portfolios still looked like a lot of money to the average citizen as well as to elected officials charged with their oversight. She quickly set in motion a series of initiatives to tell the story of foundations not just to Congress but to the press and the broader public as well.

About three decades had elapsed since passage of the Tax Reform

Act of 1969 (see Chapter 12). Two of the perhaps most salutary features of that legislation had been 1) the mandatory payout requirement for private foundations (making it impossible for them to use tax advantages for the piling up of massive reserves) and 2) much stricter prohibitions against self-dealing of all kinds.

However, Congress then turned its attention to other matters. It was the legislators' intention that the IRS would use the excise tax on private foundation investments for auditing purposes—which the IRS had failed to do. It was not the fault of the IRS; Congress was depositing those hundreds of millions of dollars each year into the general treasury.

This relatively *laissez-faire* state of affairs probably would have continued much longer, except for a combination of factors that peaked in the late 1990s. At the risk of over-simplification, it was an era of significant American wealth acquisition and what some commentators cynically described as "a widening gap between the rich and the truly rich" (see "Intergenerational Transfer of Wealth" above). Certainly foundation assets were among the beneficiaries as returns on investment climbed as high as 20-30%, while pay-out requirements remained at 5% of assets. Attorneys and other professional advisors with sophisticated understanding of tax law had at their disposal a variety of recommended incentives to encourage their clients' conversion of wealth into philanthropic assets. The number of foundations increased dramatically, the donor-advised funds at community foundations multiplied, a flood of deposits poured into newly formed commercial gifts funds (e.g., Fidelity) and "supporting organizations" increased in popularity.

As those assets increased, they began to attract the attention of some investigative reporters. Journalists from the Philadelphia *Inquirer* were among the first to begin asking questions, and soon thereafter the interest of the Boston *Globe,* the San Jose *Mercury,* and the *Wall Street Journal* was also piqued. They too began inquiring about the purpose of foundations and their value to society. In a 2006 speech to an Alabama audience of grant-makers, Lehfeldt bluntly described the time's Congressional milieu:

> Of course, the fact that many foundations—perhaps even most foundations, although no one knew for certain— were playing by the rules and behaving in utterly honorable fashion didn't particularly interest them. Instead, their probes, sadly, uncovered far less savory stories of foundations whose executives' and trustees' compensation far exceeded the total of their grant-making; stories of nepotism—the use of a foundation as the employer of last resort to give a highly paid position to the idiot daughter or son-in-law who couldn't hold a job elsewhere; the infamous story about the foundation exec who awarded himself a $200,000 salary increase and then was stupid enough to tell a reporter that he felt obligated to compensate himself in this fashion because he needed to pay for his daughter's impending and very expensive wedding.

Most of these stories tended to focus on family foundations whose donors and heirs had somehow never learned the lesson that assets placed in foundations were no longer their money to do with as they chose, but essentially were now in a quasi-public trust. However, some of our nation's largest and professionally administered foundations did not escape scrutiny for the legal but rather cavalier way in which they were wont to take their board members and senior staff on expensive fact-finding field trips around the world—always flying first-class and staying in deluxe accommodations.[15]

Not surprisingly, the Senate Finance Committee, the House Ways and Means Committee (both committees held hearings), state attorneys-general, and other regulators as well as that diminishing portion of the public that pays attention to the news were soon studying foundations with renewed interest.[16] It is instructive to recall that nobody—not even grant recipients in the not-for-profit sector—rushed to the defense of foundations.[17]

Leading the attack on the sector was Dean Zerbe, senior counsel and tax counsel for the Senate Finance Committee. By the summer of 2004, that committee had issued an 18-page, single-spaced "white paper" that proposed a rather ruthless set of new regulations to curb what the authors were convinced were widespread abuses of foundation power and independence.[18] (Zerbe, who would later return to private practice, is credited with securing passage of the modern IRS whistleblower law of 2006, establishing the IRS Whistleblower Office and creating an award program for tax whistleblowers.)

To his credit, Senator Charles Grassley of Iowa, the chair of the committee, invited the nonprofit world, under the leadership of Independent Sector and its president, Diana Aviv, to develop a rebuttal, including its own recommendations for foundation regulation. Drawing upon the work of hundreds of leaders from the sector and a series of regional town hall meetings, they did exactly that and negotiated a series of compromises about foundation regulation with Congress.[19]

During the course of this process, Lehfeldt and several representatives from Southern foundations had the opportunity for a private meeting in Washington with U.S. Representative Bill Thomas from California, then chair of the House Ways and Means Committee, during which they listened to him ruminate. That afternoon Thomas's angry attention was focused primarily upon nonprofit hospitals that he was convinced were taking advantage of their tax-exempt status to function like for-profit hospitals. However, he also posed some philosophical questions to the foundation representatives about their field that Lehfeldt recalls as being particularly thought-provoking. Why, Thomas first asked, should foundations be permitted to exist in perpetuity; and secondly, why do people need foundations in order to be generous?[20]

SECF Accountability

Accountability was rapidly becoming the watchword for the foundation field. Community foundations had set in motion the development of standards for themselves, and the regional associations of grant-makers in Michigan and Minnesota were formulating criteria for foundation behavior.[21]

Engaging the assistance of Dr. Edward L. Queen, Director of the D. Abbott Turner Program in Ethics and Servant Leadership and Coordinator of Undergraduate Studies at Emory University's Center for Ethics, SECF convened a series of regional meetings to obtain feedback from members about their readiness for greater attention to the subject of standards.[22] That led, after many drafts, to the development of a set of Guiding Principles that the board adopted in January 2005. Unlike the standards adopted in Michigan and Minnesota, subscription to the principles was not a condition of membership, but their adoption was an important first step.

However, SECF and its peers were aware that simply composing, printing, and distributing a set of philanthropic maxims did not fully discharge their responsibilities—especially during this period of increasing scrutiny of organized philanthropy. Working in concert they retained the services of David Biemesderfer to develop a series of accountability self-assessment formulas for both staffed and unstaffed private foundations.[23] Tailored to follow each foundation's own set of guiding principles, these tools could help each to determine whether it was operating according to the law. As important, though, it could also help concerned foundations to ascertain whether they were behaving not just legally but ethically, and whether they were engaging in practices that could give the impression of illegality or impropriety.

Rural Concerns

The Southern Rural Development Initiative (SRDI), based in Raleigh, North Carolina, came into being in 1994. A leading advocate for racial and economic justice in the rural South, it had received significant financial support from both the Mary Reynolds Babcock Foundation and the C. S. Mott Foundation of Flint, Michigan. Its leaders had been in touch with SECF when Robert Hull was still CEO, and the two organizations had coordinated a retreat for foundation leaders and rural experts at the Sapelo Foundation's Musgrove Retreat Center. After Lehfeldt succeeded Hull, Debbie Warren and Alan McGregor (former head of the Sapelo Foundation) approached him to promote further discussion about how to bring philanthropic resources to bear upon the needs of the rural South (which at the time was home to 40% of the poverty in the nation). Further conversations led to the formation of a consortium including SRDI, SECF, and the Foundation for the Mid South.

Lehfeldt's instincts suggested to him that it should be possible to identify a series of indices to gauge the availability of non-traditional philanthropic resources (e.g., land, timber, equipment) within rural communities themselves. He challenged his colleagues to compile some ideas. With further support from the C. S. Mott Foundation, the result was *The Philanthropic Index for Small Towns and Rural Areas*, a workbook that Lehfeldt, Alan McGregor, and Tim Murphy co-authored.

The consortium also conducted community-needs assessments, distributed educational materials via the internet, conducted board training for several organizations, and conducted an evaluation of the early program.[24] Seeking to encourage the establishment of rural philanthropic funds, McGregor often told the apocryphal story of a wealthy farmer who allegedly had sought to bequeath his estate to the local area in which he had prospered. Because no community foundation existed to manage his gift, he awarded it to the state university.

Absent the limited availability of local seed capital, rural-based philanthropy was difficult to establish. Established in 1986, the East Tennessee Foundation, under the leadership of Katharine Pearson and

Terry Holley, had some success with establishing affiliate funds in rural counties, but that work depended in part upon an urban base in Knoxville. The Community Foundation of the New River Valley, founded in 1994, in the rural area of western Virginia, was initially led by Andy Morikawa, a strong and patient advocate of servant leadership. The foundation placed as high a value on convening and promoting collaboration among organizations in its region as it did upon building endowment. It continues to be a positive force in the region. Through its hosting of small regional, national, and even international gatherings, it also helped to inspire the formation of the Black Belt Community Foundation in Selma, Alabama.

Increasing Membership

Several years into his tenure, Lehfeldt found himself alternately curious and annoyed by the fact that SECF's membership included only 340-350 of the 10,000+ foundations in the eleven-state region. However, as he tapped into Foundation Center data to explore the matter more fully, he made several useful discoveries. 1) Only about 175 foundations had assets of at least $50 million and nearly half of them already belonged to the SECF. Further pruning of the list identified about sixty that would be good prospects. 2) Another 300 foundations had assets of at least $10 million, and nearly one-fourth of them also were members. 3) Fewer than 800 of the foundations in the South had professional staff, and 20% of them were SECF members. 4) The largest block of non-member prospects were based in Florida, which already had several associations of grant-makers. (At the time he was unable to document which of the non-members belonged to the Council on Foundations or other grant-maker federations.) Lehfeldt informally shared the findings with his regional association peers and determined that they were experiencing similar levels of success with their membership building. He and his staff agreed that there still was a need for marketing and recruitment but that they need not lose sleep about the "numbers."[25]

A Charitable Windfall for the Region

Federal law requires that proceeds from the sale of tax-exempt entities go to charity. One way to satisfy this requirement is by establishing a foundation to benefit the community that had been served by the non-profit being sold. The importance of this legal provision became evident in the mid-1990s when for-profit corporations began to purchase local hospitals and healthcare plans throughout the country, but especially in the South. This buying spree continued for about a dozen years (until the Great Recession began in December, 2007). Almost from the start, these new grant-makers were referred to as health conversion foundations—a name that some of their leaders found inappropriate. As one of them put it to Lehfeldt, "Shoot, we're not even converted yet." It was not a theological assertion. Some of them had indeed not been converted (i.e., some of the assets from their sales were still being negotiated, and, in several cases, the new foundations retained partial ownership of the hospitals).

During an SECF-sponsored summer gathering of CEOs and board members from some of the conversion foundations around the South, the subject of nomenclature arose again during a lunch break.

After some discussion, leaders from the Baptist Healing Trust in Nashville recommended that they begin calling themselves health legacy foundations. They shared the suggestion with their colleagues, who applauded the idea. Thereafter, at least in the South, if a foundation came into being from the sale of a hospital or health care plan, it was a "health legacy foundation."[26]

Among the most noticeable feature of these new grant-makers was the size of their assets. They were large—their portfolios from the start could be measured in the tens or even hundreds of

Figure 1: **Foundations Formed from Health Care Conversions by State, 2015**

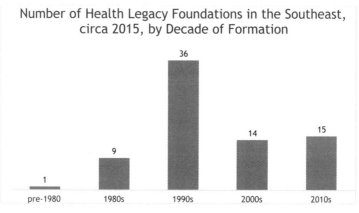

Number of Health Legacy Foundations in the Southeast, circa 2015, by Decade of Formation

Courtesy of Grantmakers in Health

millions of dollars. They dramatcally increased charitable capital in the South. Although only a barely measurable percentage of the region's foundations, they held approximately 10% of the South's charitable resources.

They dwarfed most of their peers. Many of them are based in small towns and cities where most have emerged as the principal philanthropic institutions for their service areas. For a small community suddenly to become home to a multi-million foundation was akin to it acquiring its own Woodruff Foundation or Duke Endowment.

One of Lehfeldt's first encounters with that phenomenon occurred during his first visit to Amory, Mississippi. The claim to fame of this small railroad town midway between Memphis and Birmingham included being a changing station for train crews. There he learned that the new legacy foundation had $47 million available to respond to the needs of a county with 37,000 people.[27] It was thus financially feasible, as one grant-making option the board was considering, to connect everyone in the area to the internet.[28]

A few of these new foundations elected to become community foundations,[29] but the rest are private foundations. They tend to regard the promotion and provision of health as central to their missions. However, unfettered by tradition and precedent, some chose to interpret "health" in very broad fashion, identifying non-medical, social determinants that have a profound impact on the health of individuals:

- Early in its history, the Sisters of Charity Foundation of South Carolina, based in Columbia and created in 1996, began funding a "Reducing Poverty through

Father Engagement" initiative in partnership with the South Carolina Department of Social Services. That statewide venture ripened into the South Carolina Center for Fathers and Families which supports six fatherhood programs in 12 communities.[30]

- One of the early ventures of the J. Marion Sims Foundation in Lancaster, South Carolina was to inaugurate a community-wide adult literacy program.[31]

- Foundation for a Healthy Kentucky, whose first president was Susan Zepeda, a former SECF board member, came into being in 2001 when Anthem acquired Blue Cross Blue Shield of Kentucky. From the beginning its primary emphasis has been upon development of public policy and system changes to increase health equity for all Kentuckians.[32]

- Among those foundations that have stretched the definition of "health-related" the farthest may be the Rapides Foundation Alexandria, Louisiana.[33] Like its colleagues, it conducted community assessments that led it to develop programs to improve access to health care and introduction to healthy-behavior lifestyles. However, by the early years of the 21st century, it was shaping an economic development initiative, resting upon the assumption that low unemployment and higher wages are essential to the promotion of healthy communities.

Since very few of the new health legacy foundation trustees were familiar with the rules, regulations, and culture of organized philanthropy, many of them gravitated toward SECF annual meetings. Because they had sufficient resources, they often could afford to bring the entire board membership to a conference. Urging them in that direction was Byron Harrell, the first president of Baptist Community Ministries in New Orleans, one of the early health legacies. Harrell would later become SECF board chair. Having received help from Robert Hull and SECF when his foundation began in 1995, he encouraged others to follow his lead. His volunteer "recruiting" and the value received from the Southeastern Council soon contributed to approximately 20% of the attendance and income at an annual meeting coming from the health legacy foundation delegations. It was not long before Lehfeldt and his staff began organizing annual summer gatherings whose programming was directed to the specific needs of CEOs and trustees. Included in the "curriculum" was a series of case statements written by Lehfeldt specifically for health legacy foundations. Not surprisingly, it was not long before representatives of these foundations were sharing their experience and expertise as committee members and trustees of the Southeastern Council.[34] (As described elsewhere, the health legacy growth spurt, stalled for several years by the Great Recession, appears to have resumed.)

Suzanna Stribling joined the SECF senior staff in 2004 as director of membership and operations. Her past experience had included serving as the first director of the Nonprofit Resource Center (now the Georgia Center for Nonprofits) when it was spun off as an independent organization from the Community Foundation for Greater Atlanta. In addition to staffing several member committees to provide education for SECF constituencies, she had major responsibility for strengthening the organization's technological capabilities. She further provided national and liaison leadership for a technology project that linked eight regional associations of grant-makers via a common member database, website, and knowledge base and trained SECF staff to use the new system.

Hurricane Katrina

Tumultous acts of nature were nothing new to the South—and they continue to be regular threats to people and property. Yet the magnitude of the death toll and physical damage from Hurricane Katrina in late summer of 2005 was especially startling. Many people did not take the weather warnings seriously, and the level of preparedness was low. On August 26 Lehfeldt and Stribling had just completed facilitating an SECF members' meeting in New Orleans and were sharing good-byes to the participants in front of their hotel on Canal Street. Forty-eight hours later, back in Atlanta, they watched a news reporter, standing thigh-deep in water at the same location, broadcasting his account of storm damage to the city.

George Penick, president of the Foundation for the Mid South in Jackson, Mississippi, convened a gathering of foundation leaders in Memphis to begin coordinating a response to the cataclysm. Byron

Post-Katrina Barber Shop in New Orleans
Courtesy of the Library of Congress, LC-DIG-highsm-04024

Harrell, president of Baptist Community Ministries in New Orleans, and Ted Alexander, president of the Lower Pearl River Valley Foundation in Picayune, Mississippi, were among the first philanthropic leaders to begin sharing detailed accounts of the devastation and calling for financial and other support from the foundation field. Both regional and national grant-makers responded generously to these and other solicitations. Penick and Lehfeldt co-hosted a national conference call to share information, and during the following months Lehfeldt paid several visits to the hurricane-damaged region to meet with SECF members and donor associations.[35] Reflecting on the events of that period, he took note of the importance of the region having a philanthropic infrastructure to facilitate communication and collaboration.

Changing of the Guard

During 2007, as SECF was going through a new strategic planning process, Lehfeldt informed the board of his readiness to retire in 2008 after 18 years of association with the organization, with the assurance that he would remain until his successor was in place.

Mike Howland succeeded Lehfeldt in mid-2008. He was a graduate of Jacksonville (FL) University with degrees in law and public administration from St. Louis University. For the past six years he had been president and CEO of Noble of Indiana—an organization serving 2,200 people with developmental disabilities and their families.

Howland's arrival coincided with one of the worst economic recessions in modern U.S. history—a period when many of the SECF

Table 15.3. SECF Board Chairs		
2009–10 Debra M. Jacobs	William G. Selby and Marie Selby Foundation	Sarasota, FL
2010–11 Byron R. Harrell	Baptist Community Ministries	New Orleans, LA

members experienced significant shrinkage of their investment portfolios. Reflecting on his travels through the region during that period, he recalls that the drop in assets "prompted grant-makers like the Jessie Ball duPont Fund [Jacksonville, Florida] to invest more, not less, of their assets and myriad foundations to explore incentives to foster shared services, greater collaboration, and even merger among nonprofits." Other foundations like the Wilbur and Hilda Glenn Family Foundation in Atlanta shifted their support of relatively stable organizations to not-for-profits with limited funding that provided emergency relief services to people in poverty.

During Howland's tenure he was a strong advocate of collaboration with state associations of grant-makers whom he felt were well po-

Table 15.4. SECF Annual Meetings		
2009	Peabody Hotel	Memphis, TN
2010	Battle House Renaissance	Mobile, AL

sitioned to address state policy affecting philanthropy, and he helped to establish the Georgia Grantmakers Alliance.

Howland left after less than three years to join the development staff of his undergraduate alma mater, but under his leadership, SECF started a new strategic planning process, introduced regular forums for foundation CEOs, strengthened and rebranded the Hull Fellows Program, and adopted a more assertive approach to fund raising from its members. Howland also took advantage of the weak economy to sign favorable annual meeting contracts for the next several years.[36]

Interim Leadership

When approached by the SECF board, Charles H. (Pete) McTier, the retired president of the Robert W. Woodruff Foundation, agreed to serve as the organization's interim president. It proved to be an excellent fit. McTier knew SECF very well and had been a trustee and board chair. His own office was only three blocks away from the Hurt Building. Under his direction, the search for Howland's successor began.

Greg Gerhard had been hired from SunTrust Bank as director of programs and partnerships three weeks before Howland submitted his resignation. Gerhard, filling a staff slot held by Suzanna Stribling before she became executive director of the Wilbur and Hilda Glenn Family Foundation (see above), recalls with admiration the calm and steady style that McTier brought to the SECF leadership. He further notes that McTier was "an amazing Rolodex expander" who used his large network of contacts in the business and foundation communities to identify leaders for SECF's expanding investment management and other programs for members.

As the Southeastern Council prepared for the second decade of the 21st century, it was again on solid footing, becoming acquainted with a new generation of leaders among its membership, and ready to welcome a new executive of its own.

CHAPTER 15 ENDNOTES

1   Portions of this chapter draw upon the reflections of Martin Lehfeldt, SECF President, from 1999 into 2008.

2   *https://www.bc.edu/content/dam/files/research_sites/cwp/pdf/Wealth%20Press%20Release%205.28-9.pdf.*

3   When Hull introduced his successor to the members gathered at the 1997 annual meeting in Memphis, he graciously acknowledged that Lehfeldt qualified as a Southerner. "It was not Martin's fault," he explained, "that his mother gave birth to him in New York." Source: Transcript of an oral history interview, Martin Lehfeldt, June 7, 2019.

4   During the next years, Lehfeldt systematically expanded the staff and filled new positions with European-, African-, and Asian-American individuals as well as people of varying sexual orientations. He similarly sought to promote the identification and recruitment of an increasingly diverse board.

5   Source: Transcript of an oral history interview, Martin Lehfeldt, June 7, 2019.

6   Source: Transcript of an oral history interview, Martin Lehfeldt, June 7, 2019. While still directing the Community Foundation Initiative, Lehfeldt had begun securing programs grants from national foundations and programs (e.g., Ford, C.S. Mott, W. K. Kellogg, New Ventures in Philanthropy) that totaled more than $900,000. Soon after beginning work, he successfully garnered a grant from the BellSouth Corporation for a new office telephone and computer system.

7   Much of the information in this section is drawn from Betsey Russell, "Leading the Philanthropic Future," a report composed for SECF on the occasion of the 15th anniversary of the Hull Fellows Program. Russell, a free-lance writer and long-time consultant to SECF, is President of WordOne.

8   Stephenson was the Executive Director of the J. Bulow Campbell Foundation; Pearson, long-time executive of the East Tennessee Foundation, was preparing to leave for Kenya to become the head of the Ford Foundation's East African office in Nairobi.

9   Source: Transcript of an oral history interview, Martin Lehfeldt, May 15, 2019.

10 The relationship between Zainaldin and SECF is described further in the author biographies at the end of the book.

11 Correspondence from Stephen Sherman, July 9, 2019.

12 When Lehfeldt announced his retirement in 2008, SECF published *Thinking about Things*, a compilation of these columns over an 11-year period.

13 Lehfeldt believes that business meetings always proceeded more amicably when board members had good personal relationships. "It's hard to be quarrelsome with someone when you were discussing your grandchildren and summer vacations the night before." He remembers particularly a potentially vexing debate about a dues increase that was resolved calmly the next day after "drinks and dinner on the lawn." Source: Transcript of an oral history interview, Martin Lehfeldt, June 7, 2019.

Other family-like traditions also found their way into SECF: Jane Hardesty's background as a farmer's daughter in eastern North Carolina led to her insistence (welcomed by many) that annual meeting morning meals include a full menu of eggs, grits, bacon, sausage, and fruit. (The phrase "Continental Breakfast" was stricken from the planning vocabulary!) After Dr. Ted Alexander, the colorful president of the Lower Pearl River Valley Foundation in Mississippi, attended his first annual meeting breakfast and loudly queried, "Where's the biscuits?" that item was never again missing from the buffet. Source: Transcript of an oral history interview, Martin Lehfeldt, March 7, 2019.

14 During his final year as SECF President, a time when foundations were admittedly coming under fire from Congress, the association sent a record-setting 100 people to Washington, DC, to make the case for grant-makers.

15 "People *Are* Watching You," speech to Alabama Grant-makers, February 25, 2006.

16 Senator Charles Grassley, Chair of the Senate Finance Committee was especially incensed to learn of big-game hunters traveling to Africa, bringing back the animals they killed, giving the stuffed and mounted quarry to "museums," and then claiming their hunting expenses as charitable deductions. Source: Transcript of an oral history interview, March 7, 2019.

17 It all recalled a story about Robert Hutchins, former President of the University of Chicago, who later became head of the Fund for the Republic. Learning one day that another nonprofit agency had been publicly critical of the Fund's work, Hutchins reportedly responded, "Why are they so mad at us? We never gave them a grant."

18 *https://zfffjlaw.com/about-zfffj-law/dean-zerbe/.*

19 The Council on Foundations and the Forum of Regional Associations of Grantmakers, chaired by Lehfeldt in 2003-2005, were actively engaged in this national advocacy effort. Source: Transcript of an oral history interview, Martin Lehfeldt, June 6, 2019.

20 Source: Transcript of an oral history interview, Martin Lehfeldt, June 7, 2019.

21 Only a few years earlier, Steven Minter, then the CEO of the Cleveland Foundation, proposed at the national fall conference of community foundations that the field adopt standards—what became known as the S-word. He was publicly criticized and privately pilloried for having the gall even to suggest such a ridiculous notion. Today more than 700 community foundations have documented their compliance with the rather strenuous set of national standards for their field. In 2005, the first community foundations were accredited, and today the Council on Foundations continues to provide operational support for the National Standards program. More than 700 community foundations have undergone this rigorous certification process. *https://www.cfstandards.org/about-us/our-history.*

22 Queen, a former program officer at the Lilly Endowment, is a staff member of Emory University's Ethics Center where he also serves as Director of Research for the Institute of Human Rights and co-convener of the Initiative on Religion, Conflict, and Peacebuilding. Queen received his B.A. from Birmingham-Southern College, his M.A. and Ph.D. degrees from the Divinity School of the University of Chicago, and his J.D. from the Indiana University School of Law-Indianapolis.

23 Now the CEO of the United Philanthropy Forum (see sidebar in Chapter 13).

24 *https://www.mott.org/grants/southern-rural-development-initiative-inc-philanthropy-studies-program-200000375-01/.* The consortium never was able to generate significant interest about the program among Southern foundations. SRDI disbanded operations in 2009. *https://www.wral.com/business/story/4525679/* Source: Transcript of an oral history interview, Martin Lehfeldt, June 7, 2019.

25 Stephen Sherman of the SECF staff and a former staff member of the Foundation Center estimates that no more than about 10% of all foundations today have paid staff.

26 Source: Transcript of an oral history interview, Martin Lehfeldt, June 7, 2019.

27 It has since expanded its service area.

28 The more recently formed Dogwood Health Trust in Asheville, North Carolina, with a record $1.5 billion in assets intended to be of service to approximately 900,000 people in 18 western counties of North Carolina.

29 The Gulf Coast Community Foundation of Venice, Florida; Community Foundation of the Low Country (Hilton Head, SC); and Community Foundation of Northeast Alabama (formerly Calhoun County).

30 Under the leadership of Tom Keith, president since the foundation's start and former SECF board member, the organization remains committed to addressing the causes and effects of poverty in South Carolina. *www.sistersofcharityhealth.org/foundations/.*

31 Established in 1995 with proceeds from the sale of the Elliott White Springs Memorial Hospital in Lancaster, SC. Its name honors a native of Lancaster County who would later become a pioneering, albeit controversial, figure as a physician in Alabama where he earned the reputation of being a founder of modern gynecology. The foundation's first president was James Morton, who later chaired the SECF board. *https://www.jmsims.org/history.*

32 Source: Undated correspondence from Susan Zepeda, first president of the foundation, to Martin Lehfeldt.

33 Resulted from a joint venture partnership between Rapides Regional Medical Center and Columbia HCA in 1994. Beginning with $140 million in assets, it was for a time the largest endowed charitable foundation in the state of Louisiana. Today those assets are valued at more than $250 million. Its President, Joseph R. Rosier, Jr., continues in that position. Source: Undated correspondence from Joseph R. Rosier to Martin Lehfeldt.

34 Source: Transcript of an oral history interview, Martin Lehfeldt, June 7, 2019.

35 He also agreed to chair a national board of the Hurricane Fund for the Elderly, established by Grantmakers in Aging to raise and disburse funds for programs responding to the post-hurricane needs of seniors."

36 *https://www.prweb.com/releases/2008/05/prweb940504.htm*; also correspondence from Mike Howland, April 20, 2019.

.

CHAPTER 16

Enhancing Diversity and Relevance

Completing a Half-Century of Growth

With the strong support of the Southeastern Council of Foundations during its first five decades, grant-making assets and activities in the region grew in size, scope, and effectiveness, reflecting the broad array of interests, connections, and cultures that grace the region.

Janine Lee
Courtesy of Janine Lee

Janine Lee was the first female and first African American president and CEO of the SECF. Her selection in 2011 represented the continuing determination of the board to promote increasing diversity in the organization.

A native of Kansas, Lee earned a bachelor's degree in rehabilitation services education and a master's in rehabilitation services counseling from Emporia State University, and an MBA from Rockhurst University.

She worked in counseling and prevention services before joining Project Star, a prevention education program of the Ewing Marion Kauffman Foundation in Kansas City. It was there that she first rose to prominence in philanthropy, expanding her scope of responsibility to include the foundation's broader education efforts. The Arthur M. Blank Family Foundation of Atlanta, where she focused on education programs, brought her to the Southeast.

Lee's arrival also signaled board awareness that the field was changing, a new generation of philanthropic leaders was appearing, and SECF needed to address the challenges of securing its long-term relevance. As Lee explains,

> Those earlier years were a pivotal time in the organization because we had to decide whether to maintain the status quo or move forward to embrace new and more diverse leadership and programming. We didn't want to become a dinosaur; rather we wanted to evolve with changing trends. The SECF board chose to be transformative and open to embracing younger and more diverse faces and voices in the field.[1]

Public Policy Emphasis

Under Lee's leadership and that of Karen McNeil-Miller, the organization's first African American board chair, SECF began investing significant time, money, and energy in public policy and communications In short order it partnered with the Council on Foundations to launch

"Foundations 101," meetings to acquaint U.S. Congressional and foundation staffers around the region with each other; revamped the organization's e-mail newsletter; and embraced the wider use of social media and mobile platforms.

Lee also led SECF to become more vocal on public policy matters affecting philanthropy. In 2012 the organization adopted a statement that called upon national lawmakers to preserve the full scope and value of the charitable deduction. A year later it issued another position paper urging simplification of the excise tax on private foundations. As Congress weighed the merits of tax reform in 2017, SECF publicly supported the idea of a universal charitable deduction available to all filers, provisions to promote the independence and versatility of donor-advised funds, and efforts to preserve the Johnson Amendment—the rule that prohibits 501(c)(3) organizations from endorsing, opposing, or contributing to political candidates.

SECF further developed a suite of public policy advocacy tools, called Policy in Action, and regular Public Policy Digest e-newsletter. It also connected members more closely to policy developments in Congress and statehouses by encouraging visits to in-district Congressional offices

Karen McNeill-Miller
Courtesy of Karen McNeill-Miller

KAREN MCNEIL-MILLER

While serving as president of the Kate B. Reynolds Charitable Trust in Winston-Salem, North Carolina, Karen McNeil-Miller was elected a trustee of the Southeastern Council of Foundations. In 2011 she became the first African American woman to serve as board chair of SECF. She holds a bachelor's degree and a master's degree in education from the University of North Carolina at Greensboro, and earned her PhD in education from Vanderbilt University. Before joining Kate B. Reynolds, she spent sixteen years with the Center for Creative Leadership in Greensboro, North Carolina. Since 2015 she has been president and CEO of the Colorado Health Foundation.

Source: *www.coloradohealth.org; www. secf.org/ABOUT/Our-Hiistory*

and providing online tools for tracking legislative and regulatory activity and information at both the federal and state levels. SECF continued its tradition of sending one of the largest delegations to the annual Foundations on the Hill event in Washington, D.C.

To support this increasing programming and member outreach, the organization added a full-time public policy officer to the staff in 2013. The following year further staff expansion included a full-time marketing and communications director as well as an in-house graphic designer. SECF also developed a business plan to foster and expand coordination with local and regional affinity groups throughout the Southeast.

Moving on Up

In 2015, to accommodate its expanded staff, SECF relocated to a larger suite of offices on the 20th floor of 100 Peachtree Street. The move marked an end to twenty-five years of occupancy at the historic Hurt Building, which other longtime philanthropic and not-for-profit tenants had been leaving. In the new quarters, Lee focused on building a collaborative culture among the staff and made internal professional and leadership development a priority.

Throughout her tenure, Lee has built strong connections and partnerships between SECF and other national organizations, leveraging their knowledge, expertise, and connections in order to fuel programs and projects in the Southeast. Her outreach has included service on the boards of Grantmakers for Effective Organizations (which she co-founded and chaired), the National Center for Family Philanthropy

100 Peachtree Building
Courtesy of Kevin Brittelle

the United Philanthropy Forum (formerly the Forum of Regional Associations of Grantmakers), and the Independent Sector.

In 2015 SECF established the Hull Fellows Alumni Network to promote ongoing communication among the more than three hundred veterans of that unique leadership-training program, and approved a new strategic plan to guide its work through 2020. Evidence of the organization's continued energy during a period of increased competition came in 2016, when SECF succeeded in retaining 96% of its members. A first-ever commissioned market analysis revealed that a solid majority of all eligible grant-makers in the region already belonged to the Southeastern Council.

Continued strategic planning designed under Lee's leadership enhanced and highlighted SECF's value to its membership, the region, and the broader foundation field. In 2016 the inaugural edition of the *Southern Trends Report* debuted online, positioning SECF as the "go-to" resource for research and data on philanthropic trends in the region. The organization also formally defined its value proposition, based on five key areas: Regional and National Connections; Leadership Development; Southern Perspective; Promotion and Defense of Philanthropy;

FORWARD-THINKING PHILANTHROPY

Ray C. Anderson was the founder of the modular carpet-making giant Interface and perhaps the state's leading business-based environmentalist. After Anderson's death in 2011, the Georgia legislature named an eighteen-mile stretch of interstate highway in west Georgia's Troup County after him. Soon thereafter, his daughter, Harriet, and other family members set out to make the highway (nicknamed "The Ray") as environmentally friendly as Anderson's company.

Using funds from the foundation that bears its name, the Ray (now a 501(c)(3) public charity) is becoming the first solar roadway in the country. This living laboratory offers a vision of how highways could function in the future. Grasses and plants on the side of the Ray provide pollinator habitat, carbon sinks, and soil stabilization. Other features include a tire pressure monitoring system and a charging station for electric vehicles. Solar-powered "dots" on the highway warn drivers of approaching hazards.

With continued support from the Ray C Anderson Foundation, this venture (or "an epiphany" as the foundation calls it) is an imaginative first step to correct a national pattern of U.S. highways that generate five million tons of CO_2 emissions each year and were the setting for thirty-five thousand traffic fatalities in 2015 alone.

Source: Monica Medina, "Our Daily Planet," June 22, 2018

and Best and Next Practices.

These accomplishments naturally led in 2017 to further expansion of new research projects, chief among which was the commissioned production of the report *Philanthropy as the South's Passing Gear: Fulfilling the Promise*, in partnership with MDC, Inc. of Durham, North Carolina. Its release came one decade after MDC's first *Passing Gear* report. SECF then collaborated with state grant-maker networks to convene a series of *Passing Gear* state-focused events.

SECF has continued to revise and enhance its communications in recent years. Its e-mail newsletter *Connect*, has placed stronger emphasis on highlighting work done by members in their communities. Its magazine, *Inspiration*, has evolved from a newsletter format to a focus on telling stories through longer illustrated articles. A blog, "Engage," has become a popular platform for members seeking to provide a first-person perspective on their work.

The topics of diversity, equity, and inclusion took center stage in 2018 as the organization charged a task force with developing an equity framework that would both guide SECF's work and be made available to members seeking to integrate these principles into their own operations and grant-making. Such issues also were the main focus of a special event, "Breaking Through Barriers: Forging a Path to Philanthropic Success in the South," that convened local, regional, and national funders in Atlanta for a conversation on how to promote greater equity in the region. Of that gathering, Lee wrote in 2018,

> While SECF has progressed in numerous ways during my eight years as president and CEO, this gathering would prove to be an inflection point, a moment of dramatic evolution and growth. Over two days, leaders representing dozens of foundations strengthened relationships, shared honest stories of success and frustration, and learned from one another. We asked questions regarding troubling disparities in income, education, health and other outcomes that exist nationally but are more pronounced and entrenched in the American South. Inequity, particularly race and gender inequities, are often at the root cause of these challenges. We built connections that were rooted in trust and engaged in conversations that all too often are silenced or ignored. We united under the belief that together, philanthropy can help create a better South—a South that can serve as an example to the rest of the nation.[2]

SECF has come a long way since the days when its members debated whether corporate giving programs should be permitted to join the membership. During recent years, it has broadened its definition of regional giving to make individual donors, giving circles, and state and local grant-maker associations eligible to join the Southeastern Council. It also has expanded its geographical outreach and welcomed the St. Croix Foundation for Community Development, based in the Virgin Islands, to its ranks.

From 2011 to 2018 SECF grew from a $1.5 million organization to one with an annual budget of $3.1 million. More important, it broadened its scope and mission, from that of a member-service organization

SECF Board Chairs

2011–12	Karen McNeil-Miller	Kate B. Reynolds Charitable Trust	Winston-Salem, NC
2012–13	Nina Waters	Community Foundation for Northeast Florida	Jacksonville, FL
2013–14	Jeffrey S. Cribbs Sr.	Richmond Memorial Health Foundation	Richmond, VA
2014–15	Mary Humann Judson*	Jesse Parker Williams Foundation	Atlanta, GA
2015–16	Rhett Mabry	The Duke Endowment	Charlotte, NC
2016–17	Robert M. Fockler	Community Foundation of Greater Memphis	Memphis, TN
2017–	Gilbert Miller	Belaco Foundation	Columbus, GA

*currently president of the Goizueta Foundation

to a leadership organization—one that elevates and encourages the region's best and brightest in philanthropy. As 2018 drew to a close, SECF's board, staff, and a special planning task force were deeply immersed in the design of celebrations to commemorate the fiftieth anniversary of the Southeastern Council of Foundations, which would culminate at its annual meeting, to be held in Atlanta in November 2019.

SECF Annual Meetings		
2011	The Ritz-Carlton	Amelia Island, FL
2012	Charleston Place	Charleston, SC
2013	Omni Homestead	Hot Springs, VA
2014	New Orleans Marriott	New Orleans, LA
2015	Omni Grove Park Inn	Asheville, NC
2016	The Ritz-Carlton	Amelia Island, FL
2017	Omni Orlando Resort	Championsgate, FL
2018	Louisville Marriott Downtown	Louisville, KY
2019	Hyatt Regency	Atlanta, GA

CHAPTER 16 ENDNOTES

1   Janine Lee, interview with the authors, April 10, 2019.

2   Janine Lee, "Letters to Philanthropy," *Inspiration* 27, no.2 and 3 (2018).

AFTERWORD

Continued Expansion

We conclude our narrative even as the Southeastern Council of Foundations prepares to celebrate the 50th anniversary of its founding. Of course, the story of foundations in the South will continue. Given SECF's leadership and influence, the story has the opportunity to be characterized by increased focus and impact.

The expansion of the field continues to be dramatic. When we began work on this project some six years ago, the South was home to approximately 11,000 grant-makers. That figure has since increased by about 50%; more than 16,000 of them are now active. Their numbers include huge independent foundations, nearly 150 community foundations, dozens of corporate foundations, and thousands of family foundations. Collectively, they manage total charitable assets of more than $100 billion.

Southern Billionaires and Other Donors

Twenty-seven years ago the SECF board reluctantly concluded that the era of great fortunes being transformed into super-sized foundations

ASSET LEADERS

Philanthropy's financial figures continue to fluctuate rapidly during this period. Nonetheless, it appears that for at least a while longer, North Carolina will be able to lay claim to being the home of the South's largest private charitable foundation, the largest community foundation, and the largest health legacy foundation.

The Duke Endowment of Charlotte in 2017 had an investment portfolio of approximately $3.69 billion. That same year the Foundation for the Carolinas, also based in Charlotte, reported managing $2.483 billion. The recently formed Dogwood Health Trust in Asheville, is beginning operations with approximately $1.5 billion in assets.

Sources: *https://dukeendowment. org/about/about-the-endowment*; *https://columbussurvey.cfinsights. org/dashboard/tab/top-listshttps:// dogwoodhealthtrust.org/news/*

was a phenomenon of the past. The days of James Duke and Robert Woodruff clearly had come and gone. The promotion of community foundation formation (the initiative described in chapter 14) was the only apparent way to increase the philanthropic resources of the South.

Today an ironic sequel to that story is unfolding. Atlanta alone is home to thirteen known billionaires, the majority of whom have established or are involved with personal and family foundations.[1] Even a quick spot-check of the internet reveals that other metropolitan areas of the South (like Charlotte, Jacksonville, Memphis, Miami, Nashville, and Richmond), have their share of generous billionaires.

Philanthropic growth will not be confined to the ranks of the super-wealthy. For example it is reasonable to expect that the number and asset size of women's funds at work in Atlanta Birmingham, Chattanooga, Collier County (FL) Miami, and Memphis as well as East Tennessee Kentucky, and Mississippi will continue to grow Unserved portions of the region still can benefi from the formation of community foundation and their affiliate funds.

Similarly, the arrival of new business head

quarters and other operations in the region will almost certainly stimulate the formation of new corporate foundations and giving programs.

The infrastructure of philanthropy (and the important connective tissue of communication and collaboration among donors) is certain to be enhanced by the broadening membership criteria of SECF. That inclusive organization now welcomes donor circles, grant-making public charities and operating foundations, donor-advised funds, and even philanthropic individuals to its ranks.

As a growth industry in the 21st century South, the new foundations and other forms of philanthropy obviously depend upon the availability of new wealth. From what we have observed, though, other factors contribute to the ability of philanthropy to take root and flourish. They include the presence of government marked by a commitment to justice, a social climate that embraces racial and ethnic diversity, a commitment to the strong support of public education and public health, and an appreciation of cultural variety. In this setting, enterprising business people will continue to locate and/or expand their commercial activitys and likely establish vehicles for their philanthropy. The state of the national

BLACK BELT COMMUNITY FOUNDATION

The Black Belt region of the South was a fertile plain of rich, dark soil, some thirty miles wide, stretching for three hundred miles across central Alabama and northeastern Mississippi. Pre–Civil War plantations flourished in the area and enriched their owners. Because the plantations were worked by African American slaves, the area's name in post–Civil War years came to be associated with a predominantly black population dominated by daunting white racism and deeply entrenched poverty and deprivation. Against all sorts of odds a decade ago, Carol and John Zippert, activists and newspaper publishers in Greene County, Alabama, alongside David Wilson, an administrator of Auburn University, set in motion two initiatives that became linked and led to the formation of the Black Belt Community Foundation. It now annually raises and disburses more than $1.5 million and is active in twelve Alabama counties.

Source: *blackbeltfound.org/about-us/our-history*

and global economies and population trends certainly play their roles in the continued growth of wealth and philanthropic assets in the South, but so too does the steady expansion of the region's democratic society... and as history has demonstrated, the practice of philanthropy and the building of a civil society reinforce each other.

What Philanthropy Makes Possible

Our original writing assignment stemmed from a rather modest request: compose an essay about grant-making foundations in our home-town of Atlanta. Now, as we complete a greatly expanded manuscript about the entire region, we are even more acutely aware of the powerful impact that grant-making foundations have exerted upon our metropolis. Because of them, many of us enjoy the benefits of the good life that foundation giving helps to make possible—symphonies, theaters, museums, access to excellent medical care, a network of fine private and public universities, social service agencies, recreational centers... The list is a long one. What we are describing applies at different scales to every population center in the South. Looking ahead, we can anticipate that the South's foundations will continue their tradition of strengthening the region's greatest institutions and creating new ones.

However, the current version of the New South is not the New Jerusalem. Some measure of euphoria about the rapidly expanding pool of foundation assets is understandable, but it must be tempered by a careful look at a region that still carries the historical weight of poverty and disenfranchisement for many of its citizens. For all of our economic progress, we still lead the nation in our well-catalogued deficiencies in education, health, and human services. Like the rest of the country, we also struggle with environmental decay, escalating housing costs, and challenging race relations.

Expressive vs. Instrumental Giving

One of the most helpful perspectives on generosity that we have found is Peter Frumkin's distinction between instrumental and expressive giving.[2] Joel Fleishman further amplifies the difference by describing the former approach as seeking to achieve "a particular policy objective... and to accomplish a significant impact on a specified social problem." The latter he explains as a donor's desire "to show support for a cause or an organization without necessarily expecting to achieve a noticeable impact through his or her gift."[3]

We highlight this distinction because the ultimate measure of Southern philanthropy's success will be not its dollar total but the positive change it has engineered. At several places in this book we have tried to make clear our support for all kinds of philanthropic activity. Yet we also have unapologetically expressed our particular attraction to instrumental (i.e., transformative) giving.

In 1978 (see Chap. 14), John Griffin gently rebuked his grant-making colleagues for their failure to engage in the support of social change during the 1960s. John Griffin's challenge remains valid. Will they (we) respond to our own changing times with courage or caution? In the unsettling period during which this book is appearing, how will Southern foundations interpret their responsibility to preserve the ideals of liberty and community that undergird American democracy?

A Modern Take on Maimonides

Strongly encouraged by SECF board and staff leadership, the pattern of grant-making by Southern foundations is steadily becoming more "instrumental"—exemplified by the search for and eradication of the root causes behind social malaise and the promotion of greater diversity and equity. Grant-makers can point with pride to philanthropic investments that have brought dramatically positive change to the status of individuals, organizations, and communities.

At the beginning of this book, we summarized Maimonides' stratification of giving modes. We added our translation of what that great philosopher believed to be the highest form of generosity: moving the gift recipient from dependency toward independence. Nowhere is this intention more pronounced than in the work of the Mary Reynolds Babcock Foundation. The Winston-Salem, North Carolina, grant-maker, one of the few Southern foundations that gives regionally, states its crystal-clear goal in its mission statement: "We seek to help people and places move out of poverty and achieve greater social and economic justice."[4]

New and Expanding Emphases

The increased wealth of its foundations is not sufficient to meet all the needs of the South. Grant-making constitutes only a small percentage of all charitable giving and pales into virtual insignificance when measured against tax-supported public budgets. This condition reinforces the importance of focus. We venture to offer four related opportunities for emphasis by the South's foundations:

The Strategic Embrace of Advocacy

Far too often well-intentioned grant-makers are providing direct support to address the basic human needs of food, health, and shelter while those very deficiencies—and others—are being intensified by harmful legislation and regulations. As Jera Stribling, executive director of the Joseph S. Bruno Foundation in Birmingham, Alabama, and a former SECF trustee, puts it, "Foundations will have to do more than write checks to make change."[5]

Sherry Magill, the recently retired president of the Jessie Ball duPont Fund in Jacksonville, Florida, who also has served as an SECF trustee and chaired the Council on Foundations board, is a strong supporter of place-based philanthropy, but recognizes that geographical focus can limit systems change.

"I am saddened that I don't see a lot of advocacy in Southern foundations," she says. "That's exacerbated by the fact that there's no regional policy engine, so individual states rule. If you're not willing to engage with state government to make change, you won't make a big difference. Perhaps that's not so different from other regions, but we don't have the philanthropic capital or foundation density to organize as tightly as places like California or the Northeast."[6]

Investment in the Rural South

One of the most overlooked opportunities for support of advocacy involves the rural South—still home to 40 percent of the nation's poverty. Many Southerners are still only a generation or two removed from their agrarian and small-town roots. Yet, very few foundations in the region direct their giving to the needs of rural areas. Too often ignored is the fact that emigration from these sections of economic stagnation and joblessness is the supply side of urban poverty. Helping to establish and support rural-based, nonprofit organizations that can serve as partners in both service and advocacy could extend the benefits of a civil society to far more Southern citizens.

Continued Promotion of Diversity and Inclusiveness

From what we have observed, it seems clear that Southern philanthropy has become more transformative during the past several decades precisely because growing numbers of non-privileged women and people of color have found admission to and risen to positions of leadership in the field—there to share their important insights and perspectives about the needs of the community. Part of this change can be attributed directly to the SECF's Hull Fellows Program that we have already described.

In Closing. . .

A summary challenge to the grant-makers of the South—and it is the challenge to all foundations in all of America's regions—is whether they will choose to help create the society envisioned by our nation's Founders or whether they will satisfy themselves with simply erecting gated communities for the prosperous and privileged.

In his farewell address to the nation, exiting President Ronald Reagan said:

> I've spoken of the shining city all my political life, but I
> don't know if I ever quite communicated what I saw when

I said it. . . . [I]n my mind it was a tall, proud city. . .teeming with people of all kinds living in harmony and peace. . . . And if there had to be city walls, the walls had doors and the doors were open to anyone with the will and the heart to get here. That's how I saw it, and see it still.[7]

So do we.

Martin Lehfeldt and Jamil Zainaldin

AFTERWORD ENDNOTES

1   Tim Darnell, "13 Billionaires in Georgia Make Elite *Forbes* List," *Patch Atlanta*, March 5, 2019, https://patch.com/georgia/atlanta/13-billionaires-georgia-make-elite-forbes-list.

2   Peter Frumkin, *Strategic Giving: The Art and Science of Philanthropy* (Chicago: University of Chicago Press, 2006), 156.

3   Joel L. Fleishman, *The Foundation: A Great American Secret* (New York: Public Affairs, 2007), 26.

4   One of the great success stories of the Mary Reynolds Babcock Foundation is tied to its early funding in 1977 of the Self-Help Credit Union in Durham, North Carolina. That remarkable organization has since financed more than $3.5 billion in home mortgages and loans to small businesses and is now operating in North Carolina, South Carolina, and Florida. The foundation's diverse board also is a strong advocate for the importance of involving youth and young adults in the work of philanthropy. The Babcock Foundation publishes stories about their impact on their website.

5   From unpublished portion of article by Betsey Ruseel for SECF *Interchange* in Spring, 2017.

6   Ibid.

7   To read Reagan's address, delivered January 11, 1989, see the *New York Times*, "Transcript of Reagan's Farewell Address to American People," https://www.nytimes.com/1989/01/12/news/transcript-of-reagan-s-farewell-address-to-american-people.html.

AUTHORS' ACKNOWLEDGEMENTS

We are indebted to the Board of Trustees of the Southeastern Council of Foundations and the Board of Directors of Georgia Humanities for providing financial underwriting of this book's publication. Their generous support does not necessarily convey any endorsement of the ideas and interpretations expressed by the authors.

Janine Lee and Laura McCarty, the strong chief executives of those two organizations and our successors, recognized the value of issuing the book as part of the celebration of SECF's 50th anniversary and thereby provided us with a focus for completing it. They did us the additional favor of introducing our work with their personal forewords.

During the days when the book was little more than a concept, seed grants came from three SECF members: Mildred V. Horn Foundation (Louisville, KY), Lyndhurst Foundation (Chattanooga, TN), and Self Family Foundation (Greenwood, SC). Then, as the book took shape and drew closer to publication, we received valuable support from other members: Bradley-Turner Foundation (Columbus, GA), James Graham Brown Foundation (Louisville, KY), R. Howard Dobbs Foundation (Atlanta, GA), and The Patterson Foundation (Sarasota, FL).

We would never have started, let alone finished, this book without the strong involvement of Professor David Hammack, whose scholarship has helped to shape the field of philanthropic studies. He and his colleague, Steven Rathgeb Smith, years ago launched our work by inviting us to write an essay about Atlanta foundations as part of a larger study of philanthropy in urban regions of the country. The result, with their recommended improvements, became a chapter in *American Philanthropic Foundations: Regional Difference and Change* (Indiana University Press, 2018). That experience encouraged us to attempt a deeper regional study of our own—one that also has benefitted immensely from Professor Hammack's critical review and collegiality.

Professor John Inscoe, the distinguished Albert B. Saye Professor of History AND University Professor at the University of Georgia, has provided valuable advice at many points during our research and writing.

Professor Stanley Katz, an academic leader in the fields of history, law and philanthropy, has been both mentor and friend of Jamil Zainaldin for the past forty years. We are grateful for his early encouragement when we expressed an interest in tackling the subject of Southern philanthropy.

Kelly Caudle, Vice President, Strategy and Programs, Georgia Humanities, was our most sedulous editor of both copy and substantive content. She is a former Project Director of the *New Georgia Encyclopedia*, Senior Editor of *Cooking Light*, and Managing Editor of both *The Oxford American* and The University of Georgia Press. The fact-checking and editorial advice she provided after we submitted the first draft of our manuscript to her consideration resulted in a far better product than we could have imagined.

An architect and historic preservationist by profession, and a University of Florida graduate, Beth Grashof was sufficiently intrigued by our project to volunteer her services as photo editor. She located a wide range of financially affordable illustrations in a multiplicity of archives and then secured permission for their use—a time-consuming process that she conducted with agility and thoroughness.

Our book covers many dates and historical events. However, a full understanding of grant-making is equally reliant upon the insights of its practitioners—the so-called *philanthropoids* who guide the management and charitable disbursement of charitable fortunes. Drawing upon interviews with some of them, Mark Constantine, President of the Richmond (VA) Memorial Health Foundation, has captured the insights of contemporary women and men who played a vital role in shaping the style and spirit of modern philanthropy in the South. Most are now retired, but all but one are still living and remain wise and witty.

Linetta Gilbert	Jack Murrah
Sybil Hampton	George Penick
Lynn Huntley (deceased)	Karl Stauber
James Joseph	Tom Wacaster
Sherry Magill	Gayle Williams

It is of special interest to us that all of them are Southerners. We commend to our readers Mark Constantine's *Wit and Wisdom: Unleashing the Philanthropic Imagination* (New York: Emerging Practitioners in Philanthropy, 2009).

Charles Rooks and Robert Hull, former CEOs of the Southeastern Council of Foundations, retrieved important memories and suggested corrections that enhanced the manuscript. Janine Lee and her SECF staff graciously edited the first draft of a description about her years as SECF president. Stephen Sherman, SECF's Research and Data Manager, whose research skills and statistical dexterity we had planned to use from the start, not only excavated useful items from the SECF archives but also created an excellent set of charts and tables to illustrate foundation growth in the South and then revealed himself to be an excellent copy editor as well. Danah Craft, Greg Gerhard, Michael Howland, and Suzanna Stribling furnished helpful notes.

———————

Betsey Russell shared valuable recollections and documentation from her long-time association with SECF, and Bill Bondurant (the first and uncompensated CEO) and Ben White (of counsel to SECF) reviewed those portions of the book that describe their involvement.

———————

Phil Bellury and Adam Volle of The Storyline Group encouraged our idea for this book from the start and patiently coached us through the modern-day intricacies of converting a story into a published product.

———————

Many other people, in both seemingly small and decidedly major ways, responded to our request for help. We hope that both those whose names we cite and those we may have overlooked will take pride in the book to which they contributed. Where we have achieved success, they share the credit. (Included in this list are the names of individuals to whom Beth Grashof extends her personal thanks for their assistance with the identification of photographs.)

Amber Anderson, Tiffany Atwater, Jennifer Baker, Catherine Barth, Christian Belena, David Biemesderfer, Pete Bird, Sheila Blair, Phyllis Bowen, Kevin Brittelle, Maria

Bryson, Charles and Margaret Bundy, Rebecca Byrne, Courtney Chartier, Bruz Clark, Erskine Clarke, Mike Clayborne, Anne Close, Will Close, Gene Cochrane, Christine Colburn, Rob Collier, Betsy Covington, Chris Crothers, Susie Culipher, Jeanne Cyriaque, Stephanie Davis, Tom Davis, Elizabeth B. Dunn, Charles Easley, Walter Edgar, Andrew Feiler, Bob Fockler, Penny Franklin, Caroline Gallagher, Peggy Galis, Katherine Garrett-Cox, Barbara Gilbert, Kealy Gordon, Marianne Gordon, Lloyd Gray, Todd Groce, Doreen A. Gross, Sonia Guzman, Russ Hardin, Edward A. Hatfield, Gary Hauk, Susanna Hegner, Bari Helms, Luke Hoheisel, Tim Hynes, Charles Ivey, Beth Jarrard, Beth Johnson, Dorothy Johnson, Jena P. Jones, Mary Humann Judson, Marina Klarić, Tara Keeler, Bruce Kirby, Robert Kronley, Tom Lambeth, Karen Lambert, John Lanier, Heather Larkin, Leah Lefkowitz, Moniqe Lenoir, Guy Lescault, Pat Lile, Mary Linneman, Rhett Mabry Jennifer Maddox, Sherry Magill, Michael Marsicano, Ann McCleary, Angie McCrae, Steve McDavid, Penelope McPhee, Pete McTier, Gilbert Miller, Courtney Moore, Jenny Morgan, Andy Morikawa, Jim Morton, Brittany Newberry, Kate Nielsen, Lisa Olrichs, Darcy Oman, Renee Pappous, Loretta Parham, Martha Peck, Merryll Penson, Charity Perkins, Alicia Philipp, Edward Queen, Felicia Render, Dorothy Ridings, Joe Rosier, Alan Rothschild, Jr., Mason Rummel, Maria Saporta, Joanne

Scanlan, Mat Self, Mike Shadix, Lizzy Smith, Rayman Solomon, Megan Spainhour, Karl Stauber, Chris Steed, John Stephenson, Chuck Stone, Beth Stouffer, Heidi Stover, Jera Stribling, Steve Suitts, Sarah Tanner, Bobby Thalhimer, Jet Toney, Tom Wacaster, Donnelly Walton, Kimberly Webb, Frank Wideman, III, Arden Williams, Anna Woten, Tanya Zanish-Belcher, Susan Zepeda.

———————

Members of the SECF staff whom we have not already thanked for the ways they helped to advance this project include Jaci Bertrand, Dena Chadwick, Dawaon Edwards, Matthew L. Evans, Tiffany Friesen, Marianne Gordon, David Miller, S.E. Spencer, and Roderica Williams.

———————

We extend special appreciation to the Fox Center for Humanistic Inquiry of Emory University and the Foundation Center (the newly-renamed Candid) for their contributions and encouragement.

———————

Even with all of this help, we're certain that some errors or omissions occurred. They are our responsibility, and we hope they are not too egregious.

Appendix A - Number of Foundations, U.S & Southeast 1975-2015

	1975	1980	1985	1990	1995	2000	2005	2010	2015
Southeast	2,657	2,790	3,481	4,729	5,792	8,878	12,466	13,102	15,626
U.S.	21,877	22,315	25,815	32,401	40,140	56,582	71,095	76,610	86,203

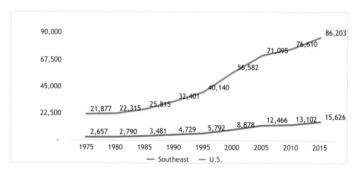

Note: Highlighted cells are estimates based on formulas and data included in the sources below.
Source for 1975 data: Southeastern Foundations: A Profile of the Region's Grantmaking Community. New York: Foundation Center, 1994
Source for 1990, 1995, 2000 data: Southeastern Foundations II: A Profile of the Region's Grantmaking Community. New York: Foundation
Source for 2005-2015 data: Foundation Center (http://data.foundationcenter.org), ca. 2018.

Appendix B - Giving by Southeast Foundations, 1975-2015

	1975	1992	1997	2000	2005	2010	2015
Southeast	$ 146,107,000	$ 1,157,181,000	$ 1,871,481,000	$ 3,360,997,000	$ 4,336,053,000	$ 6,917,185,000	$ 7,340,826,000
U.S.	$1,944,855,000	$ 10,209,453,000	$ 15,985,431,000	$ 27,563,166,000	$ 36,402,322,000	$ 45,857,616,000	$ 62,793,609,000

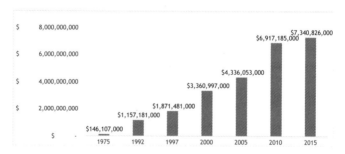

Source for 1975 data: Southeastern Foundations: A Profile of the Region's Grantmaking Community. New York: Foundation Center, 1994.
Source for 1990, 1995, 2000 data: Southeastern Foundations II: A Profile of the Region's Grantmaking Community. New York:
Foundation Center, 1999.
Source for 2005-2015 data: Foundation Center (http://data.foundationcenter.org), ca. 2018.

Appendix C - Growth in Assets of Southeast Foundations, 1975-2015

	1975	1992	1997	2000	2005	2010	2015
Southeast	$2,202,290,000	$ 18,477,053,000	$ 38,578,060,000	$ 52,580,429,000	$ 68,743,541,000	$ 70,601,344,000	$129,064,454,000
U.S.	$ 30,129,000	$176,825,000,000	$342,531,910,000	$486,085,311,000	$550,552,049,000	$643,974,334,000	$890,061,214,000

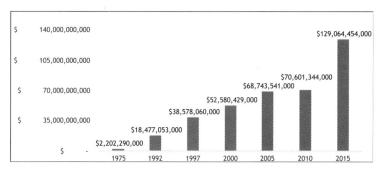

Source for 1975 data: Southeastern Foundations: A Profile of the Region's Grantmaking Community. New York: Foundation Center, 1994.

Source for 1990, 1995, 2000 data: Southeastern Foundations II: A Profile of the Region's Grantmaking Community. New York: Foundation Center, 1999.

Source for 2005-2015 data: Foundation Center (http://data.foundationcenter.org), ca. 2018.

Appendix D - SECF Board Members

FULL NAME	ORGANIZATION (AT TIME OF SERVICE)	STATE	YEAR(S) SERVED	CHAIR
John W. Red, Jr.	Smith Richardson Foundation	NC	1972	
R. Carl Hubbard	Elliott White Springs Foundation	SC	1972-1974	
William C. Archie	Mary Reynolds Babcock Foundation	NC	1972-1974	1970-1973
Carolyn Bufkin	Feild Co-Operative Association	MS	1972-1975	
John E. Eck	Self Foundation	SC	1972-1976	
John A. Griffin	Southern Education Foundation	GA	1972-1978	1977-1978
Franklyn A. Johnson	The Arthur Vining Davis Foundations	FL	1972-1978	1975-1977
Joel W. Richardson, Jr.	Memorial Welfare Foundation	TN	1972-1979	
Robert J. Sailstad	The Duke Endowment	NC	1972-1981	1978-1980
James McClure Clarke	James G.K. McClure Educational and Development Fund	NC	1972-1982	
Boisfeuillet Jones	Emily and Ernest Woodruff Fund	GA	1972-1984	1973-1975
Edwin F. Whited	Frost Foundation	LA	1974-1976	
Peggy McDonald	The Greater Birmingham Foundation	AL	1974-1978	
W.R. Broaddus III	Charles B. Keesee Educational Fund	VA	1974-1982	
H.E. Johnson	Dr. P. Phillips Foundation	FL	1974-1984	
William L. Bondurant	Mary Reynolds Babcock Foundation	NC	1975-1983	1980-1982
David R. Roberts	Edyth Bush Charitable Foundation	FL	1975-1983	
Charles A. Bundy	Elliott White Springs Foundation	SC	1975-1983 1985-1990	1982-1983
Glenn Pate	Feild Co-Operative Association	MS	1976-1984	
Frank A.M. Williams	The RosaMary Foundation	LA	1977-1979	
Frank J. Wideman, Jr.	The Self Foundation	SC	1977-1982	1984-1989
Marvin F. Vorderburg	William G. Selby and Marie Selby Foundation	FL	1979-1980	
William Kaufman	Community Foundation of Mobile	AL	1979-1984	
William T. Buice III	The Steele-Reese Foundation	KY	1979-1984	1983-1984
Flora Fenner French	Fenner Family Fund	LA	1980-1985	
Deaderick C. Montague	Memorial Welfare Foundation	TN	1980-1985	1984-1985
Hazel O. Williams	Jessie Ball duPont Religious, Charitable and Educational Fund	FL	1981-1984	
Ross M. Whipple	The Ross Foundation	AR	1981-1986	
J. Pollard Turman	J.M. Tull Foundation	GA	1982-1984	
Thomas W. Lambeth	Z. Smith Reynolds Foundation	NC	1983-1988	1985-1987
Gerald P. McCarthy	Virginia Environmental Endowment	VA	1983-1988	
Alicia Philipp	Metropolitan Atlanta Community Foundation	GA	1983-1988	
C. Thompson Wacaster	Phil Hardin Foundation	MS	1983-1988	1987-1988
Henry M. Carter, Jr.	The Winston-Salem Foundation	NC	1984-1989	1988-1989
John F. Day	The Duke Endowment	NC	1984-1989	
George D. Penick, Jr.	Mary Reynolds Babcock Foundation	NC	1984-1989	
J.W. Disher	Philip L. Van Every Foundation	NC	1985-1987	
Virginia C. Ramsey	The Greater Birmingham Foundation	AL	1985-1987	
John R. Bryden	The Steele-Reese Foundation	KY	1985-1990	
Charles H. McTier	Trebor Foundation	GA	1985-1990	1989-1990
Max K. Morris	The Arthur Vining Davis Foundations	FL	1985-1990	
Robert E. Perkins	William G. Selby and Marie Selby Foundation	FL	1985-1990	
Arthur C. Baxter	First Atlanta Foundation	GA	1985-1991	
Ida F. Cooney	The HCA Foundation	TN	1986-1991	

Blanc A. Parker	Edward G. Schlieder Educational Foundation	LA	1986-1991	
Robert C. Rhodes	The Ross Foundation	AR	1987-1989	
Jack G. Paden	Hill Crest Foundation	AL	1988-1993	
Martha G. Peck	The Burroughs Wellcome Fund	NC	1988-1993	1990-1992
Jean C. Lindsey	Chisholm Foundation	MS	1989-1991	
Valeria L. Lee	Z. Smith Reynolds Foundation	NC	1989-1994	
Darcy S. Oman	Greater Richmond Community Foundation	VA	1989-1994	
Edward L. White, Jr.	Cecil B. Day Foundation	GA	1989-1994	
Elridge W. McMillan	Southern Education Foundation	GA	1990-1993	
Ruth H. Heffron	Trident Community Foundation	SC	1990-1995	
Toney D. McMillan	The Ross Foundation	AR	1990-1995	
Jack Murrah	Lyndhurst Foundation	TN	1990-1995	1992-1993
Jere W. Witherspoon	The Duke Endowment	NC	1990-1995	
Jean W. Ludlow	Jessie Ball duPont Religious, Charitable and Educational Fund	FL	1991-1993	
Mebane M. Pritchett	Coca-Cola Scholars Foundation	GA	1991-1994	
Philip Caswell	Frank Stanley Beveridge Foundation	FL	1991-1996	
James N. Davis	Gheens Foundation	KY	1991-1996	
John W. Stephenson	J. Bulow Campbell Foundation	GA	1991-1996	1993-1995
William F. Winter	Foundation for the Mid South	MS	1992-1994	
Louis M. Freeman	The RosaMary Foundation	LA	1992-1997	
Katharine Pearson	East Tennessee Foundation	TN	1992-1997	1995-1997
Robert Hampton	Kathleen Price & Joseph M. Bryan Family Foundation	NC	1994	
Jera Stribling	Alabama Power Foundation	AL	1994; 1998-2002	
David Odahowski	Edyth Bush Charitable Foundation	FL	1994-1998	
Betsy VonBlond	The Greater Kanawha Valley Foundation	WV	1994-1998	
Leslie Lilly	Foundation for the Mid South	MS	1994-1999	
Mahlon Martin	Winthrop Rockefeller Foundation	AR	1995	
John S. Thomas	E.A. Morris Charitable Foundation	NC	1995-1997	
Sherry Magill	Jessie Ball duPont Fund	FL	1995-1998	
Sallie Adams Daniel	NationsBank	GA	1995-1998; 2003-2005	
Patricia Willis	BellSouth Foundation	GA	1995-1999	
Joyce T. Adger	Wachovia Foundation	NC	1995-2000	
Lawrence W. l'Anson, Jr.	Beazley Foundation	VA	1995-2000	1997-1999
Jacqueline Cox New	Winthrop Rockefeller Foundation	AR	1996	
James Barrett	Spartanburg County Foundation	SC	1996-1997	
Sheila Blair	Greater Birmingham Foundation	AL	1996-1997	
Martin Gatins	Katherine John Murphy Foundation	GA	1996-1997	
Jane Kendall	Kathleen Price Bryan Family Fund	NC	1996-1997	
Alice Smith	Lyndhurst Foundation	TN	1996-1997	
P. Russell Hardin	Robert W. Woodruff Foundation	GA	1996-2002	1999-2001
Sybil J. Hampton	Winthrop Rockefeller Foundation	AR	1997	
Sylvia Watson	James Graham Brown Foundation	KY	1997	
L. Evans Hubbard	A Friends' Foundation Trust	FL	1997-2002	
Juanita T. Jordan	The Peyton Anderson Foundation	GA	1997-2002	
Barry J. Flynn	The Assisi Foundation of Memphis	TN	1998-2003	
Marilyn Foote-Hudson	North Carolina GlaxoSmithKline Foundation	NC	1998-2003	
Gregory Ben Johnson	Greater New Orleans Foundation	LA	1998-2003	

Elizabeth H. Locke	The Duke Endowment	NC	1998-2004	
Frank J. Wideman, III	The Self Foundation	SC	1998-2004; 2012-2017	2001-2003
John J. Graham	Baptist Community Ministries	LA	1998-2005	2003-2005
Paul E. Arbogast	Greater Kanawha Valley Foundation	WV	1999	
JoAnn W. Kellogg	The Rapides Foundation	LA	1999-2001	
Penelope McPhee	John S. and James L. Knight Foundation	FL	1999-2001	
Linda Hyatt	Landmark Communications Foundation	VA	1999-2002	
Jonathan Howe	The Arthur Vining Davis Foundations	FL	1999-2004	
Mason Rummel	James Graham Brown Foundation	KY	1999-2005	
W.E. Gaylor	Patricia J. Buster Foundation Charitable Trust	FL	1999-2007	2005-2007
Michael Clayborne	CREATE Foundation	MS	2000-2004	
Barbara Cleveland	Tull Charitable Foundation	GA	2000-2005	
H.W. Close, Jr.	Springs Foundation	SC	2000-2006	
Brenda Rambeau	Katherine John Murphy Foundation	GA	2001-2003	
Alan E. Ronk	Foundation for Roanoke Valley	VA	2001-2003	
Richard H.C. Clay	Norton Foundation	KY	2002-2005	
Beverly Blake	David, Helen and Marian Woodward Fund	GA	2003	
Ed Furey, III	Dr. P. Phillips Foundation	FL	2003-2005	
Shannon Hull	Community Foundation for Palm Beach & Martin Counties	FL	2003-2005	
Gayle Williams	Mary Reynolds Babcock Foundation	NC	2003-2005	
Alan F. Rothschild, Jr.	Mildred Miller Fort Foundation	GA	2003-2007	
Paul A. Dresser, Jr.	Williamsburg Community Health Foundation	VA	2004	
Andrea L. Reynolds	Community Foundation for Greater Memphis	TN	2004	
William B. Johnson	Alabama Power Foundation	AL	2004-2009	
Peter F. Bird, Jr.	The Frist Foundation	TN	2004-2010	2007-2009
Thomas W. Ross	Z. Smith Reynolds Foundation	NC	2005-2006	
David D. Weitnauer	The Rockdale Foundation	GA	2005-2009	
Eugene W. Cochrane, Jr.	The Duke Endowment	NC	2005-2010	
Doyce H. Deas	Doyce H. Deas Foundation	MS	2005-2010	
Thomas C. Keith	Sisters of Charity Foundation of South Carolina	SC	2005-2010	
Allyson Rothrock	The Harvest Foundation	VA	2005-2010	
Debra M. Jacobs	William G. Selby and Marie Selby Foundation	FL	2005-2011	2009-2010
Suzanne Ward	CommunityCare Foundation	AR	2006-2007	
C. Dennis Riggs	Community Foundation of Louisville	KY	2006-2008	
Jan Young	The Assisi Foundation of Memphis	TN	2006-2009	
Ted J. Alexander	Lower Pearl River Valley Foundation	MS	2006-2011	
H. Scott Davis, Jr.	Mildred V. Horn Foundation	KY	2006-2011	
Handy L. Lindsey, Jr.	The Cameron Foundation	VA	2006-2011	
Byron R. Harrell	Baptist Community Ministries	LA	2006-2012	2010-2011
Lesley Grady	Community Foundation for Greater Atlanta	GA	2007-2010; 2012	
Louie Buntin	Louie M. & Betty M. Phillips Foundation	TN	2007-2012	
Dorothy H. Neale	IBM	TN	2007-2012	
Karen McNeil-Miller	Kate B. Reynolds Charitable Trust	NC	2007-2013	2011-2012

H. Speer Burdette, III	Fuller E. Callaway Foundation	GA	2008-2013	
Nina Waters	Community Foundation in Jacksonville	FL	2008-2014	2012-2013
Kathryn H. Dennis	Community Foundation of Central Georgia	GA	2009-2011	
Heather Larkin	Arkansas Community Foundation	AR	2009-2014	
Maria Elena Retter	The Goizueta Foundation	GA	2010-2012	
Maria S. Kennedy	The Daniel Foundation of Alabama	AL	2010-2015	
Mary Thomas	Spartanburg County Foundation	SC	2010-2015	
Leroy Davis	Jessie Ball duPont Fund	FL	2010-2017	
Susan Towler	Florida Blue Foundation	FL	2011	
Katherine Sikora	Laura Goad Turner Charitable Foundation	KY	2011-2014	
Jeffrey S. Cribbs, Sr.	Richmond Memorial Health Foundation	VA	2011-2015	2013-2014
Mary Humann Judson	The Goizueta Foundation	GA	2011-2016	2014-2015
Elizabeth A. Smith	Robert W. Woodruff Foundation	GA	2011-2016	
Susan Zepeda	Foundation for a Healthy Kentucky	KY	2012-2016	
Rhett Mabry	The Duke Endowment	NC	2012-2017	2015-2016
John Rochester	Martha Christine White Foundation	AL	2012-2017	
Marcie Skelton	The Walker Foundation	MS	2012-2017	
Damian Thorman	John S. and James L. Knight Foundation	FL		2013
Michael K. Anderson	Georgia Power Foundation	GA	2013-2015	
James T. Morton	J. Marion Sims Foundation	SC	2013-2015	
Sandra Mikush	Mary Reynolds Babcock Foundation	NC	2013-2016	
Robert M. Fockler	Community Foundation of Greater Memphis	TN	2013-2018	2016-2017
Joseph R. Rosier, Jr.	The Rapides Foundation	LA	2013-2018	
Carol Mizoguchi	Casey Family Programs	WA	2014	
Roxanne Jerde	Community Foundation of Sarasota County	FL	2014-2018	
Gilbert Miller	Beloco Foundation	GA	2014-present	2017-2019
Regan Gruber Moffitt	Winthrop Rockefeller Foundation	AR	2015-present	
Kelly Chopus	Robins Foundation	VA	2016	
Torrey DeKeyser	EyeSight Foundation of Alabama	AL	2016-2018	
Madelyn R. Adams	Kaiser Permanente of Georgia	GA	2016-present	
Jennifer A. Algire	The Greater Clark Foundation	KY	2016-present	
Alfredo A. Cruz	Foundation for Louisiana	LA	2016-present	
Stephanie K. Cooper-Lewter	Sisters of Charity Foundation of South Carolina	SC	2016-present	
Carol W. Butler	Mike & Gillian Goodrich Foundation	AL	2017-present	
Robert Dortch	Robins Foundation	VA	2017-present	
Patricia E. Lummus	The Sartain Lanier Family Foundation	GA	2017-present	
Antoinette Malveaux	Casey Family Programs	WA	2017-present	
Cabot Pyle	Dugas/Turner Family Foundations	TN	2017-present	
Claire A. Webber	May P. & Francis L. Abreu Charitable Trust	GA	2017-present	
Jane C. Alexander	Community Foundation for Mississippi	MS	2018-present	
Laura Gerald	Kate B. Reynolds Charitable Trust	NC	2018-present	
Christopher Steed	The Fullerton Foundation	SC	2018-present	
Michael Sweeney, III	Healthcare Georgia Foundation	GA	2018-present	
Mark C. Callaway	Morning Star Foundation, Inc.	GA	2019-present	
Terri Freeman	Community Foundation of Greater Memphis	TN	2019-present	
Eric M. Kelly	Quantum Foundation	FL	2019-present	
Michael Tipton	Blue Cross and Blue Shield of Louisiana Foundation	LA	2019-present	

Appendix E - Hull Fellows

Hull Class	Full Name	Affiliation at time of participation
2000	Sheryl Aikman	The Community Foundation of Western North Carolina
2000	Dawn Butler	The Fannie Mae Foundation
2000	Alfredo Cruz	John S. and James L. Knight Foundation
2000	Dori Kreiger	Community Foundation Serving Richmond & Central Virginia
2000	James Gore	The Winston-Salem Foundation
2000	Betsy Verner	J. Bulow Campbell Foundation
2000	William C. Keator	The Arthur Vining Davis Foundations
2000	Maggie Keenan	Savannah Foundation
2000	Darryl Lester	Warner Foundation
2000	Athan Lindsay	Mary Reynolds Babcock Foundation
2000	Rhett Mabry	The Duke Endowment
2000	Victoria McGovern	Burroughs Wellcome Fund
2000	Andrew McMains	McMains Foundation
2000	Jo Pauling-Jones	Sisters of Charity Foundation of South Carolina
2000	Teresa Rivero	Robert W. Woodruff Foundation
2000	W.M. Self, Jr.	The Self Family Foundation
2000	Ashley Shelton	Baton Rouge Area Foundation
2000	Allen Smart	The Rapides Foundation
2000	David Weitnauer	The Rockdale Foundation
2000	John Zell	Jacksonville Community Foundation
2001	Morgan Baldwin	CREATE Foundation
2001	Yvette Desrosiers-Alphonse	The Rapides Foundation
2001	Toni Freeman	The Duke Endowment
2001	Robert F. Hatcher, Jr.	Georgia Pine Level Foundation, Inc.
2001	Mary Holmes	Cumberland Community Foundation, Inc
2001	J.T. Hyche	Community Foundation of Greater Greenville
2001	Heather Larkin	Arkansas Community Foundation, Inc.
2001	Allen Mast	Mary Black Foundation
2001	Dodie McKenzie	James Graham Brown Foundation
2001	Scott Perry	The Memorial Foundation, Inc.
2001	Anthony Recasner	The Greater New Orleans Foundation
2001	Andrea Reynolds	Community Foundation of Greater Memphis
2001	Daphne Robinson	The Rapides Foundation
2001	Tara Scholtz	The Community Foundation of Western North Carolina
2001	Elizabeth Snyder	Balentine & Company, Wilmington Trust
2001	Marty Sonenshine	Anverse, Inc.
2001	Joy Heinsohn	Z. Smith Reynolds Foundation
2001	Laura Whitaker	CF Foundation, Inc.
2001	Kimberly Younghans	Turner Foundation, Inc.
2002	Patricia Admire	William J. & Tina Rosenberg Foundation
2002	Andrea Montag	Community Foundation for Greater Atlanta
2002	Bobbie Reynolds	Luther & Susie Harrison Foundation
2002	Ramon Rodriguez	BellSouth Foundation
2002	Elizabeth Self	The Self Family Foundation
2002	Kelley Tison	Luther & Susie Harrison Foundation
2002	Lani Rossman	The Frist Foundation
2002	Peter M. Abreu, Jr.	May P. & Francis L. Abreu Charitable Trust
2002	William Buster	Mary Reynolds Babcock Foundation
2002	Sara Collins	Foundation for the Carolinas

2002	Leigh Davis	The Norfolk Foundation
2002	Becky Farley	The Riley Foundation
2002	Lori Fuller	Kate B. Reynolds Charitable Trust
2002	Margaret Connelly	The Arthur M. Blank Family Foundation
2002	Shalondra Henry	The Arthur M. Blank Family Foundation
2002	Kristy Huntley	Benwood Foundation, Inc.
2002	Gregory Lee	Coca-Cola Scholars Foundation
2002	Charles Merritt	The Duke Endowment
2002	Joanne Pulles	The HCA Foundation
2002	Alex Spoelker	Community Foundation of Louisville, Inc.
2003	April Brumfield	Baton Rouge Area Foundation
2003	Laurie DeCuir	Baptist Community Ministries
2003	David Gibbs	Community Foundation for Greater Atlanta
2003	Mary Piepenbring	The Duke Endowment
2003	Kathleen Shields	Foundation for the Mid South
2003	Debby West	CREATE Foundation
2003	Catherine Brozowski	Washington Mutual
2003	Omisade Billie Burney	Warner Foundation
2003	Bobbi Cleveland	The Tull Charitable Foundation
2003	Kathryn Dennis	Community Foundation of Central Georgia, Inc.
2003	T. Duane Gordon	Community Foundation of Greater Jackson
2003	Milano Harden	Healthcare Georgia Foundation
2003	Kathy Hebert	The Greater New Orleans Foundation
2003	Mary H. Judson	R. Howard Dobbs, Jr. Foundation
2003	Jim Morton	J. Marion Sims Foundation, Inc.
2003	Maggie Gunther Osborn	Conn Memorial Foundation
2003	Kimberly MRussell	Community Foundation Serving Richmond & Central Virginia
2003	Daniel Shoy, Jr.	The Arthur M. Blank Family Foundation
2003	Molly Talbot-Metz	Mary Black Foundation
2003	Mark Anthony Thomas	Georgia-Pacific
2003	Tammy Wells	Springs Foundation
2004	Denise Barrett	Foundation for the Mid South
2004	Christopher Cooper	H. W. Durham Foundation
2004	Ezra Brown Crenshaw, Jr.	J. Marion Sims Foundation, Inc.
2004	Phillip Gatins	Katherine John Murphy Foundation
2004	Stephanie Liuzza	Baptist Community Ministries
2004	Phillip H. Redmond, Jr.	The Duke Endowment
2004	Katherine Williams	Sisters of Charity Foundation of South Carolina
2004	Samantha Bickham	The Greater New Orleans Foundation
2004	Nicole Buggs	Healthcare Georgia Foundation
2004	Staci Bush	AGL Resources, Inc. & the AGL Resources Private Foundation
2004	Marianne Ratcliffe	Kate B. Reynolds Charitable Trust
2004	Robyn Davis	Southern Partners Fund
2004	Tjuan Dogan	Southern Education Foundation
2004	Jennifer Ferguson	Arkansas Community Foundation, Inc.
2004	Reid THanson	The Peyton Anderson Foundation
2004	Jane Hardesty	The John H. & Wilhelmina D. Harland Charitable Foundation
2004	Jane H. Hopkins	Coca-Cola Scholars Foundation
2004	Liana Humphrey	Warner Foundation
2004	Fontella McKyer	Foundation for the Carolinas
2004	Lita Pardi	Community Foundation for Greater Atlanta
2004	Wendy Roy	The Rapides Foundation

2004	Barbara Saunders	The Arthur M. Blank Family Foundation
2004	Melissa Whitby	Community Foundation of Greater Memphis
2005	Sabrina G. Niggel	J. Marion Sims Foundation, Inc.
2005	Danielle Breslin	Blue Cross and Blue Shield of North Carolina Foundation
2005	Chris Crothers	Foundation for the Mid South
2005	Mary E. Eldridge	The Ross Foundation
2005	Robin Ganzert	Wachovia National Center of Planned Giving
2005	Elizabeth Grace	The Greater New Orleans Foundation
2005	Susan Hallett	Community Foundation Serving Richmond & Central Virginia
2005	Jennifer Koltnow	Memphis Grizzlies Charitable Foundation
2005	Susan Richardson	Kate B. Reynolds Charitable Trust
2005	Karen Rogers	The Duke Endowment
2005	Lizzy Smith	Robert W. Woodruff Foundation
2005	Christopher Stecklein	CommunityCare Foundation
2005	Anne Sterchi	J. B. Fuqua Foundation, Inc.
2005	Cheryl Tupper	The Arthur Vining Davis Foundations
2005	Cal Turner, III	Cal Turner Family Foundation
2005	Akilah Watkins-Butler	Community Foundation for Greater Atlanta
2005	Megan Watkins	JPMorgan Private Bank
2005	Pauline White	Dr. P. Phillips Foundation
2006	Michael Scott Close	The Springs Close Foundation
2006	Betty Alonso	Dade Community Foundation
2006	Louisa D'Antignac	Wilbur and Hilda Glenn Family Foundation
2006	Erin Boorn	Community Foundation for Greater Atlanta
2006	Greg Gerhard	May P. & Francis L. Abreu Charitable Trust
2006	Hazle Hamilton	Community Foundation of Central Georgia, Inc.
2006	Conaway Bernard Haskins, III	The Cameron Foundation
2006	Lin B. Hollowell, III	The Duke Endowment
2006	DiShonda Hughes	The Atlanta Women's Foundation
2006	Wanda Jenkins	Community Foundation of the Chattahoochee Valley
2006	Anita Johnson	The Cannon Foundation, Inc.
2006	Felecia Lucky	Black Belt Community Foundation
2006	Racquel Lee-Sin	Washington Mutual
2006	Jan Ross	Huey & Angelina Wilson Foundation
2006	Virginia Self Goldsmith	The Self Family Foundation
2006	Akeshia Singleton	The Rapides Foundation
2006	Katrina Spigner	Sisters of Charity Foundation of South Carolina
2006	Edgar G. Villanueva	Kate B. Reynolds Charitable Trust
2006	Lisa B. Williams	R. Howard Dobbs, Jr. Foundation
2006	Erika Williams	The Annie E. Casey Foundation
2007	Thomas P. Self	The Self Family Foundation
2007	LaToria Thomas	The Greater New Orleans Foundation
2007	Brooke Bailey	Sisters of Charity Foundation of South Carolina
2007	Evie Storey	CREATE Foundation
2007	Melanie Cianciotto	SunTrust Bank Foundations & Endowments Specialty Practice
2007	John Estes	The Harvest Foundation
2007	Lavastian Glenn	Mary Reynolds Babcock Foundation
2007	Necole Irvin	Foundation for the Mid South
2007	Erik Johnson	Robert W. Woodruff Foundation
2007	Kristen Keely-Dinger	Baptist Healing Trust
2007	Darrya Lipscomb	The Arthur M. Blank Family Foundation
2007	Lisa Medellin	Healthcare Georgia Foundation

2007	Kevin O'Halloran	Charlottesville Area Communtiy Foundation
2007	Dominique Sinyard-Smith	Wachovia Trust
2007	Genia Cayce	The Rockdale Foundation
2007	Tene Traylor	Community Foundation for Greater Atlanta
2007	Lauren Veasey	Southern Education Foundation
2007	Jillian Vukusich	Community Foundation for Palm Beach & Martin Counties
2007	Robb Webb	The Duke Endowment
2008	Ethan Clapsaddle	Cherokee Preservation Foundation
2008	Michele Pritchard	The Peyton Anderson Foundation
2008	Laurell Allen	Patterson Barclay Memorial Foundation
2008	Denise Blakney	Obici Healthcare Foundation
2008	Marco Cocito-Monoc	The Greater New Orleans Foundation
2008	Catherine Covington	SunTrust Bank Foundations & Endowments Specialty Practice
2008	Kappy deButts	The Zeist Foundation, Inc.
2008	Jennifer Evins	The Spartanburg County Foundation
2008	Rebecca Finley	The Community Foundation of Middle Tennessee
2008	Lisa Garcia	Community Foundation of the New River Valley
2008	Maria Kennedy	The Daniel Foundation of Alabama
2008	Isha Ahsan Lee	The Atlanta Women's Foundation
2008	Tina Markanda	The Duke Endowment
2008	Nadine Marsh-Carter	Richmond Memorial Health Foundation
2008	Mary Whittington	The Self Family Foundation
2008	Kathleen Shaw	The Community Foundation in Jacksonville
2008	Katy P. Smith	Piedmont Health Foundation
2008	Marvin Starks	J. Marion Sims Foundation, Inc.
2008	Lauren Welsh	Community Foundation for Greater Atlanta
2008	Joyce Yamaato	Wachovia Trust
2009	Jennifer Zuckerman	Blue Cross and Blue Shield of North Carolina Foundation
2009	Abena Asante	Kate B. Reynolds Charitable Trust
2009	Jeff Barker	St. Marys United Methodist Church Foundation, Inc.
2009	Kristina Christy	Turner Broadcasting System
2009	Diana Empsall	C. E. & S. Foundation, Inc.
2009	Lynn Collingsworth	The Joy McCann Foundation
2009	Eleanor Dunlap	Piedmont Healthcare Foundation
2009	Cynthia Elmore	John Randolph Foundation
2009	Gladys Hairston	The Harvest Foundation
2009	Ivan Hudson	Winthrop Rockefeller Foundation
2009	Richard Martinez	The Greater New Orleans Foundation
2009	Susan McConnell	The Duke Endowment
2009	Aisha Nyandoro	Foundation for the Mid South
2009	Dana Rickman	The Annie E. Casey Foundation
2009	Karen Rudolph	Lyndhurst Foundation
2009	Najmah Thomas	The Cameron Foundation
2009	Eva Tukdarian	Dr. P. Phillips Foundation
2010-2011	Michael Hubbard	A Friends' Foundation Trust
2010-2011	Stephanie K. Cooper-Lewter	Sisters of Charity Foundation of South Carolina
2010-2011	Sharon Gibbs	Community Foundation of Greenville
2010-2011	Wendi Goods Everson	Danville Regional Foundation
2010-2011	Jacqueline Innocent	The Annie E. Casey Foundation
2010-2011	Elizabeth Jarrard	J. Bulow Campbell Foundation
2010-2011	Angel Johnson-Brebner	Frances P. Bunnelle Foundation
2010-2011	Charles Lee	The Elbert W. Rogers Foundation

2010-2011	Stephan L. McDavid	The Algernon Sydney Sullivan Foundation
2010-2011	Gilbert Miller	Beloco Foundation, Inc.
2010-2011	Regan Gruber Moffitt	Winthrop Rockefeller Foundation
2010-2011	Jennifer Oldham	Baptist Healing Trust
2010-2011	Meghan Pietrantonio	SunTrust Bank Foundations & Endowments Specialty Practice
2010-2011	Deborah Ryan	The Atlanta Women's Foundation
2010-2011	Meka Sales	The Duke Endowment
2010-2011	Natalie Schmook	Hayes Family Charitable Foundation
2010-2011	Risha Stebbins	The Cameron Foundation
2010-2011	Sonia Vick	Williams Family Foundation of Georgia, Inc.
2010-2011	Catherine Warfield	Foundation for the Carolinas
2010-2011	Julia Wood	Community Foundation of Central Georgia, Inc.
2011-2012	Helen V. Harley	The Self Family Foundation
2011-2012	Charlie Myers	Cherokee Preservation Foundation
2011-2012	Amy Clarke	CF Foundation, Inc.
2011-2012	Katherine Blair	James Graham Brown Foundation
2011-2012	Erica S. Crenshaw	Black Belt Community Foundation
2011-2012	Randae Davis	Community Foundation of South Georgia
2011-2012	Belinda D. Havron	The Community Foundation of Middle Tennessee
2011-2012	Doreen A. Gross	The Arthur Vining Davis Foundations
2011-2012	Holly Furr	J. Marion Sims Foundation, Inc.
2011-2012	Ashley Harper	Community Foundation of Greater Memphis
2011-2012	David Johnson	Arkansas Community Foundation, Inc.
2011-2012	Josephine S. Maxwell	SunTrust Bank Foundations & Endowments Specialty Practice
2011-2012	Katie McDowell	Michaels Family Charitable Foundation
2011-2012	Kristina A. Morris	Community Foundation for Greater Atlanta
2011-2012	Hunter Pierson	Goldman, Sachs & Co. Foundation
2011-2012	Melinda L. Sanders	Kharis Foundation
2011-2012	Jasmine Smith	Blue Cross and Blue Shield of North Carolina Foundation
2011-2012	Kenita Williams	Southeastern Council of Foundations
2011-2012	Jane H. Wilson	Robins Foundation
2012-2013	Dwanda Moore	Foundation for the Mid South
2012-2013	Amory Scott	Scott Foundation, Inc.
2012-2013	Jehan Benton-Clark	Kate B. Reynolds Charitable Trust
2012-2013	Susie Bowie	Community Foundation of Sarasota County, Inc.
2012-2013	Tristi Charpentier	Blue Cross and Blue Shield of Louisiana Foundation
2012-2013	Deborah Cooper	Community Foundation of Greenville
2012-2013	Angela Goddard	Dugas/Turner Family Foundations
2012-2013	John Hardman	Dot & Lam Hardman Family Foundation, Inc.
2012-2013	Sara Hemingway	Marilyn & William Young Charitable Foundation
2012-2013	Kelly Hopkins	Relgalf Charitable Foundation
2012-2013	Andrea YKellum	Healthcare Georgia Foundation
2012-2013	Sarah Kinser	Arkansas Community Foundation, Inc.
2012-2013	Karen Lambert	The Peyton Anderson Foundation
2012-2013	Valerie Liggins	The Cameron Foundation
2012-2013	Sara Manning	SunTrust Bank Foundations & Endowments Specialty Practice
2012-2013	Nancy Clair McInaney	R. Howard Dobbs, Jr. Foundation
2012-2013	Josh Phillipson	Community Foundation for Greater Atlanta
2012-2013	Lora Smith	Mary Reynolds Babcock Foundation
2012-2013	Wesley Tomlinson LaRue	Community Foundation of Greater Memphis
2012-2013	Cindy Bedsole	Wiregrass Foundation
2014-2015	Rachel Cheek	Community Foundation of Greater Memphis

2014-2015	Natalie Yates	Davison Bruce Foundation
2014-2015	Kyra Cook	Williamsburg Health Foundation
2014-2015	Brad Courts	Fraser-Parker Foundation
2014-2015	Mark Crosswell	R. Howard Dobbs, Jr. Foundation
2014-2015	Nora Ferrell	Kate B. Reynolds Charitable Trust
2014-2015	Andrew Ford	Winthrop Rockefeller Foundation
2014-2015	Madeleine Frey	Healthcare Georgia Foundation
2014-2015	Renee Joyal	Huey & Angelina Wilson Foundation
2014-2015	Katie Midgley	Plough Foundation
2014-2015	Jenny Morgan	Robert W. Woodruff Foundation
2014-2015	Kelli Parker	Community Foundation of the Chattahoochee Valley
2014-2015	Emily Patteson	SunTrust Bank Foundations & Endowments Specialty Practice
2014-2015	Meshelle Rawls	Foundation for the Mid South
2014-2015	Venetia Skahen	The Cannon Foundation, Inc.
2014-2015	Tamela Spann	Hollingsworth Funds
2014-2015	Clark Tennyson	The Ross Foundation
2014-2015	Lily Zhang	The Duke Endowment
2015-2016	Keisha Williams	Kaiser Permanente
2015-2016	Jennie Blake	Cox Enterprises
2015-2016	Fuller E. Callaway, IV	Morning Star Foundation, Inc.
2015-2016	Russell Carey	Winthrop Rockefeller Foundation
2015-2016	Carrie Conway	Robert W. Woodruff Foundation
2015-2016	Nate Cousineau	Quantum Foundation
2015-2016	Karla Davis	The Assisi Foundation of Memphis, Inc.
2015-2016	Andrew Hartley	Northern Trust Corporation Foundation & Institutional Advisors
2015-2016	Stacey Keeley	Community Foundation Serving Richmond & Central Virginia
2015-2016	Alexandra Leahy	Community Foundation of Central Georgia, Inc.
2015-2016	Mark LeMaire	The Community Foundation for Northeast Florida, Inc.
2015-2016	Caitlin Nossett	The HCA Foundation
2015-2016	William Pribble	Williamsburg Health Foundation
2015-2016	Langley Shealy	Sisters of Charity Foundation of South Carolina
2015-2016	Tamika Williams	The Duke Endowment
2017-2018	Corinne Bergeron	The Frist Foundation
2017-2018	Gina Blohm	Community Foundation of Greenville
2017-2018	Amy McCrory Brown	The Goizueta Foundation
2017-2018	Catherine Callaway	Humann Family Foundation
2017-2018	Lisa Dixon	Winthrop Rockefeller Foundation
2017-2018	Shannon Gaggero	Homestead Foundation, Inc.
2017-2018	Anne Greene	J. Bulow Campbell Foundation
2017-2018	Josina P.Greene	Community Foundation of the Chattahoochee Valley
2017-2018	Sharon Hackney	Florida Blue Foundation
2017-2018	Elizabeth Jones	The Greater Clark Foundation
2017-2018	Erin Jones	Community Foundation of Sarasota County, Inc.
2017-2018	Virginia Lee	James Graham Brown Foundation
2017-2018	Alyssa Manning	Felix E. Martin Jr. Foundation
2017-2018	Jessica Mullen	Portsmouth General Hospital Foundation
2017-2018	Caroline Rakar	Coastal Community Foundation
2017-2018	Kathleen Nolte	Lyndhurst Foundation
2017-2018	Gillian Puffer	Mike & Gillian Goodrich Foundation
2017-2018	Paige Pushkin	Georgia Foundation for Public Education
2017-2018	Mary Spanburgh	Kaiser Permanente
2017-2018	Tara Weese	The Spartanburg County Foundation
2017-2018	Rhea Williams-Bishop	W.K. Kellogg Foundation

Program moved to every other year beginning in 2010

Appendix F - Columbus Survey of Community Foundations

Top 100 Community Foundations by Asset Size—2017

As of 2017, 26 of the 100 largest community foundations in the country were based in the South.[1] These are italicized below. Most of their assets have since increased.

1	Silicon Valley Community Foundation	$13,574,876,130
2	Tulsa Community Foundation	$4,437,335,394
3	Greater Kansas City Community Foundation	$3,148,672,721
4	The Chicago Community Trust	$2,828,248,897
5	The New York Community Trust	$2,806,082,837
6	*Foundation for the Carolinas*	$2,483,470,250
7	The Cleveland Foundation	$2,451,438,785
8	The Columbus Foundation	$2,266,199,489
9	The Oregon Community Foundation	$2,216,373,546
10	Marin Community Foundation	$1,774,093,000
11	California Community Foundation	$1,675,584,976
12	The San Francisco Foundation	$1,471,878,803
13	The Saint Paul & Minnesota Community Foundations	$1,251,701,000
14	The Pittsburgh Foundation	$1,249,000,000
15	Omaha Community Foundation	$1,132,915,750
16	The Boston Foundation	$1,115,286,000
17	*The Community Foundation for Greater Atlanta*	$1,099,624,149
18	Communities Foundation of Texas, Inc.	$1,098,176,000
19	Hartford Foundation for Public Giving	$1,042,810,075
20	Oklahoma City Community Foundation, Inc.	$983,180,496
21	Seattle Foundation	$965,412,953
22	The Rhode Island Community Foundation	$957,389,515
23	The Greater Milwaukee Foundation	$913,447,125
24	Community Foundation for Southeast Michigan	$912,062,338
25	San Antonio Area Foundation	$900,000,000
26	*Community Foundation Serving Richmond and Central Virginia*	$858,580,569
27	The Denver Foundation	$842,000,000
28	Arizona Community Foundation, Inc.	$828,737,930
29	Central Indiana Community Foundation, Inc.	$811,453,251
30	The Minneapolis Foundation	$761,188,506
31	Greater Houston Community Foundation	$757,057,318
32	New Hampshire Charitable Foundation	$755,511,675
33	*Baton Rouge Area Foundation*	$655,927,311
34	The Greater Cincinnati Foundation	$650,000,000
35	The Community Foundation for Greater New Haven	$620,119,557
36	Hawaii Community Foundation	$613,332,111
37	*The Winston-Salem Foundation*	$605,191,082
38	The Dayton Foundation	$541,239,254
39	Maine Community Foundation, Inc.	$532,441,519
40	Kalamazoo Community Foundation	$528,822,371
41	St. Louis Community Foundation	$505,604,828
42	The Philadelphia Foundation	$490,715,447
43	Community Foundation of Greater Des Moines	$472,321,600
44	Community Foundation of New Jersey	$468,464,818
45	Community Foundation for Greater Buffalo	$467,700,000
46	*The Community Foundation of Middle Tennessee*	$448,006,457
47	Rochester Area Community Foundation	$443,866,765
48	*East Tennessee Foundation*	$432,387,016
49	*Community Foundation of Greater Memphis, Inc.*	$429,935,073
50	The Dallas Foundation	$421,555,316

51	*The Community Foundation for Northeast Florida*	$398,034,676
52	Santa Barbara Foundation	$397,000,000
53	*The Miami Foundation*	$365,429,625
54	*Greater New Orleans Foundation*	$351,652,221
55	*Hampton Roads Community Foundation*	$340,475,627
56	Greater Washington Community Foundation	$336,785,026
57	*Arkansas Community Foundation*	$335,506,981
58	*Community Foundation of Sarasota County*	$333,577,282
59	Grand Rapids Community Foundation	$331,761,185
60	East Bay Community Foundation	$330,630,140
61	Community Foundation for the Fox Valley Region, Inc.	$325,896,309
62	Rose Community Foundation	$324,875,836
63	North Texas Community Foundation	$312,000,000
64	The Vermont Community Foundation	$310,500,000
65	Orange County Community Foundation	$301,741,000
66	*Gulf Coast Community Foundation (FL)*	$295,488,740
67	Toledo Community Foundation	$291,216,018
68	*Community Foundation of Western North Carolina*	$284,588,122
69	Stark Community Foundation	$282,637,038
70	Community Foundation of Elkhart County	$272,074,300
71	Community Foundation for Monterrey County	$267,435,208
72	Community Foundation of the Ozarks	$263,480,684
73	Amarillo Area Foundation	$261,442,470
74	Erie Community Foundation	$259,504,767
75	*Coastal Community Foundation of South Carolina*	$258,056,859
76	Fremont Area Community Foundation	$254,087,870
77	Madison Community Foundation	$248,933,893
78	*North Carolina Community Foundation*	$246,772,770
79	Greater Kanawha Valley Foundation	$246,330,955
80	Delaware Community Foundation	$241,067,084
81	Austin Community Foundation	$239,000,000
82	*Triangle Community Foundation*	$229,578,683
83	Central New York Community Foundation	$226,380,065
84	*Community Foundation of Tampa Bay, Inc.*	$224,033,958
85	*Community Foundation for Muskegon County*	$223,535,738
86	*Community Foundation of Greater Greensboro*	$221,536,015
87	*The Community Foundation of Greater Birmingham*	$221,091,852
88	*Spartanburg County Foundation*	$212,863,075
89	Community Foundation of Greater Flint	$210,542,150
90	Akron Community Foundation	$201,735,000
91	Fairfield County Community Foundation	$195,794,235
92	Harrison County Community Foundation, Inc.	$192,520,760
93	Idaho Community Foundation	$181,248,371
94	*Community Foundation of Broward, Inc.*	$180,061,743
95	Baltimore Community Foundation	$174,750,945
96	Community Foundation of St. Joseph County	$173,475,030
97	Greater Cedar Rapids Community Foundation	$173.227,883
98	*Community Foundation for Palm Beach And Martin Counties*	$162,039,649
99	Richland County Foundation	$161,942,577
100	*Givewell Community Foundation*	$160,539,842

1   https://grantcraft.org/content/blog/community-foundation-asset-growth-accelerates/. The survey is an annual census inaugurated by James Luck, CEO of The Columbus (OH) Foundation, in 1988. Actual figures and rankings can change rapidly. As an example, contributions from a coalition of local donors in 2012 to the Tulsa Community Foundation (which was not established until 1998) suddenly made it the largest community foundation in the country. A year later, a nearly $1 billion gift to the Silicon Valley Community Foundation from Facebook founder Mark Zuckerberg in 2013-14, followed by two other half-billion dollar gifts from other company founders catapulted that foundation to the top of the list.

Index

13th Amendment, 82
14th Amendment, 82, 112, 255
15th Amendment, 16, 82, 269
16th Amendment, 16, 152
1919 Paris Peace Conference, 164
1924 Indenture of Trust, 190-192
1938 Fair Labor Standards Act, 208
1963 March on Washington, 259
19th Amendment, 164
4H, 159
Abney Foundation, 235
Adams, Henry, 123, 147
Adams, John Quincy, 24, 45, 55-57, 87, 149
Addams, Jane, 170
Address to the Slaveholding States, 65
Administrative Internships, 268
Aeschylus, 25
African Methodist Episcopal Church, 94
Agnes Scott College, 230
Agrarians, 196-197
Alabama, 4, 15, 30, 33, 65, 96, 106, 116, 123, 128, 139, 171-172, 186, 188, 193, 209, 224, 244, 255, 260, 266, 297, 332, 341, 345, 350, 377, 381
Aldrich, Alfred P., 64
Alexander, Ted, 357
Alexander, Will W. 184, 186
America, 5, 15, 28, 30, 48, 129, 155, 182, 184, 214, 222, 239, 292, 382
American Baptist College, 95
American Baptist Home Mission Society, 95
American Bar Association, 127
American Cast Iron Pipe Company, 186
American Colleges and Universities, Association of, 275
American Colonization Society. See Society for the Colonization of Free People of Color of America
American Economic Association, 127, 163
American Expeditionary Force, 160
American Federation of Labor, 127
American Friends Service Committee, 160
American Historical Association, 127, 153, 278
American Hospital Association, 275
American Humane, 337
American Jewish Joint Distribution Committee, 162
American Missionary Association, 84, 94
American National Red Cross. See Red Cross
American Relief Administration, 159

American Revolution, 25

American Tobacco Company, 191

Ames, Jessie, 214

Amistad, 56, 257

Anderson Foundation, Peyton, 324

Anderson, James D., 141

Annual Meetings, 295, 302, 304, 310, 318, 332, 338, 340, 341, 355, 359, 373

Appleby, Joyce, 77

Archie, William C., 290, 293

Area Health Education Centers, 263

Arkansas Community Foundation, 321, 325

Arkansas, 4, 15, 29, 30, 66, 96, 194, 256, 280, 297, 321, 325

Ashmore, Harry, 235

Associated Grantmakers, 308

Astor, Caroline, 123

Astor, John Jacob, 76

Athenaeum, 12

Atkins, Chester Burton "Chet", 210

Atlanta AIDS Partnership Fund, 322

Atlanta and Pacific Telegraph Company, 133

Atlanta Christian Council, 186

Atlanta Compromise, 116

Atlanta University, 84, 94, 96, 110, 313, 331

Atlanta Woman's Fund, 323

Atlanta Women's Foundation, 312

Atlanta, 83, 93, 94, 96, 107, 110, 113, 116, 130, 133, 156, 176, 186-187, 209, 215, 219, 220-223, 225-226, 230, 246-248, 256-258, 268, 290-295, 301, 304, 310, 312-313, 320-321, 323, 330, 331, 334, 339, 356, 358, 366, 371, 373, 376, 378

Attorneys' and Accountants' Relief Act of 1969, 283

Aviv, Diana, 346

Babcock Foundation, Mary Reynolds, 228, 261, 290, 293, 304, 348, 380

Babock, Mary Reynolds, 228

Baptist Community Ministries, 334, 355, 357-358

Baptist Healing Trust, 352

Barnesville-Lamar Community Foundation, 324

Barton, Clara, 159

Bell, John, 63

Benton Foundation, 342

Benwood Foundation, 223

Berea College, 33, 113, 137, 139

Berresford, Susan, 333

Berry College, 230

Bethesda Orphan House and Academy, 35

Bethune, Mary McLeod, 238

Biemesderfer, David, 282, 348

Birth of a Nation, The, 156

Black Belt Community Foundation, 350, 377
Black Codes, 82, 105
Blackmon, Douglas, 105
Blaine, Anita McCormick, 251
Blank Foundation, The Arthur M., 247
Blight, David, 11
Bloody Sunday, 260
boll weevil, 193, 208
Bondurant, William L., 291, 304
Booth, John Wilkes, 70
Boston College, 317, 329, 330
Boxer Rebellion, 158
Bradley Company, W. C., 224
Bradley-Turner Foundation, 224-225
Bradley, W. C., 220, 224
Breckinridge, John C., 63
Breman Jewish Heritage Museum, 247
Bridge and Structural Iron Workers, Association of, 154
Brinkley, Robert Campbell, 92
Brook Farm, 35
Brown University, 89
Brown v. Board of Education, 216, 235, 250, 254, 256
Brown, James Graham, 246
Bruce, David, 259
Bruno Foundation, Joseph S., 381
Bryan, William Jennings, 126
Buchanan, James, 63
Buffett, Doris, 4
Bullard, Eugene, 181
Bundy, McGeorge, 283, 311
Burnett, Imani, 331, 337, 341
Burroughs Wellcome Fund, 304, 316
Burt, John, 46
Byrd, Harry F., 187
Caldwell, Erskine, 8, 195
Calhoun, John C., 55-56, 58, 149
California Community Foundation, 314, 331
California, 14, 59, 315, 317, 331, 347, 381
Callaway Foundation, 234
Callaway, Cason, 207
Callaway, Fuller E., 233
Campbell Coal Company, 230
Campbell Foundation, J. Bulow, 230-231, 291, 304, 313
Campbell, J. Bulow, 230
Campbell, John C., 134, 136
Candler, Asa, 92, 219, 222

Candler, Warren Akin, 92
Cannon Foundation, 233
Carnegie Corporation, 139, 235, 238, 276
Carnegie Libraries, 137-138
Carnegie, Andrew, 79, 86, 88, 92, 113, 137, 138
Carroll County Community Foundation, 325
Carter, Henry, 312
Carver, George Washington, 207
Cash, Wilbur J., 195
Caudill, Harry, 211
CDC Foundation, 312
Center for Civil and Human Rights Global Advisory Board, 313
Center for Educational Policy and Management, 262
Center for Research in Social Change, 301
Centers for Disease Control and Prevention, 222
Chapin Foundation, 230
Charleston, SC, 11, 31-32, 35, 50-51, 310, 338, 373
Charleston, WV, 318
Charlottesville, 11
Chattahoochee Valley Fair Fund, 319
Chernow, Ron, 78, 80
Chicago Community Trust, 276
Chicago, University of, 129, 170
Christianity, 40, 47, 52-53, 90, 108, 132, 139, 159, 161, 186, 278
Cicero, Marcus Tullius, 24
Citizenship Schools, 254
Civil Rights Act of 1875, 85
Civil Rights Act of 1964, 269
Civil Rights and Voting Rights Acts, 270
Civil rights movement, 17, 169, 174, 254-256, 259, 280, 303
Civil War, 11-13, 15, 17, 30, 32, 46, 48, 67-69, 75, 77-78, 83, 86, 94, 97, 122, 124, 130, 140, 152, 156, 163, 184, 191, 211, 237, 377
Civilian Conservation Corps, 208
Clansman, The, 156
Clark Atlanta University, 313
Clark, Jamie, 340
Clark, Kenneth, 176
Clarke, James M., 293
Clay, Cassius Marcellus, 113
Clay, Henry, 49, 59, 149
Cleveland, Bobbi, 334, 339
Cleveland, Grover, 150, 211
Clinton, Catherine, 39
Clinton, Hillary, 311
Clotfelter, Charles, 164
Cobb, James C., 36, 212, 244

Coca-Cola, 92, 219, 220, 222-226, 230, 243, 252, 268, 305
Coffin, Howard, 227
Cold War, 257, 277
Colorado Fuel and Iron Company, 154
Colorado National Guard, 154
Columbia Seminary, 38
Columbia Theological Seminary, 230, 301
Columbia University, 108, 163, 277
Commission for Relief, 158
Commission on Industrial Relations, 154
Commission on Interracial Cooperation, 176, 186, 214
Commons, John R., 155
Communicable Disease Center, 222
Communities of Coastal Georgia Foundation, 325
Community Foundation Development Project, 317
Community Foundation for Greater Atlanta, 292, 312, 320, 323, 356
Community Foundation Initiative, 317-318, 331
Community Foundation of Central Georgia, 324
Community Foundation of Coffee County, 324
Community Foundation of Greater Memphis, 270, 320
Community Foundation of Sarasota County, 319, 320, 342
Community Foundation of the Chattahoochee Valley, 319
Community Foundation of the New River Valley, 350
Confederacy, 4, 11-13, 17, 65-68, 81, 83, 85, 88, 106, 114, 181, 191, 211, 338
Confederate flag, 11, 339
Conferences on Christian Education, 139
Congress of Racial Equality, 113
Congress, 3, 16, 29, 49, 55, 60, 62, 79, 81-83, 85, 88, 96, 99, 125, 127, 130, 149, 150, 152-153, 181, 183, 187, 209, 229, 254, 269, 277, 279-280, 282, 288, 306-308, 325, 343-345, 347, 367
Connecticut, 48, 108, 130, 161, 292
Constitution, 1, 16, 24, 59, 61, 63, 111-112, 150, 152, 269
Constitutional Convention, 24, 45
Constitutional Union Party, 63
cooperative democracy, 161
cotton gin, 18, 77
Council for United Civil Rights Leadership, 259
Council of Michigan Foundations, 308
Council on Foundations, 4, 15, 282, 289, 298, 305, 308, 314, 341, 351, 366, 381
Country Training Schools, 174
Courts Foundation, 246, 313
Cox, Eugene "Goober", 277-278
Craft, Danah, 313
CREATE Foundation, 294
Crews, Harry, 196
Crimean War, 67
Cult of the Lost Cause. See Lost Cause

Cummins Engine Foundation, 260
Currier, Audrey Bruce, 258
Currier, Nathaniel, 259
Currier, Stephen, 259
Cyriaque, Jeanne, 170
Danville (VA) Regional Foundation, 10
Daughters of Charity, 67
Davidson College, 192
Davis Foundations, Arthur Vining, 291-293
Day Law, 113
De Bow's Review, 113
de Tocqueville, Alexis, 34, 36, 54, 264
DeBlanc, Alcibiades, 106
Declaration of Independence, 1, 16, 64
Delta Corporation, 260
Democratic Party, 10, 63, 150, 166, 206
Democrats, 51, 62, 98, 122, 125-126, 150, 157, 199
Deutsch, Stephanie, 171
Dickens, Charles, 86
Dickson Foundation, 230
Dillard University, 96, 252
Dix, Dorothea, 37, 67
Dixon Jr., Thomas, 156
Dixon, J. Curtis, 246, 267
Dobbs Foundation, R. Howard, 312
Donors Forum of Chicago, 308
Douglas, Stephen A., 46, 62, 63
Dover Foundation, 234
Dred Scott v. Sandford, 61
Drexel, Katharine, 132
Du Bois, W. E. B., 94, 112, 117, 165, 175, 177
Duke Endowment, 16, 190, 225, 229, 279, 291, 293, 304, 334, 337, 353, 372, 376
Duke Power Company, 191
Duke University, 192, 293
Duke, James B., 191, 317
Dunbar, Leslie, 258
Duncan, Stephen, 76
duPont Fund, Jessie Ball, 358, 381
Eagan, John J., 186, 230
Early, Jubal Anderson, 114
Eisenhower, Dwight, 225, 245
Emanuel AME Church, 11
Emerson, Ralph Waldo, 38
Emory University, 33, 93, 109, 221-222, 290, 301, 347
Emporia State University, 365
Erie Canal, 27

Esser, George, 261

Esso Education Fund, 268

European Relief Council, 159

Evans Foundation, Lettie Pate 222

Evans, Lettie Pate Whitehead, 222

Evans, Walker, 210

Everett, Edward, 63

Fair Housing Act, 269

Farmers' Alliance, 124

Faulkner, William, 8, 14, 194

FDR. See Roosevelt, Franklin D.

Federal Council of Churches, 161

Feild Co-Operative Association, 189, 291, 293

Feild, Sallie Thomas, 189

Ferguson, John Howard, 111

Field Foundation, 257, 258

Field, Marshall, 170

Field, Ruth, 284

Finkelman, Paul, 60

Finley, Robert, 49

First World War, 157-159, 163, 165, 174, 182, 184-185, 188, 220, 229, 233

Fisk University, 83, 95, 110, 174, 269

Fitzhugh, George, 58

Florida, 4, 14-15, 30, 65, 107, 152, 204, 207, 238, 244, 246, 292, 297, 301, 311, 317, 319, 320, 341, 350, 358, 372, 381

Foner, Eric, 98

Foote, Shelby, 68

Foothills Community Foundation, 319

Ford Foundation, 207, 234, 235, 257, 260-261, 277, 281, 283, 333, 342

Ford, Edsel, 205, 234

Ford, Henry, 205, 207, 234

Fort Sumter, 66, 149

Fort Valley College, 174

Forum of Regional Associations of Grantmakers, 282, 341, 369

Foundation Center, 14, 17, 278, 297, 337, 350

Foundation Directory, The, 279, 295

Foundation for the Carolinas, 292, 320-321, 325, 376

Foundation for the Mid South, 335, 349, 356

Foundations on the Hill, 341

Founders of the new American Republic, 15

Founders, the, 13, 18, 19, 25, 51, 57, 112, 193 - 2, 15, 23-25, 26, 34, 40, 60, 62, 69-70, 148, 270, 382

Franklin, Benjamin, 15, 24, 35

Fraser-Parker Foundation, 313

Freedmen's Bureau, 82-84, 93, 97

Freedom Summer, 260, 267

Freeman Foundation, Ella West, 252

Freeman, Alfred Bird ("A. B."), 252

Freeman, David, 306

Freeman, Rosa, 252

French Air Force, 181

French Croix de Guerre, 182

Fries, Francis, 190

Fugitive Slave Act, 59-60

Fulbright, J. W., 280

Furman University, 33, 192

Gaberman, Barry, 333

Gallatin, Albert, 25

Gaudiani, Claire, 6

General Education Board, 130-131, 153, 174, 190, 276

George, Henry, 108, 124, 132

Georgia Baptist Healthcare Ministry Foundation, 312

Georgia Center for Nonprofits, 323, 356

Georgia Foundation Board, University System of, 313

Georgia Health Foundation, 313

Georgia Historical Society, 11

Georgia Humanities Council, 335

Georgia Warm Springs Foundation, 205

Georgia, 4, 11-12, 14-15, 28, 30, 47, 49, 65, 92, 109, 112, 115, 125-126, 130-131, 134-135, 137, 174, 181, 195, 205-206, 212-213, 215, 220-221, 224-228, 230, 233, 239, 252, 255, 258, 262, 268, 277, 279, 280, 311, 313, 317, 319-321, 323-325, 335, 341, 356, 359, 370

Gerhard, Greg, 359

GI Bill, 245

Gilded Age, 80, 97-98, 150

Ginzburg, Ralph, 107

Girard, Stephen, 76

Girl Scouts, 159

Glen, John, 254

Glenn Family Foundation, Wilbur and Hilda, 358, 359

Glover, Staci, 185

Goff, Frederick H., 190

Goheen, Robert, 306

Goizueta Foundation, 226, 372

Goizueta, Roberto, 226

Gone With the Wind, 210

Goodwin, Doris Kearns, 245

Goodwyn, Lawrence C., 125

Gordon Fund, Joseph G., 263

Gordon, Joseph G., 263

Gordon, Marianne, 332

Gore, Albert, Sr., 281

Gorman, Arthur, 150

Gospel of Wealth, 86
Gould, Jay, 133
Grady Foundation, Henry W., 312
Grady, Henry W., 112, 115, 116
Grant, Ulysses S., 66, 98, 107
Grantmakers for Effective Organizations, 368
Grassley, Charles, 346
Gray, Bowman, 227
Great Depression, 16, 159, 190, 192-193, 203, 206-208, 214, 224, 234, 243
Great Migration, 184
Great Society, 265, 283
Greater Kanawha Valley Community Foundation, 318
Green, William D., 48
Greenwood Mills, 232, 233
Gregg-Graniteville Foundation, 231-232
Gregg, William, 231-232
Gregory, James N., 184
Griffin, John, 261, 293-294, 302, 304, 379
Grimké sisters, 39
Groce, Todd, 11
Gross Breesen, 208
Gross, Robert A., 38
Guiding Principles, 348
Hamilton, Alexander, 45, 148
Hammack, David, 39, 53, 97, 134
Hampton Institute, 83, 110, 131
Hamrick Mills Foundation, 234
Hancock, Gordon, 215
Hardesty, Jane, 313, 334
Hardin Bakeries Corporation, 262
Hardin Foundation, 262, 304
Hardin, Phillip B., 262
Hardin, Russ, 339
Harding, Warren G., 183, 187-188, 234
Harland Charitable Foundation, 334
Harlem Hellfighters, 182
Harrell, Byron, 355, 357-358
Harris, Carl V., 128
Hasson, Jim, 303
Hatcher, Claud, 224
Havens, John J., 317, 329
Hawthorne, Nathaniel, 38
Hayes, Rutherford B., 99, 108
Haygood, Atticus G., 109
Head Start, 263
Healthcare Georgia Foundation, 313

Henderson, V. W., 269

Henry, Gustavus, 46

Heyard, Nathaniel, 76

Heyrman, Christine Leigh, 52

Highlander Folk School, 251

Highlander Research and Education Center, 251, 255

Hirsch, Emil, 170

Historically Black Colleges and Universities (HBCUs), 174, 236, 265-268

Hogg Foundation, 275-276

Holley, Francis, 332

Hoover, Herbert, 158-159, 183, 206

Hope, John, 187

Howard University, 83, 110

Howe Junior College, 95

Howland, Mike, 358-359

Hull Fellows, 333-337, 359, 369, 382

Hull, Robert H., 288, 290, 301-303, 305, 307-308, 312, 317-318, 320, 330, 332, 336, 341, 348-349, 355

Hunter, David, 257

Hurricane Katrina, 356

Hurt Building, 312, 332, 359, 368

Hyde Farmlands, 208

Ichauway Plantation, 220, 223

Illinois, 46, 62, 107, 169, 258, 293

Independent Sector, 346, 369

Industrial Revolution, 7

influenza, 182

Inman-Riverdale Foundation, 230, 234

Internal Revenue Service, 289-290

Interstate Commerce Commission (ICC), 150

Ishii, Helen, 337

Jackson, Andrew, 49, 63, 150

Jaffa, Harry, 64

Janney, Caroline E., 114

Jaworski, Taylor, 212

Jeanes Fund, 174

Jeanes Supervisors, 131, 249

Jeanes Teachers Program, 137

Jeanes, Anna T., 131

Jefferson, Thomas, 23, 25, 27, 30, 45, 52, 55, 196

Jim Crow, 111, 141, 170, 173, 187, 193, 236, 246

Joanna Foundation, 234

Johns Hopkins University, 156, 194

Johnson Amendment, 367

Johnson C. Smith University, 96, 192

Johnson Foundation, Lyndon B., 262

Johnson, Andrew, 70, 81-82
Johnson, Dorothy, 308
Johnson, Lyndon B., 269
Jones, Bobby, 233
Jones, Boisfeuillet, 293, 340
Jones, Charles Colcock, 47
Jones, Montfort, 189
Jones, Thomas Jesse, 137
Jordan, Juanita, 324
Joslyn, Dan, 331
Kansas-Nebraska Act, 60
Karl, Barry, 88, 151
Katz, Stanley, 88, 151
Katznelson, Ira, 187
Kauffman Foundation, Ewing Marion, 366
Keesee Educational Fund, Charles B., 230
Keller Family Foundation, 252
Keller Jr., Charles, 252
Kellogg Foundation, 264, 282, 341
Kendall, Jane, 264
Kennedy, John F., 257, 265
Kennedy, Robert F., 257, 281
Kentucky, 4, 15, 59, 113, 137-138, 149, 194, 246, 297, 311, 354, 376
Key, Francis Scott, 49
King Jr., Martin Luther, 251, 254-255, 268, 270
Knight Foundation, John S. and James L., 311
Knights of Columbus, 161
Knights of the White Camellia, 106
Ku Klux Klan, 107, 156, 166
Ladies' Memorial Associations, 114
laissez-faire, 150, 163, 344
Lancaster and Chester Railroad, 233
Landrieu, Mitch, 13
League of Nations, 164, 183
League of Women Voters, 343
Lee, Gypsy Rose, 233
Lee, Janine, 365
Lee, Robert E., 13, 69
Lehfeldt Company, 317
Lehfeldt, Martin C., 282, 318-319, 330-333, 335, 337-339, 341-342, 345, 347, 349, 350-351, 353, 355-358
LeMoyne-Owen College, 95-96, 110
Leuchtenburg, William, 203
Levi Strauss Company, 304-305
Lewis and Clark expedition, 25
Liberia, 49, 136

Liberty Bonds, 160
Liberty Hall Academy, 56
Lilly Family School of Philanthropy, 279
Lincoln Institute, 113
Lincoln Republicans, 125
Lincoln, Abraham, 46, 62-63, 65, 69-70, 77, 81, 84, 96, 99, 113, 125, 149, 169, 252
Linwood Shull, 238
Litwack, Leon, 48
Locke, Betsy, 334
Locke, John, 24
Lockley, Timothy James, 36
Lodge, Henry Cabot, 164
London Peabody Donation fund, 91
Long, Russell, 280, 283
Los Angeles Times, 154
Lost Cause, 10, 13, 111, 113-115, 197
Louisiana, 4, 15, 25, 29, 30, 33, 65, 85, 106, 112, 132, 244, 252, 280, 283, 297, 320, 354
Ludlow Massacre, 154
Lupton, John T., 219
Lyndhurst Foundation, 223, 291, 303-305, 335
MacArthur, Charles, 233
Madison, James, 23, 25
Maimonides, Moses ben, 7, 380
Maine, 29, 203
Malaria Control in War Areas Program, 222
Manatee (FL) Community Foundation, 342
Manigault, Peter, 32
Mann, Horace, 35, 38, 89
manumission, 47, 50
March to the Sea, 12
Marshall Plan, 84
Marshall, George C., 84
Maryland, 30, 49, 67, 68, 86, 150
Mason-Dixon line, 36
Massachusetts, 34-35, 55, 59, 63, 88-89, 92, 115, 134, 164, 292, 308
Mather, Cotton, 34-35
McCarthy, Joseph, 277-278
McClure, James G. K., 296
McCully, George, 25
McGarvie, Mark D., 38
McGrath, Earl J., 266
McGregor, Alan, 349
McKinley, William, 126
McLean, George, 294
McMillan, Elridge W., 313
McNeil-Miller, Karen, 366-367, 372

McPhee, Penelope, 247
McPherson, James Alan, 138
McPherson, James M., 94
McTier, Charles H. (Pete), 304, 359, 360
McTyerie, Holland N., 91
MDC, Inc, 370
Meharry Medical College, 96, 110, 174
Mehrotra, Ajay, 163
Mellon, Andrew W., 183, 259
Memorial Welfare Foundation, 223, 291, 293
Memphis Daily Appeal, 113
Mencken, H. L., 194
Methodist Episcopal Church, South, 92, 109
Metropolitan Atlanta Arts Fund, 323
Metropolitan Atlanta Community Foundation, 291, 321
Metropolitan Foundation of Atlanta, Inc, 321
Metropolitan Interfaith Association (MIFA), 270
Michigan, 156, 207, 308, 316, 342, 347, 348
Mississippi, 4, 15, 29-30, 33, 65, 68, 76, 92, 189, 209, 222, 260, 262, 294, 297, 311, 338, 339, 353, 357, 376, 377
Missouri Compromise, 29-30, 37, 51, 60
Missouri, 4, 25, 29, 30, 37, 63, 154
Monroe, James, 45, 49
Monrovia, 49
Montana, 25
Montgomery (Alabama) Improvement Association, 255
Montgomery, David, 155
Montgomery, Walter Scott, 190
Morgan, J. Pierpont, 79
Morikawa, Andy, 350
Moton, Robert Russa, 138, 187
Mott Foundation, Charles Stewart, 316, 319, 349
Mulberry Grove, 28
Murphy Foundation, Katherine John, 313
Murphy, Tim, 349
Muscogee Creek Indians, 205
Myrdal, Gunnar, 235, 277
NAACP Legal Defense and Educational Fund, 260
Nashville Normal and Theological Institute, 95
Nashville, University of, 91
Nat Turner's rebellion, 50, 257
National Agenda for Community Foundations, 314, 331
National Association for the Advancement of Colored People (NAACP), 117, 249, 259-260, 264
National Association of Manufacturers, 127
National Catholic War Council, 162
National Center for Family Philanthropy, 368

National Civic League, 343

National Committee on Foundations and Trusts for Community Welfare. See National Council on Community Foundations

National Council on Community Foundations, 276

National Urban League, 113, 264

Near East Foundation, 161

Negro Rural School Fund, 131, 249

New Deal, 207, 212, 229, 243, 258, 277, 280

New South, 111, 113, 117, 195, 210, 269, 378

New Ventures in Philanthropy, 282

New World Foundation, 251, 257

New York Community Trust, 315

New York Southern Society, 211

New York, 27, 31, 35, 76, 86, 93, 107-108, 123, 130, 133, 136, 153, 161-162, 184, 187, 192, 204, 206, 211-212, 233-234, 251, 257-259, 276, 298, 306, 308, 315, 330

Newcomb, Josephine Louise Le Monnier, 93

NewTown Macon, 324

Nightingale, Florence, 67

Noble of Indiana, 358

Nonprofit Resource Center. See Georgia Center for Nonprofits

North Carolina Center for Nonprofits (NCCNP), 264

North Carolina Fund, 261

North Carolina, 4, 14-16, 66-67, 107, 135, 138-139, 141, 190-192, 194, 215, 225, 227, 230, 233, 234, 238, 256, 261, 263-264, 279, 290-291, 293, 296, 311, 316-318, 320, 335, 340, 343, 348, 367, 370, 376, 380

North, the, 16, 27, 30-31, 34, 36-40, 49-53, 57-58, 62, 66-67, 77-78, 85, 97, 105-106, 115, 123, 128, 176-177, 183, 211, 213, 236, 244, 281

Northern Presbyterians, 94

Norwich Free Academy, 108

Noyes Foundation, Jesse Smith, 268

Odum, Eugene, 215, 228

Odum, Howard W., 194

Oglethorpe, James, 18

Ohio, 29, 86, 190, 311

Oklahoma, 107, 280

Oman, Darcy, 315, 316

Otis, Harrison Gray, 154

Page, Walter Hines, 141

Parks, Rosa, 254, 255

Patman, Wright, 280, 281

Patterson, Frederick, 237

Patton, Randall L., 214

Payton, Benjamin F., 207

Peabody Education Fund, 88-90, 109

Peabody Fund. See Peabody Education Fund

Peabody Normal College, 95

Peabody Normal School, 91
Peabody sisters, 38
Peabody, George Foster, 130-131, 187, 204
Peabody, George, 85-92, 108, 134, 246,
Pearson, Katharine, 333, 349
Peck, Martha G., 304, 316
Pemberton, John, 219
Penick, George, 335, 356-357
Peninsula Community Foundation, 317
Pennsylvania, 78, 112, 114, 130, 153,
People's Party. See Populist Party
Perkins, Thomas, 76
Petersen, Eleanor, 308
Peterson Commission, 280
Peterson, Peter G., 280
Phelps Stokes Fund, 136-137
Phelps, Anson Greene, 136
Philipp, Alicia, 323
Phillips, Daniel W., 95
Pickett & Hatcher Educational Fund, 224
Piedmont College, 134
Pinckney, Charles C., 47
Pitkin, Timothy, 26
plantation, 28, 39, 47, 193, 220, 377
Plessy v. Ferguson, 141, 176, 250,
Plessy, Homer A., 111
Policy in Action, 367
Pollock v. Farmers' Loan & Trust Company, 152
Pontchartrain Park, 252
Ponte Vedra, 292
Populism, 126, 265
Populist Party, 125
Populists, 125-126
Poteat, William Louis, 187
Princeton, 166, 296, 330,
Progressivism, 124, 126, 140
Project Star, 366
Protestantism, 52, 97
Public Policy Digest, 367
Pullen, Ann Ellis, 214
Quakers. See Society of Friends
Queen, Edward L., 347
Rabun Gap–Nacoochee School, 230
Radical Republicans, 81-82, 115
Radicals, 82
Rangel, Charles, 308-309

Ransom, John Crowe, 196
Rapides Foundation, 354
Rauschenbusch, Walter, 132-133
Reconstruction Force Act, 107
Reconstruction, 81-82, 85, 97, 98-99, 107, 109, 112, 156
Red Cross Production Corps, 159
Red Cross, 159-160
Republican motherhood, 38
Republican Party, 62, 97, 125, 308
republican synthesis, 23
Republicans, 26, 122, 124-125, 152,
Revenue Act of 1861, 149
Revenue Act of 1913, 152
Revenue Act of 1935, 223
Revenue Cutter Service, 56, 149
Revolutionary War, 76
Reynolds Charitable Trust, Kate B., 227, 263, 367, 372
Reynolds Foundation, Z. Smith, 226, 261, 273
Reynolds, R. J., 226
Rhode Island, 89, 95, 108
Rhodes-Haverty Building, 294
Richmond Hill, 207
Ridings, Dorothy, 4, 342-343
Rockefeller Brothers Fund, 280
Rockefeller Foundation, 187, 267, 276, 280
Rockefeller Foundation, Winthrop, 321
Rockefeller III, John D., 280
Rockefeller Sr., John D., 79, 80, 88, 127, 129, 130-131, 134, 137, 153, 154
Rockefeller, Jr. John D., 237
Rockhurst University, 365
Roger Williams University, 94, 111
Rooks, Charles S., 17, 293-298, 301, 306-307
Roosevelt, Franklin D., 131, 203, 205-207, 209, 229, 237, 258, 277
Roosevelt, Franklin Delano. See Roosevelt, Franklin D.
RosaMary Foundation, 223, 252
Rosenwald Fund, 177, 187
Rosenwald schools, 173-174, 249
Rosenwald, Julius, 127, 129, 133, 177, 183 - 169-177, 247, 252, 257,
Royal Crown Cola, 224
Ruffin, Edmund, 58
Russell, Betsey, 335, 337
Russell, Richard, 213
Sage Foundation, Russell, 133-136,
Sage, Russell, 79, 133,
Salvation Army, 6, 159
Sanford, Terry, 261, 311

Sapelo Foundation, 228
Sapelo Island, 227
Savannah, GA, 12, 18, 28, 31, 35, 138, 207, 295, 338
Schervish, Paul G., 317, 329
Scott, Anne Firor, 38
Sears, Barnas, 88
Sears, Richard, 169-170
Sears, Roebuck Company, 169
SECF. See Southeastern Council of Foundations
Second Great Awakening, 52
Selby Foundation, William G. and Marie, 246
Self Family Foundation, 232
Self Foundation. See Self Family Foundation
Self, James C., 232
Seligman, Edwin R.A., 162-163
Sellers, James, 9
Senate Finance Committee, 281, 296, 346
separate but equal, 111, 216, 236, 250
Separate Car Act, 112
Serviceman's Readjustment Act of 1944. See GI Bill
Shakeley, Jack, 314-315
Shame of the Cities, The, 133
sharecropper, 29, 193
Shelby County, 113
Sherman Anti-Trust Act of 1890, 79, 153
Sherman, Stephen, 337
Sherman, William, 12, 66,
Sierra Leone, 56-57
Simms, William Gilmore, 58
Sims Foundation, J. Marion, 354
Sisters of Charity Foundation, 353
Sisters of the Blessed Sacrament, 132
sit-in movement, 256
Slater Fund, 108-109, 111, 115, 128, 134, 246
Slater, John F., 108-109
slavery, 5, 9, 12, 18, 27-28, 30, 32, 37, 40, 45-48, 51-52, 55, 57-63, 65, 82, 105, 131, 211,
Slocum, Margaret Oliver, 133, 134
Smith, Al, 206
Smith, Gid, 270
Smith, Lillian, 194, 215
Smithson, James, 54-55
Smithsonian, 55, 57
Social Darwinism, 122, 132
Social Gospel, 132, 186, 278, 294
Social Welfare Research Institute of Boston College, 329
Society for the Colonization of Free People of Color of America, 48-50, 136

Society of Friends, 131, 162

Somerville, Bill, 317

Sons of Confederate Veterans, 114

South Carolina, 4, 15, 18, 28, 31-32, 39, 47, 50-51, 55, 63-66, 76, 94, 131, 209, 230-233, 235, 238, 296, 319-321, 325, 353-354

South, the 2, 4, 8-11, 16-17, 19, 27, 31-32, 34-40, 45, 47-54, 57-59, 63, 66-68, 75, 77, 81-82, 84-85, 88-92, 94, 97-99, 105-109, 111-113, 115, 117, 123-132, 134, 136-142, 149, 151, 156, 165, 166, 169-173, 177, 183, 185, 188, 190, 192-198, 203, 207, 209-214, 216, 229, 231, 235-238, 243-244, 247, 249-250, 254-256, 258, 262, 264, 266, 269-270, 277, 279-282, 287-288, 293, 297, 303, 314, 317, 319, 330, 334, 336, 348-353, 356, 371, 375-378, 380-382

Southeastern Council of Foundations (SECF), 282, 287, 288, 291, 293-298, 301-307, 309-311, 313, 316-319, 324-325, 330-342, 347-351, 354-360, 365-373, 375, 377, 380-382

Southern Diaspora, 184

Southern Education Board, 139

Southern Education Foundation, 246, 267, 276, 294, 302

Southern Education Reporting Service, 260

Southern Highland Handicraft Guild, 136

Southern Historical Society, 114

Southern Manifesto, 281

Southern Methodist University, 92

Southern Mountain Workers Conference, 135

Southern Regional Council, 257-258

Southern Rural Development Initiative, 348

Spanish-American War, 159

Spartanburg County Foundation, 190

Spelman College, 130, 331

Spencer, Herbert, 121-122

Springs Foundation, 232

Springs, Elliott, 232-233, 292

St. Croix Foundation for Community Development, 372

Stalwart Republicans, 99

Standard Oil, 79-80

Stanfield II, John H., 177

Stauber, Karl, 10

Steffens, Lincoln, 133

Stephens, Alexander H., 12

Stephenson, John, 333

Stern Family Fund, 252

Stern Fund, 257

Stern Sr., Edgar, 252

Stokes, Carl, 281

Stokes, Caroline Phelps, 136

Stouffer, Samuel, 237

Strengthening Developing Institutions Program, 268

Stribling, Jera, 381

Stribling, Suzanna, 355-356

Strong, Josiah, 186
Struckhoff, Eugene C. ("Struck"), 315
Student Nonviolent Coordinating Committee, 259
Sullivan Foundation, Algernon Sydney, 211-212
Sun Trust Endowment and Foundations group, 313
SunTrust Bank, 313, 359
Sutherland, Robert, 275
Taconic Foundation, 257, 259, 273
Taft, William Howard, 154
Talmadge, Herman, 280
Taney, Roger Brook, 61
Tarbell, Ida, 234
Tariff of Abominations, 149
Tassava, Christopher, 214
Tax Reform Act of 1969, 280, 283, 288, 290, 293, 301, 306, 314, 316, 340, 343
Tax, 105, 124, 148-149, 150-153, 155, 158-159, 161-163, 165, 223, 212, 229, 234, 244, 277-281, 284, 295, 307-309, 327, 343-344, 346-347, 351, 367, 380
Taylor, Janet, 308
Tennessee Agricultural and Industrial State College, 174
Tennessee Valley Authority, 208
Tennessee, 4, 15, 29, 63, 66, 91, 92, 95, 106, 188, 194, 207, 222-223, 251, 254-255, 278, 281, 320, 376
Texas, 3, 11, 23, 54, 73, 83, 94, 174, 194, 195, 198 - 4, 14, 30, 66, 92, 109, 125, 244, 275-276, 280
Thalhimer Sr., William B., 208
Thomas, Benjamin F., 219, 223
Thomas, Bill, 347
Thomas, Clarence, 138
Thomas, Lowell, 233
Thornwell, James Henley, 46
Thrift, Carroll, 304
Thurmond, Strom, 281
Tomochichi, 18
trade tariffs, 148, 149
Transcontinental Railroad, 77
Trebor Foundation, 223, 226
Trinity College, 191-192
Truman, Harry, 238
Truth Seeker, 107
Tucker, Nathaniel Beverley, 58
Tulane University, 93
Tull Charitable Foundation, 313, 334
Turner, D. A., 224
Turner, Nat, 50, 257
Turner, William B. (Bill), 224
Tuskegee Institute, 94, 116, 131, 139, 171, 172, 176, 187, 207, 237, 266

U.S. Coast Guard, 149

U.S. Food Administration, 159

U.S. House Ways and Means Committee, 150, 296, 308, 347

U.S. Postal Service, 170

U.S. Public Health Service, 221

U.S. Sanitary Commission, 67

United Nations, 164

United Negro College Fund, 236-237

United Philanthropy Forum. See Forum of Regional Associations of Grantmakers

United States, 2, 3, 4, 7, 13, 14, 24, 26, 40, 54, 57, 61, 75, 76, 82, 84, 93, 97, 107, 108, 117, 122, 133, 137, 148, 157, 159, 165, 182, 193, 203, 204, 208, 213, 214, 219, 220, 232, 245, 257, 258, 266, 277, 278, 279, 292, 343,

Vanderbilt University, 95, 196, 301, 367

Vanderbilt, Alva, 123

Vanderbilt, Cornelius, 79, 80, 91, 92, 123

Vary, Renee, 337

Vesey, Denmark, 50, 257

Vinson, Carl, 213

Virginia, 4, 14, 15, 27, 30, 39, 50, 55, 66, 68, 89, 109, 114, 152, 190, 208, 211, 222, 243, 246, 251, 297, 299, 320, 332, 350,

VISTA, 263

von Blond, Betsy, 318

Voter Education Project, 257, 260, 293

Voting Rights Act, 269, 270

Wacaster, C. Thompson (Tom), 262, 304

Wake Forest College. See Wake Forest University

Wake Forest University, 187, 226, 228, 263, 290, 293, 297

Wallace, Henry, 251, 272

Walsh Commission, 154

Walsh, Frank P., 154, 155

War of 1812, 56, 149

War on Poverty, 263

War Revenue Act of 1917, 161

Warburg, Edward M. M., 259

Warren, Debbie, 349

Warren, Robert Penn, 46, 194

Washington & Lee University, 56

Washington, Booker T., 116, 117, 136, 139, 169, 170, 171, 172, 173, 175

Washington, Bushrod, 49

Washington, D.C., 30, 55, 60, 83, 110, 112, 114, 162, 246, 278, 298, 307, 368

Washington, George, 23, 26, 49, 52, 56

Watkins, William Law, 319

Watson, Tom, 125, 126

Ways Station, 207

Webster, Daniel, 59

Wellspring Fund, Toyota, 294

West Virginia, 68, 139, 150
white supremacy, 8, 30, 76, 81, 85, 106, 132, 146 - 9, 40, 97, 101, 105, 112, 141, 177, 249
White, Angela, 279
Whitefield, George, 35, 42
Whitehead Foundation, Joseph B., 223, 292, 340
Whitehead Foundation, Lettie Pate, 222, 291, 292
Whitehead, Joseph B., 219, 222
Whites Creek Pike, 95
Whitney, Eli, 27, 42
Williams College, 134
Williams Foundation, Jesse Parker, 313, 372
Wilson-Gorman Act. See Wilson-Gorman Tariff Act
Wilson-Gorman Tariff Act, 150, 152
Wilson, William, 150
Wilson, Woodrow, 141, 152, 154, 156, 158, 166, 181, 188, 234
Winston-Salem Foundation, 312
Winston-Salem, 139, 225, 227, 263,
Winthrop Rockefeller Foundation, 321
Winthrop, Charles Robert, 88
Winthrop, John, 34, 42, 88
Wisconsin, 48, 277
Wisconsin, University of, 155
Wisconsin, University of, 155
Wisdom, Mary Elizabeth (Betty), 252
Women's suffrage, 123, 140
Woodrow Wilson National Fellowship Foundation, 267, 330
Woodruff Foundation, Robert W., 222, 313, 318, 340, 353, 359,
Woodruff Fund, Ernest and Emily, 223
Woodruff Malaria Fund, 221
Woodruff, Ernest, 220
Woodruff, Robert W., 220, 221, 222, 223, 224, 240, 317, 376
Woodson, Carter G., 113
Woodward, C. Vann, 194
Woodward, Isaac, 238
Works Progress Administration, 208
World War I, 118, 157, 158, 159, 163, 165, 174, 182, 184, 185, 188, 198
World War II, 185, 223, 225, 229, 237, 240, 249, 296, 326
WWI. See First World War
Xavier University, 132
Yale College, 87
Yale University, 11, 28, 42, 71, 118, 178, 194, 226, 262
YMCA War Work Council, 186
YMCA, 102, 108, 159, 161, 176
Young Jr., Whitney M., 113
Young Men's Christian Association. See YMCA
Young Women's Christian Association, 159, 161

Zainaldin, Jamil, 335
Zerbe, Dean, 346
Zimmerman Telegram, 157
Zionism, 176

THE AUTHORS
MARTIN LEHFELDT & JAMIL ZAINALDIN

Martin Lehfeldt is a graduate of Haverford College and Union Theological Seminary in New York City. Among other roles, he has served as program officer for the Woodrow Wilson National Fellowship Foundation, vice president for development at Clark College (now Clark Atlanta University), director of development for the Atlanta University Center, president of his own consulting firm, and president of the Southeastern Council of Foundations. He is also the author of *The Sacred Call*, *Notes from a Non-Profitable Life*, and *Thinking about Things*, a compilation of his SECF newsletter columns.

Dr. Jamil Zainaldin graduated from the University of Virginia and the University of Chicago. In addition to teaching at Northwestern University and Case Western Reserve University, he has served as staff director of the Task Force on Social Security and Women of the U.S. House Select Committee on Aging, deputy director of the American Historical Association, president of the Federation of State Humanities Council, and president of the Georgia Humanities Council, from which he recently retired as president *emeritus*. He is co-author of *Law and Jurisprudence in America* and author of *Law in Antebellum Society*.

Photo of Martin Lehfeldt courtesy of Mikki Harris. Photo of Jamil Zainaldin courtesy of himself.

THE LIBERATING PROMISE OF PHILANTHROPY

THE LIBERATING PROMISE OF PHILANTHROPY

THE LIBERATING PROMISE OF PHILANTHROPY